Pro ASP.NET MVC 5 Platform

Adam Freeman

Apress®

Pro ASP.NET MVC 5 Platform

ISBN-13 (pbk): 978-1-4302-6541-2

ISBN-13 (electronic): 978-1-4302-6542-9

Distributed to the book trade worldwide by Springer Science+Business Media New York, 233 Spring Street, 6th Floor, New York, NY 10013. Phone 1-800-SPRINGER, fax (201) 348-4505, e-mail `orders-ny@springer-sbm.com`, or visit `www.springeronline.com`. Apress Media, LLC is a California LLC and the sole member (owner) is Springer Science + Business Media Finance Inc (SSBM Finance Inc). SSBM Finance Inc is a Delaware corporation.

For information on translations, please e-mail `rights@apress.com`, or visit `www.apress.com`.

Apress and friends of ED books may be purchased in bulk for academic, corporate, or promotional use. eBook versions and licenses are also available for most titles. For more information, reference our Special Bulk Sales–eBook Licensing web page at `www.apress.com/bulk-sales`.

Any source code or other supplementary material referenced by the author in this text is available to readers at `www.apress.com`. For detailed information about how to locate your book's source code, go to `www.apress.com/source-code/`.

Dedicated to my lovely wife, Jacqui Griffyth.

Contents at a Glance

Contents

About the Author

Adam Freeman is an experienced IT professional who has held senior positions in a range of companies, most recently serving as chief technology officer and chief operating officer of a global bank. Now retired, he spends his time writing and running.

About the Technical Reviewer

Fabio Claudio Ferracchiati is a senior consultant and a senior analyst/developer using Microsoft technologies. He works for Brain Force (`www.brainforce.com`) in its Italian branch (`www.brainforce.it`). He is a Microsoft Certified Solution Developer for .NET, a Microsoft Certified Application Developer for .NET, a Microsoft Certified Professional, and a prolific author and technical reviewer. Over the past ten years, he's written articles for Italian and international magazines and coauthored more than ten books on a variety of computer topics.

PART 1

Getting Ready

CHAPTER 1

Putting the ASP.NET Platform in Context

The ASP.NET platform was originally developed for use with Web Forms, and support for the MVC framework was added later. The ASP.NET platform is full of rich and useful features, but most guides to the MVC framework assumed that programmers have experience in Web Forms development and already know what the platform is capable of doing. That was a reasonable assumption when the MVC framework was new, but a new generation of ASP.NET developers has jumped right in with MVC without using Web Forms and—by implication—the features that the ASP.NET platform provides.

This book corrects the problem, detailing the features of the ASP.NET platform for the MVC framework developer who has no Web Forms experience (and no desire to acquire any). Throughout this book, I show you how the ASP.NET platform underpins the MVC framework and how you can take advantage of the platform to improve your MVC applications.

You don't *need* to know how the ASP.NET platform works to build MVC framework applications, but you will *want* to know when you learn just how much functionality is available and how it can help simplify application development, customize the way that the MVC framework operates, and scale up applications to larger numbers of users, both for local and cloud-deployed applications.

Note This book is not an MVC framework tutorial, and I assume you have a basic understanding of MVC and web application development in general. If you are new to the MVC framework, then start by reading my *Pro ASP.NET MVC 5* book, which is also published by Apress.

What Is the ASP.NET Platform?

ASP.NET was originally synonymous with Web Forms, which aims to make the web application development experience as similar as possible to developing a traditional desktop application and to abstract away the details of HTML and HTTP.

Web Forms has achieved remarkable market penetration despite having a reputation for producing hard-to-maintain applications and being bandwidth hungry. Microsoft continually improves and updates Web Forms—and it is still a widely used technology—but the broad development trend is away from abstraction and toward embracing the stateless nature of HTTP. To remain current in the web development world, Microsoft extended ASP.NET to include the MVC framework and, more recently, SignalR and Web API.

These technologies have disparate natures. The MVC framework is an alternative to Web Forms for building complete web applications (one I assume you are familiar with if you are reading this book). SignalR uses an HTML5 feature called web sockets to enable real-time communication between a browser and a server, and Web API is used to create web services and APIs that deliver JSON or XML content.

For all their differences, the ASP.NET technologies share some common characteristics, and this is where the ASP.NET platform starts to emerge. Features that are common across ASP.NET—such as the need to receive and process HTTP requests, for example—are implemented in a common foundation, which results in the technology stack shown in Figure 1-1.

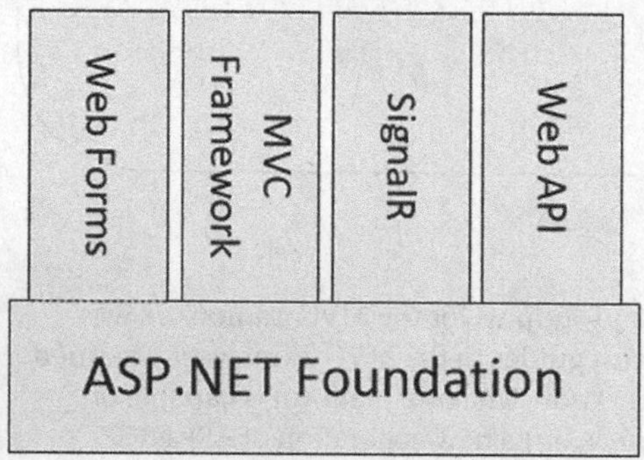

Figure 1-1. *The ASP.NET foundation*

The dotted line in the figure illustrates that some of the design decisions made when Web Forms was the only ASP.NET technology are still present in the ASP.NET foundation. For the most part, this just means that there are some odd method names in the foundation API, which I describe in Part 2 of this book.

The ASP.NET platform doesn't just provide common features to the ASP.NET technology stack; it also provides a set of services that make it easier to write web applications, such as security, state data, and caching, as illustrated by Figure 1-2.

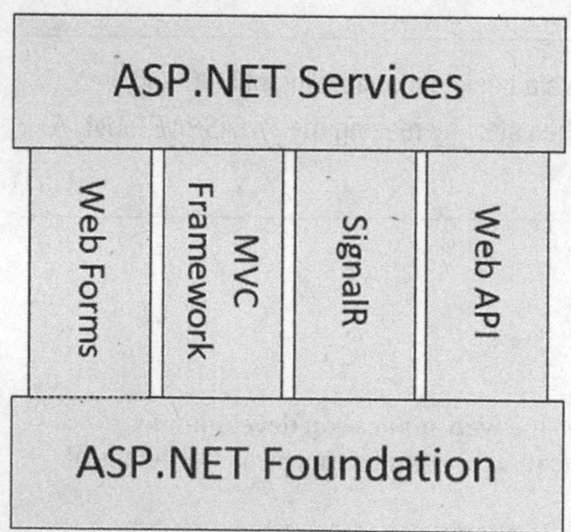

Figure 1-2. *The ASP.NET services*

When using the MVC framework, you will usually consume these services from within controllers and models, but the services themselves are not part of the MVC framework and are available across the entire ASP.NET family of technologies.

I have drawn the ASP.NET services as being separate from the ASP.NET foundation, which makes them easier to describe but doesn't accurately reflect the fact almost all of the services are integrated into the functionality provided by the foundation. This is important because the services rely on the way that the foundation handles HTTP requests in order to provide functionality to services, and it will start to make more sense once I get into the details of the ASP.NET request life cycle in Part 2 of this book.

The ASP.NET platform is the combination of the foundation and the services, and using the ASP.NET platform in MVC framework applications is the topic of this book, as illustrated by Figure 1-3.

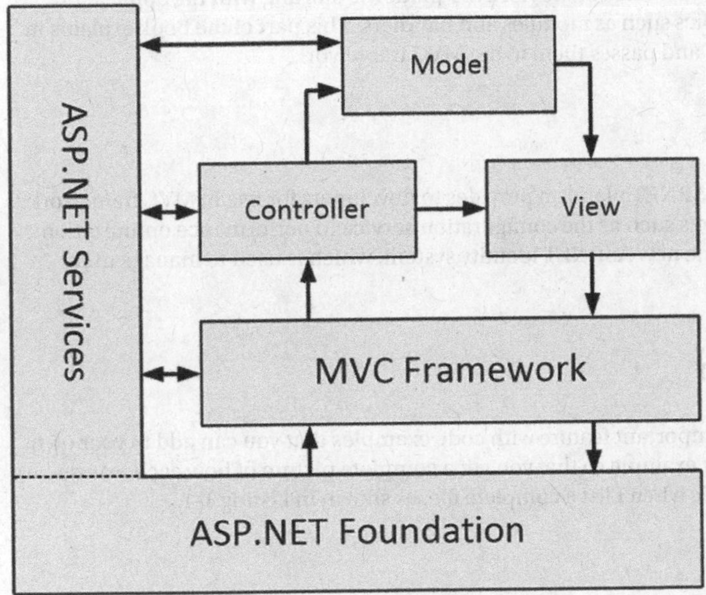

***Figure 1-3.** The relationship between the ASP.NET platform and the MVC framework*

Don't worry if the relationship between the MVC framework, the application components, and the ASP.NET platform don't make immediate sense. Everything will start to fall into place as you learn about how the platform works and the features it provides.

What Do You Need to Know?

This book is for developers who have experience in web application development using C# and the MVC framework. You should understand the nature of HTTP, HTML, and CSS and be familiar with the basic features of Visual Studio 2013 (although I provide a quick primer for how I use Visual Studio in Chapter 2).

You will find this book hard to follow if you don't have experience with the MVC framework, although there are plenty of examples that will help fill in the gaps. If you need to brush up on using the MVC framework, then I suggest my *Pro ASP.NET MVC 5* for MVC development and *The Definitive Guide to HTML5* for detailed coverage of HTML and CSS.

What's the Structure of This Book?

This book is split into three parts, each of which covers a set of related topics.

Part 1: Getting Ready

Part 1 of this book provides the information you need to get ready for the rest of the book. It includes this chapter and a primer for the tools I use in this book and for the MVC pattern.

Part 2: The ASP.NET Platform Foundation

Part 2 of this book takes you through the foundation features of the ASP.NET platform, starting with the application and request life cycle and onto more advanced topics such as modules and handlers. This part of the book explains in detail how the ASP.NET platform handles requests and passes them to the MVC framework.

Part 3: The ASP.NET Services

Part 3 of this book describes the services that the ASP.NET platform provides to developers for use in MVC framework applications. These services range from hidden gems such as the configuration service to performance optimizations, such as data and content caching. I also describe the new ASP.NET Identity system, which is used to manage user authentication and authorization.

Are There Lots of Examples?

There are *loads* of examples. I demonstrate every important feature with code examples that you can add to your own projects, and I list the contents of every file in every example so that you get a complete picture of how each feature works. I use two code styles for examples. The first is when I list a complete file, as shown in Listing 1-1.

Listing 1-1. A Complete Listing

```
using Microsoft.AspNet.Identity;
using Microsoft.AspNet.Identity.EntityFramework;
using Microsoft.AspNet.Identity.Owin;
using Microsoft.Owin;
using Users.Models;

namespace Users.Infrastructure {
    public class AppUserManager : UserManager<AppUser> {

        public AppUserManager(IUserStore<AppUser> store)
            : base(store) {
        }

        public static AppUserManager Create(
                IdentityFactoryOptions<AppUserManager> options,
                IOwinContext context) {

            AppIdentityDbContext db = context.Get<AppIdentityDbContext>();
            AppUserManager manager = new AppUserManager(new UserStore<AppUser>(db));

            return manager;
        }
    }
}
```

This listing is taken from Chapter 13—don't worry about what it does at the moment. I usually start the chapter with complete listings; then, as I make changes to show you different features, I switch to partial listings, such as Listing 1-2.

Listing 1-2. A Partial Listing

```
...
return HttpContext.GetOwinContext().GetUserManager<AppUserManager>();
...
```

This listing is also taken from Chapter 13 and shows a section of the file from Listing 1-1. I highlight the changes that I have made or the statements I want to draw your attention to. Using partial listings helps avoid endless repetitions of files that have small changes and lets me pack in more examples per page and per chapter.

Where Can You Get the Example Code?

All of the example code is contained in the text of this book, but you don't have to type it in yourself. You can download a complete set of example projects, organized by chapter, without charge from `Apress.com`.

What Software Do You Need for This Book?

The most important software you need for this book is Visual Studio 2013, which contains everything you need to get started, including a built-in application server for running and debugging MVC applications, an administration-free edition of SQL Server for developing database-driven applications, tools for unit testing, and, of course, a code editor compiler and debugger.

There are several editions of Visual Studio, but I will be using the one that Microsoft makes available free of charge, called Visual Studio Express 2013 for Web. Microsoft adds some nice features to the paid-for editions of Visual Studio, but you will not need them for this book, and all of the figures that you see throughout this book have been taken using the Express edition, which you can download from `www.microsoft.com/visualstudio/eng/products/visual-studio-express-products`. There are several versions of Visual Studio 2013 Express, each of which is used for a different kind of development. Make sure that you get the Web version, which supports ASP.NET applications.

I follow a specific approach to creating ASP.NET projects: I don't use the predefined templates that Microsoft provides, preferring to explicitly add all of the packages that I require. This means more work is required to get set up, but the benefit is that you end up with a much better understanding of how an application fits together. I provide a primer in Chapter 2 that gives an example of what you can expect.

■ **Tip** Visual Studio includes NuGet for downloading and installing software packages. I use NuGet throughout this book. So that you are sure to get the results that I demonstrate, I always specify the version of the NuGet package you require. If you are in doubt, download the source code for this book from `www.apress.com`, which contains complete projects for each chapter.

Preparing Visual Studio

Visual Studio Express contains all the features you need to create, test, and deploy an MVC framework application, but some of those features are hidden away until you ask for them. To enable all of the features, select Expert Settings from the Visual Studio Tools ➤ Settings menu.

■ **Tip** Microsoft has decided that the top-level menus in Visual Studio should be all in uppercase, which means that the menu I just referred to is really TOOLS. I think this is rather like shouting, and I will capitalize menu names like Tools is here throughout this book.

The only other preparation is to disable the Browser Link feature when you create projects. Browser Link works by establishing a connection to the server that is used to receive notifications when the project contents change. In Part 2 of this book, I spend a lot of time talking about how requests are handled, and the extra requests sent by Browser Link skew the results. Disable Browser Link by clicking the button highlighted in Figure 1-4 and deselecting the Enable Browser Link menu item.

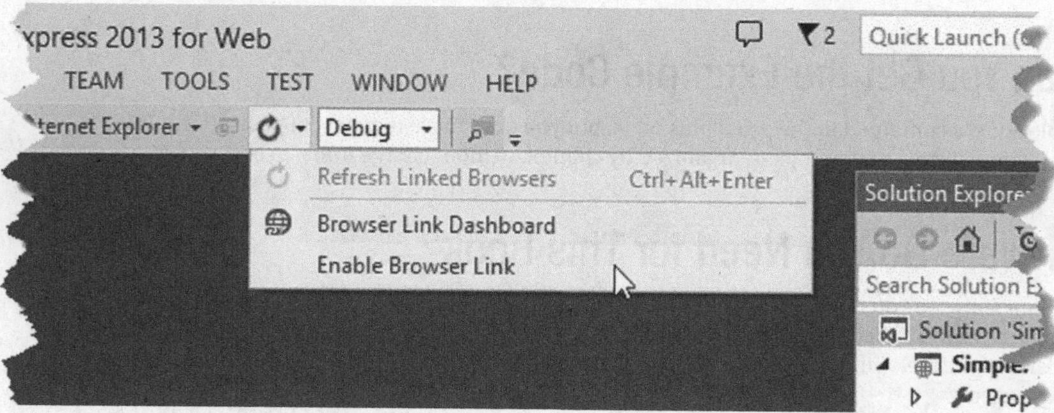

Figure 1-4. Disabling Browser Link

Getting Google Chrome

For the majority of the examples in this book, I use Internet Explorer because I know that it is always available on Windows. There are occasions when I use Google Chrome, and you will need to download it from `www.google.com/chrome` if you want to re-create the examples.

I use Chrome for two main reasons. The first reason is because it supports simple emulation of mobile devices, which is useful in Chapter 7 when I show you how to detect device capabilities. The second reason is when I show you how to differentiate requests for services like caching in Chapter 12.

Summary

In this chapter, I outlined the content and structure of this book and set out the software that is required. The next chapter refreshes your basic skills with the MVC pattern and the MVC framework before I start digging into the details in Part 2.

CHAPTER 2

Pattern and Tools Primer

In this chapter, I provide a brief overview of the pattern that the MVC framework follows and demonstrate the process for creating a simple MVC project using Visual Studio 2013. The purpose of this chapter is to refresh your memory about the nature, objectives, and benefits of the MVC pattern and to show you the process I use to create the examples in this book.

This chapter isn't a tutorial for the MVC framework. As I explained in Chapter 1, you already need to have a basic understanding of MVC framework development in order to benefit from the features and techniques I describe in this book. If you do not have experience with the MVC framework, then read *Pro ASP.NET MVC 5*, also from Apress, before continuing.

Understanding the MVC Pattern

The term *Model-View-Controller* has been in use since the late 1970s and arose from the Smalltalk project at Xerox PARC where it was conceived as a way to organize early GUI applications. Some of the details of the original MVC pattern was tied to Smalltalk-specific concepts, such as *screens* and *tools*, but the broader concepts are still applicable to applications—and are especially well-suited to web applications.

Interactions with an MVC application follow a natural cycle of user actions and view updates, where the view is assumed to be stateless. This fits nicely with the HTTP requests and responses that underpin a web application.

Further, the MVC pattern enforces a *separation of concerns*—the domain model and controller logic are decoupled from the user interface, which means that an MVC application will be split into at least three pieces:

- *Models*, which contain or represent the data that users work with. These can be simple *view models*, which just represent data being transferred between views and controllers; or they can be *domain models*, which contain the data in a business domain as well as the operations, transformations, and rules for manipulating that data.
- *Views*, which are used to render some part of the model as a user interface.
- *Controllers*, which process incoming requests, perform operations on the model, and select views to render to the user.

In the MVC framework, controllers are C# classes derived from the `System.Web.Mvc.Controller` class. Each `public` method in a class derived from `Controller` is an *action method*, which is associated with a URL defined through the ASP.NET routing system. When a request is sent to the URL associated with an action method, the statements in the controller class are executed in order to perform some operation on the domain model and then select a view to display to the client. Figure 2-1 shows the interactions between the controller, model, and view.

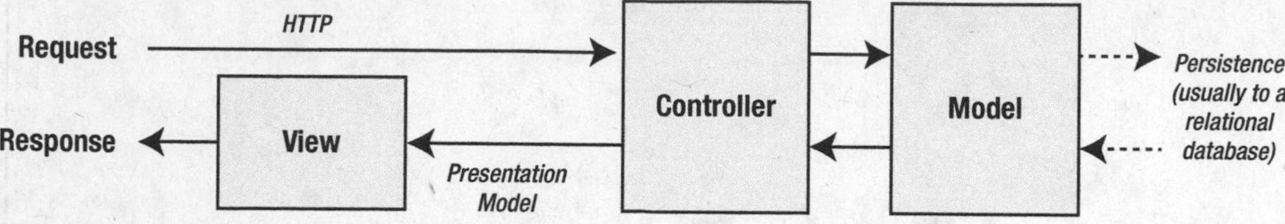

Figure 2-1. *The interactions in an MVC application*

The ASP.NET MVC framework use a *view engine*, which is the component responsible for rendering a view to generate a response for the browser. The view engine for the MVC framework is called Razor, and you'll see examples of Razor markup throughout this book. If you don't like Razor, then you can select one of the many third-party view engines that are available (although I won't be doing so in this book, not least because I find Razor to be robust and easy to work with).

Models are the definition of the universe your application works in. In a banking application, for example, the model represents everything in the bank that the application supports, such as accounts, the general ledger, and credit limits for customers—as well as the operations that can be used to manipulate the data in the model, such as depositing funds and making withdrawals from the accounts. The model is also responsible for preserving the overall state and consistency of the data—for example, making sure that all transactions are added to the ledger and that a client doesn't withdraw more money than he is entitled to or more money than the bank has.

Models are also defined by what they are *not* responsible for: Models don't deal with rendering UIs or processing requests; those are the responsibilities of *views* and *controllers. Views* contain the logic required to display elements of the model to the user—and nothing more. They have no direct awareness of the model and do not directly communicate with the model in any way. *Controllers* are the bridge between views and the model; requests come in from the client and are serviced by the controller, which selects an appropriate view to show the user and, if required, an appropriate operation to perform on the model.

The MVC framework doesn't apply any constraints on the implementation of your domain model. You can create a model using regular C# objects and implement persistence using any of the databases, object-relational mapping frameworks, or other data tools supported by .NET.

Understanding the Benefits of the MVC Pattern

Each piece of the MVC architecture is well-defined and self-contained—this is the *separation of concerns.* The logic that manipulates the data in the model is contained *only* in the model; the logic that displays data is *only* in the view, and the code that handles user requests and input is contained *only* in the controller. This separation is at the heart of the benefits imparted by the MVC pattern—and by implication—the MVC framework.

The first benefit is *scale*, not in terms of how many users a web application can support but in terms of how complex it can be. Technologies such as Web Forms can be used to build complex applications, of course, but doing so requires detailed planning and attention to detail, and many projects end up as a morass of code that duplicates functionality and markup in multiple places, making extending or fixing the application difficult. It is possible to get into the same kind of mess with the MVC framework, but only by ignoring the MVC pattern. Most developers produce MVC projects that can scale in complexity without much difficulty and that are easy to maintain and extend (and if you do find yourself in a mess, the separation of concerns in an MVC framework application makes it easier to refactor the application back onto a stable footing).

The second benefit is *unit testing*. The module nature of the MVC framework makes it easy to perform unit testing, aided by the testing support provided by Visual Studio (although many other testing toolkits are available).

The third benefit is *flexibility*. The separation of concerns makes it relatively easy to respond to changes in requirements throughout the life of the application. This is a hard benefit to quantify and comes in part from the MVC pattern and in part from the convention-over-configuration approach that the MVC framework has adopted, but once the fundamental pieces of an application have been developed, it is a simple task to modify or rearrange them to respond to requests in new ways.

■ **Note** If there is one drawback of the MVC framework, it is that there is an initial investment of time required to create and arrange components in an application before you start seeing results. This is time well spent for large projects but not for quick and simple prototyping. In these situations, I still use Web Forms because it can be used to create simple applications in just a few minutes, despite lacking all of the long-term benefits that the MVC framework provides.

Creating the Example Project

In this section, I am going to walk through the process of creating a simple MVC framework application. Not only will this act as a quick primer for how Visual Studio supports MVC development, but it will also allow me to demonstrate the way that I like to create projects. Visual Studio is set up to add default template content to most projects, but I prefer to start with a minimal project and explicitly add the features I require.

■ **Note** You will need to have downloaded and installed Visual Studio if you want to create this example yourself. See Chapter 1 for details.

To get started, I created a new Visual Studio project. Select File ➤ New Project to open the New Project dialog window. Navigate through the Templates section to select the Visual C# ➤ Web ➤ ASP.NET Web Application template and set the name of the project to SimpleApp, as shown in Figure 2-2.

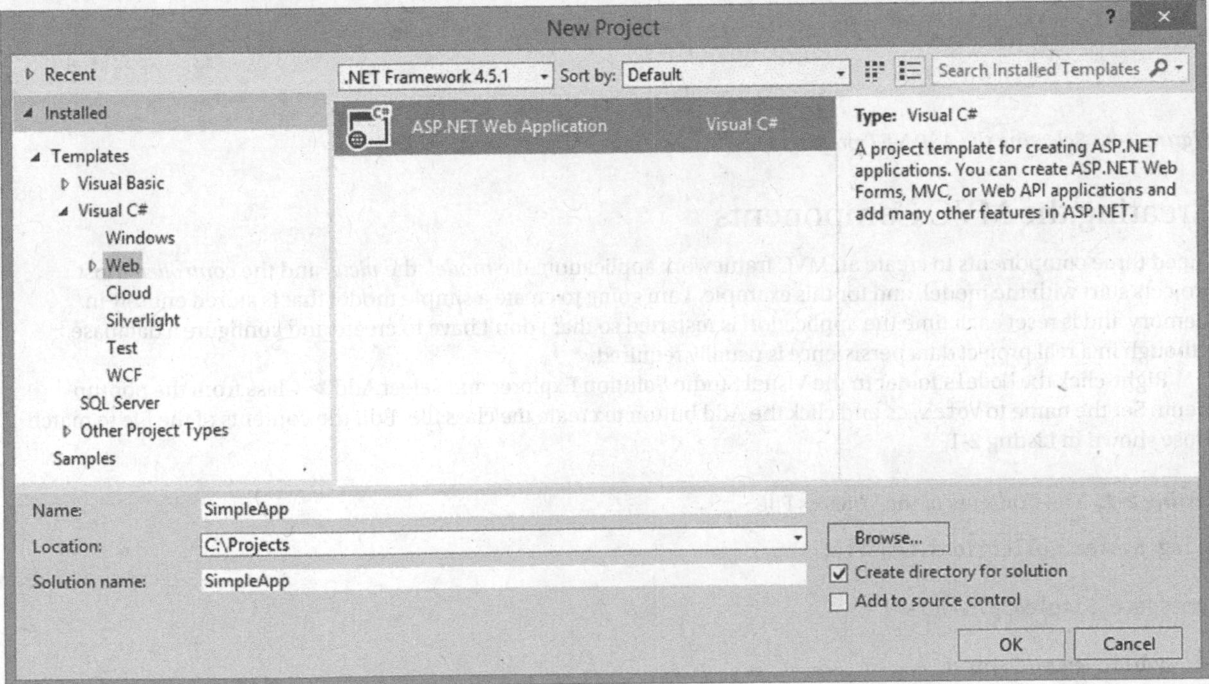

Figure 2-2. Creating the Visual Studio project

Click the OK button to move to the New ASP.NET Project dialog window. Ensure that the Empty option is selected and check the MVC option, as shown in Figure 2-3. Click the OK button, and Visual Studio will create a new project called SimpleApp.

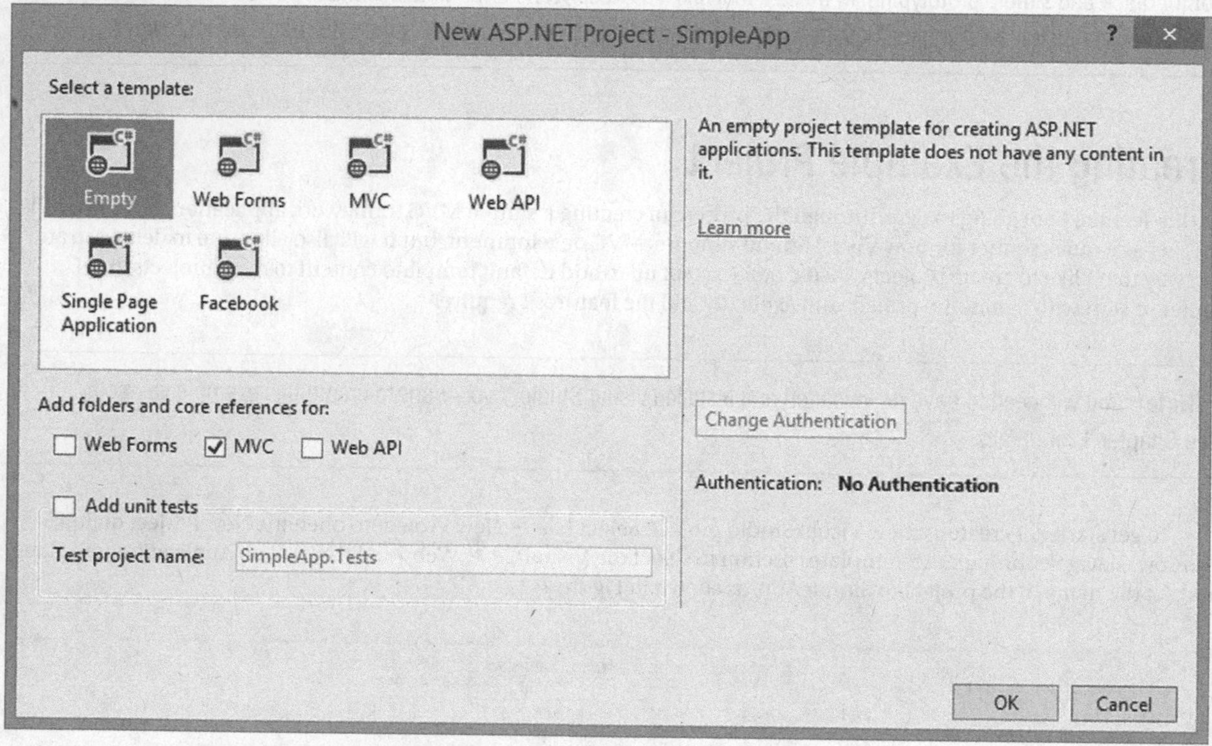

Figure 2-3. *Selecting the ASP.NET project type*

Creating the MVC Components

I need three components to create an MVC framework application: the *model*, the *view*, and the *controller*. Most projects start with the model, and for this example, I am going to create a simple model that is stored entirely in memory and is reset each time the application is restarted so that I don't have to create and configure a database, although in a real project data persistence is usually required.

Right-click the `Models` folder in the Visual Studio Solution Explorer and select Add ➤ Class from the pop-up menu. Set the name to `Votes.cs` and click the Add button to create the class file. Edit the contents of the file to match those shown in Listing 2-1.

Listing 2-1. The Contents of the Votes.cs File

```
using System.Collections.Generic;

namespace SimpleApp.Models {

    public enum Color {
        Red, Green, Yellow, Purple
    };
```

```
public class Votes {
    private static Dictionary<Color, int> votes = new Dictionary<Color, int>();

    public static void RecordVote(Color color) {
        votes[color] = votes.ContainsKey(color) ? votes[color] + 1 : 1;
    }

    public static void ChangeVote(Color newColor, Color oldColor) {
        if (votes.ContainsKey(oldColor)) {
            votes[oldColor]--;
        }
        RecordVote(newColor);
    }

    public static int GetVotes(Color color) {
        return votes.ContainsKey(color) ? votes[color] : 0;
    }
  }
}
```

■ **Tip** You don't have to type the example code to see the example projects in this book. The complete source code for every chapter is available in a free download from `www.apress.com`.

My example application will allow users to vote for their favorite color. This isn't an exciting demonstration, but it will provide me with a simple application that I can use to demonstrate where the ASP.NET framework stops and the MVC framework starts when I extend the project in later chapters.

I have defined an `enum` of colors that users can vote for and a `Votes` class that records and reports on the votes for each color. The methods presented by the `Votes` class are static, and the data, which is stored in a dictionary collection, will be lost when the application is stopped or restarted.

■ **Note** Using static data and methods in the `Votes` class means I don't have to use a technique called *dependency injection* to provide instances of `Votes` to application components that require them. I wouldn't use the static approach in a real project because dependency injection is a useful technique that helps create an easy-to-manage code base. See my *Pro ASP.NET MVC 5* book for details of setting up and using dependency injection. For this chapter, I need a simple MVC application and don't have to consider long-term maintenance or testing.

The controller is the component that defines the logic for receiving HTTP requests from the browser, updating the model, and selecting the view that will be displayed to the user.

An MVC framework controller provides one or more action methods that are targeted by individual URLs. The mapping between URLs and action methods is handled through the URL routing feature, and the default routing configuration specifies that requests to the default URL (the / URL) for the application are mapped to the `Index` action method in a controller called `Home`.

I am not going to get into the details of the URL routing system in this book, but the default configuration is sufficient for my example application as long as I create a controller with the right name.

Right-click the Controllers folder in the Visual Studio Solution Explorer and select Add ➤ Controller from the pop-up menu. Select MVC 5 Controller – Empty from the list of options and click the Add button. Set the name to be HomeController and click the Add button to create the Controllers/HomeController.cs file. Edit the new file to match Listing 2-2.

Listing 2-2. The Contents of the HomeController.cs File

```
using System.Web.Mvc;
using SimpleApp.Models;

namespace SimpleApp.Controllers {
    public class HomeController : Controller {

        public ActionResult Index() {
            return View();
        }

        [HttpPost]
        public ActionResult Index(Color color) {
            Color? oldColor = Session["color"] as Color?;
            if (oldColor != null) {
                Votes.ChangeVote(color, (Color)oldColor);
            } else {
                Votes.RecordVote(color);
            }
            ViewBag.SelectedColor = Session["color"] = color;
            return View();
        }
    }
}
```

■ **Note** The URL routing system is actually part of the ASP.NET platform rather than the MVC framework, but I described URL routing in detail in my *Pro ASP.NET MVC 5* book, and I am not going to repeat the information here.

One useful feature of controllers is the ability to define multiple action methods with the same name and then differentiate them through the use of attributes. In the listing, I have applied the HttpPost attribute to the Index action method that takes an argument, which tells the MVC framework that the method should be used to handle HTTP POST requests. HTTP GET requests will be handled by the Index method that takes no arguments.

The goal of an action method is to update the model and select a view to be displayed to the user. I don't need to update my model when dealing with GET requests, so I just return the result from calling the View method, which selects the default view associated with the action method. I need to update the vote tally when dealing with POST requests, either by registering a new vote or, if the user has voted already, by changing an existing vote. I keep track of whether a user has voted through the Session property, which allows me to maintain state data for the duration of the user's browser session.

The final component is the *view*, which generates the HTML that is displayed to the user as the response to an HTTP request. Both of the action methods in the Home controller call the View method without any arguments, which tells the MVC framework to look for a view whose name matches the action method name. The MVC framework will search for an Index view with different file extensions and in different folder locations, one combination of which is /Views/Home/Index.cshtml. The Views folder is the conventional location of views in an MVC application, the Home folder is the conventional location for views used by the Home controller, and the .cshtml file extension specifies that the view contains C# Razor annotations.

To create the view for the example application, right-click either of the action methods in the `HomeController` class and select Add View from the pop-up menu to open the Add View dialog window. Set the Name field to Index, set the Template field to Empty (without model), and ensure that the Create as a partial view and Use a layout page options are not checked, as shown in Figure 2-4.

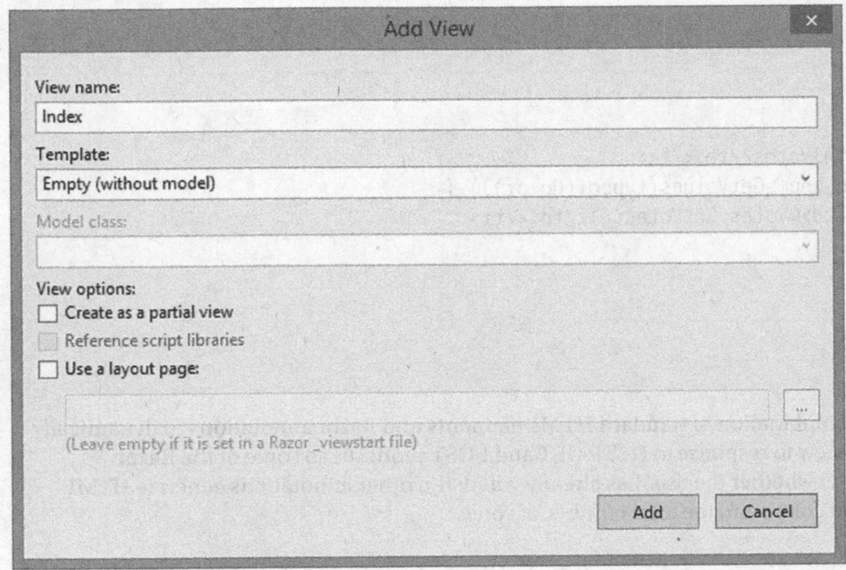

Figure 2-4. *Creating the view*

Click the Add button, and Visual Studio will create a file called `Index.cshtml` in the `Views/Home` folder. Edit this file so that it matches Listing 2-3.

Listing 2-3. The Contents of the Index.cshtml File

```
@using SimpleApp.Models
@{ Layout = null; }

<!DOCTYPE html>
<html>
<head>
    <meta name="viewport" content="width=device-width" />
    <title>Vote</title>
</head>
<body>
    @if (ViewBag.SelectedColor == null) {
        <h4>Vote for your favorite color</h4>
    } else {
        <h4>Change your vote from @ViewBag.SelectedColor</h4>
    }
```

```
    @using (Html.BeginForm()) {
        @Html.DropDownList("color",
                new SelectList(Enum.GetValues(typeof(Color))), "Choose a Color")
        <div>
            <button type="submit">Vote</button>
        </div>
    }
    <div>
        <h5>Results</h5>
        <table>
            <tr><th>Color</th><th>Votes</th></tr>
            @foreach (Color c in Enum.GetValues(typeof(Color))) {
                <tr><td>@c</td><td>@Votes.GetVotes(c)</td></tr>
            }
        </table>
    </div>
</body>
</html>
```

An MVC framework view uses a combination of standard HTML elements and Razor annotations to dynamically generate content. I am using a single view to response to HTTP GET and POST requests, so some of the Razor annotations adapt the content to reflect whether the user has already voted; the other annotations generate HTML elements based on the enumeration of colors and the total number of votes.

Testing the Application

Once you have created the three components in the previous section, you can test them by selecting Start Debugging from the Visual Studio Debug menu. Visual Studio will open a browser window and navigate to the application URL, allowing you to select a color and vote. Figure 2-5 illustrates the voting process.

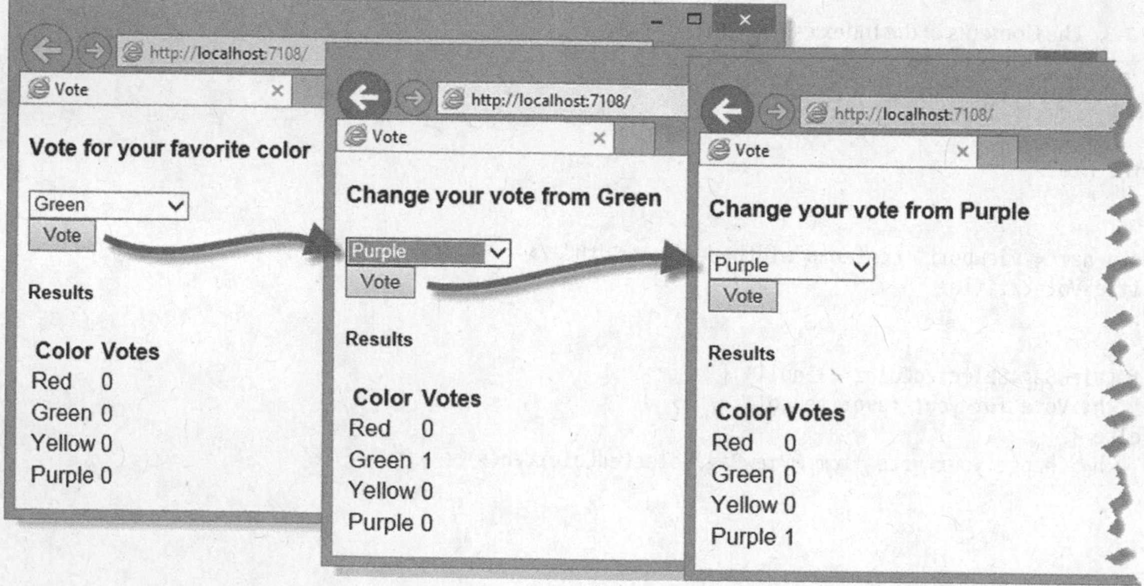

***Figure 2-5.** Using the application*

■ **Note** I refer to the Visual Studio Debug menu, but it is really the DEBUG menu because Microsoft has adopted an all-capitals policy to menu names. I think this is an odd thing to do, and I will refer to menu items in mixed case in this book.

Adding Packages to the Project

As I explained earlier in the chapter, I prefer to create a basic Visual Studio project and then explicitly add the features I need. This is less work than you might expect because Visual Studio supports NuGet, which is a package manager that provides access to a wide catalog of packages for .NET application development. The integration into Visual Studio allows for the automatic downloading, installation, and dependency management of packages and has transformed the process of using standard libraries in .NET development.

The NuGet package catalog, which you can browse at `www.nuget.org`, is extensive and includes many popular open source web application packages. Microsoft has given tacit support to some of these packages by including them in the Visual Studio templates for new ASP.NET projects, but you can use NuGet directly to install these packages without getting the rest of the (generally useless) template content.

One package that Microsoft has adopted with the MVC 5 release is Bootstrap, which is an excellent CSS and JavaScript library for styling HTML that grew out of a project at Twitter. I have absolutely no design skills at all, and I like using Bootstrap because it lets me style content during the early stages of development without making too much of a mess. I like to work with professional designers on real projects (and I recommend you do the same), but in this book I'll use Bootstrap to make some the examples easier to understand and to highlight specific results and features.

■ **Note** Bootstrap is only one of the packages that Microsoft has adopted, and I only briefly describe its use in this chapter. For full details of client-side development for MVC framework projects, see my *Pro ASP.NET MVC 5 Client Development* book, which is published by Apress.

I'll show you how I use Bootstrap later in this chapter, but in this section I will show you how to use the Visual Studio support for NuGet to download and install the Bootstrap package.

■ **Note** Bootstrap isn't directly related to the MVC Framework or the ASP.NET platform. In this chapter I use it to demonstrate how to install a NuGet package and in later chapters to make the examples easier to follow. If you are familiar with NuGet and Bootstrap (or are not interested in either), then you can move directly to Part 2 of this book, where I turn to the details of the ASP.NET platform.

Visual Studio provides a graphical interface that lets you navigate through the package catalog, but I prefer to use the console feature that accepts NuGet commands directly in Visual Studio. Open the console by selecting Package Manager Console from the Tools ➤ Library Package Manager menu and enter the following command:

```
Install-Package -version 3.0.3 bootstrap
```

The `Install-Package` command instructs Visual Studio to add a new package to the project. When you press the Enter key, Visual Studio will download and install the Bootstrap package and any other packages that it depends on. Bootstrap depends only on the popular jQuery library, which Visual Studio added automatically when setting up the project, along with some additional JavaScript files that use jQuery to handle form validation.

■ **Tip** The -version argument allows me to specify a particular version of the package, and version 3.0.3 is the current version of Bootstrap available as I write this. The latest version of the package will be installed if you omit the -version argument when using the Install-Package command. I use specific versions of packages in this book to ensure that you are able to re-create the examples.

The Bootstrap NuGet package adds some CSS files to the Content folder (which is the home of static content in an MVC framework application) and some JavaScript files to the Scripts folder. Bootstrap mainly works through CSS files, but there are some JavaScript enhancements for more complex interactions. (The Bootstrap package also creates a fonts folder. Not all open source libraries fit neatly into the ASP.NET project structure, so occasionally you will see artifacts like this to support assumptions made by the library about the layout of its files.)

Using Bootstrap

I don't want to get into too much detail about Bootstrap because it isn't the topic of this book, and I will be using it only to make the examples easier to understand. To demonstrate the basic Bootstrap features, I have applied some of the most useful styles to the Views/Home/Index.cshtml file, as shown in Listing 2-4.

Listing 2-4. Applying Bootstrap Styles to the Index.cshtml File

```
@using SimpleApp.Models
@{ Layout = null; }

<!DOCTYPE html>
<html>
<head>
    <meta name="viewport" content="width=device-width" />
    <title>Vote</title>
    <link href="~/Content/bootstrap.min.css" rel="stylesheet" />
    <link href="~/Content/bootstrap-theme.min.css" rel="stylesheet" />
</head>
<body class="container">
    <div class="panel panel-primary">
        @if (ViewBag.SelectedColor == null) {
            <h4 class="panel-heading">Vote for your favorite color</h4>
        } else {
            <h4 class="panel-heading">Change your vote from @ViewBag.SelectedColor</h4>
        }

        <div class="panel-body">

            @using (Html.BeginForm()) {
                @Html.DropDownList("color",
                        new SelectList(Enum.GetValues(typeof(Color))), "Choose a Color",
                            new { @class = "form-control" })
```

```
            <div>
                <button class="btn btn-primary center-block"
                    type="submit">Vote</button>
            </div>
        }

    </div>
</div>

<div class="panel panel-primary">
    <h5 class="panel-heading">Results</h5>
    <table class="table table-condensed table-striped">
        @foreach (Color c in Enum.GetValues(typeof(Color))) {
            <tr><td>@c</td><td>@Votes.GetVotes(c)</td></tr>
        }
    </table>
</div>
</body>
</html>
```

The first changes in the view are the addition of `link` elements to import the `bootstrap.min.css` and `bootstrap-theme.min.css` files into the HTML document. Bootstrap includes a set of base CSS classes that are supplemented by replaceable themes. The base classes are in the `bootstrap.min.css` file, and I have used the default theme that is defined by the bootstrap-`theme.min.css` file and that is installed by the NuGet package.

■ **Tip** I am using the *minified* versions of the Bootstrap files in this example, which have been processed to remove whitespace, comments, and other optional content. Minified files are used in deployment to reduce bandwidth requirements or (as here) when using third-party packages that you do not need to debug. The NuGet package also installs the human-readable files if you want to take a look at how Bootstrap works.

The other changes apply the Bootstrap CSS classes to style the HTML content that the view will generate. Bootstrap includes a lot of CSS classes, and I am only using some of the most basic, but they are representative of the examples you will see throughout this book. Figure 2-6 shows the effect that the changes in Listing 2-4 have on the application, which will provide some useful context.

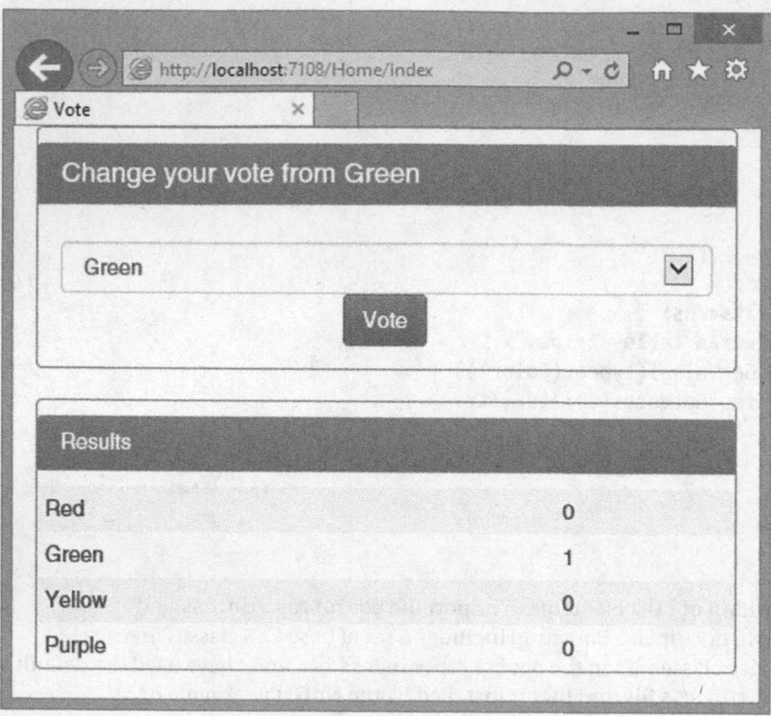

Figure 2-6. *The effect of using Bootstrap on the example application*

■ **Note** Bootstrap functionality is largely provided through CSS classes but is supplemented with some JavaScript additions. I don't need to use the JavaScript features for this example and am only using the CSS classes.

I am not going to describe the individual Bootstrap classes in detail, but I have provided a quick summary of those that I have used in Listing 2-4 in Table 2-1 so that you can see how I created the effect shown in the figure.

Table 2-1. *The Bootstrap Classes Applied to the Index.cshtml File*

Name	Description
`Btn`	Styles `button` or a elements as Bootstrap buttons. This class is usually applied in conjunction with a button theme class, such as `btn-primary`.
`btn-primary`	Used in conjunction with the `btn` class to apply a theme color to a button. The other button theme classes are `btn-default`, `btn-success`, `btn-info`, `btn-warning`, and `btn-danger`.
`center-block`	Centers elements. I used this class in the view to position the Vote button.
`container`	Centers the contents of the element it is applied to. In the listing, I applied this class to the body element so that all of the HTML content is centered.
`form-control`	Styles a Bootstrap form element. There is only one form element in the listing, but this class usefully sizes and aligns elements to present a form.

(continued)

Table 2-1. (*continued*)

Name	Description
panel	Groups related content together. Used with the panel-body and panel-heading classes to denote the sections of the panel and, optionally, with a class that applies a theme color, such as panel-primary.
panel-body	Denotes the content section of a panel.
panel-heading	Denotes the heading section of a panel.
panel-primary	Used in conjunction with the panel class to apply a theme color to a panel. The other theme classes are panel-default, panel-success, panel-info, panel-warning, and panel-danger.
table	Styles a Bootstrap table.
table-condensed	Used in conjunction with the table class to create a compact table layout.
table-striped	Used in conjunction with the table class to color alternate rows in a table.

The Bootstrap classes are simple to use and can quickly create a consistent layout for the HTML in a view. For the most part, I applied the classes to the static HTML elements in the view in Listing 2-4, but I have also used a Bootstrap class with the HTML helper method that generates the select element from the enumeration of color values, like this:

```
...
@Html.DropDownList("color", new SelectList(Enum.GetValues(typeof(Color))),
    "Choose a Color", new { @class = "form-control" })
...
```

The HTML helpers are convenience methods used in Razor views to generate HTML elements from model data. All of the helper methods are overridden so that there is a version that accepts an object that is used to apply attributes to the elements that are created. The properties of the object are used for the attribute names, and the values for the attributes are taken from the property values. For the DropDownList helper in the example, I have passed in a dynamic object that defines a class property that applies the Bootstrap form-control class to the select element that the helper creates.

■ **Tip** I have to prefix the property name with @ because class is a C# keyword. The @ symbol is a standard C# feature that allows the use of keywords without confusing the compiler.

Summary

In this chapter, I started by refreshing your memory as to the nature and purpose of the MVC pattern. Understanding the MVC pattern will provide some useful context when considering the design and application of the platform features that I describe in Part 2 of this book.

I also showed you how to create a simple MVC framework application using Visual Studio. Visual Studio is a feature-rich and flexible development tool, and there are many choices about how projects are created and built. As this chapter demonstrated, I prefer a basic starting point from which I can add the functionality and features that I require, such as the Bootstrap library that I added to the example project with NuGet and that I briefly described. In Part 2 of this book, I begin to describe the ASP.NET platform in detail, starting with the two life cycles of an ASP.NET application.

PART 2

The ASP.NET Platform Foundation

CHAPTER 3

The ASP.NET Life Cycles

The ASP.NET platform defines two important life cycles that underpin the MVC framework. The first is the *application life cycle*, which tracks the life of a web application from the moment it starts to the moment it is terminated. The second is the request life cycle, which defines the path that an HTTP request follows as it moves through the ASP.NET platform from the point at which the initial request is received until the response is sent. In this chapter, I describe both life cycles and the context objects that the ASP.NET platform uses to describe them and the overall state of the application. Table 3-1 summarizes the chapter.

Table 3-1. *Chapter Summary*

Problem	Solution	Listing
Perform actions when the application starts and stops.	Use the special `Application_Start` and `Application_End` methods in the global application class.	1–3
Monitor or modify a request as it is processed.	Handle the events that define the request life cycle.	4–8
Get information about the state of the application, the current request, or the response associated with it.	Use the properties defined by the context objects.	9–11, 13

Preparing the Example Project

For this chapter, I am going to continue use the SimpleApp project I created in Chapter 2 and that allows the user to vote for a color. You will find that most of the MVC framework applications that I build in this book are pretty simple because my focus is on the ASP.NET platform.

Tip Don't forget that you can download the source code for all the examples in this book for free from `www.apress.com`.

The ASP.NET Application Life Cycle

As an MVC framework developer, you are used to starting an application and letting it handle requests, using Visual Studio during development or on a production platform after deployment. At some later time, the application is stopped—perhaps for maintenance or an upgrade—and requests are no longer processed.

These two moments—the point at which an application starts and stops receiving requests—define the application life cycle, the management of which provides the most fundamental features for ASP.NET web applications. ASP.NET provides notifications when the application starts and when it is stopped in a controlled way, and these notifications are the topic of this section of this chapter. Table 3-2 puts the application life-cycle notifications in context.

Table 3-2. *Putting the Application Life-Cycle Notification in Context*

Question	Answer
What is it?	The application life-cycle notifications allow you to perform actions when the application starts and when it is shut down in a controlled way.
Why should I care?	The notifications are useful if you have one-off configuration tasks or if you need to release resources when the application is stopped. The most common use of the application life cycle by MVC framework developers is to configure a dependency injection container.
How is it used by the MVC framework?	The MVC framework uses the application life cycle to perform configuration tasks that affect all requests, such as setting up routes, areas, and content bundles.

Understanding the Application Life Cycle

The life cycle of an ASP.NET application begins the moment the application is started and continues while HTTP requests are received from clients and processed to generate responses. It includes matching requests to controllers and actions and rendering content from Razor views. The life cycle ends when the application is stopped.

The ASP.NET platform provides notifications of the two stages of the life cycle through methods defined by the *global application class*. The global application class has been around since the earliest versions of ASP.NET and consists of two files: `Global.asax` and `Global.asax.cs`.

Strictly speaking, the `Global.asax` file is the global application class, and the `Global.asax.cs` file is the associated *code-behind* file. This is the classic Web Forms approach to splitting declarative and programmatic code and is an artifact of the origins of ASP.NET. The `Global.asax` file used to be more important in ASP.NET applications, but it is just there for compatibility these days, even in Web Forms projects. Listing 3-1 shows the content of the `Global.asax` file from the example project, although you will never need to edit this file for an MVC framework project.

Listing 3-1. The Contents of the Global.asax File

```
<%@ Application Codebehind="Global.asax.cs" Inherits="SimpleApp.MvcApplication" Language="C#" %>
```

■ **Tip** To see the contents of this file, right-click `Global.asax` in the Solution Explorer and select View Markup from the pop-up menu.

This is an example of a Web Forms directive that tells ASP.NET that the associated code file is called `Global.asax.cs` and that it is written in C#. (Remember that ASP.NET applications can be written in any .NET language and that Visual Basic is still widely used.)

The Global.asax file may be a mildly interesting artifact left over from earlier versions of ASP.NET, but for this chapter it is the Global.asax.cs file that is important. The role of these files has gradually changed as ASP.NET has matured, and now the term *global application class* is usually used to refer to the Global.asax.cs file to the extent that when you double-click Global.asax in the Solution Explorer, it is the Global.asax.cs file that opens in the editor.

Listing 3-2 shows the contents of the Global.asax.cs file that Visual Studio created for the example project.

Listing 3-2. The Contents of the Global.asax.cs File

```
using System;
using System.Collections.Generic;
using System.Linq;
using System.Web;
using System.Web.Mvc;
using System.Web.Routing;

namespace SimpleApp {
    public class MvcApplication : System.Web.HttpApplication {
        protected void Application_Start() {
            AreaRegistration.RegisterAllAreas();
            RouteConfig.RegisterRoutes(RouteTable.Routes);
        }
    }
}
```

The default global application class is called MvcApplication and is derived from the System.Web.HttpApplication class. You'll see many more classes from the System.Web namespace in this book because it is the home of the bulk of the ASP.NET platform functionality.

The MvcApplication class is instantiated by the ASP.NET framework, and the methods it defines are called at key moments in the application life cycle (and, as you'll learn, in the request life cycle).

The default implementation of the MvcApplication class contains only one method, called Application_Start, but there is another method available, and I describe them both in the following sections.

Receiving Notifications When the Application Starts and Ends

The global application class supports two special methods that define the start and end of the application life cycle, as described by Table 3-3.

Table 3-3. *The Global Application Class for Application Life-Cycle Notifications*

Name	Description
Application_Start()	Called when the application is started
Application_End()	Called when the application is about to be terminated

The Application_Start method is called when the application is first started and provides an opportunity to perform one-off configuration tasks that affect the entire application. In Listing 3-2, you can see that Visual Studio has added statements to the Application_Start method that set up MVC areas and URL routes. When I created the example project in Chapter 2, I selected the option for the minimal initial project content, but additional statements would have been added to the Application_Start method if I had selected one of the other template options.

The `Application_End` method is called just before the application is terminated and is an opportunity to release any resources that the application maintains and to generally tidy up. The usual reason given for using this method is to release persistent database connections, but most modern web applications don't manage connections directly, and I rarely find it necessary to implement the `Application_End` method in my own projects. Databases are pretty good at managing their own connections these days, which is good because the `Application_End` method is called only when the application is shut down in an orderly manner. You can't rely on the method being called if the server fails or there is some other kind of sudden, unexpected problem such as a power outage.

I refer to these methods as being *special* because they are implemented in an odd way. These methods are not defined by the base for the global application class (which is `System.Web.HttpApplication`), so you don't have to use the `override` keyword to implement them. In fact, the ASP.NET framework uses reflection to look for the methods by name. You won't receive an error if you mistype the method names; ASP.NET just assumes you don't want to be notified when the application starts or stops. For this reason, it is important to ensure that you test that your code is being called, which I demonstrate later in this chapter.

■ **Tip** You will sometimes see the `Application_Start` and `Application_End` methods defined with object `Object` and `EventArgs` arguments, following the convention for a C# event handler method. This is optional, and the ASP.NET framework is able to locate and call these methods with or without these arguments.

Calls to the `Application_Start` and `Application_End` methods bookend the life cycle of the application, and between those method calls ASP.NET receives and processes requests, as described in Figure 3-1. I'll return to this diagram as I detail the request life cycle and show you how everything fits together.

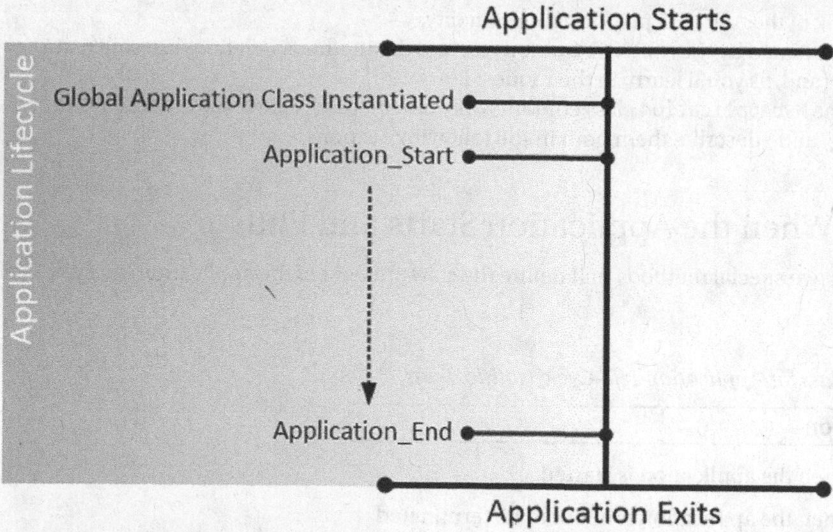

***Figure 3-1.** The application life cycle*

Testing the Start and Stop Notifications

You can use the Application_Start and Application_End methods directly in your applications to perform one-off startup and shutdown activities, just as the MVC framework does. In this section, I'll show you how to use the debugger to ensure that the methods are being called—something that is important when your custom code doesn't work the way you expect.

The simplest way to check that these methods are being called is to use the Visual Studio debugger. In Listing 3-3 you can see how I have added calls to the static System.Diagnostics.Debugger.Break method to the Application_Start and Application_End methods, which has the same effect as setting a breakpoint using the Visual Studio code editor, but with the benefit of ensuring that you will get the same result I describe here if you re-create this example.

Listing 3-3. Breaking the Debugger in the Global.asax.cs File

```
using System;
using System.Collections.Generic;
using System.Linq;
using System.Web;
using System.Web.Mvc;
using System.Web.Routing;

namespace SimpleApp {
    public class MvcApplication : System.Web.HttpApplication {

        protected void Application_Start() {
            AreaRegistration.RegisterAllAreas();
            RouteConfig.RegisterRoutes(RouteTable.Routes);
            System.Diagnostics.Debugger.Break();
        }

        protected void Application_End() {
            System.Diagnostics.Debugger.Break();
        }
    }
}
```

I have added a call to the Break method in the existing Application_Start method and added the Application_End method (which contains only a call to Break since my application doesn't have any cleanup code and none is required by the MVC framework).

Testing the Start Notification

Testing the Application_Start method is simple. Select Start Debugging from the Visual Studio Debug menu, and Visual Studio will open a browser window. The ASP.NET framework begins initializing the application, creates an instance of the global application class, discovers the Application_Start method, and invokes it, which leads to the Break method being called. The execution of the application is halted, and control is passed to the debugger, as shown in Figure 3-2.

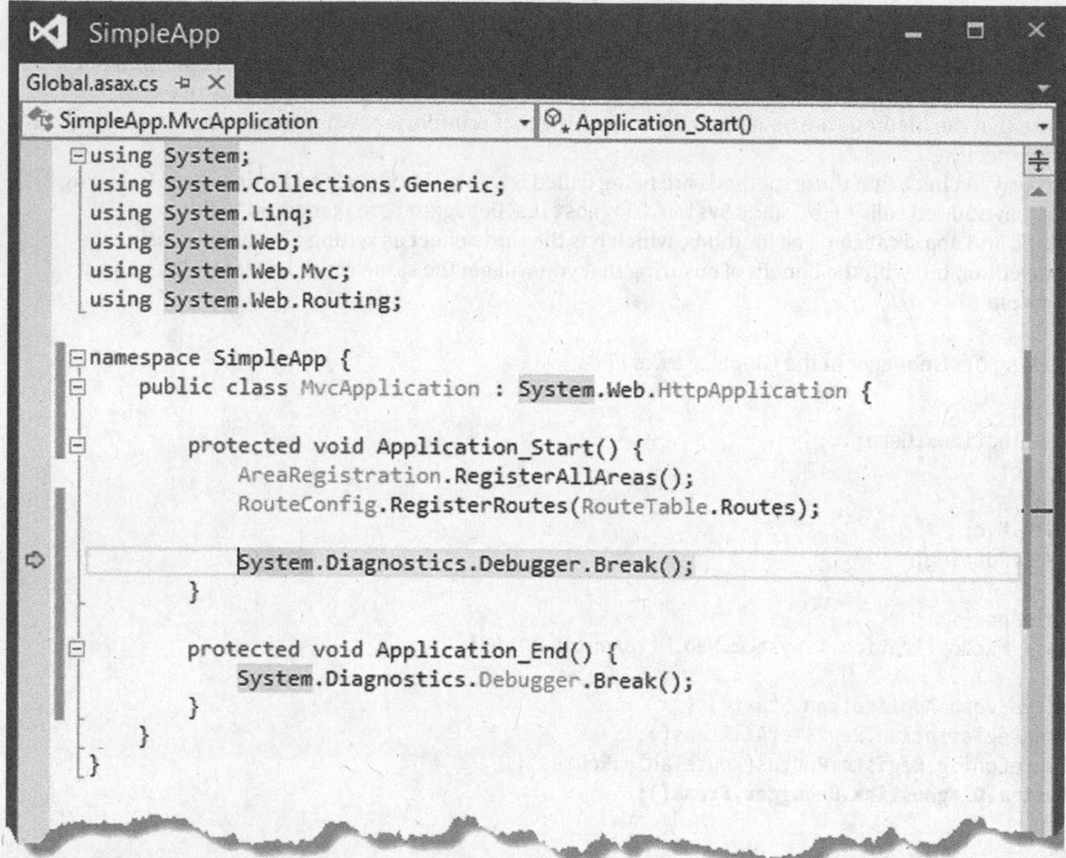

Figure 3-2. *Control is passed to the debugger when the Application_Start method is called*

Select Continue from the Visual Studio Debug menu, and execution of the application will resume. The request from the browser is processed, generating an HTML response that allows the user to vote for a color.

Testing the Stop Notification

Testing the `Application_End` method is a little trickier because selecting Stop Debugging detaches the debugger from the application before the `Application_End` method is called. The browser window is closed, the debugger is terminated, and Visual Studio returns to its default state—but the `Debugger.Break` method isn't invoked.

To test the code in the `Application_End` method, you must work with IIS Express directly, rather than through Visual Studio. IIS Express is a cut-down version of the IIS application server included with Visual Studio and is used to run ASP.NET applications during development.

Execution of the application will continue, and the time and day of the week will be displayed by the browser.

Locate the IIS Express icon on the Windows taskbar and right-click to make the pop-up menu appear. You will see a menu item for the SimpleApp project, and when you select it, you will see a Stop Site menu item, as shown in Figure 3-3.

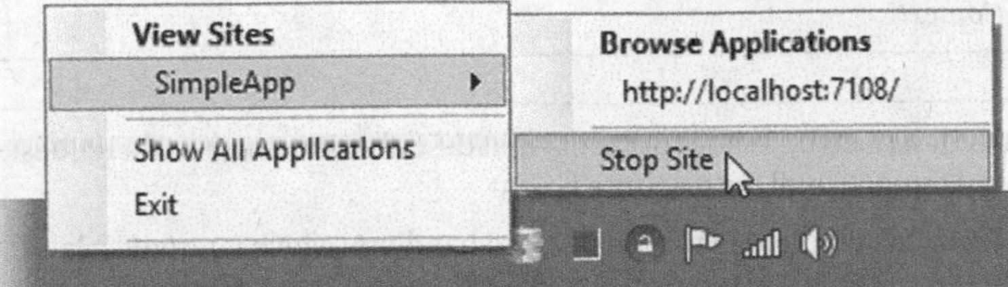

Figure 3-3. Stopping an application using IIS Express

When you select Stop Site, IIS Express will stop the application, and as part of this process, the `Application_End` method will be called. For my example, this means the `Debugger.Break` call is executed, as shown in Figure 3-4.

```
        AreaRegistration.RegisterAllAreas();
        RouteConfig.RegisterRoutes(RouteTable.Routes);

        System.Diagnostics.Debugger.Break();
    }

    protected void Application_End() {
        System.Diagnostics.Debugger.Break();
    }
}
```

Figure 3-4. Testing the code in the Application_End method

The ASP.NET Request Life Cycle

The global application class is also used to track the life cycle of individual requests, allowing you to follow each request as it passes through the ASP.NET platform into the MVC framework. The ASP.NET framework creates instances of the `MvcApplication` class defined in the `Global.asax.cs` file and uses the events it defines to shepherd the request through until the point where the response is generated and sent back to the browser. These events are not just for use by the application developer; they are used by the ASP.NET framework and the MVC framework to perform request handling (this will become clearer as I dig deeper into the detail). Table 3-4 puts the request life cycle in context.

Table 3-4. *Putting the Request Life Cycle in Context*

Question	Answer
What is it?	The request life cycle is described by a series of events that describe the progress of a request from when it is received through until the response is sent.
Why should I care?	The events are used when creating your own modules and handlers (which I introduce later in this chapter and describe properly in Chapters 4 and 5). You can also use these events to debug complex problems caused by interactions between ASP.NET components.
How is it used by the MVC framework?	The MVC framework includes a module and a handler. The module blocks requests for view files, and the handler is the component that locates the controller and action method that will process the request and renders the view that the action method selects.

Understanding the Request Life Cycle

The `Application_Start` and `Application_End` methods are not called on the `MvcApplication` instances that ASP.NET creates to handle requests. Instead, the ASP.NET framework triggers the sequence of events described in Table 3-5. These events describe the *request life cycle.*

Table 3-5. *The Request Life Cycle Events Defined by the Global Application Class*

Name	Description
`BeginRequest`	This is triggered as the first event when a new request is received.
`AuthenticateRequest` `PostAuthenticateRequest`	The `AuthenticateRequest` event is triggered to identify the user who has made the request. When all of the event handlers have been processed, `PostAuthenticateRequest` is triggered.
`AuthorizeRequest`	`AuthorizeRequest` is triggered to authorize the request. When all of the event handlers have been processed, `PostAuthorizeRequest` is triggered.
`ResolveRequestCache` `PostResolveRequestCache`	`ResolveRequestCache` is triggered to resolve the request from cached data. I describe the caching features in Chapters 11 and 12. When the event handlers have been processed, `PostResolveRequestCache` is triggered.
`MapRequestHandler` `PostMapRequestHandler`	`MapRequestHandler` is triggered when the ASP.NET framework wants to locate a handler for the request. I introduce handlers later in this chapter and cover them in depth in Chapter 5. The `PostMapRequestHandler` event is triggered once the handler has been selected.
`AcquireRequestState` `PostAcquireRequestState`	`AcquireRequestState` is triggered to obtain the state data associated with the request (such as session state). When all of the event handlers are processed, `PostAcquireRequestState` is triggered. I explain the different kinds of state data in Chapter 10.
`PreRequestHandlerExecute` `PostRequestHandlerExecute`	These events are triggered immediately before and immediately after the handler is asked to process the request.
`ReleaseRequestState` `PostReleaseRequestState`	`ReleaseRequestState` is triggered when the state data associated with the request is no longer required for request processing. When the event handlers have been processed, the `PostReleaseRequestState` event is triggered.

(*continued*)

Table 3-5. (*continued*)

Name	Description
UpdateRequestCache	This event is triggered so that modules responsible for caching can update their state. I introduce the role of modules later in this chapter and describe them in depth in Chapter 4. I describe the built-in support for caching in Chapters 11 and 12.
LogRequest PostLogRequest	This event is triggered to provide an opportunity for details of the request to be logged. When all of the event handlers have been processed, PostLogRequest is triggered.
EndRequest	This event is triggered when the request has been processed and the response is ready to be sent to the browser.
PreSendRequestHeaders	This event is triggered just before the HTTP headers are sent to the browser.
PreSendRequestContent	This event is triggered after the headers have been sent but before the content is sent to the browser.
Error	This event is triggered when an error is encountered; this can happen at any point in the request process. See Chapter 6 for details about error handling.

THE LIFE OF A REQUEST LIFE CYCLE HTTPAPPLICATION OBJECT

The ASP.NET framework will create multiple instances of the `MvcApplication` class to process requests, and these instances can be reused so that they process several requests over their lifetime. The ASP.NET framework has complete freedom to create `MvcApplication` instances as and when they are required and to destroy them when they are no longer needed. This means your global application class *must* be written so that multiple instances can exist concurrently and that these instances can be used to process several requests sequentially before they are destroyed. The only thing you can rely on is that each instance will be used to process one request at a time, meaning you have to worry only about concurrent access to data objects that are shared (I show you an example of this issue when I introduce application-wide state data in Chapter 10).

The ASP.NET framework triggers these events to chart the path of a request through the processing life cycle. You can handle these events in the global application class, in a *module*, or in a *handler*. I introduce modules and handlers in the following section and describe them in depth in Chapters 4 and 5.

Understanding Modules and Handlers

In the following sections, I show you how to respond to the request life-cycle events directly in the global application class. This is a good start for exploring the life-cycle events, but it is suitable for only the simplest of interactions with requests. Any serious request handling functionality tends to consume a number of life-cycle events, which means that the global application class quickly becomes a morass of code that handles the same events to handle requests in different ways. The ASP.NET framework deals with this by supporting *modules*, which are self-contained classes that receive the life-cycle events and can monitor and manipulate requests. Many of the most important ASP. NET platform services rely on the module functionality to prepare a request early in its life cycle. Examples are the state data and security services, which include modules that respond to events such as `AcquireRequestState` and `AuthenticateRequest` to add data to a request before it is handled by the MVC framework. Modules can interact with requests—and the associated responses—at any point in the life cycle, and I describe them in detail in Chapter 4.

The ASP.NET framework also supports a component called a *handler*. Handlers are responsible for generating a response for a request. The handler for the MVC framework is the component responsible for locating a controller and action method to service a request and rendering the view that the action method specifies. The ASP.NET framework supports multiple handlers, which is why it is possible to mix and match development frameworks such as MVC, Web API, and Web Forms within the same application. The handler is linked to four of the request life-cycle events. The `MapRequestHandler` and `PostMapRequestHandler` events are triggered before and after a handler is selected for the request, and the `PreRequestHandlerExecute` and `PostRequestHandlerExecute` events are triggered before and after the handler is asked to generate a response for the request. I describe how handlers work in detail in Chapter 5.

The reason that I have introduced modules and handlers in this chapter is because doing so allows me to illustrate the request life cycle more completely, as shown in Figure 3-5.

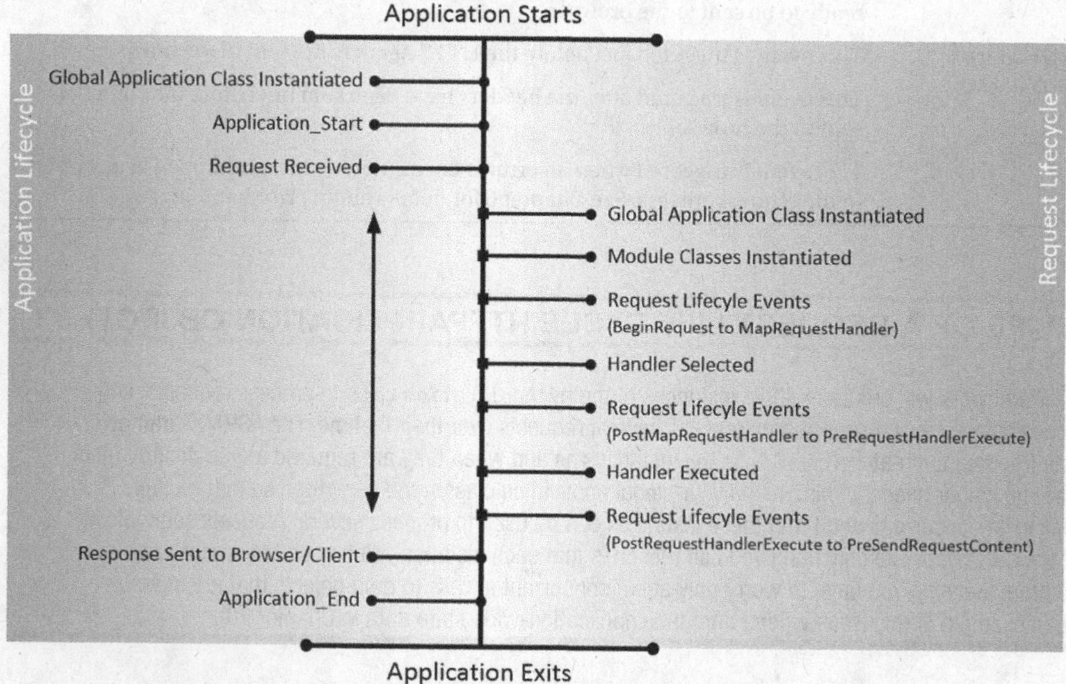

Figure 3-5. *Adding the request handling process to the life-cycle diagram*

Don't worry if this seems complex; it will start to make sense as I explain how these events are handled and as you see how various ASP.NET platform services are implemented.

Notice that the global application class is instantiated by both the application and request life cycles. Not only does the ASP.NET framework create multiple instances to service parallel requests, but it also creates separate instances to support each life cycle. You will see the practical impact of this in the "Handling Property Exceptions" section later in this chapter.

Handling Request Life-Cycle Events Using Special Methods

To handle these events in the global application class, you create a method with a name that starts with `Application_`, followed by the event name, such as `Application_BeginRequest`, for example. As with the `Application_Start` and `Application_End` methods, the ASP.NET framework finds the methods and invokes them when the event they correspond to is triggered. In Listing 3-4, you can see how I have updated the global application class so it handles some of the events in the table (and removed the statements that cause the debugger to break).

Listing 3-4. Handling Request life-Cycle Events in the Global.asax.cs File

```
using System;
using System.Collections.Generic;
using System.Linq;
using System.Web;
using System.Web.Mvc;
using System.Web.Routing;

namespace SimpleApp {
    public class MvcApplication : System.Web.HttpApplication {

        protected void Application_Start() {
            AreaRegistration.RegisterAllAreas();
            RouteConfig.RegisterRoutes(RouteTable.Routes);
        }

        protected void Application_BeginRequest() {
            RecordEvent("BeginRequest");
        }

        protected void Application_AuthenticateRequest() {
            RecordEvent("AuthenticateRequest");
        }

        protected void Application_PostAuthenticateRequest() {
            RecordEvent("PostAuthenticateRequest");
        }

        private void RecordEvent(string name) {
            List<string> eventList = Application["events"] as List<string>;
            if (eventList == null) {
                Application["events"] = eventList = new List<string>();
            }
            eventList.Add(name);
        }
    }
}
```

I have defined a method called `RecordEvent` that accepts the name of an event and stores it using one of the ASP.NET state management features. I describe these features in detail in Chapter 10, but the one I have used in this example—accessed via the `Application` property of the `HttpApplication` class—stores data in a way that makes it available throughout the application.

■ **Caution** Don't use the `Application` property without reading Chapter 10. I am using this feature without taking precautions that are essential in real projects.

I call the RecordEvent method from three other methods I added to the global application class. These events will be called when the BeginRequest, AuthenticateRequest, and PostAuthenticateRequest events are triggered. I don't have to explicitly register these methods as event handlers; the ASP.NET framework locates and invokes these methods automatically.

Displaying the Event Information

To display information about the events that my code receives, I need to make changes to the Home controller and its Index view. In Listing 3-5, you can see how I retrieve the event state data and pass it to the view as the model object in the Home controller.

Listing 3-5. Getting the Event Information in the Controllers/HomeController.cs File

```
using System.Web.Mvc;
using SimpleApp.Models;

namespace SimpleApp.Controllers {
    public class HomeController : Controller {

        public ActionResult Index() {
            return View(HttpContext.Application["events"]);
        }

        [HttpPost]
        public ActionResult Index(Color color) {
            Color? oldColor = Session["color"] as Color?;
            if (oldColor != null) {
                Votes.ChangeVote(color, (Color)oldColor);
            } else {
                Votes.RecordVote(color);
            }
            ViewBag.SelectedColor = Session["color"] = color;
            return View(HttpContext.Application["events"]);
        }
    }
}
```

To access the data I stored in the global application class, I have to use the HttpContext.Application property, which I describe later in this chapter as part of the context objects that the ASP.NET framework provides and whose functionality I describe in Chapter 10. In Listing 3-6, you can see how I have updated the Razor view associated with the controller so that details of the events are displayed in the browser.

Listing 3-6. Displaying the Event Information in the Views/Home/Index.cshtml File

```
@using SimpleApp.Models
@model List<string>
@{ Layout = null; }

<!DOCTYPE html>
<html>
```

```
<head>
    <meta name="viewport" content="width=device-width" />
    <title>Vote</title>
    <link href="~/Content/bootstrap.min.css" rel="stylesheet" />
    <link href="~/Content/bootstrap-theme.min.css" rel="stylesheet" />
</head>
<body class="container">
    <div class="panel panel-primary">
        @if (ViewBag.SelectedColor == null) {
            <h4 class="panel-heading">Vote for your favorite color</h4>
        } else {
            <h4 class="panel-heading">Change your vote from @ViewBag.SelectedColor</h4>
        }

        <div class="panel-body">

            @using (Html.BeginForm()) {
                @Html.DropDownList("color",
                        new SelectList(Enum.GetValues(typeof(Color))), "Choose a Color",
                            new { @class = "form-control" })
                <div>
                    <button class="btn btn-primary center-block"
                            type="submit">
                        Vote
                    </button>
                </div>
            }

        </div>
    </div>

    <div class="panel panel-primary">
        <h5 class="panel-heading">Results</h5>
        <table class="table table-condensed table-striped">
            @foreach (Color c in Enum.GetValues(typeof(Color))) {
                <tr><td>@c</td><td>@Votes.GetVotes(c)</td></tr>
            }
        </table>
    </div>

    <div class="panel panel-primary">
        <h5 class="panel-heading">Events</h5>
        <table class="table table-condensed table-striped">
            @foreach (string eventName in Model) {
                <tr><td>@eventName</td></tr>
            }
        </table>
    </div>
</body>
</html>
```

The list of event names is passed to the view as the model object, and I use a Razor `foreach` loop to generate rows in an HTML `table` element. The result is that the view generates HTML that describes the events that have been recorded by the global application class, as shown in Figure 3-6.

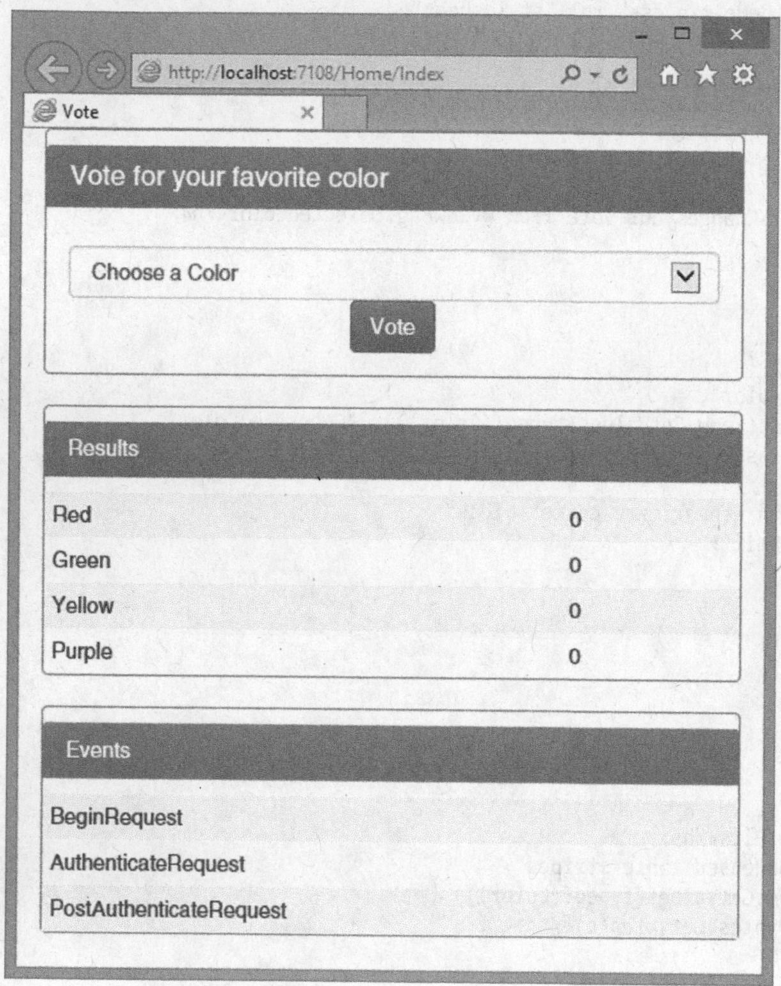

***Figure 3-6.** Displaying details of life-cycle events*

■ **Tip** This technique can be used only for events up to `PreRequestHandlerExecute` in the sequence shown in Table 3-5. This is because the action method in the controller is called between the `PreRequestHandlerExecute` and `PostRequestHandlerExecute` events and so subsequent events are triggered after the response has been produced.

Handling Request Life-Cycle Events Without Special Methods

The HttpApplication class, which is the base for the global application class, defines regular C# events that can be used instead of special methods, as shown in Listing 3-7. The choice between the standard C# events and the special methods is a personal one, and you can mix and match techniques if you want.

Listing 3-7. Using C# Events in the Global.asax.cs File

```
using System;
using System.Collections.Generic;
using System.Linq;
using System.Web;
using System.Web.Mvc;
using System.Web.Routing;

namespace SimpleApp {
    public class MvcApplication : System.Web.HttpApplication {

        public MvcApplication() {
            BeginRequest += (src, args) => RecordEvent("BeginRequest");
            AuthenticateRequest += (src, args) => RecordEvent("AuthentucateRequest");
            PostAuthenticateRequest += (src, args) =>
                RecordEvent("PostAuthenticateRequest");
        }

        protected void Application_Start() {
            AreaRegistration.RegisterAllAreas();
            RouteConfig.RegisterRoutes(RouteTable.Routes);
        }

        private void RecordEvent(string name) {
            List<string> eventList = Application["events"] as List<string>;
            if (eventList == null) {
                Application["events"] = eventList = new List<string>();
            }
            eventList.Add(name);
        }
    }
}
```

I have added a constructor to the MvcApplication class and have used it to set up event handlers for three of the request life-cycle events. For all three events I have used lambda expressions that call the RecordEvent method, storing the name of the event so that it can be read back by the controller, just as in the previous example.

■ **Tip** There are no standard C# events to replace the Application_Start and Application_End methods. You can receive these notifications only via special methods.

Using a Single Method to Handle Multiple Events

You can use two properties defined by the SystemWeb.HttpContext class if you want to use a single method to handle multiple life-cycle events without relying on lambda expressions. The HttpContext class provides details of the current request and the state of the application, and I describe it later in this chapter. For the moment, however, the two properties that relate to processing life-cycle events are shown in Table 3-6.

Table 3-6. *The HttpContext Properties for Determining the Current Application Event*

Name	Description
CurrentNotification	This property indicates the current application event using a value from the System.Web.RequestNotification enumeration.
IsPostNotification	This property returns true if the current application event is the Post<Name> variant of the event returned by the CurrentNotification property.

These two properties are a little odd because both must be used to figure out which event is being handled. The CurrentNotification property returns a value from the RequestNotification enumeration, which defines a subset of the HttpApplication events. The value that this property returns is used with the IsPostNotification property to figure out whether the event that has been triggered is an event like AcquireRequestState or its paired event, PostAcquireRequestState. The HttpApplication class provides access to an HttpContext object through the Context property, and Listing 3-8 shows how to handle events in this way.

Listing 3-8. Handling Life-Cycle Events in a Single Method in the Global.asax.cs File

```
using System;
using System.Collections.Generic;
using System.Linq;
using System.Web;
using System.Web.Mvc;
using System.Web.Routing;

namespace SimpleApp {
    public class MvcApplication : System.Web.HttpApplication {

        public MvcApplication() {
            BeginRequest += RecordEvent;
            AuthenticateRequest += RecordEvent;
            PostAuthenticateRequest += RecordEvent;
        }

        protected void Application_Start() {
            AreaRegistration.RegisterAllAreas();
            RouteConfig.RegisterRoutes(RouteTable.Routes);
        }
```

```
        private void RecordEvent(object src, EventArgs args) {
            List<string> eventList = Application["events"] as List<string>;
            if (eventList == null) {
                Application["events"] = eventList = new List<string>();
            }
            string name = Context.CurrentNotification.ToString();
            if (Context.IsPostNotification) {
                name = "Post" + name;
            }
            eventList.Add(name);
        }
    }
}
```

I changed the signature of the RecordEvent method so that it accepts the standard event handler arguments: an object that represents the source of the event and an EventArgs object that describes the event. I don't use these, however, since the information about the event is exposed through the Context.CurrentNotification and Context.IsPostNotification properties.

I don't know why Microsoft has implemented the events this way, but this is the approach you must use if you don't like special methods or lambda expressions. Notice that in this listing I had to call the ToString method on the Context.CurrentNotification method; this is required because the CurrentNotification property returns a value from the System.Web.RequestNotification enumeration, which I have described in Table 3-7.

Table 3-7. *The Values of the RequestNotification Enumeration*

Value	Description
BeginRequest	Corresponds to the BeginRequest event
AuthenticateRequest	Corresponds to the AuthenticateRequest and PostAuthenticateRequest events
AuthorizeRequest	Corresponds to the AuthorizeRequest event
ResolveRequestCache	Corresponds to the ResolveRequestCache and PostResolveRequestCache events
MapRequestHandler	Corresponds to the MapRequestHandler and PostMapRequestHandler events
AcquireRequestState	Corresponds to the AcquireRequestState and PostAcquireRequestState event
PreExecuteRequestHandler	Corresponds to the PreExecuteRequestHandler event
ExecuteRequestHandler	Corresponds to the ExecuteRequestHandler event
ReleaseRequestState	Corresponds to the ReleaseRequestState and PostReleaseRequestState event
UpdateRequestCache	Corresponds to the UpdateRequestCache event
LogRequest	Corresponds to the LogRequest event
EndRequest	Corresponds to the EndRequest event
SendResponse	Indicates that the response is being sent—corresponds loosely to the PreSendRequestHeaders and PreSendRequestContent events

The ASP.NET Context Objects

ASP.NET provides a set of objects that are used to provide context information about the current request, the response that will be returned to the client, and the web application itself; indirectly, these context objects can be used to access core ASP.NET framework features. Table 3-8 summarizes the context objects.

***Table 3-8.** Putting the Request Life Cycle in Context*

Question	Answer
What are they?	The context objects provide information about the application, the current request, and the response that is being prepared for it. They also provide access to the most important ASP.NET platform services such as security and state data.
Why should I care?	You use the context objects within MVC framework controllers and views to vary your application responses based on the request or the state of the application. You also use these objects when creating modules and handlers, which I describe in Chapters 4 and 5.
How are they used by the MVC framework?	The MVC framework uses the context objects to process requests and build on ASP.NET services such as mobile device detection (which I describe in Chapter 7).

Understanding the ASP.NET Context Objects

The class at the heart of the context is `System.Web.HttpContext`. It is universally available throughout the ASP.NET framework and the MVC framework, and it acts as a gateway to other context objects and to ASP.NET platform features and services. In fact, the `HttpContext` class is so central to the ASP.NET framework that the most important properties are like a map to the rest of this book, as Table 3-9 illustrates.

***Table 3-9.** The Most Commonly Used HttpContext Members*

Name	Description
`Application`	Returns the `HttpApplicationState` object used to manage application state data (see Chapter 10).
`ApplicationInstance`	Returns the `HttpApplication` object associated with the current request (described later in this chapter).
`Cache`	Returns a `Cache` object used to cache data. See Chapter 11 for details.
`Current`	(Static.) Returns the `HttpContext` object for the current request.
`CurrentHandler`	Returns the `IHttpHandler` instance that will generate content for the request. See Chapter 5 for details of handlers and Chapter 6 for information about how to preempt the handler selection process used by the ASP.NET platform.
`IsDebuggingEnabled`	Returns `true` if the debugger is attached to the ASP.NET application. You can use this to perform debug-specific activities, but if you do, take care to test thoroughly without the debugger before deployment.
`Items`	Returns a collection that can be used to pass state data between ASP.NET framework components that participate in processing a request.
`GetSection(name)`	Gets the specified configuration section from the `Web.config` file. I show you how to work with the `Web.config` files in Chapter 9.

(continued)

Table 3-9. (*continued*)

Name	Description
Request	Returns an HttpRequest object that provides details of the request being processed. I describe the HttpRequest class later in this chapter.
Response	Returns an HttpResponse object that provides details of the response that is being constructed and that will be sent to the browser. I describe the HttpResponse object later in this chapter.
Session	Returns an HttpSession state object that provides access to the session state. This property will return null until the PostAcquireRequestState application event has been triggered. See Chapter 10 for details.
Server	Returns an HttpServerUtility object that can contain utility functions, the most useful being the ability to control request handler execution (see Chapter 6).
Timestamp	Returns a DateTime object that contains the time at which the HttpContext object was created.
Trace	Used to record diagnostic information. See Chapter 8.

The HttpContext class also defines methods and properties that can be used to manage the request life cycle—like the CurrentNotification and IsPostNotification properties I used when handling life-cycle events with a single method in the previous section. I'll show you the different context object features, including those defined by HttpContext, in the chapters that are related to their functionality.

As you saw in Listing 3-8, you can get an instance of the HttpContext class using the Context property from within the global application class. This property name is not universal; you will need to use the HttpContext property from within a controller class or a view, for example. If all else fails, you can get the HttpContext object associated with the current request by using the static HttpContext.Current property. For quick reference, Table 3-10 summarizes the ways in which you can get an HttpContext object in the different parts of an application.

Table 3-10. *Obtaining an HttpContext in Different ASP.NET/MVC Components*

Component	Technique
Controller	Use the HttpContext property defined by Controller, which is the base class for MVC framework controllers.
View	Use the Context property defined by WebViewPage, which is the base class used to compile Razor views.
Global Application Class	Use the Context convenience property defined by the HttpApplication class (which is the base for the global application class).
Module	The Init method is passed an HttpContext object when it is invoked, and the life-cycle event handlers are passed an HttpApplication object, which defines a Context property. See Chapter 4 for details of modules.
Handler	The ProcessRequest method is passed an HttpContext object when it is invoked. See Chapter 5 for details of handlers.
Universally	You can always get the HttpContext object associated with the current request through the static HttpContext.Current property.

■ **Tip** A new set of context objects is created for every request, and when you obtain HttpRequest or HttpResponse objects, you will receive the instances that relate to the request being processed by the current instance of the global application class. Or, in other words, you don't have to worry about locating the context objects that relate to a specific request.

Notice that I have not included the model in the list of application components in Table 3-10. You *can* obtain the HttpContext object for the current request in the model through the static HttpContext.Current property, but I suggest that you don't because it blurs the separation of concerns between the model and the controller. If the model needs information about a request, then obtain this information from the context objects in the controller and pass it as method arguments to the model. This will ensure that the model doesn't meddle in the business of controllers and will allow the model to be unit tested without any reference to ASP.NET or the MVC framework.

CONTEXT, BASE, AND WRAPPER CLASSES

The properties that I listed in Table 3-10 do not all return the same type. The properties used in the pre-MVC framework components (the global application class, handlers, and modules) return an HttpContext object, just as you would expect).

These context objects predate the MVC framework and make it hard to perform unit testing because they are tightly coupled, requiring you to create entire sets of context objects each time you want to perform a test.

The properties defined by the MVC framework components—the controller and the view—are used to get context objects and return instances of different classes that are derived from the context classes but provide support for easy unit testing. The HttpContext property in the Controller class returns an instance of the HttpContextBase class. All the context objects are represented by a class with Base appended to the name (HttpRequestBase, HttpResponseBase, and so on) and can more readily instantiated, configured, and mocked for testing purposes.

You will sometimes need to create a Base object from an ASP.NET object; for example, you might have an HttpRequest object but need to call a method that takes an HttpRequestBase object. The ASP.NET class library includes classes with Wrapper appended to the name: HttpContextWrapper, HttpRequestWrapper, and so on. These classes are derived from the Base classes and are used by the MVC framework to present the ASP.NET context classes in an MVC-friendly Base class (so HttpContextWrapper is derived from HttpContextBase, which accepts an instance of HttpContext as constructor arguments). The Wrapper class constructors take context objects as arguments and the properties, and methods of the HttpContextWrapper are passed to the HttpContext instance that it contains.

You can't unwrap a Base object—converting from HttpRequestBase to HttpRequest, for example. But you can always get the context object you require through the static HttpContext.Current property, which returns an HttpContext object that presents the properties shown in Table 3-9. You will have to use the fully qualified name for this property (System.Web.HttpContext.Current) within controller classes because they define an HttpContext property that returns an HttpContextBase object. In this book, I treat the ASP.NET framework context classes and the MVC Base classes as being identical.

Working with HttpApplication Objects

Many of the classes that you will use in the ASP.NET framework provide convenience properties that are mapped to those defined by the HttpContext class. A good example of this overlap can be seen in HttpApplication, which is the base for the global application class. In Table 3-11, you can see the properties and methods defined by the HttpApplication class, many of which are similar to those defined by HttpContext.

***Table 3-11.** The Members Defined by the HttpApplication Class*

Name	Description
Application	Maps to the HttpContext.Application property, which provides access to application-wide state data, as described in Chapter 10.
CompleteRequest()	Abandons the life cycle for the current request and moves directly to the LogRequest event. See Chapter 6 for details.
Context	Returns the HttpContext object for the current request.
Init()	Called when the Init method has been called on each of the registered modules; see Chapter 4 for details of modules.
Modules	Returns an HttpModuleCollection object that details the modules in the application; see Chapter 4 for details of modules.
RegisterModule(type)	Static method that registers a new module; see Chapter 4 for an example.
Request	Returns the HttpContext.Request value, but throws an HttpException if the value is null.
Response	Returns the HttpContext.Response value, but throws an HttpException if the value is null.
Server	Maps to the HttpContext.Server property. See Chapter 6.
Session	Returns the HttpContext.Session value, but throws an HttpException if the value is null. See Chapter 10.

Most of these members are convenience properties that map to the properties of the HttpContext class, but there are some points to note, as discussed in the following section.

Handling Property Exceptions

The Request, Response, Session, and User properties all return the value of the corresponding properties from the HttpContext class, but with a wrinkle—all of these properties will throw an HttpException if the value they get from HttpContext is null.

This happens because the HttpApplication class receives notifications for two different life cycles: the application life cycle and the request life cycle. Objects that describe a single request are not available when an instance of the global application class is being used to handle application-level events, so the HttpException is thrown if you try to access request-related properties when handling application-level notifications.

The policy of throwing an exception is harsh because it makes it hard to deal with HttpApplication objects of unknown provenance. You can see an example of this issue in Listing 3-9, which shows changes to the global application class.

Listing 3-9. Writing Code That Deals with Both Kinds of HttpApplication Objects in the Global.asax.cs File

```
using System;
using System.Collections.Generic;
using System.Linq;
using System.Web;
using System.Web.Mvc;
using System.Web.Routing;

namespace SimpleApp {
    public class MvcApplication : System.Web.HttpApplication {

        public MvcApplication() {
            PostAcquireRequestState += (src, args) => CreateTimeStamp();
        }

        protected void Application_Start() {
            AreaRegistration.RegisterAllAreas();
            RouteConfig.RegisterRoutes(RouteTable.Routes);
            CreateTimeStamp();
        }

        private void CreateTimeStamp() {
            string stamp = Context.Timestamp.ToLongTimeString();
            if (Session != null) {
                Session["request_timestamp"] = stamp;
            } else {
                Application["app_timestamp"] = stamp;
            }
        }
    }
}
```

I have removed the code that registers and handles some of the request life-cycle events and have defined a new method that creates a timestamp and stores it as state data. I describe the ASP.NET framework support for state data (including the objects returned by `Session` and `Application` properties used here) in Chapter 10, but for now it is enough to know that the `Session` property will return an object for storing state for individual requests.

■ **Tip** Notice that I create the request timestamp in response to the `PostAcquireRequestState` event. This is because the modules that provide state data services for requests are not asked to do so until the `AcquireRequestState` event; therefore, the `Session` property will return `null`, even if the global application class instance has been created to process events for a request. Don't worry if this doesn't make sense now; I explain how modules work in Chapter 4 and describe the different types of state data in Chapter 10.

The new method, called `CreateTimeStamp`, aims to reduce code duplication by dealing with application-level and request-level timestamps with the same set of statements. This code will throw an exception as soon as the application is started because it attempts to read the `Session` property for an instance of the global application class that has been created to deal with the `Application_Start` method being called.

I could address this by using `try...catch` blocks, but that would be bad practice because exception handling should not be used to manage the regular and expected flow of an application. Instead, I can use the equivalent properties directly on `HttpContext`, as shown in Listing 3-10. This allows me to use one method to create both kinds of timestamps in a single method without having to worry about exceptions.

Listing 3-10. Using the Properties Defined by the HttpContext Class in the Global.asax.cs File

```
...
private void CreateTimeStamp() {
    string stamp = Context.Timestamp.ToLongTimeString();
    if (Context.Session != null) {
        Session["request_timestamp"] = stamp;
    } else {
        Application["app_timestamp"] = stamp;
    }
}
...
```

■ **Caution** The change in Listing 3-10 won't work until you have also applied the changes in Listing 3-11.

Notice that I only have to change the initial check for the `Session` property; if it isn't `null`, I can use the `Session` property defined by the `HttpApplication` class. The `Application` property will always return an `HttpApplicationState` object because, as I explain in Chapter 10, the state management feature it provides is application-wide and is initialized when the application is started.

You need to pay attention to this issue only when working directly with the global application class where you can be working with objects that are not associated with an individual request. Elsewhere in ASP.NET, and especially within MVC framework controller classes, you will always be working with context objects that represent a request. As an example, Listing 3-11 shows the changes I made to the `HomeController` class to display the timestamps created in the previous listing.

Listing 3-11. Displaying Timestamps in the HomeController.cs File

```
using System.Collections.Generic;
using System.Web.Mvc;
using SimpleApp.Models;

namespace SimpleApp.Controllers {
    public class HomeController : Controller {

        public ActionResult Index() {
            return View(GetTimeStamps());
        }

        [HttpPost]
        public ActionResult Index(Color color) {
            Color? oldColor = Session["color"] as Color?;
            if (oldColor != null) {
                Votes.ChangeVote(color, (Color)oldColor);
            } else {
                Votes.RecordVote(color);
            }
```

```
            ViewBag.SelectedColor = Session["color"] = color;
            return View(GetTimeStamps());
        }

        private List<string> GetTimeStamps() {
            return new List<string> {
                string.Format("App timestamp: {0}",
                    HttpContext.Application["app_timestamp"]),
                string.Format("Request timestamp: {0}", Session["request_timestamp"]),
            };
        }
    }
}
```

I have used the C# string composition feature, available through the static `String.Format` method, to create a list of messages that will be passed to the view. The `Controller` class that is the base for MVC framework controllers provides a `Session` convenience property that corresponds to `HttpContext.Session` (but I have to access `HttpContext.Application` directly since there is no corresponding convenience property).

You can see the timestamps by starting the application, as illustrated by Figure 3-7. Both values will be the same initially, but if you reload the browser window a few times, you will see that the application timestamp remains constant while the request timestamp is updated each time.

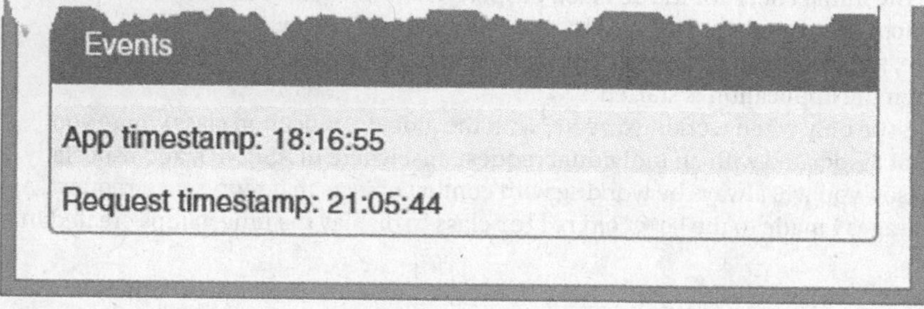

***Figure 3-7.** Displaying application and request timestamps*

■ **Note** If you find that both timestamps update for every request, then you may have forgotten to disable the Visual Studio Browser Link feature as described in Chapter 1. The Browser Link feature relies on injecting JavaScript code into the HTML sent to the browser that establishes a connection back to the server and waits for a change notification. The global application class handles *all* requests and not just those intended for the MVC framework, so the `GetTimeStamps` method is called twice for each request. Browser Link uses a feature called *sessionless controllers* that prevents the `Context.Session` property from ever being set, which has the effect of confusing the code in Listing 3-10 and updating the application-level timestamp. I describe sessionless controllers in Chapter 10.

Working with HttpRequest Objects

The HttpRequest object describes a single HTTP request as it is being processed. Table 3-12 describes the HttpRequest properties that provide information about the current request. (The HttpRequest class defines methods and some other properties, but I describe these in later chapters in the context of the platform features they correspond to.)

***Table 3-12.** The Descriptive Properties Defined by the HttpRequest Class*

Name	Description
AcceptTypes	Returns a string array containing the MIME types accepted by the browser.
Browser	Returns an HttpBrowserCapabilities object that describes the capabilities of the browser; see Chapter 7 for more details.
ContentEncoding	Returns a System.Text.Encoding object that represents the character set used to encode the request data.
ContentLength	Returns the number of bytes of content in the request.
ContentType	Returns the MIME type of the content included in the request.
CurrentExecutionFilePathExtension	Returns the file extension component of the requested URL.
Headers	Returns a collection containing the request headers.
HttpMethod	Returns the HTTP method used to make the request (GET, POST, and so on).
InputStream	Returns a stream that can be used to read the contents of the request.
IsLocal	Returns true when the request has originated from the local machine.
MapPath(path)	Translates a file name within the project to an absolute path. See Chapter 11 for an example.
RawUrl	Returns the part of the URL that follows the hostname. In other words, for http://apress.com:80/books/Default.aspx, this property would return /books/Default.aspx.
RequestContext	Returns a RequestContext object that provides access to the routing information for a request. I demonstrate the use of the RequestContext object in Chapter 6.
Url	Returns the request URL as a System.Uri object.
UrlReferrer	Returns the referrer URL as a System.Uri object.
UserAgent	Returns the user-agent string supplied by the browser.
UserHostAddress	Returns the IP address of the remote client, expressed as a string.
UserHostName	Returns the DNS name of the remote client.
UserLanguages	Returns a string array of the languages preferred by the browser/user.

To demonstrate the use of the HttpRequest class, I have modified the Index.cshtml view so that it displays some of the request properties, as shown in Listing 3-12.

Listing 3-12 Displaying Request Details in the Index.cshtml File

```
@using SimpleApp.Models
@model List<string>
@{ Layout = null; }

<!DOCTYPE html>
<html>
<head>
    <meta name="viewport" content="width=device-width" />
    <title>Vote</title>
    <link href="~/Content/bootstrap.min.css" rel="stylesheet" />
    <link href="~/Content/bootstrap-theme.min.css" rel="stylesheet" />
</head>
<body class="container">
    <div class="panel panel-primary">
        @if (ViewBag.SelectedColor == null) {
            <h4 class="panel-heading">Vote for your favorite color</h4>
        } else {
            <h4 class="panel-heading">Change your vote from @ViewBag.SelectedColor</h4>
        }

        <div class="panel-body">

            @using (Html.BeginForm()) {
                @Html.DropDownList("color",
                        new SelectList(Enum.GetValues(typeof(Color))), "Choose a Color",
                            new { @class = "form-control" })
                <div>
                    <button class="btn btn-primary center-block"
                            type="submit">
                        Vote
                    </button>
                </div>
            }
        </div>
    </div>

    <div class="panel panel-primary">
        <h5 class="panel-heading">Results</h5>
        <table class="table table-condensed table-striped">
            @foreach (Color c in Enum.GetValues(typeof(Color))) {
                <tr><td>@c</td><td>@Votes.GetVotes(c)</td></tr>
            }
        </table>
    </div>
```

```
    <div class="panel panel-primary">
        <h5 class="panel-heading">Request Properties</h5>
        <table class="table table-condensed table-striped">
            <tr><th>Property</th><th>Value</th></tr>
            <tr><td>HttpMethod</td><td>@Request.HttpMethod</td></tr>
            <tr><td>IsLocal</td><td>@Request.IsLocal</td></tr>
            <tr><td>RawURL</td><td>@Request.RawUrl</td></tr>
        </table>
    </div>
</body>
</html>
```

Notice that I am able to access the HttpRequest object using a property called Request, like this:

```
...
<tr><td>HttpMethod</td><td>@Request.HttpMethod</td></tr>
...
```

The HttpRequest object is so frequently used that some application components, including Razor views, provide convenience properties so that you don't have to obtain an HttpContext object just to get an instance of HttpRequest. Table 3-13 summarizes the convenience properties that are available for HttpRequest objects.

***Table 3-13.** Obtaining an HttpRequest Object in Different ASP.NET/MVC Components*

Component	Technique
Controller	Use the Request convenience property.
View	Use the Request convenience property.
Global Application Class	Use the Request convenience property.
Module	No convenience property is available. Use the HttpContext.Request property. (Modules are described in Chapter 4.)
Handler	No convenience property is available. Use the HttpContext.Request property. (Handlers are described in Chapter 5.)
Universally	You can always get the HttpRequest object for the current request through the static HttpContext.Current.Request property.

Figure 3-8 shows the request property values displayed by the view, for both an initial GET request and the POST request that results when the user selects a color and clicks the Vote button.

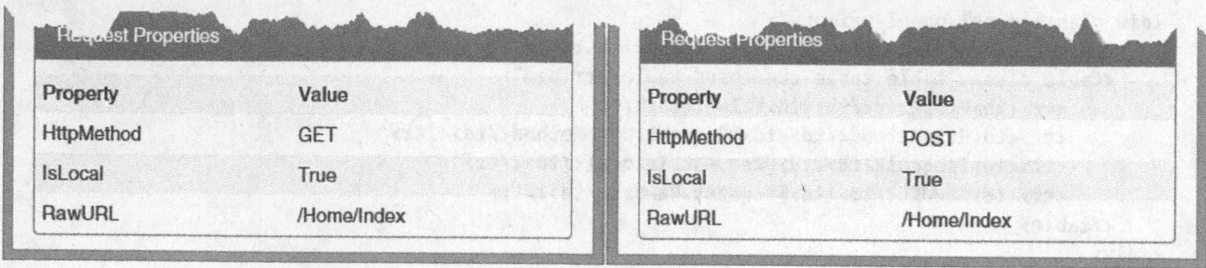

Figure 3-8. *Displaying details of the request*

In addition to the properties shown in Table 3-12, there are some properties that provide access to the data included in a request. I have shown these in Table 3-14, but they are not usually used directly in MVC controllers because model binding, which I describe in *Pro ASP.NET MVC 5*, is easier to work with. These properties are sometimes used in modules, however.

Table 3-14. *Additional Properties Defined by the HttpRequest Class*

Name	Description
`Files`	Returns a collection of files sent by the browser in a form.
`Form`	Provides access to the raw form data.
`Params`	A collection of the combined data items from the query string, form fields, and cookies. You can also use an array-style indexer directly on the `HttpRequest` object, such that `Request["myname"]` is the same as `Request.Params["myname"]`.
`QueryString`	Returns a collection of the query string parameters; this property isn't usually used directly in MVC applications.

Working with HttpResponse Objects

The `HttpResponse` object is the counterpart to `HttpRequest` and represents the response as it is being constructed. It also provides methods and properties that let you customize the response, something that is rarely required when using MVC views but that can be useful when working with other components, such as modules and handlers (described in Chapters 4 and 5).

Like `HttpRequest`, this class is essential to the way that ASP.NET processes requests and is used extensively within the MVC framework to generate the HTML (or other data) that is returned to clients. I have described the most important methods and properties in Table 3-15.

***Table 3-15.** The Most Useful Members of the HttpResponse Class*

Name	Description
`AppendHeader(name, val)`	Convenience method to add a new header to the response.
`BufferOutput`	Gets or sets a value indicating whether the request should be buffered completely before it is sent to the browser. The default value is `true`. Changing this to `false` will prevent subsequent modules and handlers from being able to alter the response.
`Cache`	Returns an `HttpCachePolicy` object that specifies the caching policy for the response. I describe the ASP.NET caching services in Chapters 11 and 12.
`CacheControl`	Gets or set the `cache-control` HTTP header for the response.
`Charset`	Gets or sets the character set specified for the response.
`Clear()` `ClearContent()`	The `Clear` and `ClearContent` methods are equivalent, and they remove any content from the response.
`ClearHeaders()`	Removes all of the headers from the response.
`ContentEncoding`	Gets or sets the encoding used for content in the response.
`Headers`	Returns the collection of headers for the response.
`IsClientConnected`	Returns `true` if the client is still connected to the server.
`IsRequestBeingDirected`	Returns `true` if the browser will be sent a redirection.
`Output`	Returns a `TextWriter` that can be used to write text to the response.
`OutputStream`	Returns a `Stream` that can be used to write binary data to the response.
`RedirectLocation`	Gets or sets the value of the HTTP `Location` header.
`Status`	Gets or sets the status for the response; the default is `200 (OK)`.
`StatusCode`	Gets or sets the numeric part of the status; the default is `200`.
`StatusDescription`	Gets or sets the text part of the status; the default is `(OK)`.
`SuppressContent`	When set to `true`, this property prevents the response content from being sent to the client.
`Write(data)`	Writes data to the response output stream.
`WriteFile(path)`	Writes the contents of the specified file to the output stream.

In Table 3-16, I have summarized the convenience properties for a range of ASP.NET and MVC framework components.

***Table 3-16.** Obtaining an HttpResponse Object in Different ASP.NET/MVC Components*

Component	Technique
Controller	Use the `Response` convenience property.
View	Use the `Response` convenience property.
Global Application Class	Use the `Response` convenience property.
Module	No convenience property is available. Use the `HttpContext.Response` property. (Modules are described in Chapter 4.)
Handler	No convenience property is available. Use the `HttpContext.Response` property. (Handlers are described in Chapter 5.)
Universally	You can always get the current `HttpResponse` object through the static `HttpContext.Current.Response` property.

Summary

In this chapter, I described the application and request life cycles, which provide the foundation for much of the functionality provided by the ASP.NET platform—and, by implication, the MVC framework. I introduced the global application class and explained the role of the special `Application_Start` and `Application_End` methods and their relationship to the application life cycle. I also described the request life-cycle events and explained how they are used to move a request through ASP.NET, something that will become clearer once I have described modules and handlers in later chapters. I finished the chapter by providing an overview of the context objects that ASP.NET provides for describing the state of the application, the current request being processed, and the response that is being prepared for it. You'll see these context objects throughout the book because they underpin so much of what ASP.NET can do. In the next chapter, I describe modules, which are self-contained components that handle the request life-cycle events.

CHAPTER 4

Modules

In the previous chapter, I showed you how to handle life-cycle requests in the global application class. The problem with this approach is that the code quickly becomes a mess, especially when you are trying to perform different kinds of work driven by the same set of events. In this chapter, I describe *modules*, which are self-contained components that receive and handle life-cycle requests and which can monitor or modify a request and its response. Not only do modules avoid a morass of code in the global application class, but they can be packaged up and used in multiple applications, providing a useful mechanism for creating reusable features for customizing or debugging the ASP.NET request handling process.

In this chapter, I explain how modules work, how you can create them, and how they fit into the request life cycle. In Chapter 5, I explain how modules can be used to provide services to *handlers*, which are the component responsible for generating content for a request. Table 4-1 summarizes this chapter.

***Table 4-1.** Chapter Summary*

Problem	Solution	Listing
Create a module.	Implement the `IHttpModule` interface.	1-2
Register a module.	Create an `add` element in the `system.webServer/modules` section of the `Web.config` file or apply the `PreApplicationStartMethod` attribute.	3-5
Provide functionality to other modules.	Define a module event.	6
Consume functionality from other modules.	Locate the module via the `HttpApplication` instance and register a handler for the events it defines.	7-10

Preparing the Example Project

I am going to continue using the SimpleApp project I created in Chapter 2 and modified in Chapter 3. At the end of the previous chapter, I demonstrated how to display details about the current HTTP request using the `HttpRequest` object. To prepare for this chapter, I have removed the `table` element that displays information from the `Views/Home/Index.cshtml` file, as shown in Listing 4-1.

Listing 4-1. The Contents of the Index.cshtml File

```
@using SimpleApp.Models
@{ Layout = null; }

<!DOCTYPE html>
<html>
<head>
    <meta name="viewport" content="width=device-width" />
    <title>Vote</title>
    <link href="~/Content/bootstrap.min.css" rel="stylesheet" />
    <link href="~/Content/bootstrap-theme.min.css" rel="stylesheet" />
</head>
<body class="container">
    <div class="panel panel-primary">
        @if (ViewBag.SelectedColor == null) {
            <h4 class="panel-heading">Vote for your favorite color</h4>
        } else {
            <h4 class="panel-heading">Change your vote from @ViewBag.SelectedColor</h4>
        }

        <div class="panel-body">
            @using (Html.BeginForm()) {
                @Html.DropDownList("color",
                        new SelectList(Enum.GetValues(typeof(Color))), "Choose a Color",
                            new { @class = "form-control" })
                <div>
                    <button class="btn btn-primary center-block"
                            type="submit">
                        Vote
                    </button>
                </div>
            }

        </div>
    </div>

    <div class="panel panel-primary">
        <h5 class="panel-heading">Results</h5>
        <table class="table table-condensed table-striped">
            @foreach (Color c in Enum.GetValues(typeof(Color))) {
                <tr><td>@c</td><td>@Votes.GetVotes(c)</td></tr>
            }
        </table>
    </div>

</body>
</html>
```

The example application contains some other remnants from the previous chapter, such as the global application class generating timestamps in response to application life-cycle notifications and request life-cycle events, but I am going to ignore those for the moment. Figure 4-1 shows how the browser displays the view rendered by the example application.

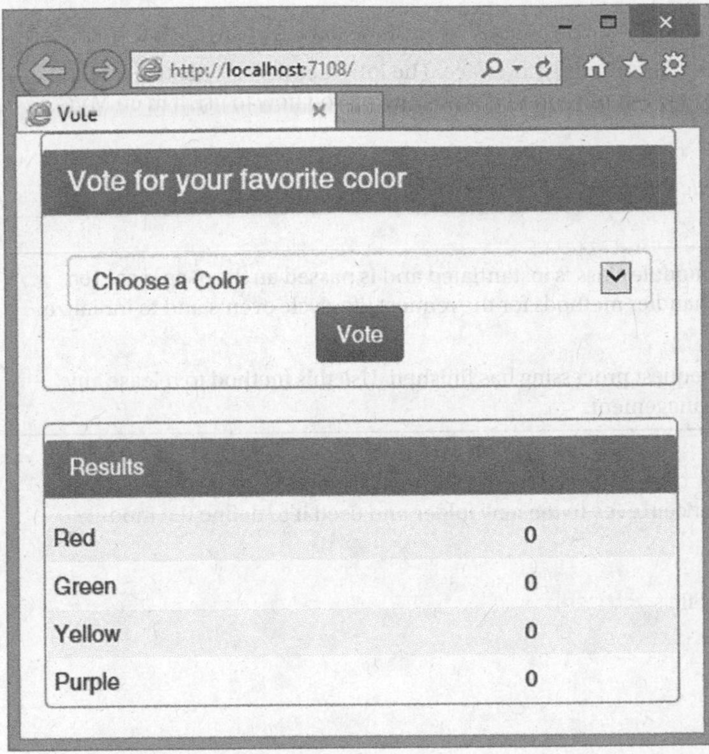

Figure 4-1. *The example application*

ASP.NET Modules

In this section, I introduce you to the interface that defines modules, show you how to create your own module, and explain the process for registering modules with the ASP.NET platform. Table 4-2 puts modules in context.

Table 4-2. *Putting Modules in Context*

Question	Answer
What is it?	Modules are classes that handle life-cycle events to monitor or manipulate requests or responses. Modules can also provide services to handlers, which I describe in Chapter 5.
Why should I care?	Modules are one of the easiest ways to take control of the ASP.NET request handling process, which allows you to customize the way that ASP.NET works or provide custom services to your MVC framework applications.
How is it used by the MVC framework?	The MVC framework includes a module that prevents requests for view files. In addition, MVC relies on several ASP.NET platform services, which are delivered using modules and which are described in Part 3.

Creating a Module

Modules are classes that implement the `System.Web.IHttpModule` interface. The interface defines the two methods described in Table 4-3. I am going to begin by creating a simple module and showing you how to use it in an MVC framework application.

Table 4-3. *The Methods Defined by the IHttpModule Interface*

Name	Description
`Init(app)`	This method is called when the module class is instantiated and is passed an `HttpApplication` object, which is used to register handler methods for the request life-cycle events and to initialize any resources that are required.
`Dispose()`	This method is called when the request processing has finished. Use this method to release any resources that require explicit management.

I started by creating a folder called `Infrastructure`, which is where I like to put supporting classes in an MVC framework project. I added a class file called `TimerModule.cs` to the new folder and used it to define the module shown in Listing 4-2.

Listing 4-2. The Contents of the TimerModule.cs File

```
using System;
using System.Diagnostics;
using System.Web;

namespace SimpleApp.Infrastructure {

    public class TimerModule : IHttpModule {
        private Stopwatch timer;

        public void Init(HttpApplication app) {
            app.BeginRequest += HandleEvent;
            app.EndRequest += HandleEvent;
        }

        private void HandleEvent(object src, EventArgs args) {
            HttpContext ctx = HttpContext.Current;
            if (ctx.CurrentNotification == RequestNotification.BeginRequest) {
                timer = Stopwatch.StartNew();
            } else {
                ctx.Response.Write(string.Format(
                    "<div class='alert alert-success'>Elapsed: {0:F5} seconds</div>",
                    ((float) timer.ElapsedTicks) / Stopwatch.Frequency));
            }
        }

        public void Dispose() {
            // do nothing - no resources to release
        }
    }
}
```

■ **Tip** Be careful if you use Visual Studio to implement the interface in a module class (by right-clicking the interface name on the class definition and selecting Implement Interface from the pop-up menu). Visual Studio will add method implementations that throw a `NotImplementedException`, and a common mistake is to forget to remove the exception from the `Dispose` method. The ASP.NET platform will invoke the `Dispose` method even if you don't have any resource to release. Remove the `throw` statement from the method body and replace it with a comment, as shown in Listing 4-2.

This module uses the high-resolution `Stopwatch` timer class in the `System.Diagnostics` namespace to measure the elapsed time between the `BeginRequest` and `EndRequest` life-cycle events. Since this is the first module I have demonstrated, I will walk through the way it works in detail.

■ **Tip** The `Stopwatch` class expresses elapsed time in *ticks*, which are based on the underlying timing mechanism available to the .NET Framework on the machine on which the code is executing. I have to use the static `Frequency` property when I display the result, which tells me how many ticks the timer makes per second.

Setting Up the Event Handlers

Modules are instantiated when the ASP.NET framework creates an instance of the global application class. The module `Init` method is invoked so that the module can prepare itself to handle requests, which usually means registering event handlers with the `HttpApplication` object that is passed as the method's argument. In the `TimerModule`, I use the `Init` method to register the `HandleEvent` method as a handler for the `BeginRequest` and `EndRequest` events, like this:

```
...
public void Init(HttpApplication app) {
    app.BeginRequest += HandleEvent;
    app.EndRequest += HandleEvent;
}
...
```

■ **Caution** As I explained in Chapter 3, the ASP.NET framework creates multiple instances of the global application class, some of which will exist at the same time so that HTTP requests can be processed concurrently. Each global application class instance is given its own set of module objects, which means you must write your module code such that multiple instances can exist simultaneously in harmony and that each module can handle multiple requests sequentially.

The `Init` method is called only when a module object is instantiated, which means you must use the `Init` method only to perform one-off configuration tasks such as setting up event handlers. You must *not* perform configuration tasks that are required to process individual requests, which is why I don't instantiate the timer object in the `Init` method of this module.

Handling the BeginRequest Event

The BeginEvent life-cycle event is my cue to start the timer. I use the same method to handle both of the events I am interested in, which means I have to use the HttpContext.CurrentNotification property, which I described in Chapter 3, to work out which event I have received, as follows:

```
...
private void HandleEvent(object src, EventArgs args) {
    HttpContext ctx = HttpContext.Current;
    if (ctx.CurrentNotification == RequestNotification.BeginRequest) {
        timer = Stopwatch.StartNew();
    } else {
        ctx.Response.Write(string.Format(
            "<div class='alert alert-success'>Elapsed: {0:F5} seconds</div>",
            ((float) timer.ElapsedTicks) / Stopwatch.Frequency));
    }
}
...
```

The src object passed to event handlers for life-cycle events is an instance of the HttpApplication class, which you can use to get an HttpContext object, but I find it easier to use the static HttpContext.Current property. I instantiate and start a new timer if the CurrentNotification property indicates that I have received the BeginRequest event.

■ **Tip** This is a per-request configuration task, which means it should not be performed in the Init method, as described in the previous section. The ASP.NET framework is free to create and destroy instances of modules as it sees fit, and there is no way of telling how many requests an instance of a module class will be used to service (although you can be sure that each instance will be used to service only one request at a time).

Handling the EndRequest Event

Receiving the EndRequest event tells me that the request has been marshaled through the request life cycle and the MVC framework has generated a response that will be sent to the browser. The response has not been sent when the EndRequest event is triggered, which allows me to manipulate it through the HttpResponse context object. In this example, I append a message to the end of the response that reports the elapsed time between the BeginRequest and EndRequest, as follows:

```
...
private void HandleEvent(object src, EventArgs args) {
    HttpContext ctx = HttpContext.Current;
    if (ctx.CurrentNotification == RequestNotification.BeginRequest) {
        timer = Stopwatch.StartNew();
    } else {
        ctx.Response.Write(string.Format(
            "<div class='alert alert-success'>Elapsed: {0:F5} seconds</div>",
            ((float) timer.ElapsedTicks) / Stopwatch.Frequency));
    }
}
...
```

I use the HttpResponse.Write method to add a string to the response. I format the string as HTML and use the Bootstrap alert and alert-success CSS classes to style the content as an inline alert box.

Registering a Module

Unlike the MVC framework, the ASP.NET platform doesn't discover classes dynamically, which means you have to explicitly register a module with the ASP.NET framework before it takes effect. Modules are registered in the Web.config file, as shown in Listing 4-3.

Listing 4-3. Registering a Module in the Web.config File

```
<?xml version="1.0" encoding="utf-8"?>
<configuration>
  <appSettings>
    <add key="webpages:Version" value="3.0.0.0" />
    <add key="webpages:Enabled" value="false" />
    <add key="ClientValidationEnabled" value="true" />
    <add key="UnobtrusiveJavaScriptEnabled" value="true" />
  </appSettings>
  <system.web>
    <compilation debug="true" targetFramework="4.5.1" />
    <httpRuntime targetFramework="4.5.1" />
  </system.web>
  <system.webServer>
    <modules>
      <add name="Timer" type="SimpleApp.Infrastructure.TimerModule"/>
    </modules>
  </system.webServer>
</configuration>
```

I describe the Web.config file in detail in Chapter 9, but for the moment it is enough to know that modules are registered in the system.webServer/modules section and that each module is defined using the add element. The attributes for the add element are name, which is a unique name that describes the module, and type, which is the fully qualified name of the module class.

Testing the Module

All that remains is to start the application and see the effect the module has. Each time the ASP.NET framework receives an HTTP request, the TimerModule class will be sent the BeginRequest event, which starts the clock. After the request has proceeded through its life cycle, the module is sent the EndRequest event, which stops the clock and adds the time summary to the response, as illustrated by Figure 4-2.

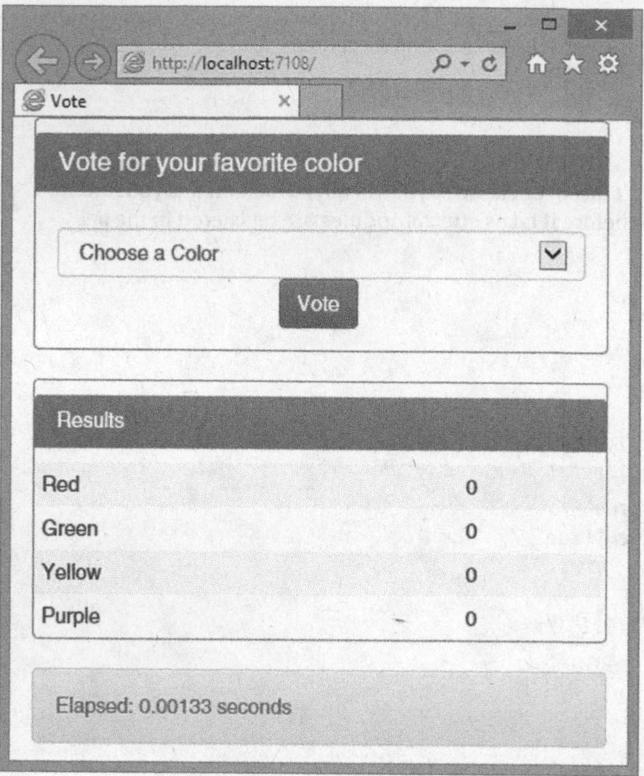

Figure 4-2. *The effect of the module*

If you look at the HTML that has been sent to the browser (by right-clicking in the browser window and selecting View Source from the pop-up menu), you will see how the message from the module has been added to the response:

```
...
    <div class="panel panel-primary">
        <h5 class="panel-heading">Results</h5>
        <table class="table table-condensed table-striped">
                <tr><td>Red</td><td>0</td></tr>
                <tr><td>Green</td><td>0</td></tr>
                <tr><td>Yellow</td><td>0</td></tr>
                <tr><td>Purple</td><td>0</td></tr>
        </table>
    </div>
</body>
</html>
<div class='alert alert-success'>Elapsed: 0.00133 seconds</div>
```

Notice that the `div` element that the module adds to the response appears after the closing `html` tag. This happens because the ASP.NET framework doesn't care about the kind of data that an HTTP response contains and so there is no special support for ensuring that HTML is properly formatted. The main part of the response is generated by the handler, which I describe in Chapter 5, and additions to the response by modules either precede or follow the content that the handler generates.

■ **Tip** Browsers are incredibly tolerant to badly formatted HTML because there is so much of it on the Internet. It is bad practice to rely on a browser being able to figure out how to handle bad data, but I admit that I often do just that when I am using modules to debug request processing or performance problems.

Creating Self-registering Modules

One of the benefits modules confer is that they can be reused across multiple projects. A common approach to module development is to define them in a separate project from the rest of the web application so that the output from the project can be used multiple times.

Creating a module project is a simple task, except for the process of registering the modules. You can define a fragment of XML that has to be inserted into the `Web.config` file, but this puts you at the mercy of the developer or administrator who sets up the web application—something that I generally like to avoid, especially when I have several modules that work together to deliver functionality. A better approach is to create modules that register themselves automatically using an assembly attribute called `PreApplicationStartMethod`. This attribute allows an assembly to define a method that is executed before the `Application_Start` method in the global application class is invoked, which is exactly when modules need to be registered. In the sections that follow, I'll walk through the process of using the `PreApplicationStartMethod`, which is summarized by Table 4-4.

Table 4-4. *Putting the PreApplicationStartMethod Attribute in Context*

Question	Answer
What is it?	The `PreApplicationStartMethod` attribute allows assemblies to specify a method that will be executed when the web application is started, prior to the global application class `Application_Start` method being invoked.
Why should I care?	This attribute makes it easy to perform one-off configuration tasks in class library projects so that additions to the `Web.config` file are not required.
How is it used by the MVC framework?	The MVC framework uses the attribute to configure a range of features, including registering HTML helper methods and setting up authentication providers for Facebook and other services. (See Part 3 for details of ASP.NET authentication.)

Creating the Project

I am going to create a second project called CommonModules within the Visual Studio solution that contains the SimpleApp project. This is not a requirement of using the `PreApplicationStartMethod` attribute, but it makes it easier for me to demonstrate the technique and use the output from the CommonModules project as a dependency of the SimpleApp project.

Right-click the Solution item in the Visual Studio Solution Explorer and select Add ➤ New Project from the pop-up menu. Visual Studio will display the Add New Project dialog window; select the Installed ➤ Visual C# ➤ Class Library project type, set the name to CommonModules, and click the OK button to create the project.

I need to add the `System.Web` assembly to the CommonModules project so that I have access to the `IHttpModule` interface and the context objects. Click the CommonModules project in the Solution Explorer and select Add Reference from the Visual Studio Project menu. Locate the `System.Web` assembly (you'll find it in the Assemblies ➤ Framework section) and check the box next it, as shown in Figure 4-3. Click the OK button to dismiss the dialog box and add the assembly reference to the project.

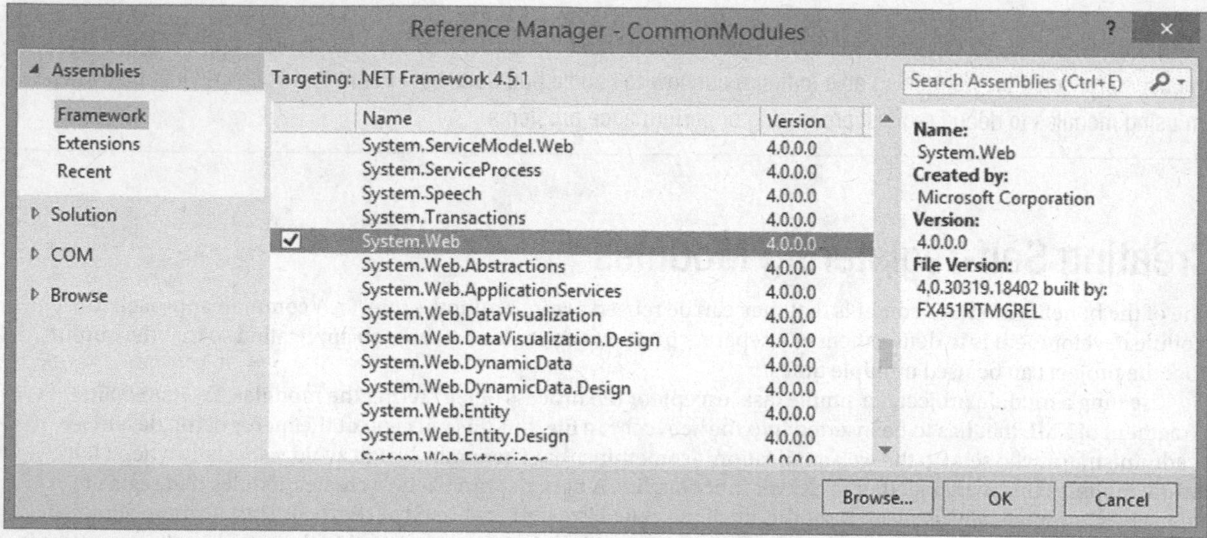

Figure 4-3. *Adding the System.Web assembly to the CommonModules project*

I need to add a reference from the SimpleApp project to the CommonModules project so that the module I create will be available in the web application. Select the SimpleApp project in the Solution Explorer and select Add Reference from the Project menu. Click the Solution section and check the box next to the CommonModules entry, as shown in Figure 4-4. Click the OK button to dismiss the dialog box and add the assembly reference to the project.

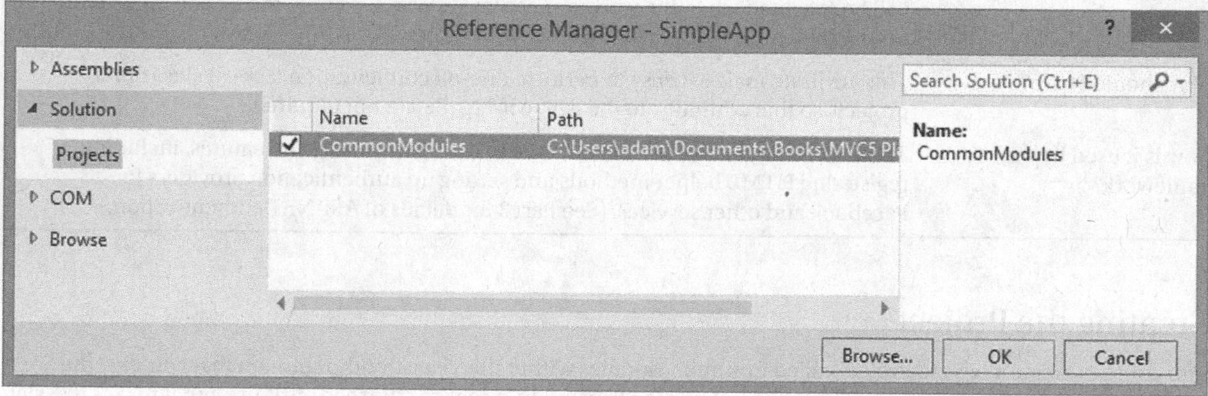

Figure 4-4. *Adding a reference to the CommonModules project*

Now that there are two projects in the solution, I need to tell Visual Studio which one I want to start when I run the debugger. Right-click the SimpleApp project in the Solution Explorer and select Set As StartUp Project from the pop-up menu.

Creating the Module

Visual Studio adds a class file called `Class1.cs` to the new project. Rename this file to `InfoModule.cs` and edit the contents to match Listing 4-4.

Listing 4-4. The Contents of the InfoModule.cs File

```
using System.Web;

namespace CommonModules {

    public class InfoModule : IHttpModule {

        public void Init(HttpApplication app) {
            app.EndRequest += (src, args) => {
                HttpContext ctx = HttpContext.Current;
                ctx.Response.Write(string.Format(
                    "<div class='alert alert-success'>URL: {0} Status: {1}</div>",
                    ctx.Request.RawUrl, ctx.Response.StatusCode));
            };
        }

        public void Dispose() {
            // do nothing - no resources to release
        }
    }
}
```

This module handles the EndRequest event and appends a fragment of HTML to the response, which details the URL that was requested and the status code sent to the browser. I have handled the event using a lambda expression (just for variety), but the overall structure/nature of the module is similar to the TimerModule module I created in the previous section.

Creating the Registration Class

To automatically register a module, I need to create a method that calls the static HttpApplication.RegisterModule method and then apply the PreApplicationStartMethod attribute to call this method when the application starts. I like to define a separate class to register the module because it means I can register all of the modules in the project in a single place. I added a class file called ModuleRegistration.cs to the CommonModules project. Listing 4-5 shows the contents of the new file.

Listing 4-5. The Contents of the ModuleRegistration.cs File

```
using System.Web;

[assembly: PreApplicationStartMethod(typeof(CommonModules.ModuleRegistration),
    "RegisterModule")]

namespace CommonModules {
    public class ModuleRegistration {

        public static void RegisterModule() {
            HttpApplication.RegisterModule(typeof(CommonModules.InfoModule));
        }
    }
}
```

The arguments for the PreApplicationStartMethod are the type of the class that contains the method that will be executed when the application starts and the name of that method, expressed as a string. I have applied the attribute in the file that contains the class and the method, as follows:

```
...
[assembly: PreApplicationStartMethod(typeof(CommonModules.ModuleRegistration),
    "RegisterModule")]
...
```

The method must be public and static and cannot take any arguments. You are free to put any statements in the method, but it is good practice to only perform tasks that configure the code in the project to work with the web application, such as registering modules.

Testing the Module

You can test the effect of the PreApplicationStartMethod attribute by selecting Start Debugging from the Visual Studio Debug menu. Visual Studio will build both projects, start the application, and load the module from the CommonModules project. You can see the message that the module adds to the response in Figure 4-5.

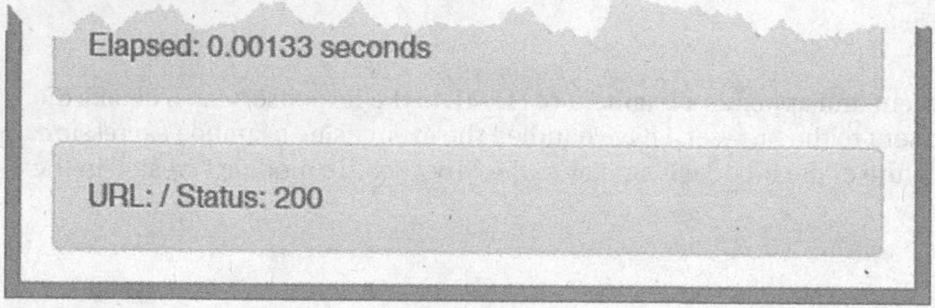

Figure 4-5. *The output from the InfoModule*

Using Module Events

My timer module is a nice demonstration of the way that modules can participate in the request processing life cycle and—optionally—manipulate the response sent to the client, but it has one problem: The timing information that it generates is locked away, which will force me to duplicate functionality if I need to do something similar in another module. Not only does this create a code maintenance concern—an anathema in MVC applications—but it also adds to the amount of time taken to process each request, leading to inconsistencies in the timing information within different modules.

What I need is the ability to share the timing information with other modules so that I can build on my core functionality, which I can do by creating a module event. Module events allow modules to coordinate their activities and share data. Table 4-5 puts module events in context.

Table 4-5. *Putting Module Events in Context*

Question	Answer
What are they?	Module events are standard C# events that are triggered to share data or coordinate activities between modules.
Why should I care?	Using module events allows you to create more complex functionality without needing to duplicate functionality in multiple modules.
How are they used by the MVC framework?	The MVC framework doesn't use module events directly.

Defining the Module Event

I am going to create a new module that keeps track of the total amount of time taken to process requests. Obviously, this requires me to measure the time taken for individual requests, which would duplicate the functionality of the TimerModule that I created at the start of the chapter.

Rather than duplicate the TimerModule functionality, I am going to extend it by adding an event that is triggered when timing information is available. To this end, you can see the changes I have made to the TimerModule.cs file in Listing 4-6.

Listing 4-6. Adding an Event to the TimerModule.cs File

```
using System;
using System.Diagnostics;
using System.Web;

namespace SimpleApp.Infrastructure {

    public class RequestTimerEventArgs : EventArgs {
        public float Duration { get; set; }
    }

    public class TimerModule : IHttpModule {
        public event EventHandler<RequestTimerEventArgs> RequestTimed;
        private Stopwatch timer;

        public void Init(HttpApplication app) {
            app.BeginRequest += HandleEvent;
            app.EndRequest += HandleEvent;
        }

        private void HandleEvent(object src, EventArgs args) {
            HttpContext ctx = HttpContext.Current;
            if (ctx.CurrentNotification == RequestNotification.BeginRequest) {
                timer = Stopwatch.StartNew();
            } else {
                float duration = ((float) timer.ElapsedTicks) / Stopwatch.Frequency;
                ctx.Response.Write(string.Format(
                    "<div class='alert alert-success'>Elapsed: {0:F5} seconds</div>",
                    duration));
```

```
                if (RequestTimed != null) {
                    RequestTimed(this,
                        new RequestTimerEventArgs { Duration = duration });
                }
            }
        }

        public void Dispose() {
            // do nothing - no resources to release
        }
    }
}
```

I have defined an event called `RequestTimed` that sends a `RequestTimerEventArgs` object to its handlers. This object defines a `float` value that provides access to the time taken for the request to be processed.

Creating the Consuming Module

My next step is to create a module that will handle the event from `TimerModule` and gather details of the overall amount of time spent handling requests. I could create this module in either of the projects in the solution, but it makes sense to keep modules that depend on one another together, so I added a class file called `TotalTimeModule.cs` to the `Infrastructure` folder of the `SimpleApp` project. Listing 4-7 shows the module I defined in the new file.

Listing 4-7. The Contents of the TotalTimeModule.cs File

```
using System.IO;
using System.Web;
using System.Web.UI;

namespace SimpleApp.Infrastructure {
    public class TotalTimeModule : IHttpModule {
        private static float totalTime = 0;
        private static int requestCount = 0;

        public void Init(HttpApplication app) {
            IHttpModule module = app.Modules["Timer"];
            if (module != null && module is TimerModule) {
                TimerModule timerModule = (TimerModule)module;
                timerModule.RequestTimed += (src, args) => {
                    totalTime += args.Duration;
                    requestCount++;
                };
            }

            app.EndRequest += (src, args) => {
                app.Context.Response.Write(CreateSummary());
            };
        }
```

```
    private string CreateSummary() {
        StringWriter stringWriter = new StringWriter();
        HtmlTextWriter htmlWriter = new HtmlTextWriter(stringWriter);
        htmlWriter.AddAttribute(HtmlTextWriterAttribute.Class,
            "table table-bordered");
        htmlWriter.RenderBeginTag(HtmlTextWriterTag.Table);
            htmlWriter.AddAttribute(HtmlTextWriterAttribute.Class, "success");
            htmlWriter.RenderBeginTag(HtmlTextWriterTag.Tr);
                htmlWriter.RenderBeginTag(HtmlTextWriterTag.Td);
                    htmlWriter.Write("Requests");
                    htmlWriter.RenderEndTag();
                    htmlWriter.RenderBeginTag(HtmlTextWriterTag.Td);
                    htmlWriter.Write(requestCount);
                htmlWriter.RenderEndTag();
            htmlWriter.RenderEndTag();
                htmlWriter.AddAttribute(HtmlTextWriterAttribute.Class, "success");
                htmlWriter.RenderBeginTag(HtmlTextWriterTag.Tr);
                    htmlWriter.RenderBeginTag(HtmlTextWriterTag.Td);
                    htmlWriter.Write("Total Time");
                    htmlWriter.RenderEndTag();
                    htmlWriter.RenderBeginTag(HtmlTextWriterTag.Td);
                    htmlWriter.Write("{0:F5} seconds", totalTime);
                htmlWriter.RenderEndTag();
            htmlWriter.RenderEndTag();
        htmlWriter.RenderEndTag();
        return stringWriter.ToString();
    }

    public void Dispose() {
        // do nothing
    }
  }
}
```

The module looks more complicated than it really is because of the way I have chosen to create the HTML fragment that is inserted into the response to the browser. I'll explain how this works in the "Generating HTML" section later in the chapter. The most important part of this example is the technique for setting up the handler for the event defined by the `TimerModule` class.

The `HttpApplication` class defines a property called `Modules` that returns a collection of modules objects, indexed by the name with which they were registered, either in the `Web.config` file or using the `PreApplicationStartMethod` attribute. This allows me to locate the `TimerModule`, which was registered using the name `Timer` in Listing 4-3, like this:

```
...
IHttpModule module = app.Modules["Timer"];
if (module != null && module is TimerModule) {
    TimerModule timerModule = (TimerModule)module;
    timerModule.RequestTimed += (src, args) => {
        totalTime += args.Duration;
        requestCount++;
    };
}
...
```

■ **Tip** The collection returned by the Modules property is also indexed by position so that, for example, Modules[0] and Modules[1] return the first two modules that were registered.

Once I have located the module I want, I cast the object and add a handler to the event that I defined in the previous section. All modules require registration, and in Listing 4-8 you can see the addition I made to the Web.config file to register the TotalTimeModule class.

Listing 4-8. Registering the Module in the Web.config File

```
<?xml version="1.0" encoding="utf-8"?>
<configuration>
  <appSettings>
    <add key="webpages:Version" value="3.0.0.0" />
    <add key="webpages:Enabled" value="false" />
     <add key="ClientValidationEnabled" value="true" />
    <add key="UnobtrusiveJavaScriptEnabled" value="true" />
  </appSettings>
  <system.web>
    <compilation debug="true" targetFramework="4.5.1" />
    <httpRuntime targetFramework="4.5.1" />
  </system.web>
  <system.webServer>
    <modules>
      <add name="Timer" type="SimpleApp.Infrastructure.TimerModule"/>
      <add name="Total" type="SimpleApp.Infrastructure.TotalTimeModule"/>
    </modules>
  </system.webServer>
</configuration>
```

■ **Tip** All of the registered module classes are instantiated before their Init methods are invoked. The order in which modules are registered determines the order in which life-cycle requests are sent to modules but doesn't have an impact on locating other modules through the HttpApplication.Modules property.

You can see the new module consuming the event from the Timer module by starting the application, as illustrated by Figure 4-6.

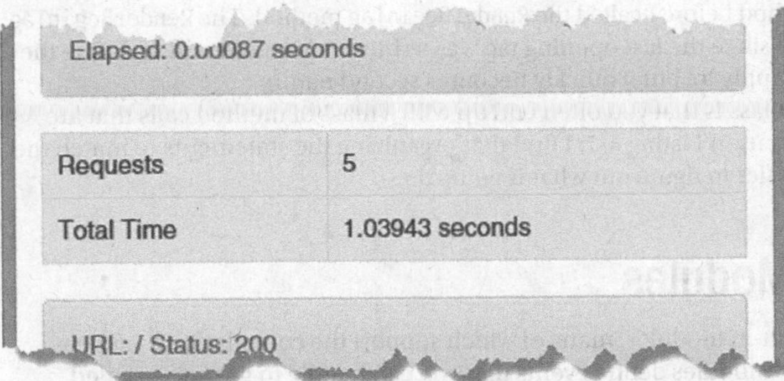

***Figure 4-6.** Generating diagnostic data based on an event in another module*

Generating HTML

The modules I created in this chapter add some HTML content to the response sent to the browser. This isn't the only thing you can do with modules, of course, and you'll get a sense of what's possible when I describe the built-in modules later in this chapter and show you how modules can provide custom services to handlers in Chapter 5—but I find adding diagnostic fragments to be helpful in solving complex problems.

I used two different techniques for generating the HTML fragments. The first, which I used in the `TimerModule` class, is to use the standard C# string composition feature, like this:

```
...
string.Format("<div class='alert alert-success'>Elapsed: {0:F5} seconds</div>",
    duration));
...
```

This approach is fine for tiny pieces of HTML, but it becomes difficult to manage for anything other than single elements. The problem is that you need to create strings that can be safely processed twice: once by the .NET runtime and once by the browser. Careful attention must be paid to getting the single and double quotes right, escaping dangerous characters, and making sure that the data values with which the HTML string is composed are safe to display.

The other technique I used was to apply the `HtmlTextWriter` class, which is defined in the `System.Web.UI` namespace. The namespace contains a lot of Web Forms classes, but the `HtmlTextWriter` can be used in any ASP.NET application, and it takes a much more structured approach to creating HTML. The result is correctly structured HTML, but the code is more verbose and takes a little time to get used to. Table 4-6 shows the `HtmlTextWriter` methods that I used in Listing 4-7.

***Table 4-6.** The HtmlTextWriter Methods Used in the TotalTimeModule*

Name	Description
`AddAttribute(attr, value)`	Sets an attribute that will be applied to the next element that is rendered. The attribute is specified as a value from the `HtmlTextWriterAttribute` enumeration.
`RenderBeginTag(tag)`	Writes the opening tag of an HTML element specified as a value from the `HtmlTextWriterTag` enumeration.
`RenderEndTag()`	Writes the ending tag to match the most recently written opening tag.
`Write(content)`	Writes content to the response. There are overloaded versions of this method for strings and the C# primitive types (`int`, `bool`, `long`, and so on).

Notice that I had to call the AddAttribute method before I called the RenderBeginTag method. The RenderBeginTag method will write out all of the attributes I defined since the last opening tag was written. It is a little odd to define the attributes before specifying the element that they apply to, but it quickly becomes second nature.

The main problem with the HtmlTextWriter class is that you often end up with a mass of method calls that are hard to read. This is why I indented the C# statements in Listing 4-7; I find that organizing the statements to match the structure of the HTML I am generating makes it easier to figure out what is going on.

Understanding the Built-in Modules

The ASP.NET framework contains a number of built-in modules, many of which support the core platform services that I describe in Part 3 of this book. Some of these modules define events that you can handle to get fine-grained information about their activities, although for the most part, you interact with the functionality they provide through the context objects that I described in Chapter 3. In this section, I am going to show you how to enumerate the modules, explain what each of them does, and describe the events that some of them define. To generate the list of modules, I have added a new action method to the Home controller, as shown in Listing 4-9.

Listing 4-9. Adding an Action Method to the HomeController.cs File

```
using System;
using System.Collections.Generic;
using System.Linq;
using System.Web.Mvc;
using SimpleApp.Models;

namespace SimpleApp.Controllers {
    public class HomeController : Controller {

        public ActionResult Index() {
            return View(GetTimeStamps());
        }

        [HttpPost]
        public ActionResult Index(Color color) {
            Color? oldColor = Session["color"] as Color?;
            if (oldColor != null) {
                Votes.ChangeVote(color, (Color)oldColor);
            } else {
                Votes.RecordVote(color);
            }
            ViewBag.SelectedColor = Session["color"] = color;
            return View(GetTimeStamps());
        }

        public ActionResult Modules() {
            var modules = HttpContext.ApplicationInstance.Modules;
            Tuple<string, string>[] data =
                modules.AllKeys
                    .Select(x => new Tuple<string, string>(
                        x.StartsWith("__Dynamic") ? x.Split('_',',')[3] : x,
                        modules[x].GetType().Name))
                    .OrderBy(x => x.Item1)
```

```
                .ToArray();
            return View(data);
        }

        private List<string> GetTimeStamps() {
            return new List<string> {
                string.Format("App timestamp: {0}",
                    HttpContext.Application["app_timestamp"]),
                string.Format("Request timestamp: {0}", Session["request_timestamp"]),
            };
        }
    }
}
```

The new action method is called `Modules`, and it uses LINQ to generate an array of `Tuple<string, string>` objects from the module objects returned by the `HttpApplication.Module` property. Modules registered using the `PreApplicationStartMethod` URL are done so using the fully qualified class name prefixed with `__Dynamic_`, and the LINQ methods locate and reformat the names to make them more readable. The result is an array of tuples that are sorted by name that I pass to the `View` method, which tells the MVC framework to render the view default associated with the action method.

■ **Tip** Notice that to get the `HttpApplication` object, I have to use the `HttpContext` convenience property (defined by the `Controller` base class) to get an `HttpContext` object and then read the `ApplicationInstance` property. I described the convenience context objects and the convenience properties available in Chapter 3.

To create this view, right-click the `Modules` action method in the code editor and select Add View from the pop-up menu. Ensure View Name is set to Modules, select Empty (without model) for Template, and uncheck the option boxes. Click Add to create the `Views/Home/Modules.cshtml` file and add the markup shown in Listing 4-10.

Listing 4-10. The Contents of the Modules.cshtml File

```
@model Tuple<string, string>[]
@{
    Layout = null;
}

<!DOCTYPE html>

<html>
<head>
    <meta name="viewport" content="width=device-width" />
    <title>Modules</title>
    <link href="~/Content/bootstrap.min.css" rel="stylesheet" />
    <link href="~/Content/bootstrap-theme.min.css" rel="stylesheet" />
</head>
<body class="container">
    <table class="table table-bordered table-striped">
        <thead>
            <tr><th>Name</th><th>Type</th></tr>
        </thead>
```

```
        <tbody>
            @foreach (Tuple<string, string> x in Model) {
                <tr><td>@x.Item1</td><td>@x.Item2</td></tr>
            }
        </tbody>
    </table>
</body>
</html>
```

The view consists of a table element that I have styled using Bootstrap and that contains a row for each of the `Tuple` objects passed from the controller. You can see the list of built-in modules by starting the application and requesting the `/Home/Modules` URL, as illustrated by Figure 4-7.

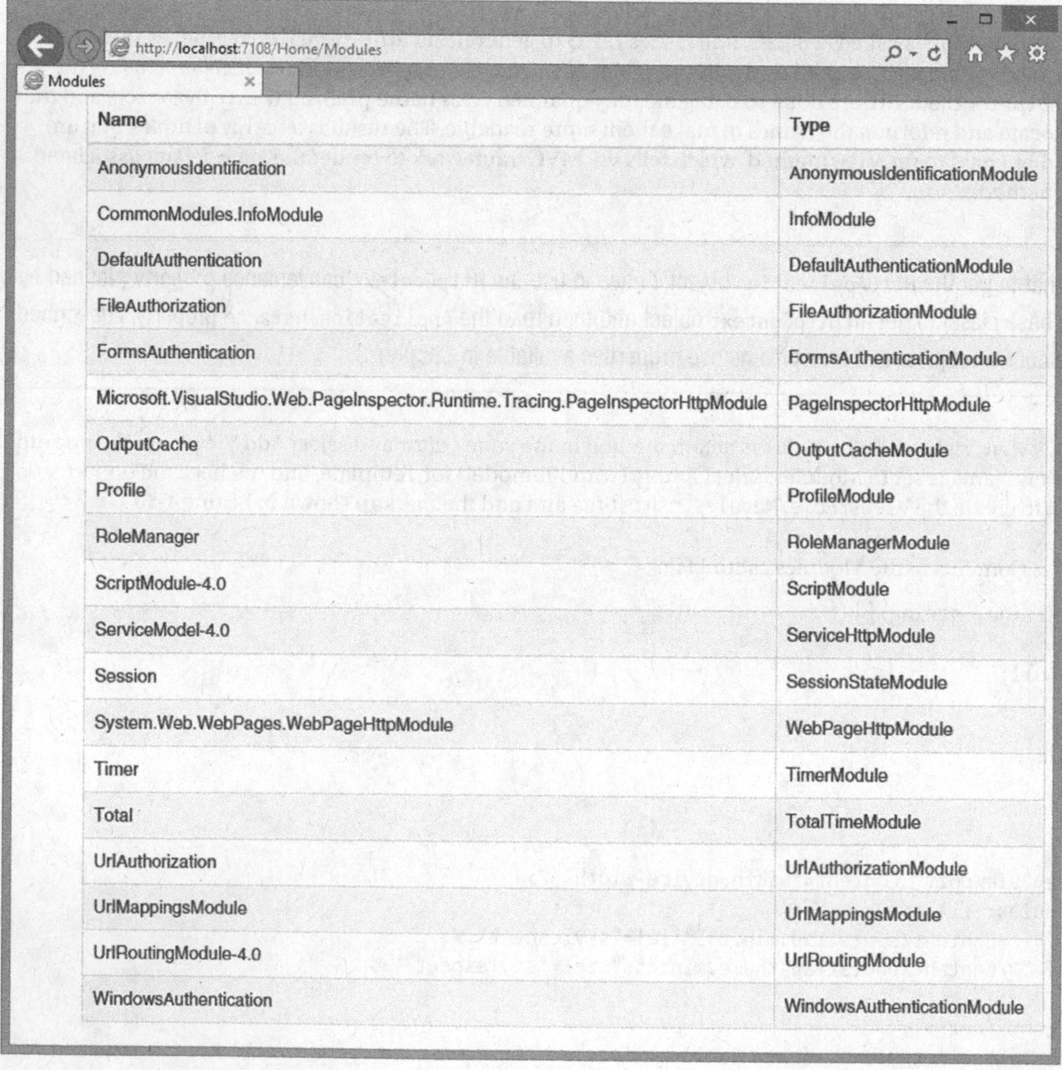

Name	Type
AnonymousIdentification	AnonymousIdentificationModule
CommonModules.InfoModule	InfoModule
DefaultAuthentication	DefaultAuthenticationModule
FileAuthorization	FileAuthorizationModule
FormsAuthentication	FormsAuthenticationModule
Microsoft.VisualStudio.Web.PageInspector.Runtime.Tracing.PageInspectorHttpModule	PageInspectorHttpModule
OutputCache	OutputCacheModule
Profile	ProfileModule
RoleManager	RoleManagerModule
ScriptModule-4.0	ScriptModule
ServiceModel-4.0	ServiceHttpModule
Session	SessionStateModule
System.Web.WebPages.WebPageHttpModule	WebPageHttpModule
Timer	TimerModule
Total	TotalTimeModule
UrlAuthorization	UrlAuthorizationModule
UrlMappingsModule	UrlMappingsModule
UrlRoutingModule-4.0	UrlRoutingModule
WindowsAuthentication	WindowsAuthenticationModule

Figure 4-7. *Displaying a list of the built-in modules*

It can be hard to read the details of the modules from the figure, so I have repeated the information in Table 4-7 and described each module.

Table 4-7. *The Modules in an ASP.NET Framework Application*

Name	Type
`AnonymousIdentification`	This module is implemented by the `System.Web.Security.AnonymousIdentificationModule` class and is responsible for uniquely identifying requests so that features such as user data can be used even when the user has not been authenticated.
`DefaultAuthentication`	This module is implemented by the `System.Web.Security.DefaultAuthenticationModule` class and is responsible for ensuring that the `User` property of the `HttpContext` object is set to an object that implements the `IPrincipal` interface if this has not been done by one of the other authentication modules. See Part 3 for details of authentication.
`FileAuthorization`	This module is implemented by the `System.Web.Security.FileAuthorizationModule` class and ensures that the user has access to the file the request relates to when Windows authentication is used. I describe authentication in Part 3, but I don't describe Windows authentication in this book because it is not widely used.
`FormsAuthentication`	This module is implemented by the `System.Web.Security.FormsAuthenticationModule` class and sets the value of the `HttpContext.User` property when forms authentication is used. I explain authentication in Part 3.
`CommonModules.InfoModule`	This is one of the example modules I created earlier in the chapter.
`OutputCache`	This module is implemented by the `System.Web.Caching.OutputCacheModule` class and is responsible for caching responses sent to the browser. I explain how the ASP.NET framework caching features work in Chapters 11 and 12.
`PageInspectorHttpModule`	This module supports the Visual Studio Page Inspector feature, which allows for HTML and CSS content to be debugged within Visual Studio. I don't describe this feature and find that the developer tools in modern web browsers are more useful.
`Profile`	This module is implemented by the `System.Web.Profile.ProfileModule` class and is responsible for associating user profile data with a request. See Part 3 for details of authentication. (This module supports the obsolete Membership API.)
`RoleManager`	This module is implemented by the `System.Web.Security.RoleManagerModule` class and is responsible for assigning details of the roles that a user has been assigned to a request. (This module supports the obsolete Membership API.)
`ScriptModule-4.0`	This module is implemented by the `System.Web.Handlers.ScriptModule` class and is responsible for supporting Ajax requests. This module has been outmoded by support for Ajax requests in the MVC framework and, more recently the Web API.
`ServiceModel-4.0`	This module is implemented by the `System.ServiceModel.Activation.ServiceHttpModule` class. This module is used to activate ASP.NET web services, which have been outmoded by the MVC framework and the Web API.
`Session`	This module is implemented by the `System.Web.SessionState.SessionStateModule` class and is responsible for associating session data with a request. See Chapter 10 for details of using session data.

(continued)

Table 4-7. *(continued)*

Name	Type
`Timer`	This is the `TimerModule` class that I created earlier in the chapter.
`Total`	This is the `TotalTimeModule` class that I created earlier in the chapter.
`UrlAuthorization`	This module is implemented by the `System.Web.Security.UrlAuthorizationModule` class and ensures that users are authorized to access the URLs they request.
`UrlMappingsModule`	This module is implemented by the `System.Web.UrlMappingsModule` class and is responsible for implementing the URL Mappings feature, which is not used in MVC framework applications.
`UrlRoutingModule-4.0`	This module is implemented by the `System.Web.Routing.UrlRoutingModule` class and is responsible for implementing the URL routing feature.
`WebPageHttpModule`	This module intercepts requests for MVC framework view files and displays an error when they are asked for (for example with a URL for `/Views/Home/Index.cshtml`). Views can be rendered only as a result of a URL that targets an action method in a controller.
`WindowsAuthentication`	This module is implemented by the `System.Web.Security.WindowsAuthenticationModule` class and is responsible for setting the value of the `HttpContext.User` property when Windows authentication is used. I don't describe Windows authentication in this book because it is no longer widely used.

■ **Tip** Some of the modules that are described in Table 4-7 are part of the membership system, which provides authentication and user management features. This has been replaced with the Identity API, which I describe in Part 3.

Some of the built-in modules define events that can be handled to receive notifications when important changes occur. I have listed these modules and their events in Table 4-8.

Table 4-8. The Built-in Modules That Define Events

Module	Description
AnonymousIdentification	Defines the event Creating, which provides an opportunity to override the identification. The Creating event sends an instance of the AnonymousIdentificationEventArgs class to event handlers.
DefaultAuthentication	This module defines the Authenticate event that is triggered when the module sets the User property and that sends an instance of the DefaultAuthenticationEventArgs class to event handlers.
FormsAuthentication	This module defines the Authenticate event that lets you override the value of the User property. Event handlers are sent a FormsAuthenticationEventArgs object.
Profile	The MigrateAnonymous event is triggered when an anonymous user logs in and sends a ProfileMigrateEventArgs object to handlers. The Personalize event is triggered when the profile data is being associated with the request and provides an opportunity to override the data that is used (handlers are sent a ProfileEventArgs object).
RoleManager	This module defines the GetRoles event that allows you to override the role information associated with a request. Event handlers are sent a RoleManagerEventArgs object.
Session	The Start event is triggered when a new session is started, and the End event is triggered when an event expires. Both events sent standard EventArgs objects to handlers.

The most widely used events are those defined by the Session module because they allow applications to associate default state data with sessions when they are created. I explain how ASP.NET sessions and state data work in Chapter 10.

Summary

In this chapter, I described the role that modules play in ASP.NET request handling. I showed you how to create modules by implementing the IHttpModule interface and how to register those modules with ASP.NET, both through the Web.config file and by using the PreApplicationStartMethod assembly attribute. I showed you how modules can provide services by defining events and demonstrated the process for locating another module and creating an event handler. I completed the chapter by describing the built-in modules, many of which provide services that I describe in Part 3 of this book. In the next chapter, I describe the handler component, which is responsible for generating responses for HTTP requests.

CHAPTER 5

Handlers

Handlers are responsible for generating the response content for an HTTP request. In this chapter, I explain how handlers generate content, demonstrate how to create custom handlers, and show you how modules can provide services to handlers. Table 5-1 summarizes this chapter.

Table 5-1. *Chapter Summary*

Problem	Solution	Listing
Create a handler.	Implement the `IHttpHandler` interface.	1–3
Register a handler using a URL route.	Create an implementation of the `IRouteHandler` interface that returns the handler from its `GetHttpHandler` method and use it as an argument to the `RouteCollection.Add` method.	4
Register a handler using the `Web.config` file.	Add handlers to the `system.webServer/handlers` section.	5, 6
Create a handler that generates content asynchronously.	Derive from the `HttpTaskAsyncHandler` class.	7, 8
Provide a service from one module to another.	Define events and use a declarative interface.	9–15
Control the instantiation of handler classes.	Create a custom handler factory.	16–21

Preparing the Example Project

I am going to continue using the SimpleApp project I created in Chapter 2 and have been using ever since. I defined three modules that add fragments of HTML to the response in Chapter 4, which has the effect of cluttering up the response in the browser window and which I don't need in this chapter. Listing 5-1 shows how I commented out the module registration elements in the `Web.config` file.

Listing 5-1. Disabling Modules in the Web.config File

```
<?xml version="1.0" encoding="utf-8"?>
<configuration>
  <appSettings>
    <add key="webpages:Version" value="3.0.0.0" />
    <add key="webpages:Enabled" value="false" />
```

```
      <add key="ClientValidationEnabled" value="true" />
      <add key="UnobtrusiveJavaScriptEnabled" value="true" />
   </appSettings>
   <system.web>
      <compilation debug="true" targetFramework="4.5.1" />
      <httpRuntime targetFramework="4.5.1" />
   </system.web>
   <system.webServer>
      <modules>
         <!--<add name="Timer" type="SimpleApp.Infrastructure.TimerModule"/>-->
         <!--<add name="Total" type="SimpleApp.Infrastructure.TotalTimeModule"/>-->
      </modules>
   </system.webServer>
</configuration>
```

Listing 5-2 shows how I commented out the PreApplicationStartMethod in the ModuleResigstration.cs file in the CommonModules project.

Listing 5-2. Disabling the Module in the ModuleRegistration.cs File

```
using System.Web;

//[assembly: PreApplicationStartMethod(typeof(CommonModules.ModuleRegistration),
//     "RegisterModule")]

namespace CommonModules {
    public class ModuleRegistration {

        public static void RegisterModule() {
            HttpApplication.RegisterModule(typeof(CommonModules.InfoModule));
        }
    }
}
```

Adding the System.Net.Http Assembly

Later in the chapter, I will be using the System.Net.Http.HttpClient class that is defined in the System.Net.Http assembly. The assembly isn't added to ASP.NET projects by default, so select the SimpleApp project in the Solution Explorer and then select Add Reference from the Visual Studio Project menu; then locate the System.Net.Http assembly in the Assemblies ➤ Framework section and check the box next to it, as shown in Figure 5-1. Click the Add button to add the assembly reference and close the dialog box.

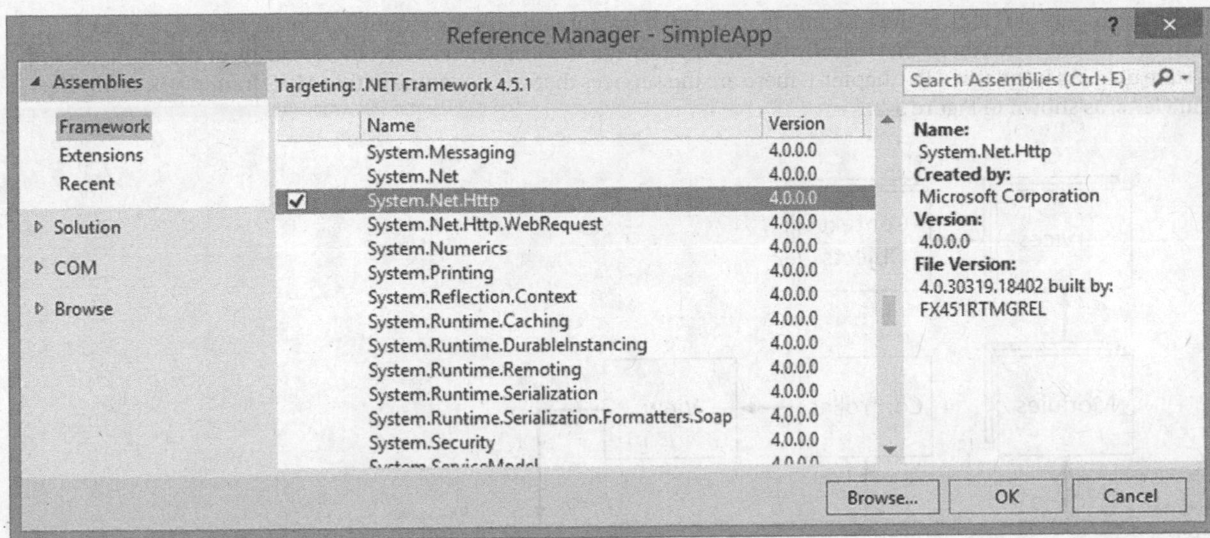

***Figure 5-1.** Adding the System.Net.Http assembly to the project*

ASP.NET Handlers

As part of the request handling life cycle, ASP.NET selects a handler to generate the content that will be returned to the client. The ASP.NET platform doesn't care what form the content takes or what process the handler uses to generate the content; it just treats the content as an opaque chunk of data that needs to be sent to the client at the end of the request life cycle. This opacity is the key to how ASP.NET is able to support different approaches to web application development: There are handlers for the MVC framework, Web Forms, SignalR, and the Web API, and the ASP.NET platform treats them all equally. Table 5-2 puts handlers into context.

***Table 5-2.** Putting Handlers in Context*

Question	Answer
What are they?	Handlers are the ASP.NET request handling component that is responsible for generating the response content for requests.
Why should I care?	Handlers are one of the key extensibility points of the ASP.NET platform and can be used to customize request handling for existing technology stacks or to create completely new ones.
How is it used by the MVC framework?	The MVC framework uses a handler to manage the process of selecting and invoking an action method and rendering a view to generate response content.

Understanding Handlers in the Request Life Cycle

A common source of confusion when working with the ASP.NET platform is the difference between modules and handlers, so it is important I explain the role of each component before digging into the details of how handlers work.

The best way to understand each component is within the scope of the request life cycle. As I explained in Chapter 4, modules have two roles in request handling. They can be used flor diagnosis and debugging, or they can provide services used by other components. The modules I created in Chapter 4 fall into the diagnosis category: They added fragments of HTML to the response that provided insight into how the request was processed. By contrast, most of the built-in modules that come with ASP.NET provide services, such as caching, security, or the management of state data. As I explained in Chapter 1, these are the services that you consume within MVC framework controllers and views, as shown in Figure 5-2.

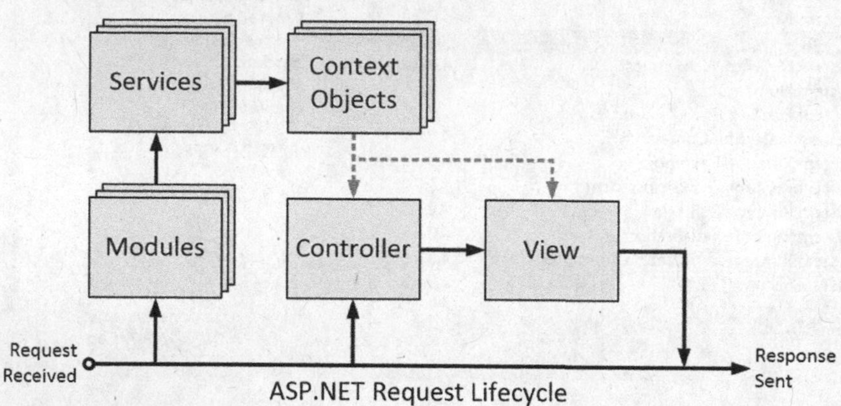

Figure 5-2. *The relationship between module services and MVC framework controllers*

This figure is a refinement of one I showed you in Chapter 1, expanded to show more details about the ASP.NET components and request life cycle. As the figure illustrates, modules are instantiated at the start of the request handling process, and they set up services that are consumed through the ASP.NET context objects by the MVC framework controller and view in order to generate the response that will be sent to the client.

In Figure 5-1, I have shown the MVC framework programmer's view of the controller and view, but, as you may have guessed, the MVC functionality is integrated into the ASP.NET platform through a handler, as shown in Figure 5-3.

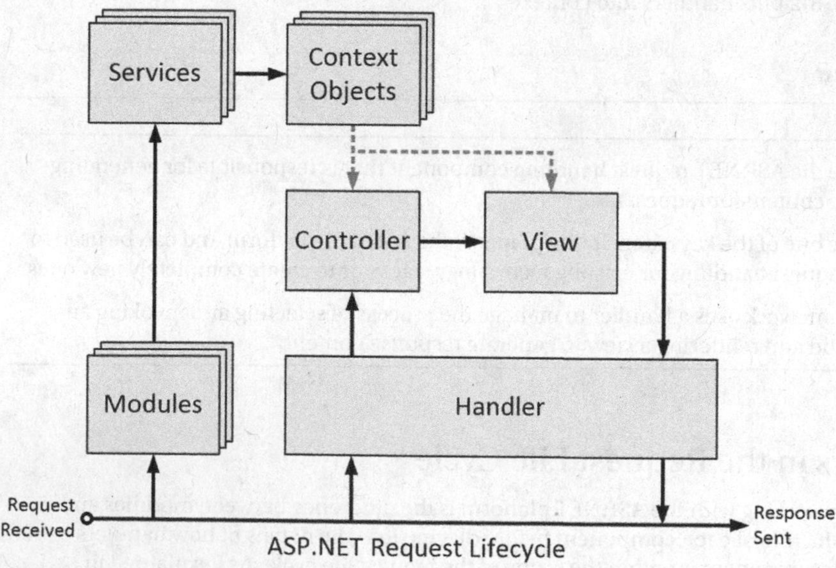

Figure 5-3. *Showing the handler in the request life cycle*

The first thing to notice is that there are multiple modules for each request but only one handler. The reason I am being so emphatic about the relationship between these components is because I want to be clear about they mesh with the request life-cycle events: The modules are created as soon as the request life cycle begins, but the selection and creation of the handler are built right into the life cycle, as shown in Figure 5-4.

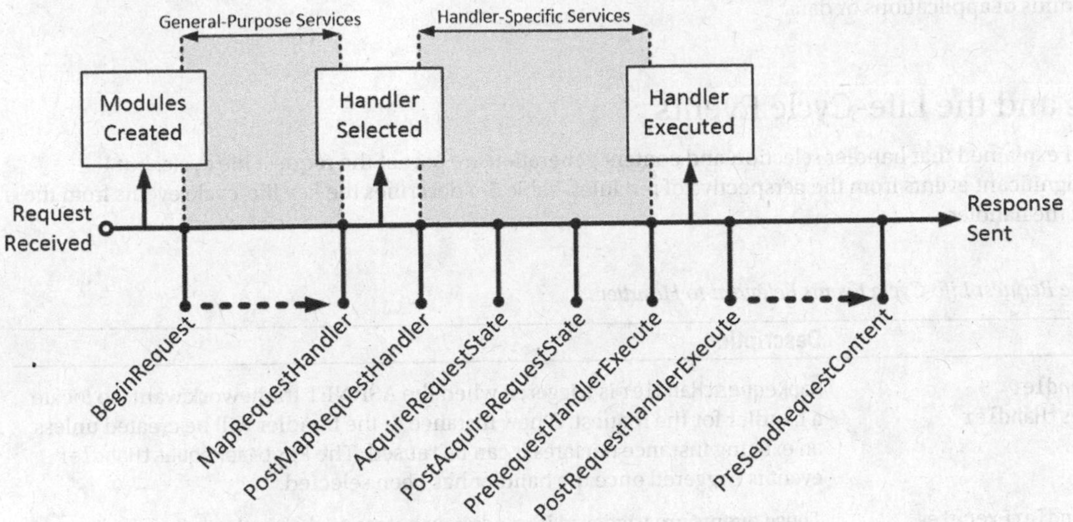

***Figure 5-4.** The relationship between life-cycle events, modules, and handlers*

The `MapRequestHandler` event is triggered before the ASP.NET platform locates the handler that will generate the content for the request, the process for which I describe in the "Creating a Handler" section later in this chapter. The `PostMapRequestHandler` event is triggered once the handler has been identified and instantiated. However, the handler isn't asked to generate the content until the `PreRequestHandlerExecute` event is triggered, which means that modules have an opportunity to respond to the handler selection and provide services that are unique to that handler, as shown in the figure. You'll see how this all works in the "Targeting a Specific Handler" section later in this chapter. (Modules can also override the handler selection process, as described in Chapter 6.)

Understanding Handlers

Handlers are classes that implement the `System.Web.IHttpHandler` interface, which defines the two methods that I have described in Table 5-3.

***Table 5-3.** The Members Defined by the IHttpHandler Interface*

Name	Description
`ProcessRequest(context)`	This method is called when the ASP.NET framework wants the handler to generate a response for a request. The parameter is an `HttpContext` object, which provides access to details of the request.
`IsReusable`	This property tells the ASP.NET framework whether the handler can be used to handle further requests. If the property returns `false`, then the ASP.NET framework will create new instances for each request. In most situations, returning a value of `true` doesn't mean that handlers will be reused unless you implement a custom handler factory, which I describe in the "Custom Handler Factories" section of this chapter.

The ProcessRequest method is passed an HttpContext object, which can be used to inspect the request and the state of the application through the properties I described in Chapter 3.

Handlers can generate any kind of content that can be delivered over HTTP, and the ASP.NET platform does not impose any constraints on how the content is created. ASP.NET includes a set of default handlers that support the Web Forms, the MVC framework, SignalR, and Web API technology stacks, but custom handlers can be used to support new kinds of applications or data.

Handlers and the Life-Cycle Events

In Figure 5-3, I explained that handler selection and content generation are part of the request life cycle, but I describe the significant events from the perspective of modules. Table 5-4 describes the key life-cycle events from the perspective of the handler.

Table 5-4. *The Request Life-Cycle Events Relevant to Handlers*

Name	Description
MapRequestHandler PostMapRequestHandler	MapRequestHandler is triggered when the ASP.NET framework wants to locate a handler for the request. A new instance of the handler will be created unless an existing instance declares it can be reused. The PostMapRequestHandler event is triggered once the handler has been selected.
PreRequestHandlerExecute PostRequestHandlerExecute	These events are triggered immediately before and after the call to the handler ProcessRequest method.

The life cycle of a handler is interwoven with the request and module life cycles. This may seem over complicated, but it provides for flexible interactions between handlers and modules (or the global application class if that's where you have defined your event handlers). All of this will start to make more sense as you see some examples of handlers and the way they can be used.

The MapRequestHandler and PostMapRequestHandler events are different from the other pairs of events in the life cycle. Normally, the first event in a pair is a request for a module to provide a service, and the second event signals that phase of the life cycle is complete. So, for example, the AcquireRequestState event is a request for modules that handle state data to associate data with the request, and the PostAcquireRequestState event signals that all of the modules that handled the first event have finished responding.

The MapRequestHandler event isn't an invitation for a module to supply a handler for a request; that's a task that ASP.NET handles itself, and the event just signals that the selection is about to be made (a process I describe in the next section). The PostMapRequestHandler event signals that the handler has been selected, which allows modules to respond to the handler choice—generally by setting up services or data specific to the chosen handler.

The handler's ProcessRequest method is called between the PreRequestHandlerExecute and PostRequestHandlerExecute events. Modules can use these events as the last opportunity to manipulate the context objects before the content is generated by the handler and the first opportunity to manipulate the response once the handler is done.

Creating a Handler

It is time to create a handler now that you understand the purpose of handlers and the context in which they exist. I created a class file called `DayOfWeekHandler.cs` in the `Infrastructure` folder and used it to define the handler shown in Listing 5-3.

Listing 5-3. The Contents of the DayOfWeekHandler.cs File

```
using System;
using System.Web;

namespace SimpleApp.Infrastructure {
    public class DayOfWeekHandler: IHttpHandler {

        public void ProcessRequest(HttpContext context) {
            string day = DateTime.Now.DayOfWeek.ToString();

            if (context.Request.CurrentExecutionFilePathExtension == ".json") {
                context.Response.ContentType = "application/json";
                context.Response.Write(string.Format("{{\"day\": \"{0}\"}}", day));
            } else {
                context.Response.ContentType = "text/html";
                context.Response.Write(string.Format("<span>It is: {0}</span>", day));
            }
        }

        public bool IsReusable {
            get { return false; }
        }
    }
}
```

When content is required for a request, the ASP.NET platform calls the `ProcessRequest` method and provides the handler with an `HttpContext` object. After that, it is up to the handler to figure out what's needed; that can be a complex process such as the one used by the MVC framework to locate and invoke an action method and render a view, or as simple as generating simple string responses, which is what this example handler does.

I want to demonstrate that the ASP.NET platform doesn't restrict the content that the handler generates, so I use the `HttpResponse.CurrentExecutionFilePathExtension` property to detect requests for URLs whose file component ends with `.json` and return the current day of the week as JSON data. For all other requests, I assume that the client requires a fragment of HTML.

■ **Note** The JavaScript Object Notation (JSON) format is commonly used in web applications to transfer data using Ajax requests. The structure of JSON is similar to the way that JavaScript data values are defined, which makes it easy to process in the browser. I don't get into the details of JSON in this book, but I dig into the details of generating and processing JSON data in my *Pro ASP.NET MVC Client Development* book, which is published by Apress.

Registering a Handler Using URL Routing

Handlers must be registered before they can be used to generate content for requests, and there are two ways in which this can be done. The firs technique for registering a handler is to use the routing system. In Listing 5-4, you can see how I have edited the RouteConfig.cs file to set up a route that matches URLs that start with /handler to my DayOfWeekHandler class.

Listing 5-4. Setting Up a Route for a Custom Handler in the RouteConfig.cs File

```
using System;
using System.Collections.Generic;
using System.Linq;
using System.Web;
using System.Web.Mvc;
using System.Web.Routing;
using SimpleApp.Infrastructure;

namespace SimpleApp {
    public class RouteConfig {
        public static void RegisterRoutes(RouteCollection routes) {
            routes.IgnoreRoute("{resource}.axd/{*pathInfo}");

            routes.Add(new Route("handler/{*path}",
                new CustomRouteHandler {HandlerType = typeof(DayOfWeekHandler)}));

            routes.MapRoute(
                name: "Default",
                url: "{controller}/{action}/{id}",
                defaults: new { controller = "Home", action = "Index",
                    id = UrlParameter.Optional }
            );
        }
    }

    class CustomRouteHandler : IRouteHandler {

        public Type HandlerType { get; set; }

        public IHttpHandler GetHttpHandler(RequestContext requestContext) {
    return (IHttpHandler)Activator.CreateInstance(HandlerType);
        }
    }
}
```

The RouteCollection.Add method creates a route and associates it with an implementation of the IRouteHandler interface, which defines the GetHttpHandler method. This method is responsible for returning an instance of the IHttpHandler interface that will be used to generate content for the request. My implementation of

IRouteHandler is configured with a C# type that I instantiate using the System.Activator class. This allows me to tie a specific custom handler to a URL pattern, like this:

```
...
routes.Add(new Route("handler/{*path}",
    new CustomRouteHandler {HandlerType = typeof(DayOfWeekHandler)}));
...
```

Registering a Handler Using the Configuration File

Using the routing system to set up custom handlers is workable, but it isn't the approach that I use in my own projects. Instead, I use the Web.config file to register my handlers, in part because not all ASP.NET projects use the routing system (and, in part, out of habit because I have been writing web applications for a long time, and the routing system is a relatively new addition to ASP.NET). Listing 5-5 shows the additions I made to the Web.config file to register my custom handler.

Listing 5-5. Registering a Handler in the Web.config File

```
<?xml version="1.0" encoding="utf-8"?>
<configuration>
  <appSettings>
    <add key="webpages:Version" value="3.0.0.0" />
    <add key="webpages:Enabled" value="false" />
    <add key="ClientValidationEnabled" value="true" />
    <add key="UnobtrusiveJavaScriptEnabled" value="true" />
  </appSettings>
  <system.web>
    <compilation debug="true" targetFramework="4.5.1" />
    <httpRuntime targetFramework="4.5.1" />
  </system.web>
  <system.webServer>
    <modules>
      <!--<add name="Timer" type="SimpleApp.Infrastructure.TimerModule"/>-->
      <!--<add name="Total" type="SimpleApp.Infrastructure.TotalTimeModule"/>-->
    </modules>
    <handlers>
      <add name="DayJSON" path="/handler/*.json" verb="GET"
           type="SimpleApp.Infrastructure.DayOfWeekHandler"/>
      <add name="DayHTML" path="/handler/day.html" verb="*"
           type="SimpleApp.Infrastructure.DayOfWeekHandler"/>
    </handlers>
  </system.webServer>
</configuration>
```

Handlers are registered in the system.webServer/handlers section of the Web.config file, through the use of the add element, which defines the attributes shown in Table 5-5. (The set of handlers is a configuration *collection*, which I explain in Chapter 9 when I describe the ASP.NET configuration system in detail.)

Table 5-5. *The Attributes Defined by the handlers/add Attribute*

Name	Description
name	Defines a name that uniquely identifies the handler.
path	Specifies the URL path for which the handler can process.
verb	Specifies the HTTP method that the handler supports. You can specify that all methods are supported by using an asterisk (*), specify that a single method is supported (GET), or use comma-separated values for multiple methods ("GET,POST"). When using comma-separated values, be sure not to use spaces between values.
type	Specifies the type of the IHttpHandler or IHttpHandlerFactory implementation class. (I describe the IHttpHandlerFactory interface in the "Custom Handler Factories" section later in this chapter.)

■ **Tip** Some additional attributes relate to IIS and file access. They are not often used, and I don't describe them in this book, but you can get details at `http://msdn.microsoft.com/en-us/library/ms691481(v=vs.90).aspx`.

You can be as general or as specific as you want when you register a custom handler, and you can create any number of configuration entries for each handler. I created two entries in the `Web.config` file to set up the new handler. This isn't essential for such a simple handler, but I wanted to demonstrate that a handler can be set up to support multiple types of request. The first entry registers the custom handler to deal with requests with URLs that start with `/handler` *and* have the JSON extension *and* are made using the GET method. The second entry registers the same handler class, but only for requests made using any HTTP method for the `/handler/day.html` URL.

There is one more configuration step, and that's to stop the URL routing feature from intercepting requests that I want to go to my custom handler. The default routing configuration that Visual Studio adds to ASP.NET projects assumes that all incoming requests will routed and sends a `404 - Not Found` error to the client when a request can't be matched to a route. To avoid this problem, I have edited the `App_Start/RouteConfig.cs` file to tell the routing system to ignore any requests intended for my custom handler, as shown in Listing 5-6.

Listing 5-6. Ignoring Requests for the Custom handler in the RouteConfig.cs File

```
using System;
using System.Collections.Generic;
using System.Linq;
using System.Web;
using System.Web.Mvc;
using System.Web.Routing;
using SimpleApp.Infrastructure;

namespace SimpleApp {
    public class RouteConfig {
        public static void RegisterRoutes(RouteCollection routes) {
            routes.IgnoreRoute("{resource}.axd/{*pathInfo}");

            //routes.Add(new Route("handler/{*path}",
            //     new CustomRouteHandler {HandlerType = typeof(DayOfWeekHandler)}));

            routes.IgnoreRoute("handler/{*path}");
```

```
        routes.MapRoute(
            name: "Default",
            url: "{controller}/{action}/{id}",
            defaults: new { controller = "Home", action = "Index",
                id = UrlParameter.Optional }
        );
    }
}

class CustomRouteHandler : IRouteHandler {
    public Type HandlerType { get; set; }

    public IHttpHandler GetHttpHandler(RequestContext requestContext) {
        return (IHttpHandler)Activator.CreateInstance(HandlerType);
    }
}
}
```

The `RouteCollection.IgnoreRoute` method tells the routing system to ignore a URL pattern. In the listing, I used the `IgnoreRoute` method to exclude any URL whose first segment is `/handler`. When a URL pattern is excluded, the routing system won't try to match routes for it or generate an error when there is no route available, allowing the ASP.NET platform to locate a handler from the `Web.config` file.

Testing the Handler

To test the custom handler, start the application and request the `/handler/day.html` URL. This request will select the `DayOfWeekHandler` to generate the content, and the handler will return an HTML fragment, as shown in Figure 5-5.

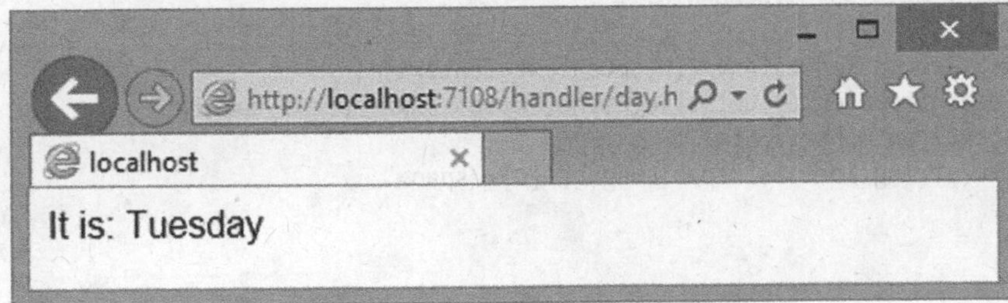

Figure 5-5. *Generating an HTML fragment from the custom handler*

The custom handler will also generate a JSON response. To test this, you can request any URL that starts with `/handler` and ends with `.json`, such as `/handler/day.json`. Internet Explorer won't display JSON content in the browser window, and you will be prompted to open a file that contains the following content:

```
{"day": "Tuesday"}
```

Creating Asynchronous Handlers

If your handler needs to perform asynchronous operations, such as making a network request, for example, then you can create an *asynchronous handler*. Asynchronous handlers prevent a request handling thread from waiting for an operation to complete, which can improve the overall throughput of a server.

■ **Note** Asynchronous programming is an advanced topic that is beyond the scope of this book. Don't use asynchronous features unless you understand how they work because it is easy to get into trouble. If you want more details about the .NET support for asynchronous programming, then see my *Pro .NET Parallel Programming in C#* book, which is published by Apress.

Asynchronous handlers implement the `IHttpAsyncHandler` interface, but this interface follows the old style of .NET asynchronous programming of having `Begin` and `End` methods and relying on `IAsyncResult` implementations. C# and .NET have moved on in recent years, and a much simpler approach is to derive the handler from the `HttpTaskAsyncHandler` class, which allows the use of `Task` objects and the `async` and `await` keywords. To demonstrate creating an asynchronous handler, I created a class file called `SiteLengthHandler.cs` in the `Infrastructure` folder and used it to define the handler shown in Listing 5-7.

Listing 5-7. The Contents of the SiteLengthHandler.cs File

```
using System.Net.Http;
using System.Threading.Tasks;
using System.Web;

namespace SimpleApp.Infrastructure {

    public class SiteLengthHandler : HttpTaskAsyncHandler {

        public override async Task ProcessRequestAsync(HttpContext context) {
            string data = await new HttpClient().GetStringAsync("http://www.apress.com");
            context.Response.ContentType = "text/html";
            context.Response.Write(string.Format("<span>Length: {0}</span>",
                data.Length));
        }
    }
}
```

Asynchronous handlers override the `ProcessRequestAsync` method, which is passed an `HttpContext` object and which must return a `Task` that represents the asynchronous operation. I have annotated the method with the async keyword, which allows me to use `await` in the method body and avoid working directly with `Tasks`.

■ **Tip** The `await` and `async` keywords are recent additions to C# and are processed by the compiler to standard Task Parallel Library objects and methods.

My example handler uses the HttpClient class to make an asynchronous HTTP request to www.apress.com and determine how many characters the result contains. In real projects, a more likely asynchronous operation would be to read from a file or query a database, but I want to keep this example as simple as possible. Asynchronous handlers are registered in just the same way as regular handlers, as shown in Listing 5-8.

Listing 5-8. Registering the Asynchronous Handler in the Web.config File

```
<?xml version="1.0" encoding="utf-8"?>
<configuration>
  <appSettings>
    <add key="webpages:Version" value="3.0.0.0" />
    <add key="webpages:Enabled" value="false" />
     <add key="ClientValidationEnabled" value="true" />
    <add key="UnobtrusiveJavaScriptEnabled" value="true" />
  </appSettings>
  <system.web>
    <compilation debug="true" targetFramework="4.5.1" />
    <httpRuntime targetFramework="4.5.1" />
  </system.web>
  <system.webServer>
    <modules>
      <!--<add name="Timer" type="SimpleApp.Infrastructure.TimerModule"/>-->
      <!--<add name="Total" type="SimpleApp.Infrastructure.TotalTimeModule"/>-->
    </modules>
    <handlers>
      <add name="DayJSON" path="/handler/*.json" verb="GET"
           type="SimpleApp.Infrastructure.DayOfWeekHandler"/>
      <add name="DayHTML" path="/handler/day.html" verb="*"
           type="SimpleApp.Infrastructure.DayOfWeekHandler"/>
      <add name="SiteLength" path="/handler/site" verb="*"
           type="SimpleApp.Infrastructure.SiteLengthHandler"/>
    </handlers>
  </system.webServer>
</configuration>
```

■ **Tip** I don't need to add an IgnoreRoute method call to the RouteConfig.cs file for this handler because the URL it supports is already covered by the URL pattern that I used in Listing 5-6.

To test the asynchronous handler, start the application and request the /handler/site URL. The exact length of the content returned from www.apress.com changes often, but you can see an example of the output in Figure 5-6.

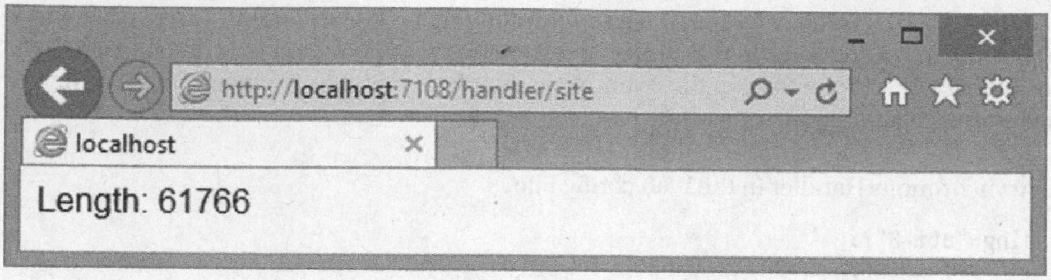

Figure 5-6. *The content generated by the asynchronous handler*

Creating Modules That Provide Services to Handlers

Now that you have seen the basic mechanism for defining a registering a handler, it is time to show you how to coordinate the actions of modules and handlers within an ASP.NET application.

Modules can provide services to handlers by assigning data values to the context objects. You can set a value for one of the predefined context object properties, such as `HttpContext.Session`, for example, if you are implementing a session state feature. Using the predefined properties generally means you are replacing one of the built-in features, but a module can also pass arbitrary data to the handler using the `HttpContext.Items` property. The `Items` property returns an `IDictionary` implementation that can be used to store any data that the handler requires access to.

■ **Tip** If you are replacing one of the built-in services, then you will need to disable the service's module in one of the ASP.NET configuration files that are outside of the project. I explain how these files work and tell you how to find them in Chapter 9.

To demonstrate how the `Items` property can be used, I created a class file called `DayModule.cs` in the `Infrastructure` folder and used it to define the module shown in Listing 5-9.

Listing 5-9. The Contents of the DayModule.cs File

```
using System;
using System.Web;

namespace SimpleApp.Infrastructure {
    public class DayModule : IHttpModule {

        public void Init(HttpApplication app) {
            app.BeginRequest += (src, args) => {
                app.Context.Items["DayModule_Time"] = DateTime.Now;
            };
        }

        public void Dispose() {
            // nothing to do
        }
    }
}
```

This module handles the BeginRequest life-cycle event and adds data to the Items collection. The name of the property is DayModule_Time, and I assign the value of the DateTime.Now property, which is the current date and time. In Listing 5-10, you can see how I registered the module in the Web.config file.

Listing 5-10. Registering the Module in the Web.config File

```
<?xml version="1.0" encoding="utf-8"?>
<configuration>
  <appSettings>
    <add key="webpages:Version" value="3.0.0.0" />
    <add key="webpages:Enabled" value="false" />
     <add key="ClientValidationEnabled" value="true" />
    <add key="UnobtrusiveJavaScriptEnabled" value="true" />
  </appSettings>
  <system.web>
    <compilation debug="true" targetFramework="4.5.1" />
    <httpRuntime targetFramework="4.5.1" />
  </system.web>
  <system.webServer>
    <modules>
      <!--<add name="Timer" type="SimpleApp.Infrastructure.TimerModule"/>-->
      <!--<add name="Total" type="SimpleApp.Infrastructure.TotalTimeModule"/>-->
      <add name="DayPrep" type="SimpleApp.Infrastructure.DayModule"/>
    </modules>
    <handlers>
      <add name="DayJSON" path="/handler/*.json" verb="GET"
          type="SimpleApp.Infrastructure.DayOfWeekHandler"/>
      <add name="DayHTML" path="/handler/day.html" verb="*"
          type="SimpleApp.Infrastructure.DayOfWeekHandler"/>
      <add name="SiteLength" path="/handler/site" verb="*"
          type="SimpleApp.Infrastructure.SiteLengthHandler"/>
    </handlers>
  </system.webServer>
</configuration>
```

■ **Tip** There is no segregation of the data in the Items collection, which means that care had to be taken to ensure that two modules don't assign data using the same keys. The way I do this is to include the name of the module class in the Items key, as shown in Listing 5-9, where I used the key DayModule_Time to indicate that the data value was set by the DayModule module.

Consuming the Items Data

The same Items collection that the module uses is available to the handler via the HttpContext.Items property. Listing 5-11 shows how I have updated the DayOfWeekHandler so that it consumes the data provided by DayModule.

Listing 5-11. Consuming Module Data in the DayOfWeekHandler.cs File

```
using System;
using System.Web;

namespace SimpleApp.Infrastructure {
    public class DayOfWeekHandler : IHttpHandler {

        public void ProcessRequest(HttpContext context) {

            if (context.Items.Contains("DayModule_Time")
                && (context.Items["DayModule_Time"] is DateTime)) {

                string day = ((DateTime)context.Items["DayModule_Time"])
                    .DayOfWeek.ToString();

                if (context.Request.CurrentExecutionFilePathExtension == ".json") {
                    context.Response.ContentType = "application/json";
                    context.Response.Write(string.Format("{{\"day\": \"{0}\"}}", day));
                } else {
                    context.Response.ContentType = "text/html";
                    context.Response.Write(string.Format("<span>It is: {0}</span>",
                        day));
                }

            } else {
                context.Response.ContentType = "text/html";
                context.Response.Write("No Module Data Available");
            }
        }

        public bool IsReusable {
            get { return false; }
        }
    }
}
```

Caution is required when retrieving the data from the Items collection. First, you must establish that the data has been added to the collection because there is no guarantee that a specific module has been registered in the Web.config file. Second, you must ensure that the data is of the expected type because there is nothing to prevent modules from adding different data to the Items collection using the same key. Once you have established that the data exists and is of the correct type, you can read the value from the Items collection and use it to generate content for a request. In the example, I get the DataTime value provided by the module and use it to generate my HTML and JSON fragments.

Targeting a Specific Handler

The module that I defined in Listing 5-9 adds data to the Items collection for every request, whether or not the handler that is selected will use it. That doesn't present a problem when the data is as easy to create as the current date and time, but it becomes a problem if there is significant time or expense required to obtain or generate the data. As an example, you won't want to query a database in the module to obtain data that will be ignored by most handlers. To avoid this, you can respond to the PostMapRequestHandler life-cycle event in the module and add data to the Items collection only if the handler that ASP.NET has selected is one that will consume the data. In Listing 5-12, I have modified the DayModule so that it will add data to the collection only when DayOfWeekHandler is selected to generate content for the request.

Listing 5-12. Targeting a Specific Handler in the DayModule.cs File

```
using System;
using System.Web;

namespace SimpleApp.Infrastructure {
    public class DayModule : IHttpModule {

        public void Init(HttpApplication app) {
            app.PostMapRequestHandler += (src, args) => {
                if (app.Context.Handler is DayOfWeekHandler) {
                    app.Context.Items["DayModule_Time"] = DateTime.Now;
                }
            };
        }

        public void Dispose() {
            // nothing to do
        }
    }
}
```

The module now handles the PostMapRequestHandler event, which is triggered after the handler has been selected to generate content for the request and uses the HttpContext.Handler property to check the type of the selected handler. The module adds a DateTime value to the Items collection if the handler is an instance of DayWeekHandler, but not otherwise.

Decoupling Components Using Declarative Interfaces

The basic approach shown in Listing 5-12 works, but it creates a situation where the module and handler are tightly coupled (meaning that they are harder to test and maintain) and where the module can provide a service only to a single handler class. A more flexible approach is to identify handlers that a module will provide services to using declarative interfaces, which are regular C# interfaces that define no methods and exist just so a handler can declare that it requires a specific service.

To demonstrate the use of a declarative interface, I added a class file called IRequiresDate.cs to the Infrastructure folder and used it to define the interface shown in Listing 5-13.

Listing 5-13. The Contents of the IRequiresDate.cs File

```
namespace SimpleApp.Infrastructure {

    public interface IRequiresDate {
        // this interface is declarative and defines no members
    }
}
```

I can then apply the declarative interface to the DayOfWeekHandler class, as shown in Listing 5-14.

Listing 5-14. Applying the Declarative Interface in the DayOfWeekHandler.cs File

```
...
namespace SimpleApp.Infrastructure {
    public class DayOfWeekHandler : IHttpHandler, IRequiresDate {
...
```

And finally, I can update DayModule so that it looks for the declarative interface rather than the handler class, as shown in Listing 5-15.

Listing 5-15. Updating the Module to Use the Declarative Interface in the DayModule.cs File

```
using System;
using System.Web;

namespace SimpleApp.Infrastructure {
    public class DayModule : IHttpModule {

        public void Init(HttpApplication app) {
            app.PostMapRequestHandler += (src, args) => {
                if (app.Context.Handler is IRequiresDate) {
                    app.Context.Items["DayModule_Time"] = DateTime.Now;
                }
            };
        }

        public void Dispose() {
            // nothing to do
        }
    }
}
```

Not only does this make it easier to test and maintain both the handler and the module, it also allows any handler that implements the declarative interface to receive the services that the module provides.

■ **Note** A good declarative interface example can be found in the module responsible for session state. As I will demonstrate in Chapter 10, you can elect to store session state in a database in order to reduce memory consumption on the server and improve data persistence. The process of retrieving session data and associating it with the request can slow down request processing, so the session module will undertake this work only if the handler implements the IRequiresSessionState interface, which is contained in the System.Web.SessionState namespace. I describe how the session state feature works in detail in Chapter 10.

Custom Handler Factories

Handler factories are the ASP.NET component responsible for creating instances of handlers to service requests. ASP.NET includes a default handler factory that creates a new instance of the handler class, but you can take more control of the process by creating a custom factory. There are three reasons you may require a custom handler factory:

- You need to take control of the way that custom handler classes are instantiated.
- You need to choose between different custom handlers for the same request type.
- You need to reuse handlers rather than create a new one for each request.

I'll show you how to address each of these issues in the sections that follow. Table 5-6 puts custom handler factories into context.

***Table 5-6.** Putting Handler Factories in Context*

Question	Answer
What are they?	Custom handler factories are responsible for providing instances of handler classes to the ASP.NET platform in order to generate content for requests.
Why should I care?	Custom handler classes allow you to customize the handler instantiation process to address one of the situations listed earlier.
How is it used by the MVC framework?	The MVC framework doesn't use custom handler factories.

■ **Tip** Handler factories are used only when handlers are selected using the `Web.config` file registrations. They are not involved in the process of creating handlers through the URL routing policy, which I demonstrated in the "Registering a Handler Using URL Routing" section earlier in this chapter.

Handler factories are classes that implement the `IHttpHandlerFactory` interface and that are registered like a handler in the `Web.config` file. The `IHttpHandlerFactory` interface defines the methods described in Table 5-7.

***Table 5-7.** The Methods Defined by the IHttpHandlerFactory Interface*

Name	Description
`GetHandler(context, verb, url, path)`	Called when the ASP.NET framework requires a handler for a request that matches the `Web.confing` registration
`ReleaseHandler(handler)`	Called after a request, providing the factory with the opportunity to reuse the handler

The `GetHandler` method is called when the ASP.NET framework requires a handler to process a request. A single factory can support multiple types of handler, so the `GetHandler` method is passed details of the request so that the right kind of handler can be returned. I have described each of the parameters to the `GetHandler` method in Table 5-8.

Table 5-8. *The Parameters of the IHttpHandlerFactory.GetHandler Method*

Name	Description
context	An HttpContext object through which information about the request and the state of the application can be obtained
verb	A string containing the HTTP method used to make the request (GET, POST, and so on)
url	A string containing the request URL
path	A string that combines the directory to which the application has been deployed and the request URL

Controlling Handler Instantiation

The simplest kind of handler factory is one that controls the way that custom handlers are instantiated. The best example I have seen of this kind of factory is the one that handles requests for Web Form files, which involves a complex parsing and compilation process to generate a class that can return a response to the browser. This is similar to the process that the MVC framework uses for Razor views but is implemented using a handler factory.

Needing to generate and compile handler classes is pretty unusual; the most common kind of handler that requires a factory is one that requires some kind of initialization or a constructor argument for resource configuration, such as a database connection or a license key.

To keep the example focused on the handler factory, I am going to demonstrate how to create instances of a handler that requires a constructor argument—something that the default handler can't resolve. I added a class file called CounterHandler.cs to the Infrastructure folder and used it to define the handler shown in Listing 5-16.

Listing 5-16. The Content of the CounterHandler.cs File

```
using System.Web;

namespace SimpleApp.Infrastructure {
    public class CounterHandler : IHttpHandler {
        private int handlerCounter;

        public CounterHandler(int counter) {
            handlerCounter = counter;
        }

        public void ProcessRequest(HttpContext context) {
            context.Response.ContentType = "text/plain";
            context.Response.Write(string.Format("The counter value is {0}",
                handlerCounter));
        }

        public bool IsReusable {
            get { return false; }
        }
    }
}
```

This handler takes an int constructor argument, which prevents it from being instantiated by the built-in handler. In Listing 5-17, you can see the contents of the CounterHandlerFactory.cs file, which I added to the Infrastructure folder to define a handler factory that can provide the CounterHandler with the constructor argument it needs.

Listing 5-17. The Contents of the CounterHandlerFactory.cs File

```
using System.Web;

namespace SimpleApp.Infrastructure {
    public class CounterHandlerFactory : IHttpHandlerFactory {
        private int counter = 0;

        public IHttpHandler GetHandler(HttpContext context, string verb,
                string url, string path) {
            return new CounterHandler(++counter);
        }
        public void ReleaseHandler(IHttpHandler handler) {
            // do nothing - handlers are not reused
        }
    }
}
```

ASP.NET doesn't care how the GetHandler method provides it with a handler, just as long as it does. In this simple example, the handler factory increments a counter and uses it as the constructor argument to create a new instance of CounterHandler.

Registering the Handler Factory

Handler factories are registered in the Web.config file, just as you would register a handler. When ASP.NET looks at the interfaces implemented by the type, it matches from the list of registered handlers and knows the difference between IHttpHandler and IHttpHandlerFactory implementations. Listing 5-18 shows the addition I made to the Web.config file to register the CounterHandlerFactory.

Listing 5-18. Registering a Handler Factory in the Web.config File

```
<?xml version="1.0" encoding="utf-8"?>
<configuration>
  <appSettings>
    <add key="webpages:Version" value="3.0.0.0" />
    <add key="webpages:Enabled" value="false" />
     <add key="ClientValidationEnabled" value="true" />
    <add key="UnobtrusiveJavaScriptEnabled" value="true" />
  </appSettings>
  <system.web>
    <compilation debug="true" targetFramework="4.5.1" />
    <httpRuntime targetFramework="4.5.1" />
  </system.web>
  <system.webServer>
    <modules>
      <!--<add name="Timer" type="SimpleApp.Infrastructure.TimerModule"/>-->
      <!--<add name="Total" type="SimpleApp.Infrastructure.TotalTimeModule"/>-->
      <add name="DayPrep" type="SimpleApp.Infrastructure.DayModule"/>
    </modules>
```

```
    <handlers>
      <add name="DayJSON" path="/handler/*.json" verb="GET"
           type="SimpleApp.Infrastructure.DayOfWeekHandler"/>
      <add name="DayHTML" path="/handler/day.html" verb="*"
           type="SimpleApp.Infrastructure.DayOfWeekHandler"/>
      <add name="SiteLength" path="/handler/site" verb="*"
           type="SimpleApp.Infrastructure.SiteLengthHandler"/>
      <add name="CounterFactory" path="/handler/counter" verb="*"
          type="SimpleApp.Infrastructure.CounterHandlerFactory"/>
    </handlers>
  </system.webServer>
</configuration>
```

■ **Tip** You don't register handlers in the `Web.config` file when they are instantiated by a custom handler factory.

I have registered the handler factory so that it will be used for the URL `/handler/counter`. You can test the factory and handler by starting the application and requesting this URL. The content generated by the handler will display an incrementing counter for each request, as shown in Figure 5-7.

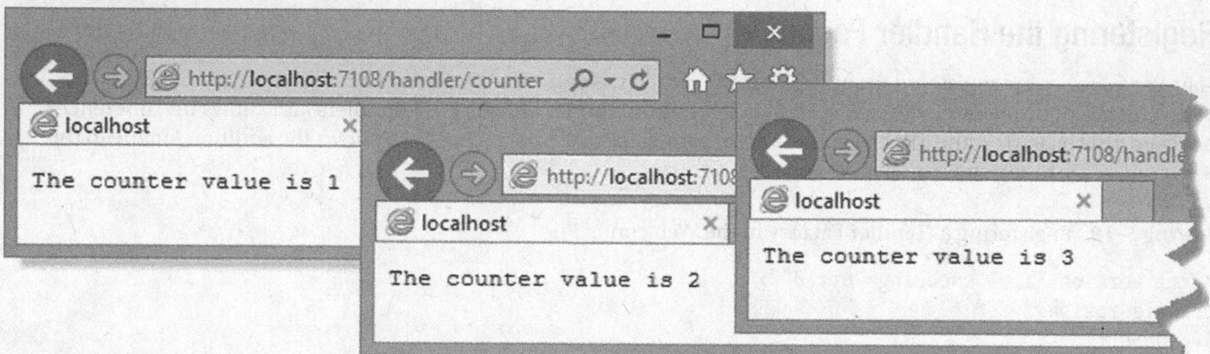

***Figure 5-7.** Creating instances of handlers in a handler factory*

■ **Tip** What happens when you create and register a class that implements the `IHttpHandler` and `IHttpHandlerFactory` interfaces? ASP.NET checks for the `IHttpHandler` interface first, which means your class will be treated as a handler and the methods defined by the `IHttpHandlerFactory` interface will never be called.

Selecting Handlers Dynamically

The `Web.config` file can be used to match handlers to combinations of HTTP method and URL, but that is the limit of the built-in support for matching handlers to requests. For more complex selections, a handler factory is required. Listing 5-19 shows how I have changed the `CounterHandlerFactory` to instantiate different handlers based on the browser that makes the request.

Listing 5-19. Dynamically Selecting Handlers Based on Request Details in the CounterHandlerFactory.cs File

```
using System.Web;

namespace SimpleApp.Infrastructure {
    public class CounterHandlerFactory : IHttpHandlerFactory {
        private int counter = 0;

        public IHttpHandler GetHandler(HttpContext context, string verb,
                string url, string path) {
            if (context.Request.UserAgent.Contains("Chrome")) {
                return new SiteLengthHandler();
            } else {
                return new CounterHandler(++counter);
            }
        }
        public void ReleaseHandler(IHttpHandler handler) {
            // do nothing - handlers are not reused
        }
    }
}
```

As I explained earlier, ASP.NET doesn't care how the handler factory creates handlers, but neither does it care *which* handlers are created. In this case, I use the context objects to get the user agent string that the browser sends as part of the HTTP request and select the SiteLengthHandler for requests made by the Google Chrome browser users and the CounterHandler otherwise. (I created the SiteLengthHandler in the "Creating Asynchronous Handlers" section earlier in this chapter.) You can see the effect of requesting the /handler/counter URL in Internet Explorer and Chrome in Figure 5-8.

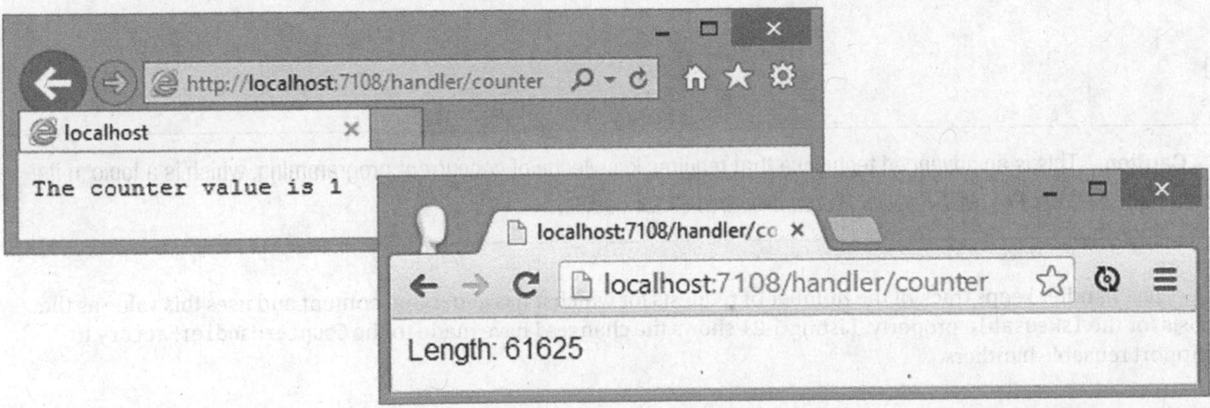

Figure 5-8. *Selecting handlers dynamically*

Reusing Handlers

The IHttpHandler interface defines the IsReusable property, which allows handlers to indicate that they can be used to generate content for multiple requests in sequence. The built-in handler factory ignores the IsReuseable property value and always creates new handlers for each request.

The main situation where reusing handlers is attractive is when they require significant time or resources to create, typically because they need to load or generate substantial amounts of data before they are able to generate any content. Listing 5-20 shows how I have modified the `CounterHandler` so that it can be reused, but only for three requests. This isn't a common scenario, but I want to emphasize the way that handler instances can control their own reuse through the `IsReusable` property.

Listing 5-20. Creating a Reusable Handler in the CounterHandler.cs File

```
using System.Web;

namespace SimpleApp.Infrastructure {
    public class CounterHandler : IHttpHandler {
        private int handlerCounter;
        private int requestCounter = 0;

        public CounterHandler(int counter) {
            handlerCounter = counter;
        }

        public void ProcessRequest(HttpContext context) {
            requestCounter++;
            context.Response.ContentType = "text/plain";
            context.Response.Write(
                string.Format("The counter value is {0} (Request {1} of 3)",
                    handlerCounter, requestCounter));
        }

        public bool IsReusable {
            get { return requestCounter < 2; }
        }
    }
}
```

■ **Caution** This is an advanced technique that requires knowledge of concurrent programming, which is a topic in its own right. See my *Pro .NET Parallel Programming in C#* for details.

The handler keeps track of the number of requests for which it has generated content and uses this value as the basis for the `IsReusable` property. Listing 5-21 shows the changes I have made to the `CounterHandlerFactory` to support reusable handlers.

Listing 5-21. Reusing Handlers in the CounterHandlerFactory.cs File

```
using System.Collections.Concurrent;
using System.Web;

namespace SimpleApp.Infrastructure {
    public class CounterHandlerFactory : IHttpHandlerFactory {
        private int counter = 0;
        private int handlerMaxCount = 3;
```

```
            private int handlerCount = 0;
            private BlockingCollection<CounterHandler> pool
                = new BlockingCollection<CounterHandler>();

            public IHttpHandler GetHandler(HttpContext context, string verb,
                    string url, string path) {

                    CounterHandler handler;
                    if (!pool.TryTake(out handler)) {
                        if (handlerCount < handlerMaxCount) {
                            handlerCount++;
                            handler = new CounterHandler(++counter);
                            pool.Add(handler);
                        } else {
                            handler = pool.Take();
                        }
                    }
                    return handler;
            }
            public void ReleaseHandler(IHttpHandler handler) {
                if (handler.IsReusable) {
                    pool.Add((CounterHandler)handler);
                } else {
                    handlerCount--;
                }
            }
        }
    }
```

The handler factory uses a BlockingCollection to maintain a pool of handlers, each of which will be used for three requests. The pool contains a maximum of three handlers, and requests are queued up until a handler is available.

■ **Note** In reality, the pool can contain more than three handlers because I don't guard against multiple simultaneous requests from creating new handlers if one isn't available and there is space in the pool.

Summary

In this chapter, I introduced the handler component and explained how it relates to modules and the request life-cycle events. I demonstrated how to create and register a custom handler, how to create handlers that perform asynchronous operations, and how modules can provide handlers with services. I finished the chapter by exploring handler factories, which allow you to control how handlers are created and used. In the next chapter, I describe techniques for interrupting the normal flow of the request life cycle.

CHAPTER 6

Disrupting the Request Life Cycle

In previous chapters, I described the ASP.NET request life cycle and explained how the global application class, modules, and handlers work together to process requests and generate content. In this chapter, I am going to explain how to disrupt the normal flow of a request and take direct control of the life cycle.

Disrupting the life cycle can be useful for optimizing the performance of a web application or taking fine-grained control over the way that particular requests are processed. The life cycle is also disrupted when unhandled exceptions occur, and knowing the nature of the disruption means you can receive notifications when this happens.

Disrupting the request life cycle can also be useful for changing the behavior of an application without having to modify any of its code, through the addition of a module or a handler. There are a lot of badly designed and implemented ASP.NET applications in the world, and if you inherit one of them, you may find that making even the slightest change triggers unexpected problems that are hard to predict and difficult to debug and test. Such applications are *brittle*, and being able to change the way that requests are handled by adding custom modules or handlers can help extend the life of the application. All brittle applications eventually throw up problems that can't be patched, but the techniques I show you in this chapter can help keep things ticking along while a properly designed replacement is developed. Table 6-1 summarizes this chapter.

Table 6-1. *Chapter Summary*

Problem	Solution	Listing
Optimize redirections.	Call one of the redirection methods defined by the `HttpResponse` class in a module or custom handler.	1–5
Preempt the normal handler selection process.	Call the `RemapHandler` method before the `MapRequestHandler` event has been triggered.	6–8
Transfer a request to a new handler.	Call the `TransferRequest` method.	9–11
Prevent the normal life cycle from completing.	Call the `CompleteRequest` method.	12, 13
Receive notification when the life cycle has been disrupted by an exception.	Handle the `Error` event.	14–16

Preparing the Example Project

I am going to create a new project called RequestFlow for this chapter. To get started, select New Project from the File menu to open the New Project dialog window. Navigate through the Templates section to select the Visual C# ➤ Web ➤ ASP.NET Web Application template and set the name of the project to Request, as shown in Figure 6-1.

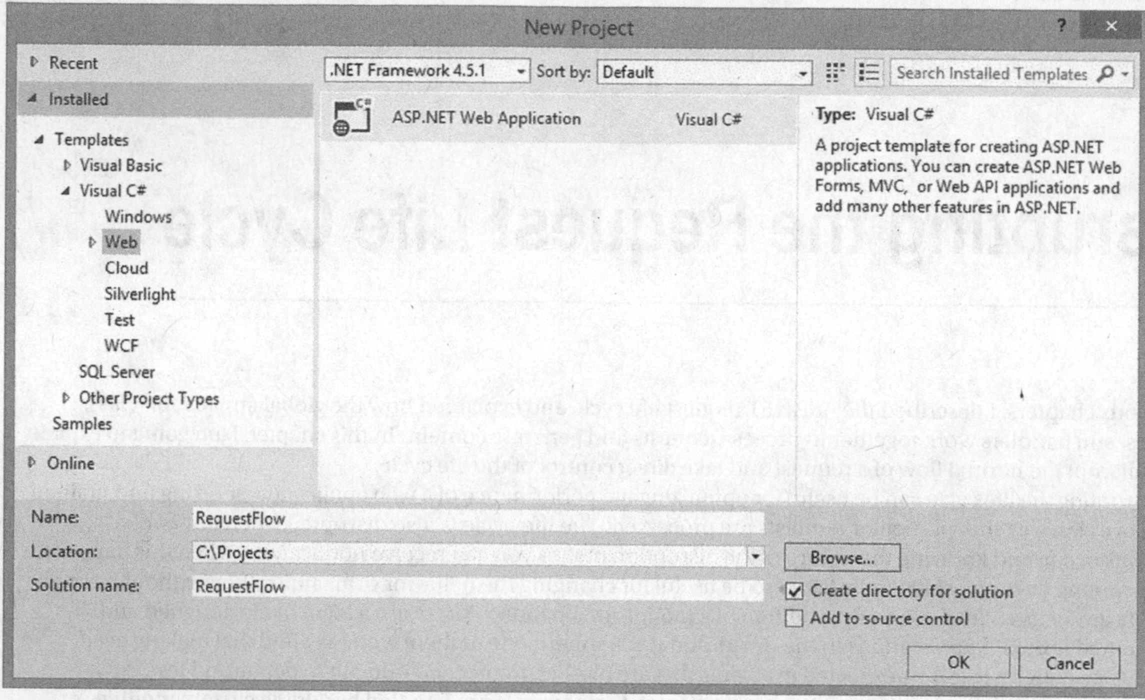

Figure 6-1. Creating the Visual Studio project

Click the OK button to move to the New ASP.NET Project dialog window. Ensure that the Empty option is selected and check the MVC option, as shown in Figure 6-2.

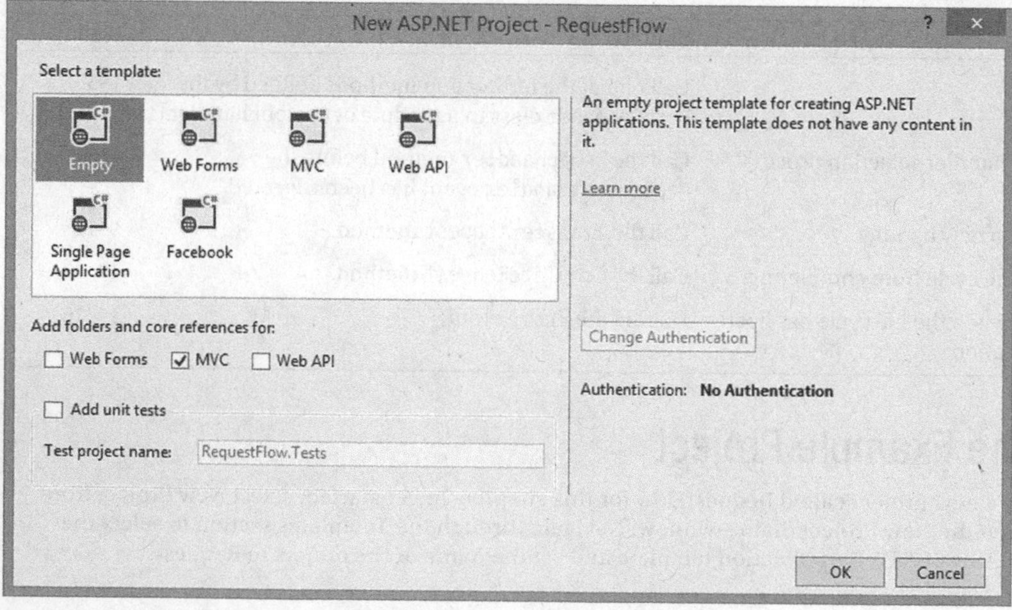

Figure 6-2. Configuring the ASP.NET project

Click the OK button, and Visual Studio will create a new project called RequestFlow.

Adding the Bootstrap Package

Open the console by selecting Package Manager Console from the Tools ➤ Library Package Manager menu and enter the following command:

```
Install-Package -version 3.0.3 bootstrap
```

Visual Studio will download and install the Bootstrap library into the RequestFlow project.

Creating the Controller

Right-click the `Controllers` folder in the Visual Studio Solution Explorer and select Add ➤ Controller from the pop-up menu. Select MVC 5 Controller – Empty from the list of options and click the Add button. Set the name to be HomeController and click the Add button to create the `Controllers/HomeController.cs` file. Edit the new file to match Listing 6-1.

Listing 6-1. The Contents of the HomeController.cs File

```
using System.Web.Mvc;

namespace RequestFlow.Controllers {
    public class HomeController : Controller {

        public ActionResult Index() {
            return View();
        }
    }
}
```

The controller contains a single action method, called `Index`. The action method contains no logic and simply returns the result from the `View` method to have the MVC framework render the default view.

Creating the View

Right-click the `Index` action method in the code editor and select Add View from the pop-up menu. Ensure that View Name is Index, that Template is set to Empty (without model), and that the boxes are unchecked, as shown in Figure 6-3.

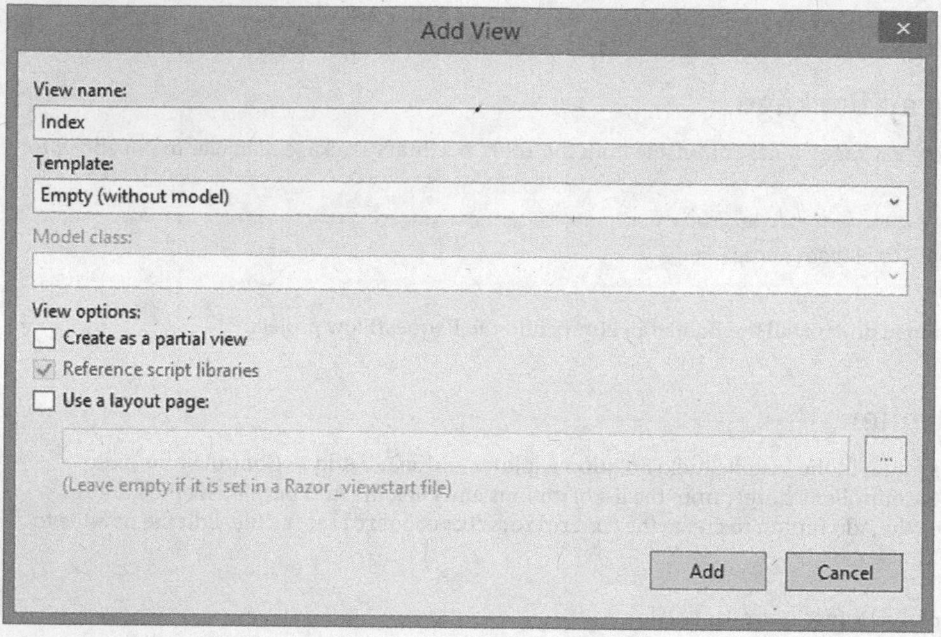

Figure 6-3. *Creating the view*

Click the Add button to create the `Views/Home/Index.cshtml` file. Edit the file to match Listing 6-2. The view simply reports that the content has been rendered from the `Index` view associated with the `Home` controller, which is all that I will need to demonstrate the techniques for managing request execution.

Listing 6-2. The Contents of the Index.cshtml File

```
@{
    Layout = null;
}

<!DOCTYPE html>

<html>
<head>
    <meta name="viewport" content="width=device-width" />
    <title>Index</title>
    <link href="~/Content/bootstrap.min.css" rel="stylesheet" />
    <link href="~/Content/bootstrap-theme.min.css" rel="stylesheet" />
</head>
<body>
    <div class="container">
        <h3 class="text-primary">This is the Home/Index view</h3>
    </div>
</body>
</html>
```

Testing the Example Application

To test the example application, select Start Debugging from the Visual Studio Debug menu. The example application displays a simple message in the browser, as shown in Figure 6-4.

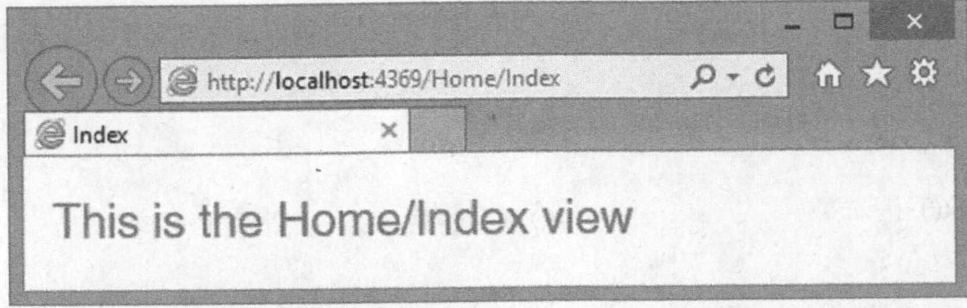

Figure 6-4. *Testing the example application*

Using URL Redirection

I am going start with a simple technique to demonstrate how you can control request handling to achieve tasks that would otherwise be handled deep within the MVC framework. If you have been using the MVC framework for a while, you will know that you can redirect requests to alternate URLs by returning the result from methods such as `Redirect` and `RedirectPermanent`.

The MVC framework provides a set of redirection methods that can target a literal URL, a URL route, or another action method, and these redirections can be combined with other logic such that redirections happen only under certain circumstances (such as when requests contain particular form data values or originate from mobile devices).

However, in mature projects, the most common reason for adding new redirections to action methods is to hide changes in the application structure. An example that I have seen a lot lately comes when a project switches from performing authentication locally to relying on a third-party such as Microsoft, Google, or Facebook. This could be addressed by changes in the routing configuration, but often the routes become so complex that performing the redirection in the controller is seen as the safer option. The action methods that would usually have received the authentication requests are replaced with redirections to new URLs that can initiate the third-party authentication process.

■ **Tip** I demonstrate how to authenticate users through third parties in Part 3.

In this section, I am going to explain how redirections normally work in the MVC framework and how you can optimize this process by disrupting request execution and perform the redirection in a module. Table 6-2 puts module redirection in context.

Table 6-2. *Putting Module Redirection in Context*

Question	Answer
What is it?	Module redirection is the process of intercepting requests and redirecting them in a module, rather than letting the request be handled by the MVC framework.
Why should I care?	Action methods that perform only redirection incur relatively high overheads that can be avoided by using a module.
How is it used by the MVC framework?	This technique is about disrupting the normal request life cycle and is not used by the MVC framework.

Understanding the Normal Redirection Process

I have added a new action method to the Home controller that contains a redirection, as shown in Listing 6-3.

Listing 6-3. Adding an Action Method to the HomeController.cs File

```
using System.Web.Mvc;

namespace RequestFlow.Controllers {
    public class HomeController : Controller {

        public ActionResult Index() {
            return View();
        }

        public ActionResult Authenticate() {
            return RedirectToAction("Index", "Home");
        }
    }
}
```

The action method I added is called Authenticate, and it represents the scenario that I described: an action method whose original implementation has been replaced with a redirection. In this example, I perform the redirection by returning the result of the RedirectToAction method, which allows me to specify the names of the action method and the controller that the client will be redirected to.

You can see the effect of targeting the Authenticate action method by starting the application and requesting the /Home/Authenticate URL in the browser. You can see the sequence of requests to the application and the responses that are returned using the browser F12 developer tools (so called because they are accessed by pressing the F12 key), as illustrated by Figure 6-5.

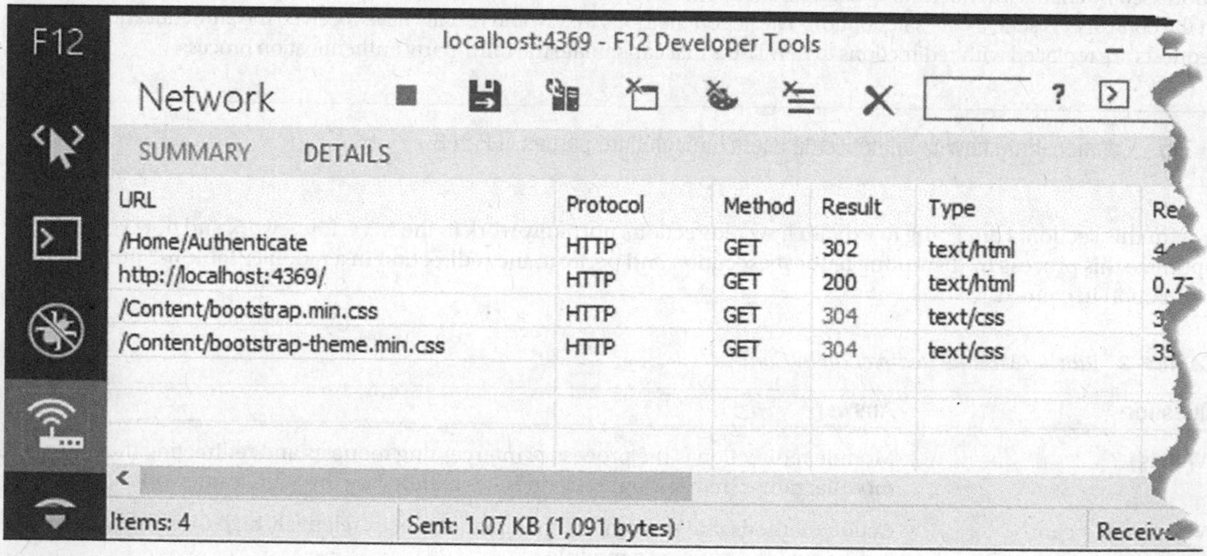

Figure 6-5. *Tracing the requests and responses in a redirection*

■ **Tip** To see all the requests and responses, you must disable the Clear Entries on Navigate option at the top of the developer tools window.

The sequence of requests and responses is exactly like you would expect. The browser asks the server for `/Home/Authenticate` but receives a 302 response, which tells the browser to request a different URL. I specified the `Index` action method in the `Home` controller, which corresponds to the default URL (`/`) in the default routing configuration, and that's what the browser is redirected to. The browser makes the second request, and the server sends the content generated by the `Index` action method, which includes `link` elements for Bootstrap CSS files. The sequence is completed when the browser requests and receives the content of CSS files.

If the only thing that an action method is doing is issuing a redirection, then it becomes an expensive operation—something that is easy to forget about, especially when refactoring a mature application where the focus is on the new functionality. The MVC framework is flexible and configurable, and it has to do a lot of work to get to the point where the `RedirectToAction` method in Listing 6-3 is invoked and the result is evaluated. The list includes the following:

- Locating and instantiating the controller factory
- Locating and instantiating the controller activator
- Locating and instantiating the action invoker
- Identifying the action method
- Examining the action method for filter attributes
- Invoking the action method
- Invoking the `RedirectToAction` method

At every stage, the MVC framework has to figure out which implementation is required and usually has to create some new objects, all of which takes time and memory. The `RedirectToAction` method creates a new `RedirectToRouteResult` object, which is evaluated and does the work of performing the redirection.

Simplifying the Redirection Process

The result of all the work that the MVC framework has to go through to produce the `RedirectToRouteResult` object is one of the methods described in Table 6-3 being invoked on the `HttpResponse` context object associated with the request.

***Table 6-3.** The Redirection Methods Defined by the HttpResponse Class*

Name	Description
`Redirect(url)` `Redirect(url, end)`	Sends a response with a 302 status code, directing the client to the specified URL. The second argument is a `bool` that, if `true`, immediately terminates the request handling process by calling `HttpApplication.CompleteRequest` (which I describe later in this chapter). The single-argument version is equivalent to setting the second parameter to `true`.
`RedirectPermanent(url)` `RedirectPermanent(url, end)`	Like the `Redirect` method, but the response is sent with a 301 status code.
`RedirectToRoute(name)`	Sends a response with a 302 status code to a URL generated from a URL route.
`RedirectToRoutePermanent(name)`	Sends a response with a 301 status code to a URL generates from a URL route.

I can avoid having the MVC framework do all of that work by instead performing the redirection in a module. To demonstrate how this works, I created a folder called `Infrastructure` and added to it a class file called `RedirectModule.cs`. You can see the contents of the class file in Listing 6-4.

Listing 6-4. The Contents of the RedirectModule.cs File

```
using System;
using System.Web;
using System.Web.Mvc;
using System.Web.Routing;

namespace RequestFlow.Infrastructure {
    public class RedirectModule : IHttpModule {

        public void Init(HttpApplication app) {
            app.MapRequestHandler += (src, args) => {

                RouteValueDictionary rvd
                    = app.Context.Request.RequestContext.RouteData.Values;

                if (Compare(rvd, "controller", "Home")
                    && Compare(rvd, "action", "Authenticate")) {
                        string url = UrlHelper.GenerateUrl("", "Index", "Home", rvd,
                            RouteTable.Routes, app.Context.Request.RequestContext, false);
                        app.Context.Response.Redirect(url);
                }
            };
        }

        private bool Compare(RouteValueDictionary rvd, string key, string value) {
            return string.Equals((string)rvd[key], value,
                StringComparison.OrdinalIgnoreCase);
        }

        public void Dispose() {
            // do nothing
        }
    }
}
```

This module handles the `MapRequestHandler` life-cycle event, which means the handler has been selected and is about to be asked to generate the content for the request. Prior to this event, the `UrlRoutingModule` processes the request in order to match it to a route and, as part of this process, creates and associates a `RequestContext` object with the `HttpRequest` instance.

■ **Tip** You might be wondering how I know that the UrlRoutingModule processes the request before the MapRequestHandler event. In fact, I looked at the source code for the module class and found that the request is processed in response to the PostResolveRequestCache event, which proceeds MapRequestHandler in the life cycle I described in Chapter 3. You can get the source code for the .NET Framework, including the ASP.NET platform from http://referencesource.microsoft.com/netframework.aspx. This is separate from the source code for the MVC framework and the Web API, which are available from http://aspnetwebstack.codeplex.com. Be sure to read the licenses carefully because there are restrictions on how the source code can be used, especially for the .NET Framework code.

The RequestContext object provides information about the URL route that has matched the request and is accessed through the HttpRequest.RequestContext property. The RequestContext class defines the properties described in Table 6-4.

***Table 6-4.** The Properties Defined by the RequestContext Class*

Name	Description
HttpContext	Returns the HttpContext object for the current request. This isn't useful in this scenario because the HttpContext is used to obtain the RequestContext object.
RouteData	Returns a System.Web.Routing.RouteData object that describes the route matches to the request by UrlRoutingModule.

It is the RouteData object that gives me access to the information that I need, and I have described the three useful properties that RouteData defines in Table 6-5.

***Table 6-5.** The Properties defined by the RouteData Class*

Name	Description
Route	Returns the Route object that represents the route that has matched the request.
RouteHandler	Returns the IRouteHandler implementation that specifies the IHttpHandler that will generate content for the request. See Chapter 5 for an example of using the IRouteHandler interface.
Values	Returns a RouteValueDictionary that contains the values extracted from the request to match the route variables.

In my module, I use the RouteValueDictionary to determine the controller and action route values, which are used by the MVC framework to identify the controller and action method that the request will target. If the values match the Authenticate action on the Home controller, then I perform a redirection, like this:

```
...
if (Compare(rvd, "controller", "Home") && Compare(rvd, "action", "Authenticate")) {
    string url = UrlHelper.GenerateUrl("", "Index", "Home", rvd,
        RouteTable.Routes, app.Context.Request.RequestContext, false);
    app.Context.Response.Redirect(url);
}
...
```

I could have specified the target URL for the redirection as a literal string value, but that would mean my module would have to be updated every time the routing configuration for the application changed, which is just the kind of thing that leads to brittle applications in the first place. Instead, I have used the `UrlHelper` class from the `System.Web.Mvc` namespace to generate a URL based on the name of the action method and controller that I want to target, as follows:

```
...
if (Compare(rvd, "controller", "Home") && Compare(rvd, "action", "Authenticate")) {
    string url = UrlHelper.GenerateUrl("", "Index", "Home", rvd,
        RouteTable.Routes, app.Context.Request.RequestContext, false);
    app.Context.Response.Redirect(url);
}
...
```

Once I have generated the URL from the routing configuration, I call the `HttpResponse.Redirect` method to send the response to the client and terminate any further request handling. Listing 6-5 shows how I registered the module in the `Web.config` file using the same approach I described in Chapter 4.

Listing 6-5. Registering the Module in the Web.config File

```
<?xml version="1.0" encoding="utf-8"?>

<configuration>
  <appSettings>
    <add key="webpages:Version" value="3.0.0.0" />
    <add key="webpages:Enabled" value="false" />
     <add key="ClientValidationEnabled" value="true" />
    <add key="UnobtrusiveJavaScriptEnabled" value="true" />
  </appSettings>
  <system.web>
    <compilation debug="true" targetFramework="4.5.1" />
    <httpRuntime targetFramework="4.5.1" />
  </system.web>
  <system.webServer>
    <modules>
      <add name="Redirect" type="RequestFlow.Infrastructure.RedirectModule"/>
    </modules>
  </system.webServer>
</configuration>
```

To test the module, start the application and request the `/Home/Authenticate` URL. You can set a debugger breakpoint on the `Authenticate` action method in the controller class to prove that the method isn't invoked when a request is redirected.

Managing Handler Selection

An alternative way to manage request flow is to control the selection of the handler. This allows you to preempt the normal handler selection process or to transfer a request from one handler to another. Table 6-6 puts handler selection in context.

Table 6-6. Putting Handler Selection in Context

Question	Answer
What is it?	Handler selection lets you override the process that would usually match a handler to a request.
Why should I care?	Controlling handler selection lets you create applications that are more adaptable and flexible than would otherwise be possible.
How is it used by the MVC framework?	The MVC framework relies on a module to implement URL routing. The routing module preempts handler selection to ensure that handlers defined by routes are used to process requests—including the `MvcHttpHandler` class, which is the handler for MVC framework requests.

Preempting Handler Selection

Preempting the handler selection allows you to explicitly select a handler and bypass the process by which ASP.NET locates a handler for a request. The `HttpContext` class defines several members that relate to handler selection, as described by Table 6-7. The `RemapHandler` method allows me to override the normal selection process and explicitly specify the handler that will be used to generate content for the current request.

Table 6-7. The HttpContext Members That Manage Handler Selection

Name	Description
`CurrentHandler`	Returns the handler to which the request has been transferred.
`Handler`	Returns the handler originally selected to generate a response for the request.
`PreviousHandler`	Returns the handler from which the request was transferred.
`RemapHandler(handler)`	Preempts the standard handler selection process. This method must be called before the `MapRequestHandler` event is triggered.

First, I need to create a handler so that I have something to select with the `RemapHandler` method. I added a class file called `InfoHandler.cs` to the `Infrastructure` folder and used it to define the handler shown in Listing 6-6.

Listing 6-6. The Contents of the InfoHandler.cs File

```
using System.Web;

namespace RequestFlow.Infrastructure {
    public class InfoHandler : IHttpHandler {

        public void ProcessRequest(HttpContext context) {
            context.Response.Write("Content generated by InfoHandler");
        }

        public bool IsReusable {
            get { return false; }
        }
    }
}
```

I can now create a module that explicitly selects the handler for certain requests. I added a class file called `HandlerSelectionModule.cs` to the `Infrastructure` folder and used it to define the module shown in Listing 6-7.

Listing 6-7. The Contents of the HandlerSelectionModule.cs File

```
using System;
using System.Web;
using System.Web.Routing;

namespace RequestFlow.Infrastructure {
    public class HandlerSelectionModule : IHttpModule {

        public void Init(HttpApplication app) {
            app.PostResolveRequestCache += (src, args) => {
                if (!Compare(app.Context.Request.RequestContext.RouteData.Values,
                    "controller", "Home")) {
                        app.Context.RemapHandler(new InfoHandler());
                }
            };
        }

        private bool Compare(RouteValueDictionary rvd, string key, string value) {
            return string.Equals((string)rvd[key], value,
                StringComparison.OrdinalIgnoreCase);
        }

        public void Dispose() {
            // do nothing
        }
    }
}
```

■ **Tip** You can also preempt normal handler selection by using the URL routing system, which calls the `RemapHandler` method when it matches a request to a route. This was what happened in Chapter 5 when I registered a handler using a route.

I have used the routing values in order to detect requests that target controllers other than `Home`. For such requests, I preempt the handler selection by calling the `RemapHandler` method and passing an instance of the handler class that I want to use, which is `InfoHandler`. I have to call the `RemapHandler` *before* the `MapRequestHandler` event is triggered, so my module is set up to perform its preemption in response to the `PostResolveRequestCache` event, which preceded `MapRequestHandler` in the sequence I described in Chapter 3.

In Listing 6-8, you can see that I have registered the module in the `Web.config` file. I don't need to register the handler because the module instantiates it directly.

Listing 6-8. Registering a Module in the Web.config File

```
<?xml version="1.0" encoding="utf-8"?>

<configuration>
  <appSettings>
    <add key="webpages:Version" value="3.0.0.0" />
    <add key="webpages:Enabled" value="false" />
     <add key="ClientValidationEnabled" value="true" />
    <add key="UnobtrusiveJavaScriptEnabled" value="true" />
  </appSettings>
  <system.web>
    <compilation debug="true" targetFramework="4.5.1" />
    <httpRuntime targetFramework="4.5.1" />
  </system.web>
  <system.webServer>
    <modules>
      <add name="Redirect" type="RequestFlow.Infrastructure.RedirectModule"/>
      <add name="Select" type="RequestFlow.Infrastructure.HandlerSelectionModule"/>
    </modules>
  </system.webServer>
</configuration>
```

You can test the selection preemption by starting the application and requesting a URL such as `/Test`. This request will be matched to the default URL routing configuration in the `App_Start/RouteConfig.cs` file but doesn't target the `Home` controller. This means that the `HandlerSelectionModule` will preempt the normal selection process (which would have led to the MVC framework handler being asked to generate content) and force `InfoHandler` to be used instead, as illustrated by Figure 6-6.

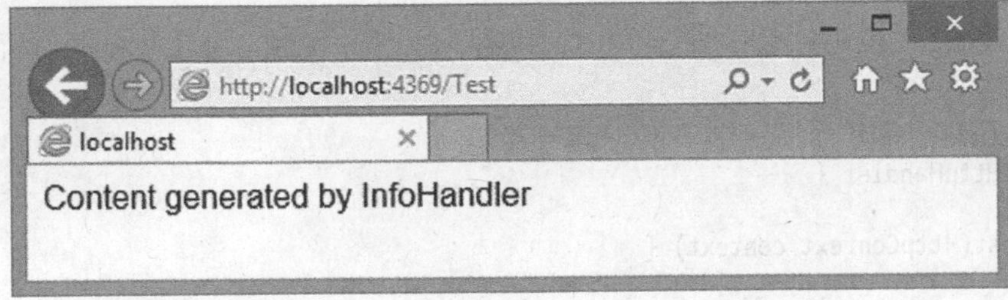

Figure 6-6. *Preempting handler selection*

Transferring a Request to a Different Handler

Handlers can decide that they are not best suited to generate the content for a request and pass the request on to a different handler for processing. This is equivalent to redirecting a request within ASP.NET without sending a redirection response to the client and is useful when you need finer-grained control over handler selection than is possible through the `Web.config` registration of handlers. Requests are transferred using the `HttpServerUtility.TransferRequest` method, which is available in the overloaded versions described by Table 6-8.

Table 6-8. *The HttpServerUtility TransferRequest Method*

Name	Description
`TransferRequest(url)`	Transfers the request to the handler for the specified URL, which need not be the URL from the current request.
`TransferRequest(url, preserve)`	Transfers the request to the handler for the specified URL. The form and query string data are passed to the new handler if the `preserve` argument is `true`.
`TransferRequest(url, preserve, method, headers)`	Like with the previous version, except that the `method` argument specifies the HTTP method for the transferred request, and the `headers` collection specifies the headers.
`TransferRequest (url, preserve, method, headers, preserveUser)`	Like with the previous version, except that the `preserveUser` argument will preserve the user identity associated with the request when set to `true`. See Part 3 for details of user identities.

■ **Tip** The `HttpServerUtility` class also defines a `Transfer` method, but this can be used only with Web Forms and skips a number of the life cycle events after generating content for a request. Use with caution.

To demonstrate the use of the `TransferRequest` method, I have modified the `InfoHandler` class from the previous section to transfer the request for a specific URL, as shown in Listing 6-9.

Listing 6-9. Transferring a Request in the InfoHandler.cs File

```
using System.Web;
using System.Web.Mvc;
using System.Web.Routing;

namespace RequestFlow.Infrastructure {
    public class InfoHandler : IHttpHandler {

        public void ProcessRequest(HttpContext context) {

            if (context.Request.RawUrl == "/Test/Index") {
                context.Server.TransferRequest("/Home/Index");
            } else {
                context.Response.Write("Content generated by InfoHandler");
            }
        }

        public bool IsReusable {
            get { return false; }
        }
    }
}
```

I decide whether to transfer the request based on the value of the HttpRequest.RawUrl property. In a real project, I tend to use the routing information as demonstrated in the previous section (see Listing 6-7), but I have used the RawUrl property for simplicity in this example.

If the URL that has been requested is /Test/Index, then I obtain an instance of the HttpServerUtility class through the HttpContext.Server property and call the TransferRequest method, specifying a URL that will target the MVC framework Home controller in the example application. You can see the effect by starting the application and requesting the /Test/Index URL. If you monitor the HTTP requests made by the browser using the F12 developer tools, you will see that no HTTP redirections are sent to the client. Instead, the client requests the /Test/Index URL but gets the content from the /Home/Index URL instead, as shown in Figure 6-7.

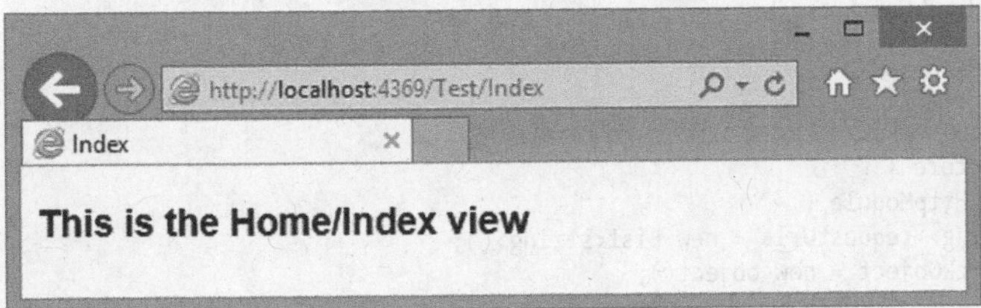

Figure 6-7. *Transferring a request from one handler to another*

Terminating Requests

The HttpApplication.CompleteRequest method can be used to terminate the normal flow of a request through its life cycle and jump straight to the LogRequest event. This technique is useful if you are able to respond to a request entirely within a module and don't want other modules or a handler to alter the response that will be sent to the client, essentially bypassing the rest of the application. Table 6-9 summarizes terminating request handling using the CompleteRequest method.

Table 6-9. *Terminating Request Handler Context*

Question	Answer
What is it?	The CompleteRequest method terminates the normal request handling life cycle and jumps directly to the LogRequest event.
Why should I care?	Using the CompleteRequest method stops other modules from processing the request and prevents handler selection and content generation.
How is it used by the MVC framework?	This method is not used by the MVC framework.

You can use the CompleteRequest method in any situation when you can service the request completely from within a module. I use this technique in two main ways: to create special debug URLs that provide insights into the application during development and to prevent requests from being processed by a troublesome component in a brittle application.

Responding to a Special URL

It can often be helpful to get insight into the overall state of the application during development, especially when tracking down bugs. There are some useful tools for understanding how an ASP.NET application is running, some which I describe in Chapter 8, but they tend to be general in nature. Sometimes you need a snapshot of specific information, and a module can help provide useful insights without requiring a lot of additional development. The use of the `CompleteRequest` method allows you to create modules that service special URLs without touching the rest of the application. As a demonstration, I added a class file called `DebugModule.cs` to the `Infrastructure` folder and used it to define the module shown in Listing 6-10.

Listing 6-10. The Contents of the DebugModule.cs File

```
using System.Collections.Generic;
using System.Web;

namespace RequestFlow.Infrastructure {
    public class DebugModule : IHttpModule {
        private static List<string> requestUrls = new List<string>();
        private static object lockObject = new object();

        public void Init(HttpApplication app) {

            app.BeginRequest += (src, args) => {
                lock (lockObject) {
                    if (app.Request.RawUrl == "/Stats") {
                        app.Response.Write(
                            string.Format("<div>There have been {0} requests</div>",
                                requestUrls.Count));
                        app.Response.Write("<table><tr><th>ID</th><th>URL</th></tr>");
                        for (int i = 0; i < requestUrls.Count; i++) {
                            app.Response.Write(
                                string.Format("<tr><td>{0}</td><td>{1}</td></tr>",
                                    i, requestUrls[i]));
                        }
                        app.CompleteRequest();
                    } else {
                        requestUrls.Add(app.Request.RawUrl);
                    }
                }
            };
        }

        public void Dispose() {
            // do nothing
        }
    }
}
```

■ **Caution** Be sure to disable your debug modules before deploying the application because they can represent a security risk. If you need to enable the modules in production to track down live problems (which is something you should do only as a last resort for serious issues that you can't reproduce in the test environment), then make sure you restrict access to authorized users with the techniques I described in Part 3.

This module looks for requests for the `/Stats` URL and responds by generating details of the requests that the application has received since it started and then calling the `CompleteRequest` method to terminate request handling.

For all other requests, the URL that has been asked for is added to a static collection. The collection must be static so that all instances of the module class can store details of the requests they are asked to process. ASP.NET processes requests concurrently, so I have taken the precaution of using the `lock` keyword to synchronize access to the collection object. Listing 6-11 shows the registration of the module in the `Web.config` file.

Listing 6-11. Registering the Module in the Web.config File

```
<?xml version="1.0" encoding="utf-8"?>

<configuration>
  <appSettings>
    <add key="webpages:Version" value="3.0.0.0" />
    <add key="webpages:Enabled" value="false" />
    <add key="ClientValidationEnabled" value="true" />
    <add key="UnobtrusiveJavaScriptEnabled" value="true" />
  </appSettings>
  <system.web>
    <compilation debug="true" targetFramework="4.5.1" />
    <httpRuntime targetFramework="4.5.1" />
  </system.web>
  <system.webServer>
    <modules>
      <add name="Redirect" type="RequestFlow.Infrastructure.RedirectModule"/>
      <add name="Select" type="RequestFlow.Infrastructure.HandlerSelectionModule"/>
      <add name="Debug" type="RequestFlow.Infrastructure.DebugModule"/>
    </modules>
  </system.webServer>
</configuration>
```

■ **Caution** You should be wary of using synchronization in web applications because it limits the concurrent throughput of your servers. The `lock` keyword in the listing ensures that I get accurate debug data, but it does so by allowing only one module instance update the collection at a time. Make sure you disable any modules that rely on synchronization once you have finished debugging. See Chapter 8 for details of collecting statistics without causing this kind of performance problem.

You can test the module by starting the application and requesting other URLs such as `/Home/Index` and `/Test/Index` followed by `/Stats`. You can see a typical result in Figure 6-8.

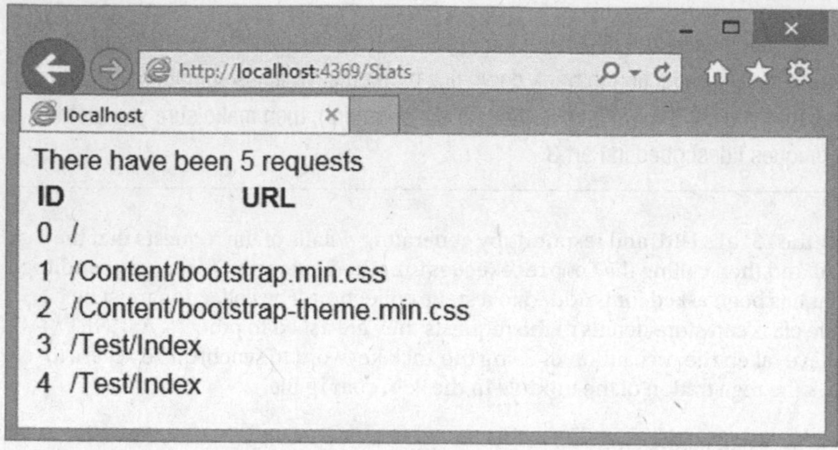

Figure 6-8. *The output from a module that services a special URL*

Avoiding Brittle Application Components

The second use for the `CompleteRequest` method is to prevent requests from being processed by some part of a brittle application. The details will vary in different applications, but to give a sense of the kind of code I sometimes require, I added a class file called `DeflectModule.cs` to the `Infrastructure` folder and used it to define the module shown in Listing 6-12.

Listing 6-12. The Contents of the DeflectModule.cs File

```
using System.Web;

namespace RequestFlow.Infrastructure {
    public class DeflectModule : IHttpModule {

        public void Init(HttpApplication app) {
            app.BeginRequest += (src, args) => {
                if (app.Request.RawUrl.ToLower().StartsWith("/home")) {
                    app.Response.StatusCode = 500;
                    app.CompleteRequest();
                }
            };
        }

        public void Dispose() {
            // do nothing
        }
    }
}
```

The module looks for requests that begin with `/Home`. When such a request is received, I set the status code to `500`, which indicates a server error and call the `CompleteRequest` method to terminate request handling. You can apply this technique anywhere in the request life cycle, and, of course, you don't have to send the client an error message—what's important is that you can use the `CompleteRequest` method to terminate the request life cycle before the components you are concerned about are reached. Listing 6-13 shows the registration of the new module in the `Web.config` file.

Listing 6-13. Registering a Module in the Web.config File

```
<?xml version="1.0" encoding="utf-8"?>

<configuration>
  <appSettings>
    <add key="webpages:Version" value="3.0.0.0" />
    <add key="webpages:Enabled" value="false" />
     <add key="ClientValidationEnabled" value="true" />
    <add key="UnobtrusiveJavaScriptEnabled" value="true" />
  </appSettings>
  <system.web>
    <compilation debug="true" targetFramework="4.5.1" />
    <httpRuntime targetFramework="4.5.1" />
  </system.web>
  <system.webServer>
    <modules>
      <add name="Redirect" type="RequestFlow.Infrastructure.RedirectModule"/>
      <add name="Select" type="RequestFlow.Infrastructure.HandlerSelectionModule"/>
      <add name="Debug" type="RequestFlow.Infrastructure.DebugModule"/>
      <add name="Deflect" type="RequestFlow.Infrastructure.DeflectModule"/>
    </modules>
  </system.webServer>
</configuration>
```

To test the module, start the application and request the /Home/Index URL. Rather than seeing the view associated with the action method, the browser will display the error message shown in Figure 6-9.

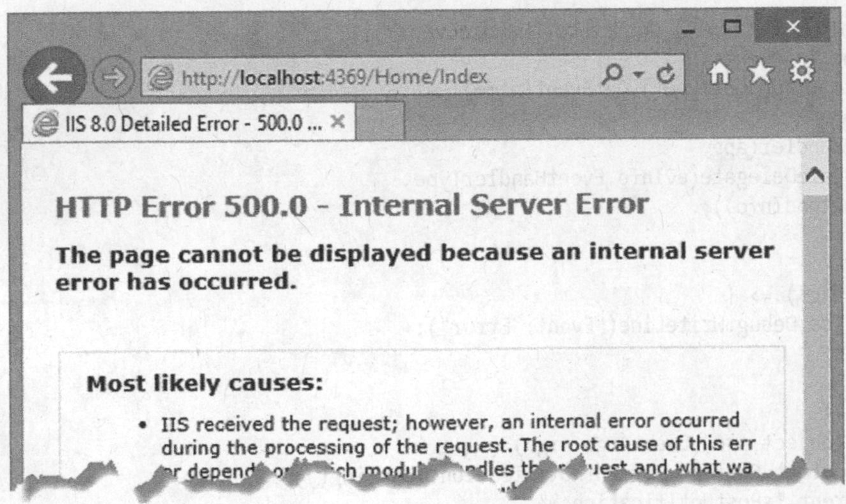

Figure 6-9. *Displaying an error message in the browser*

Handling Error Notifications

The final way to disrupt the regular flow of life cycle events is to throw an unhandled exception. When the ASP.NET platform receives an exception that has propagated from a handler or a module, it abandons the request, triggers the `Error` event, and jumps to the `LogRequest` event and completes the request. To demonstrate the effect on request handling, I created a class file called `EventListModule.cs` in the `Infrastructure` folder and used it to define the module shown in Listing 6-14.

Listing 6-14. The Contents of the EventListModule.cs File

```
using System;
using System.Reflection;
using System.Web;

namespace RequestFlow.Infrastructure {
    public class EventListModule : IHttpModule {

        public void Init(HttpApplication app) {

            string[] events = { "BeginRequest", "AuthenticateRequest",
                "PostAuthenticateRequest", "AuthorizeRequest", "ResolveRequestCache",
                "PostResolveRequestCache", "MapRequestHandler", "PostMapRequestHandler",
                "AcquireRequestState", "PostAcquireRequestState",
                "PreRequestHandlerExecute", "PostRequestHandlerExecute",
                 "ReleaseRequestState", "PostReleaseRequestState",
                "UpdateRequestCache", "LogRequest", "PostLogRequest",
                "EndRequest", "PreSendRequestHeaders", "PreSendRequestContent"};

            MethodInfo methodInfo = GetType().GetMethod("HandleEvent");
            foreach (string name in events) {
                EventInfo evInfo = app.GetType().GetEvent(name);

                evInfo.AddEventHandler(app,
                    Delegate.CreateDelegate(evInfo.EventHandlerType,
                        this, methodInfo));
            }

            app.Error += (src, args) => {
                System.Diagnostics.Debug.WriteLine("Event: Error");
            };
        }

        public void HandleEvent(object src, EventArgs args) {
            string name = HttpContext.Current.CurrentNotification.ToString();
            if (HttpContext.Current.IsPostNotification &&
                !HttpContext.Current.Request
                    .CurrentExecutionFilePathExtension.Equals("css")) {
                name = "Post" + name;
            }
```

```
            if (name == "BeginRequest") {
                System.Diagnostics.Debug.WriteLine("----------------");
            }
            System.Diagnostics.Debug.WriteLine("Event: {0}", new string[] { name });
        }

        public void Dispose() {
            // do nothing
        }
    }
}
```

This module uses reflection to register a handler for all the life cycle events and writes out the name of the event as it is received. The names are written using the `System.Diagnostics.Debug.WriteLine` method, which is visible in the Visual Studio Output window. (Select View ➤ Output if the window isn't available.) Listing 6-15 shows how I registered the new module in the `Web.config` file and disabled the `DeflectModule` from the previous section.

Listing 6-15. Registering and Disabling Modules in the Web.config File

```
...
<system.webServer>
  <modules>
    <add name="Redirect" type="RequestFlow.Infrastructure.RedirectModule"/>
    <add name="Select" type="RequestFlow.Infrastructure.HandlerSelectionModule"/>
    <add name="Debug"  type="RequestFlow.Infrastructure.DebugModule"/>
    <!--<add name="Deflect" type="RequestFlow.Infrastructure.DeflectModule"/>-->
    <add name="EventList" type="RequestFlow.Infrastructure.EventListModule"/>
  </modules>
</system.webServer>
...
```

■ **Note** You will notice that there are two handlers in this example: a lambda expression for the `Error` event and the `HandleEvent` method for all the others. The `HandleEvent` method uses the `HttpContect.CurrentNotificiation` property to determine which event is being handled, but the value of this property isn't set correctly for the `Error` event and remains set to whichever event was triggered before the event occurred. To create accurate results, I had to create a separate handler for the `Error` event so that I know for certain when it has been triggered.

In Listing 6-16, I have added an action method to the `Home` controller that throws an exception. This is a common error, where a default value is assigned to an action method parameter to simplify the code. The action method works as long as the request includes a value that the model binding process can use for the parameter but fails when the request omits a value.

Listing 6-16. Adding a Broken Action Method to the HomeController.cs File

```
using System.Web.Mvc;

namespace RequestFlow.Controllers {
    public class HomeController : Controller {

        public ActionResult Index() {
            return View();
        }

        public ActionResult Authenticate() {
            return RedirectToAction("Index", "Home");
        }

        public ActionResult Calc(int val = 0) {
            int result = 100 / val;
            return View("Index");
        }
    }
}
```

I select the Index view as the result of the action method, but the reason that this action method exists is to throw an exception that will propagate up through the MVC framework and into the ASP.NET platform. To see the event sequence for a regular request, start the application and request the URL /Home/Index. You will see the following in the Visual Studio Output window:

```
Event: BeginRequest
Event: AuthenticateRequest
Event: PostAuthenticateRequest
Event: AuthorizeRequest
Event: ResolveRequestCache
Event: PostResolveRequestCache
Event: MapRequestHandler
Event: PostMapRequestHandler
Event: AcquireRequestState
Event: PostAcquireRequestState
Event: PreExecuteRequestHandler
Event: PostExecuteRequestHandler
Event: ReleaseRequestState
Event: PostReleaseRequestState
Event: UpdateRequestCache
Event: LogRequest
Event: PostLogRequest
Event: EndRequest
Event: SendResponse
Event: SendResponse
```

■ **Tip** To simplify the output, the module I defined in Listing 6-14 ignores requests for CSS files.

This is the regular sequence of life-cycle events I described in Chapter 3. To see the effect of an uncaught exception, request the /Home/Calc URL. The Visual Studio debugger will break to handle the exception. Press F5 to resume execution, and you will see the following in the Output window:

```
Event: BeginRequest
Event: AuthenticateRequest
Event: PostAuthenticateRequest
Event: AuthorizeRequest
Event: ResolveRequestCache
Event: PostResolveRequestCache
Event: MapRequestHandler
Event: PostMapRequestHandler
Event: AcquireRequestState
Event: PostAcquireRequestState
Event: PreExecuteRequestHandler
Event: Error
Event: LogRequest
Event: PostLogRequest
Event: EndRequest
Event: SendResponse
Event: SendResponse
```

The important point to note is that the ASP.NET platform jumps to the LogRequest event after triggering the Error event, which means that modules that depend on later events won't receive them and may be left in an undesirable state. Modules that need to update the state of the application or release resources when events are triggered should handle the Error event so they know that a request has encountered problems and is being terminated.

■ **Tip** You can get information about the exception that disrupted the life cycle through the HttpContext.Error property.

Summary

In this chapter, I showed you how to interrupt the normal request life cycle to avoid performing unnecessary work and to work around the dangerous parts of brittle applications. I showed you how to perform redirections earlier in the request life cycle, how to control the selection and execution of the request handler, how to terminate requests so that difficult components are not executed, and how to receive notifications of errors. These are not techniques that you will need every day, but knowing what is possible will help you build better applications and can help keep old ones up and running. In the next chapter, I describe the ASP.NET platform facilities for identifying and adapting to the capabilities of browsers, which can help ensure that your application runs on the widest possible range of devices.

CHAPTER 7

Detecting Device Capabilities

Just a few years ago, the world of web clients consisted of browsers running on desktops and browsers running on mobile devices. The desktop browsers offered the best support for HTML, CSS, and JavaScript and made their requests over fast and reliable network connections. The mobile browsers had limited support for the web standards, made requests over slow and unreliable cellular networks, and displayed their content on small screens running on underpowered hardware. In those days, it was important for web applications to be able to work out what kind of client had made a request because mobile devices could support only the simplest of applications.

The situation is different today. Smartphones and tablets run the same browsers as desktops, have high-resolution and high-density displays, and support a range of touch interactions. And functionality has started to migrate from the smartphone to the desktop: The latest versions of Windows support touch on the desktop, and more desktop monitors are being sold with touch sensors.

The term *mobile client* is still shorthand for describing a broad classification of devices, but any complex web application has to take a more nuanced view of what each client is capable of and respond appropriately.

Web applications can deal with device capabilities in a range of ways. The simplest approach is to ignore the differences and let the user figure it out. This isn't as bad as it sounds because smartphone and tablet browsers have become adept at presenting all kinds of content to users and users have become adept at navigating content that isn't optimized for their devices. A better approach is to use *responsive design*, which relies on features in CSS version 3 to adapt content based on the device, a technique that is usually supplemented by JavaScript code that adds support for different kinds of interaction when they are supported, such as touch and orientation sensors.

In this chapter, I show a different approach, which is to adapt the application at the server. I show you the facilities that the ASP.NET platform provides for classifying requests based on device capabilities and demonstrate how you can use these in your MVC framework applications to differentiate your content to create the best user experience. Table 7-1 summarizes this chapter.

Table 7-1. Chapter Summary

Problem	Solution	Listing
Determine the capabilities of the browser used to make a request.	Read the properties of the `HttpBrowserCapabilities` object accessible through the `HttpRequest.Browser` property.	1-5
Define custom capabilities data.	Define new browser files or create a capabilities provider class.	6-8
Replace the built-in capabilities data.	Install data from a third-party provider.	9-11
Alter the content generated by the application based on the browser capabilities.	Use a Razor conditional statement in the view or select partial views through the `Html.Partial` helper.	12, 14-17
Adapt content to device screen size and orientation.	Use responsive design.	13
Automate the selection of partial views based on browser capabilities.	Use display modes.	18, 19

Preparing the Example Project

I am going to create a new project called Mobile for chapter, following the same approach that I have used for earlier examples. I used the Visual Studio ASP.NET Web Application template, selected the Empty option, and added the core MVC references. You should be familiar with the process by now, but see Chapter 6 if you want step-by-step instructions. I'll be using Bootstrap again in this chapter, so enter the following command into the Package Manager Console:

```
Install-Package -version 3.0.3 bootstrap
```

Listing 7-1 shows the content of the `Programmer.cs` file, which I created in the `Models` folder.

Listing 7-1. The Contents of the Programmer.cs File

```
namespace Mobile.Models {

    public class Programmer {

        public Programmer(string firstName, string lastName, string title,
                string city, string country, string language) {
            FirstName = firstName; LastName = lastName; Title = title;
            City = city; Country = country; Language = language;
        }
        public string FirstName { get; set; }
        public string LastName { get; set; }
        public string Title { get; set; }
        public string City { get; set; }
        public string Country { get; set; }
        public string Language { get; set; }
    }
}
```

This will be the model class for the application, and I'll be using it to demonstrate how to adapt content to different kinds of devices. Listing 7-2 shows the contents of the HomeController.cs file, which I used to define the default controller for the project in the Controllers folder.

Listing 7-2. The Contents of the HomeController.cs File

```
using System.Web.Mvc;
using Mobile.Models;

namespace Mobile.Controllers {

    public class HomeController : Controller {

        private Programmer[] progs = {
            new Programmer("Alice", "Smith", "Lead Developer", "Paris", "France", "C#"),
            new Programmer("Joe", "Dunston", "Developer", "London", "UK", "Java"),
            new Programmer("Peter", "Jones", "Developer", "Chicago", "USA", "C#"),
            new Programmer("Murray", "Woods", "Jnr Developer", "Boston", "USA", "C#")
        };

        public ActionResult Index() {
            return View(progs);
        }
    }
}
```

The controller creates an array of Programmer objects and passes them to the View method. I created a view by right-clicking the action method in the code editor and selecting Add View from the pop-up menu. I called the view Index.cshtml, selected the Empty (without model) template, and unchecked all of the view option boxes. You can see the content I defined in the view in Listing 7-3.

Listing 7-3. The Contents of the Index.cshtml File

```
@using Mobile.Models
@model Programmer[]
@{
    Layout = null;
}
<!DOCTYPE html>
<html>
<head>
    <meta name="viewport" content="width=device-width" />
    <title>Mobile Devices</title>
    <link href="~/Content/bootstrap.min.css" rel="stylesheet" />
    <link href="~/Content/bootstrap-theme.min.css" rel="stylesheet" />
    <style>
        body { padding-top: 10px; }
    </style>
</head>
<body>
    <div class="alert alert-success">
        This is the /Views/Home/Index.cshtml view
    </div>
```

```
    <div class="panel panel-primary">
        <div class="panel-heading">Programmers</div>
        <table class="table table-striped">
            <tr>
                <th>First Name</th><th>Last Name</th><th>Title</th>
                <th>City</th><th>Country</th><th>Language</th>
            </tr>
            @foreach (Programmer prog in Model) {
                <tr>
                    <td>@prog.FirstName</td>
                    <td>@prog.LastName</td>
                    <td>@prog.Title</td>
                    <td>@prog.City</td>
                    <td>@prog.Country</td>
                    <td>@prog.Language</td>
                </tr>
            }
        </table>
    </div>
</body>
</html>
```

The layout generates a table display of the `Programmer` objects, styled using CSS classes. You can see how the view is rendered by starting the application, as illustrated by Figure 7-1.

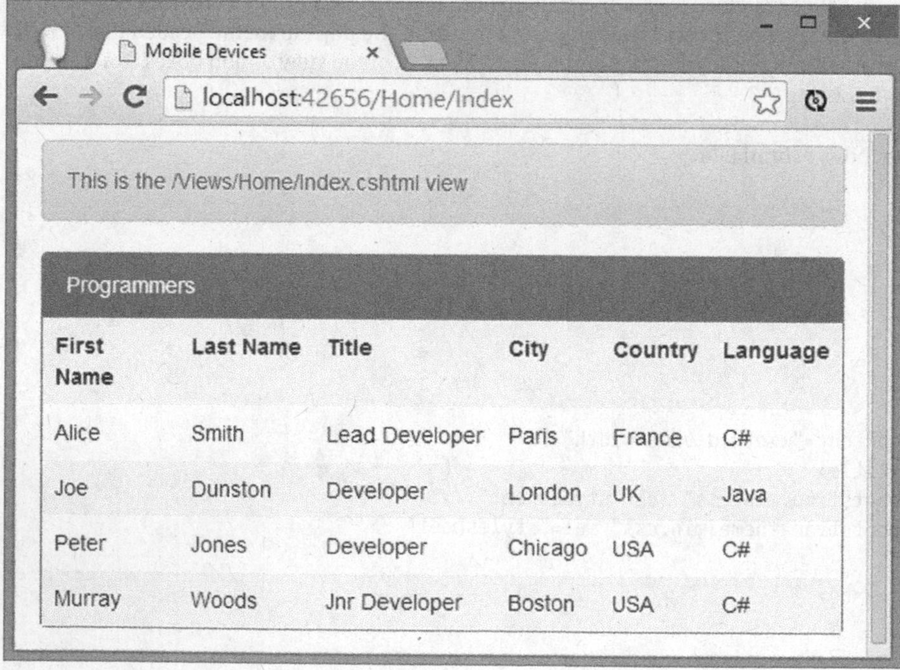

***Figure 7-1.** Testing the example application*

As the figure shows, I have switched from Internet Explorer to Google Chrome to display the output from the example application in this chapter. Recent versions of Chrome have added support for emulating a range of devices, which I'll be using to demonstrate techniques in this chapter. Chrome can be downloaded from `http://google.com/chrome`.

To enable device simulation, press the F12 key to open the developer tools window, click the Show Drawer button (the one with the > character and three horizontal lines), and select the Emulation tab.

■ **Tip** If you don't see the Emulation tab, then open the Settings window by clicking the cog icon in the developer tools window and enable the Show Emulation View in the Console Drawer option.

Select Apple iPhone 5 from the list of devices and click the Emulate button. Figure 7-2 shows the way that the output from the application is displayed when Chrome simulates an iPhone 5. Smartphone and tablet browsers are pretty good at laying out HTML content automatically. I stacked this example in my favor by using a table because they present a difficult layout problem. Scaling the content so that the table is entirely visible makes the content unreadable, and reformatting the table so that each row spans multiple lines is often confusing to the user.

This is the /Views/Home/Index.cshtml view

Programmers

First Name	Last Name	Title	City	Cour
Alice	Smith	Lead Developer	Paris	Fran
Joe	Dunston	Developer	London	UK
Peter	Jones	Developer	Chicago	USA
Murray	Woods	Jnr Develope	Boston	USA

***Figure 7-2.** Emulating an iPhone 5 using Google Chrome*

I have cropped the figure because tall thin screenshots take up a lot of space on the page, but even so, you can see that the table doesn't display well on the narrow iPhone screen. Throughout this chapter, I'll show you different ways that you can adapt the content to the capabilities of the device that it is being displayed on.

EMULATING AND TESTING MOBILE DEVICES

I have used Google Chrome to emulate mobile devices in this chapter because it is simple and free and gives a pretty good idea of how different capabilities affect the way content will be rendered by the target browsers. Since Google introduced the emulation features, I find myself using them at the start of projects as I create the main building blocks of functionality. Having Chrome installed locally means that the emulator performs well and is always available for quick tests without delay. The limitation of this approach is that the Chrome rendering engine is always used, which means you can get a sense of how content is affected by screen size, for example, but not how different implementations of CSS properties or JavaScript APIs affect an application.

As I get further into the detail of a project, I switch to using a remote browser test suite. I use `browserstack.com`, but there are others available. These test suites allow you to run your application using emulators for popular mobile devices. This isn't perfect, of course, but it starts to give you a sense of where browser implementation issues are going to be a problem. (To be clear: I don't have any relationship with `browserstack.com` other than as a customer. I pay the standard fees and don't receive any special support or features.) The drawback of using a testing service is that the emulators are running remotely and it takes a while to create a session, start the emulator, and load the application. This can be a tedious process when you want to make rapid changes, which is why I start with Chrome for the major functionality areas and don't switch to the emulators until I have a solid foundation in place.

I start testing with real devices when all of the major functionality is complete. No emulator can re-create the feel of interacting with an application through a touch screen, and I spend some time making sure that gestures feel natural and that the application gives the user a sense of context about where they are in the application. I adjust the fit and finish of the application until I produce something that works well. I don't have hardware for every device, but I keep a small pile of the most popular and representative devices, most of which I purchased used or refurbished. Testing with real devices is a laborious process, which is why I wait until the end of the development process before using them.

Detecting Device Capabilities

The starting point for adapting to different devices is to access their capabilities. In this section, I show you how ASP.NET provides information about different devices and how you can customize and improve this information that is available. Table 7-2 puts the process of detecting device capabilities into context.

Table 7-2. *Putting Detecting Device Capabilities in Context*

Question	Answer
What is it?	Device capabilities provide you with information about the browser and device from which a request originates.
Why should I care?	Not all devices can cope with complex content or implement the latest HTML and CSS features. Assessing capabilities allows you to tailor the content and behavior of your application to reach the widest possible audience.
How is it used by the MVC framework?	The MVC framework implements the display modes feature, which is commonly used in conjunction with capabilities data. See the "Using Display Modes" section later in the chapter for details.

Getting Browser Capabilities

The ASP.NET platform focuses on the browser, rather than the underlying device, although the two are usually one in the same when it comes to smartphones and tablets. The `HttpRequest.Browser` property returns a `System.Web.HttpBrowserCapabilities` object that describes the capabilities of the device that has made the request. The `HttpBrowserCapabilities` class defines a great many properties, but only a few are truly useful, and I have described them in Table 7-3. You can see a complete list of the properties defined by the `HttpBrowserCapabilities` class at `http://msdn.microsoft.com/en-us/library/system.web.httpbrowsercapabilities(v=vs.110).aspx`. Later in the chapter, I'll explain how you can extend the set of properties using freely available third-party data.

***Table 7-3.** The Most Useful Properties Defined by the HttpBrowserCapabilities Class*

Name	Description
`Browser`	Returns the browser name.
`IsMobileDevice`	Returns `true` if the device is mobile. There is no fixed definition of what constitutes a mobile device, and it is the responsibility of the provider of capability data to make the assessment. As a general rule, you can expect this property to return `true` if the device is handheld, is battery powered, and connects via a wireless or cellular network.
`MobileDeviceManufacturer`	Returns the name of the device manufacturer.
`MobileDeviceModel`	Returns the name of the device.
`ScreenPixelsHeight`	Returns the size of the screen in pixels.
`ScreenPixelsWidth`	Returns the width of the screen in pixels.
`Version`	Returns the version number of the browser.

■ **Note** I have included two properties defined by the `HttpBrowserCapabilities` class that look more useful than they really are: `ScreenPixelsHeight` and `ScreenPixelsWidth`. I listed them because they are so widely used and so that I can highlight the problems they cause. The root issue is that the quality of information about screen size is patchy and doesn't always take into account the pixel density of the display. Making decisions about the content sent to a client based on the value of these properties can cause a lot of issues, especially for clients that support resizable browser windows that don't correlate directly to the size of the screen (commonly the case for desktop clients). The short version is that you should not categorize clients based on the `ScreenPixelsHeight` and `ScreenPixelsWidth` properties.

To demonstrate the basic use of the `HttpBrowserCapabilities` class, I added a new action method to the `Home` controller, as shown in Listing 7-4.

***Listing 7-4.** Adding a New Action Method to the HomeController.cs File*

```
using System.Web.Mvc;
using Mobile.Models;

namespace Mobile.Controllers {

    public class HomeController : Controller {
```

```
        private Programmer[] progs = {
            new Programmer("Alice", "Smith", "Lead Developer", "Paris", "France", "C#"),
            new Programmer("Joe", "Dunston", "Developer", "London", "UK", "Java"),
            new Programmer("Peter", "Jones", "Developer", "Chicago", "USA", "C#"),
            new Programmer("Murray", "Woods", "Jnr Developer", "Boston", "USA", "C#")
        };

        public ActionResult Index() {
            return View(progs);
        }

        public ActionResult Browser() {
            return View();
        }
    }
}
```

The action, called Browser, simply asks the MVC framework to render the default view, which I created by right-clicking the action method in the code editor and selecting Add View from the pop-up menu. You can see the contents of the view file I created in Listing 7-5.

Listing 7-5. The Contents of the Browser.cshtml File

```
@model IEnumerable<Tuple<string, string>>
@{
    Layout = null;
}
<!DOCTYPE html>
<html>
<head>
    <meta name="viewport" content="width=device-width" />
    <title>Device Capabilities</title>
    <link href="~/Content/bootstrap.min.css" rel="stylesheet" />
    <link href="~/Content/bootstrap-theme.min.css" rel="stylesheet" />
</head>
<body class="container">
    <div class="panel panel-primary">
        <div class="panel-heading">Capabilities</div>
        <table class="table table-striped table-bordered">
            <tr><th>Property</th><th>Value</th></tr>
            <tr><td>Browser</td><td>@Request.Browser.Browser</td></tr>
            <tr><td>IsMobileDevice</td><td>@Request.Browser.IsMobileDevice</td></tr>
            <tr>
                <td>MobileDeviceManufacturer</td>
                <td>@Request.Browser.MobileDeviceManufacturer</td>
            </tr>
            <tr>
                <td>MobileDeviceModel</td>
                <td>@Request.Browser.MobileDeviceModel</td>
            </tr>
```

```
            <tr>
                <td>ScreenPixelsHeight</td>
                <td>@Request.Browser.ScreenPixelsHeight</td>
            </tr>
            <tr>
                <td>ScreenPixelsWidth</td>
                <td>@Request.Browser.ScreenPixelsWidth</td>
            </tr>
            <tr><td>Version</td><td>@Request.Browser.Version</td></tr>
        </table>
    </div>
</body>
</html>
```

The view populates a table with rows that contain the property names and values from the `HttpBrowserCapabilities` object. You can see the data generated for the iPhone in Figure 7-3.

Capabilities

Property	Value
Browser	Safari
IsMobileDevice	True
MobileDeviceManufacturer	Apple
MobileDeviceModel	IPhone
ScreenPixelsHeight	480
ScreenPixelsWidth	640
Version	7.0

***Figure 7-3.** The ASP.NET browser capabilities properties for the iPhone*

■ **Caution** Notice that the values of the `ScreenPixelsHeight` and `ScreenPixelsWidth` properties are wrong. ASP.NET will default to reporting a screen size of 640 by 480 pixels when there is no information available. This is why you should not use these properties to adapt the content you sent to the device: You can't tell whether the information is accurate or just not available.

Improving Capability Data

ASP.NET uses the user-agent string sent as part of the HTTP request to identify a client. As an example, here is the user-agent string that Chrome sends when it is emulating an iPhone 5:

```
Mozilla/5.0 (iPhone; CPU iPhone OS 7_0 like Mac OS X; en-us) AppleWebKit/537.51.1 (KHTML, like
Gecko) Version/7.0 Mobile/11A465 Safari/9537.53
```

You may see a slightly different string because the version number of the browser or the operating system may change. To populate the `HttpBrowserCapabilities` properties, ASP.NET processes the user-agent string using a set of *browser files*, which are contained in the following location:

```
%SystemRoot%\Microsoft.NET\Framework\<version>\CONFIG\Browsers
```

For me, this means that the files are in the `C:\Windows\Microsoft.NET\Framework\v4.0.30319\Config\Browsers` folder. I'll explain the format of these files in the "Creating a Custom Browser File" section later in the chapter, but for now it is enough to understand that the browser doesn't send details of its capabilities to the application. Instead, the ASP.NET platform has to be able to translate user-agent strings into meaningful capabilities and present them to the application. There is some useful information in a user-agent string, such as the version of the browser or operating system being used, but most of the useful information, such as whether a request has originated from a mobile device, has to be obtained by the browser files.

Microsoft includes the browser files in the .NET Framework because there has to be some initial reference point from which translating between user-agent strings and capabilities can begin. But .NET isn't updated all that often, and the information in the browser files is rudimentary and gets stale quickly given the vibrant market for smartphones and tablets. If you rely on just the built-in browser files, then you'll find that new devices can mislead an application because of the way that ASP.NET describes the characteristics of devices that it doesn't recognize. As an example, Figure 7-4 shows the `HttpBrowserCapabilities` values displayed for a request from a second-generation Google Nexus 7 tablet, which sends a user-agent string that the built-in browser files don't contain information for.

Capabilities

Property	Value
Browser	Chrome
IsMobileDevice	False
MobileDeviceManufacturer	Unknown
MobileDeviceModel	Unknown
ScreenPixelsHeight	480
ScreenPixelsWidth	640
Version	29.0

***Figure 7-4.** Misleading data for an unrecognized device*

There are obviously some problems with this data. The browser has been correctly recognized as Chrome, but the manufacturer and model are unknown, the screen size is incorrect, and the `IsMobileDevice` property returns `false`, even though tablets are generally considered to be mobile. In the sections that follow, I'll show you different ways to improve the accuracy of the ASP.NET capabilities data.

Creating a Custom Browser File

The first technique for improving the ASP.NET capabilities data is to create custom browser files that supplement the built-in ones. A browser file describes one or more new browsers. To create a new browser file, right-click the project in the Solution Explorer and select Add ➤ Add ASP.NET Folder ➤ App_Browsers from the pop-up menu. This is the location that ASP.NET looks in for custom browser files. To create a new file, right-click the App_Browsers folder and select Add ➤ Browser File from the pop-up menu. Set the name of the new file to Nexus and click the OK button to create the `App_Browsers/Nexus.browser` file. In Listing 7-6, you can see how I used the browser file to define capabilities for the Nexus 7 tablet.

Listing 7-6. The Contents of the Nexus.browser File

```
<browsers>
  <browser id="Nexus" parentID="Chrome">

    <identification>
      <userAgent match="Nexus" />
    </identification>

    <capture>
      <userAgent match="Nexus (?'model'\d+)" />
    </capture>

    <capabilities>
      <capability name="MobileDeviceManufacturer" value="Google" />
      <capability name="MobileDeviceModel" value="Nexus ${model}" />
      <capability name="isMobileDevice" value="true" />
    </capabilities>
  </browser>

  <browser id="Nexus7" parentID="Nexus">
    <identification>
      <userAgent match="Nexus 7" />
    </identification>

    <capabilities>
      <capability name="ScreenPixelsHeight" value="1900" />
      <capability name="ScreenPixelsWidth" value="1200" />
    </capabilities>
  </browser>

</browsers>
```

■ **Tip** I only describe the XML elements that I use in this example, but there is a complete description of the browser file schema at `http://msdn.microsoft.com/en-us/library/ms228122(v=vs.85).aspx`.

Browser files are XML. The top-level element is browsers, and individual browser definitions are denoted by the browser element. New browser definitions can build on existing ones. In the example, I used the id attribute to define a new browser called Nexus that builds on the built-in definition for the Chrome browser, which is specified by the parentID attribute. (The built-in browser files contain definitions for all the mainstream browsers.)

The identification attribute tells ASP.NET how to determine that a request originates from the browser. I have used the most common option, which is to perform a regular expression match on the user-agent string, specified with the userAgent element and the match attribute. My browser definition matches any request that contains Nexus. You can also identify browsers using headers, but the Nexus products include the information I need in the user-agent string, like this:

```
Mozilla/5.0 (Linux; Android 4.3; Nexus 7 Build/JSS15Q) AppleWebKit/537.36 (KHTML, like Gecko)
Chrome/29.0.1547.72 Safari/537.36
```

The capture element allows me to pull out information from the request that I will use to set the value for capability properties later. I want to be able to accurately report the model of a Nexus device, so I use the userAgent element to match the digits that follow Nexus in the user-agent string and assign them to a temporary variable called model:

```
...
<capture>
    <userAgent match="Nexus (?'model'\d+)" />
</capture>
...
```

The capabilities element contains one or more capability elements that generate values for the HttpBrowserCapabilities object. I use literal values to set MobileDeviceManufacturer and isMobileDevice but include the model variable from the capture section to set the MobileDeviceModel property, as follows:

```
...
<capabilities>
    <capability name="MobileDeviceManufacturer" value="Google" />
    <capability name="MobileDeviceModel" value="Nexus ${model}" />
    <capability name="isMobileDevice" value="true" />
</capabilities>
...
```

The result is that all requests that have a user-agent string that contains Nexus will report the built-in capabilities defined for the Chrome browser, with the exception of the three properties I redefined using capability elements. The second browser element further refines the capabilities for the Nexus 7 device. If the user-agent string contains Nexus 7, then set the value of the ScreenPixelsHeight and ScreenPixelsWidth properties. Figure 7-5 shows the capabilities reported when Google Chrome is used to emulate the Nexus 5 phone and Nexus 7 tablet.

Capabilities	
Property	**Value**
Browser	Chrome
IsMobileDevice	True
MobileDeviceManufacturer	Google
MobileDeviceModel	Nexus 7
ScreenPixelsHeight	1900
ScreenPixelsWidth	1200
Version	29.0

Capabilities	
Property	**Value**
Browser	Chrome
IsMobileDevice	True
MobileDeviceManufacturer	Google
MobileDeviceModel	Nexus 5
ScreenPixelsHeight	480
ScreenPixelsWidth	640
Version	18.0

Figure 7-5. *The effect of creating a custom browser file*

■ **Note** I am using the screen size properties to demonstrate another problem they represent. You can create custom browser definitions to override the default values from the built-in files, but it is still hard to provide useful data. In this case, the values I have set for the properties are accurate for the second-generation Nexus 7, but the first generation used the same user-agent string and has a smaller screen, meaning that inaccurate capabilities will be reported for requests that come from the earlier devices.

Creating a Capability Provider

Creating individual browser files works well, but it can quickly get fiddly if you have to maintain a lot of capabilities data. A more flexible approach is to create a *capability provider*, which is a class that is derived from the `System.Web.Configuration.HttpCapabilitiesProvider` class and provides ASP.NET with capability information about requests. A custom provider allows you to use C# code to define capabilities, rather than XML elements.

To demonstrate creating a custom capabilities provider, I created a folder called `Infrastructure` in the example project and created a new class file called `KindleCapabilities.cs`. Listing 7-7 shows how I used the class file to define a provider for Amazon Kindle Fire tablets, which I selected because Google Chrome will emulate them and because there is no definition for them in the browser files.

Listing 7-7. The Contents of the KindleCapabilities.cs File

```
using System.Web;
using System.Web.Configuration;

namespace Mobile.Infrastructure {
    public class KindleCapabilities : HttpCapabilitiesProvider {

        public override HttpBrowserCapabilities
                GetBrowserCapabilities(HttpRequest request) {
```

```
            HttpCapabilitiesDefaultProvider defaults =
                new HttpCapabilitiesDefaultProvider();
            HttpBrowserCapabilities caps = defaults.GetBrowserCapabilities(request);

            if (request.UserAgent.Contains("Kindle Fire")) {
                caps.Capabilities["Browser"] = "Silk";
                caps.Capabilities["IsMobileDevice"] = "true";
                caps.Capabilities["MobileDeviceManufacturer"] = "Amazon";
                caps.Capabilities["MobileDeviceModel"] = "Kindle Fire";
                if (request.UserAgent.Contains("Kindle Fire HD")) {
                    caps.Capabilities["MobileDeviceModel"] = "Kindle Fire HD";
                }
            }
            return caps;
        }
    }
}
```

The `HttpCapabilitiesProvider` class requires subclasses to implement the `GetBrowserCapabilities` method, which receives an `HttpRequest` object and returns the `HttpBrowserCapabilities` object that describes the browser. There can be only one instance of the `HttpCapabilitiesProvider` class for an application and so the most common approach is to implement the `GetBrowserCapabilities` method so that it supplements the data produced by the `HttpCapabilitiesDefaultProvider` class, which is the default capabilities provider and is responsible for processing the browser files. In the listing, you can see how I get the capabilities of the browser using the default provider and add to them only for the Kindle devices. The overall effect is that my capabilities are drawn from a combination of the built-in browser files, the custom browser file I created for the Nexus devices, and the code in the `KindleCapabilities` provider class.

The provider must be registered with ASP.NET during application initialization, and in Listing 7-8 you can see how I have used the `Application_Start` method in the global application class to tell ASP.NET that I want to use the `KindleCapabilities` class as the browser capabilities provider. (I described the role that the `Application_Start` method plays in the ASP.NET life cycle in Chapter 3.)

Listing 7-8. Registering the Capabilities Provider in the Global.asax.cs File

```
using System;
using System.Collections.Generic;
using System.Linq;
using System.Web;
using System.Web.Configuration;
using System.Web.Mvc;
using System.Web.Routing;
using Mobile.Infrastructure;

namespace Mobile {
    public class MvcApplication : System.Web.HttpApplication {
        protected void Application_Start() {
            AreaRegistration.RegisterAllAreas();
            RouteConfig.RegisterRoutes(RouteTable.Routes);
            HttpCapabilitiesBase.BrowserCapabilitiesProvider = new KindleCapabilities();

        }
    }
}
```

The static `HttpCapabilitiesBase.BrowserCapabilitiesProvider` property sets the capabilities provider for the application, and in the listing I have applied an instance of my `KindleCapabilities` class. Figure 7-6 shows the effect of requesting the `/Home/Browser` URL using Chrome while it is emulating one of the Kindle Fire tablets before and after the addition of the custom capabilities provider.

Capabilities

Property	Value
Browser	Mozilla
IsMobileDevice	True
MobileDeviceManufacturer	Unknown
MobileDeviceModel	Linux
ScreenPixelsHeight	480
ScreenPixelsWidth	640
Version	0.0

Capabilities

Property	Value
Browser	Silk
IsMobileDevice	True
MobileDeviceManufacturer	Amazon
MobileDeviceModel	Kindle Fire HD
ScreenPixelsHeight	480
ScreenPixelsWidth	640
Version	0.0

***Figure 7-6.** The effect of creating a custom capabilities provider*

Using Third-Party Capabilities Data

Using a custom capabilities provider can be more flexible than using XML files, but you still have to provide all of the capabilities data for the devices that you want to support. Keeping track of all the devices that are released can be a lot of work, which is why you may choose to use a third-party source for the device data. There are three main suppliers of capabilities data, and two of them provide no-cost options for using their data. I have listed all three companies in Table 7-4.

***Table 7-4.** The Types of Web Forms Code Nuggets*

Name	Description
`51degrees.mobi`	Offers freely available data that can be used in most projects. The free data contains a subset of the capability properties in the commercial offering and delays adding new device data for three months. See the next section for details of use.
Scientiamobile	Freely available data from `http://wurfl.sourceforge.net` and a commercial offering that includes cloud access to data (which has a free option for up to 5,000 requests per month).
Device Atlas	Commercial-only offering of on-site data and cloud service.

The `51degrees.mobi` data is the most popular because it is easy to integrate into an ASP.NET project and because the data is pretty good. The free data is well-maintained and extends the core set of capabilities defined by the built-in browser files, but it doesn't offer the depth of additional capabilities that the paid-for option has, which differentiates between smartphones and tablets, for example. (The other limitation is that new devices are not added to the free data for three months, which can present a problem when requests from popular new devices start to arrive before the capabilities data has been released.)

■ **Caution** You must keep third-party data up-to-date, which generally means downloading a new data file and publishing an update of the application. An alternative is to use one of the cloud service offerings, which have the benefit of always being current but are outside of your control and require a commercial contract.

Installing the Module and Data File

The 51degrees data is most easily installed through the NuGet package called `51Degrees.mobi`, but I don't use this option because the package installs extra features that go beyond device capabilities and get in the way of features such as ASP.NET *display modes* (which I detail later in this chapter). Instead, I prefer to download a .NET assembly and the latest data file from `http://51degrees.codeplex.com/releases/view/94175`.

To add the 51degrees data to the example application, go to the URL just mentioned and download the `51Degrees.mobi DLL Website Enhancer` file. This is a zip file from which you will need to copy the `FiftyOne.Foundation.dll` file from the `NET4\bin` into the application's `bin` folder.

The DLL file contains a module that adds the capabilities data to `HttpRequest` objects and that is registered using the `PreApplicationStartMethod` attribute, which I described in Chapter 4.

The DLL also contains device data, but it isn't updated as frequently as the separate data file listed on the same CodePlex web page, so download the latest version of the binary data file, rename it to be `51Degrees.mobi.dat`, and copy it into the `App_Data` folder.

■ **Tip** You will have to use the Windows File Explorer to copy the files. Neither file will show up in the Solution Explorer window by default. The `bin` folder isn't usually shown, but you can show the data file by right-clicking the `App_Data` folder, selecting Add ➤ Existing Item from the pop-up menu, and locating the `51Degrees.mobi.dat` file. The module and data file will work even if you don't perform this step.

Configuring the Module

The next step is to create a configuration file that tells the module to use the separate data file. Right-click the Mobile project item in the Solution Explorer and select Add ➤ New Item from the pop-up menu. Select the Web Configuration File template item from the Web category, set the name of the file to be `51degrees.mobi.config`, and click the Add button to create the file. Edit the file that Visual Studio creates to match Listing 7-9.

Listing 7-9. The Contents of the 51degrees.mobi.config File

```
<?xml version="1.0"?>
<configuration>
  <configSections>
    <sectionGroup name="fiftyOne">
      <section name="detection"
               type="FiftyOne.Foundation.Mobile.Detection.Configuration.DetectionSection,
                   FiftyOne.Foundation"
               requirePermission="false"
               allowDefinition="Everywhere"
```

```
            restartOnExternalChanges="false"
            allowExeDefinition="MachineToApplication"/>
    </sectionGroup>
  </configSections>
  <fiftyOne>
    <detection binaryFilePath="~/App_Data/51Degrees.mobi.dat"/>
  </fiftyOne>
</configuration>
```

This configuration file specifies the location of the device data file. The `51degrees.mobi` developers have extended the standard configuration file schema to define their own configuration sections, a technique that I describe in Chapter 9.

Disabling the Custom Capabilities Provider

Setting a custom capabilities provider overrides the `51degrees.mobi` data, so I have to comment out the statement in the global application class that sets up the `KindleCapabilities` object from the previous section. Listing 7-10 shows the commented-out statement.

Listing 7-10. Disabling the Custom Capabilities Provider in the Global.asax.cs File

```
using System;
using System.Collections.Generic;
using System.Linq;
using System.Web;
using System.Web.Configuration;
using System.Web.Mvc;
using System.Web.Routing;
using Mobile.Infrastructure;

namespace Mobile {
    public class MvcApplication : System.Web.HttpApplication {
        protected void Application_Start() {
            AreaRegistration.RegisterAllAreas();
            RouteConfig.RegisterRoutes(RouteTable.Routes);
            // HttpCapabilitiesBase.BrowserCapabilitiesProvider
            //      = new KindleCapabilities();
        }
    }
}
```

Displaying Additional Properties

The final step is to demonstrate that the third-party capabilities data is being used. The `51degrees.mobi` data defines a number of additional properties, and in Listing 7-11 you can see how I have extended the markup in the `Browser.cshtml` view to display two of them.

Listing 7-11. Adding Capability Properties to the Browser.cshtml File

```
@model IEnumerable<Tuple<string, string>>
@{
    Layout = null;
}
<!DOCTYPE html>
<html>
<head>
    <meta name="viewport" content="width=device-width" />
    <title>Device Capabilities</title>
    <link href="~/Content/bootstrap.min.css" rel="stylesheet" />
    <link href="~/Content/bootstrap-theme.min.css" rel="stylesheet" />
</head>
<body class="container">
    <div class="panel panel-primary">
        <div class="panel-heading">Capabilities</div>
        <table class="table table-striped table-bordered">
            <tr><th>Property</th><th>Value</th></tr>
            <tr><td>Browser</td><td>@Request.Browser.Browser</td></tr>
            <tr><td>IsMobileDevice</td><td>@Request.Browser.IsMobileDevice</td></tr>
            <tr>
                <td>MobileDeviceManufacturer</td>
                <td>@Request.Browser.MobileDeviceManufacturer</td>
            </tr>
            <tr>
                <td>MobileDeviceModel</td>
                <td>@Request.Browser.MobileDeviceModel</td>
            </tr>
            <tr>
                <td>ScreenPixelsHeight</td>
                <td>@Request.Browser.ScreenPixelsHeight</td>
            </tr>
            <tr>
                <td>ScreenPixelsWidth</td>
                <td>@Request.Browser.ScreenPixelsWidth</td>
            </tr>
            <tr><td>Version</td><td>@Request.Browser.Version</td></tr>
            <tr><td>CssColumn</td><td>@Request.Browser["CssColumn"]</td></tr>
            <tr><td>CssFlexbox</td><td>@Request.Browser["CssFlexbox"]</td></tr>
        </table>
    </div>
</body>
</html>
```

■ **Tip** You can see a complete set of additional properties at `http://51degrees.mobi/Products/DeviceData/PropertyDictionary.aspx`. Most of the properties listed are available only with the commercial data, but there are some useful additions in the free data as well.

These two capabilities, `CssColumn` and `CssFlexbox`, indicate whether a browser supports two CSS3 layouts. The `HttpBrowserCapabilities` object doesn't define properties that correspond to these capabilities, but you can get their values by treating it as a collection indexed by name, like this:

```
...
<tr><td>CssColumn</td><td>@Request.Browser["CssColumn"]</td></tr>
...
```

Figure 7-7 shows the additional capabilities when Google Chrome is used to emulate an iPhone 5.

Capabilities

Property	Value
Browser	Safari
IsMobileDevice	True
MobileDeviceManufacturer	Apple
MobileDeviceModel	IPhone
ScreenPixelsHeight	480
ScreenPixelsWidth	320
Version	7.0
CssColumn	True
CssFlexbox	False

***Figure 7-7.** Using third-party capabilities data*

■ **Tip** You may have to refresh the browser tab to change the browser emulation.

Adapting to Capabilities

The first part of this chapter was all about identifying devices and adding capabilities, and with that out of the way, I can turn to the different ways in which you can use the capabilities data in an application to adapt to different devices.

Avoiding the Capabilities Trap

I am going to start by showing you the most common mistake with capability data, which is to reduce the amount of content sent to mobile devices in order to make difficult layouts fit on the screen. Listing 7-12 shows how I have edited the `Index.cshtml` file to reduce the number of columns in the table of programmers.

Listing 7-12. Adapting Content for Mobile Devices in the Index.cshtml View

```
@using Mobile.Models
@model Programmer[]
@{
    Layout = null;
}
<!DOCTYPE html>
<html>
<head>
    <meta name="viewport" content="width=device-width" />
    <title>Mobile Devices</title>
    <link href="~/Content/bootstrap.min.css" rel="stylesheet" />
    <link href="~/Content/bootstrap-theme.min.css" rel="stylesheet" />
    <style>
        body { padding-top: 10px; }
    </style>
</head>
<body>
    <div class="alert alert-success">
        This is the /Views/Home/Index.cshtml view
    </div>
    <div class="panel panel-primary">
        <div class="panel-heading">Programmers</div>
        <table class="table table-striped">
            <tr>
                <th>First Name</th>
                @if (!Request.Browser.IsMobileDevice) {
                    <th>Last Name</th>
                    <th>Title</th>
                }
                <th>City</th>
                @if (!Request.Browser.IsMobileDevice) {
                    <th>Country</th>
                }
                <th>Language</th>
            </tr>
            @foreach (Programmer prog in Model) {
                <tr>
                    <td>@prog.FirstName</td>
                    @if (!Request.Browser.IsMobileDevice) {
                        <td>@prog.LastName</td>
                        <td>@prog.Title</td>
                    }
```

```
                    <td>@prog.City</td>
                    @if (!Request.Browser.IsMobileDevice) {
                        <td>@prog.Country</td>
                    }
                    <td>@prog.Language</td>
                </tr>
            }
        </table>
    </div>
</body>
</html>
```

Razor makes it easy to build logic into views that alters the HTML sent to the browser based on the device capabilities, and it is simple and easy to get some effective results. In the listing, I have used the `IsMobileDevice` property to reduce the number of table columns, and you can see the result when the view is rendered for an iPhone in Figure 7-8.

This is the /Views/Home/Index.cshtml view

Programmers

First Name	City	Language
Alice	Paris	C#
Joe	London	Java
Peter	Chicago	C#
Murray	Boston	C#

***Figure 7-8.** Adapting content to support device capabilities*

The problem with this approach is that it isn't adapting to the device capabilities in a useful way. The `IsMobileDevice` property doesn't convey any information about the device screen size or screen orientation, just that the device is likely to run on battery and use cellular networks. Equating mobility with a narrow screen doesn't make sense for today's smartphones and tablets, not least because they allow the user to view content in two orientations. Figure 7-9 shows the same view rendered for the Nexus 7 tablet in landscape screen orientation.

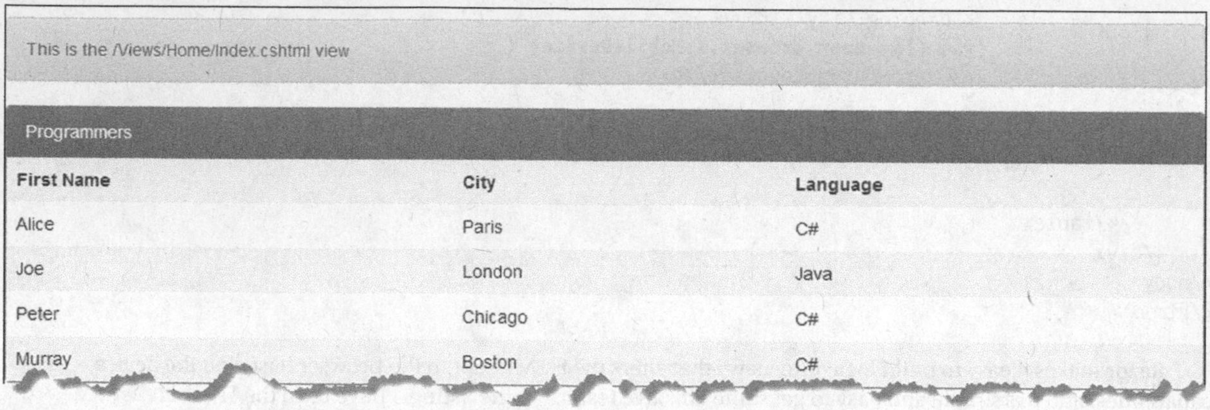

This is the /Views/Home/Index.cshtml view

Programmers

First Name	City	Language
Alice	Paris	C#
Joe	London	Java
Peter	Chicago	C#
Murray	Boston	C#

Figure 7-9. Content displayed on a tablet

The result is that all mobile devices get the same user experience, even those that are capable of displaying all of the content. That's not to say that the `IsMobileDevice` property can't be useful when it used appropriately, but it is important to understand that the definition of the property depends on the source of the capabilities data and that it can be relied on to make assessments of display size.

Using Responsive Design Instead of Capabilities

The browser knows the size and orientation of the device screen and is far better placed to alter the layout to suit the display capabilities of the device through responsive design. Responsive design relies on CSS *media queries*, which change CSS property values based on the current characteristics of the device, including the screen. And, since media queries are performed at the browser, they allow content to be adapted dynamically, such as when the user changes the orientation of the device. I get into the topic of responsive design in detail in my *Pro MVC 5 Client Development* book, but you don't have to understand advanced CSS features when you are working with a framework such as Bootstrap because it includes convenience CSS classes that take care of the work for you. In Listing 7-13, you can see that I have removed the conditional Razor statements from the `Index.cshtml` view and added a CSS class to `th` and `td` elements.

Listing 7-13. Creating a Responsive Table in the Index.cshtml File

```
@using Mobile.Models
@model Programmer[]
@{
    Layout = null;
}
<!DOCTYPE html>
<html>
<head>
    <meta name="viewport" content="width=device-width" />
    <title>Mobile Devices</title>
    <link href="~/Content/bootstrap.min.css" rel="stylesheet" />
    <link href="~/Content/bootstrap-theme.min.css" rel="stylesheet" />
    <style>
        body { padding-top: 10px; }
    </style>
</head>
```

```
<body>
    <div class="alert alert-success">
        This is the /Views/Home/Index.cshtml view
    </div>
    <div class="panel panel-primary">
        <div class="panel-heading">Programmers</div>
        <table class="table table-striped">
            <tr>
                <th>First Name</th>
                <th class="hidden-xs">Last Name</th>
                <th class="hidden-xs">Title</th>
                <th>City</th>
                <th class="hidden-xs">Country</th>
                <th>Language</th>
            </tr>
            @foreach (Programmer prog in Model) {
                <tr>
                    <td>@prog.FirstName</td>
                    <td class="hidden-xs">@prog.LastName</td>
                    <td class="hidden-xs">@prog.Title</td>
                    <td>@prog.City</td>
                    <td class="hidden-xs">@prog.Country</td>
                    <td>@prog.Language</td>
                </tr>
            }
        </table>
    </div>
</body>
</html>
```

Bootstrap includes a set of responsive CSS classes that show and hide elements based on the width of the screen. The `hidden-xs` class, which I used in the listing, hides an element when the width of the screen is less than 768 pixels. The result of the changes I made in Listing 7-13 is that narrow screens show fewer columns but wider screens display the full table, as shown in Figure 7-10.

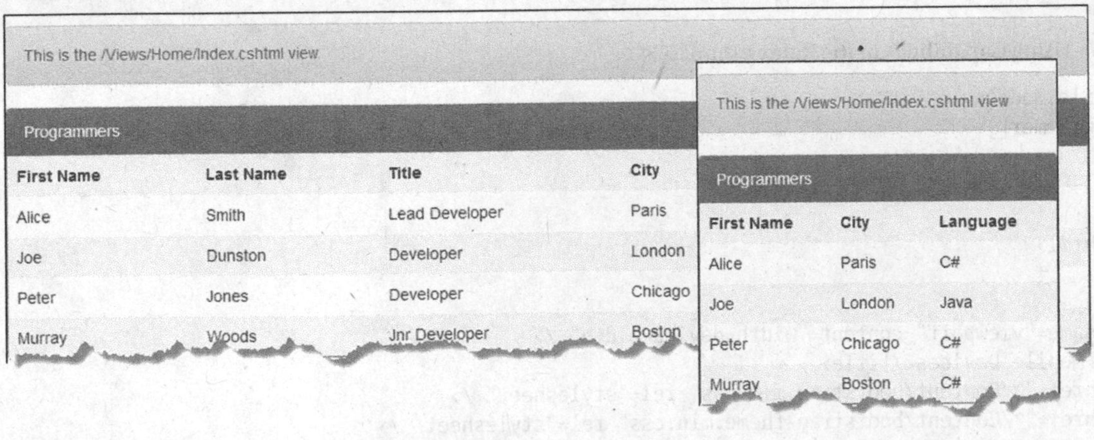

Figure 7-10. *The effect of responsive design*

■ **Caution** If you are going to use the `IsMobileDevice` to offer a variation of the application to all mobile devices, then you should also provide a mechanism by which the user can elect to switch back to the full-fat version. This means you won't alienate those users who don't share your assessment of the capabilities of their device. I usually do this by adding a simple switch or button to the HTML layout and keeping track of a user's choice through the session state data feature (which I describe in Chapter 10) or the user data feature (which I describe in Chapter 15.

Tailoring Content to Match Devices

Having shown you the common pitfall with capabilities data, I want to show you that there are useful ways in which to adapt your application to support different devices but, importantly, based on the actual capabilities of the device, rather than a loose proxy such as the value from the `IsMobileDevice` property.

Adapting views works best when you focus on the capabilities of specific devices or browsers. HTML and CSS provide many opportunities for this kind of adaptation as different generations of browsers implement aspects of the standards at different paces.

In effect, capabilities can be used to work around deficiencies of specific devices, especially older devices whose built-in browsers don't support recent HTML and CSS features. I find this especially useful for dealing with older versions of Internet Explorer, which are notoriously difficult to support because they were produced during the dark days of Microsoft's embrace-and-extend approach to web standards. Tools such as jQuery and Bootstrap can go a long way to helping support old browsers, but complex applications can still encounter problems, and that's where device capabilities can be useful.

I don't want to get into the process of setting up test rigs for old versions of Internet Explorer, so I am going to simulate the problem by identifying a particular browser that Google Chrome can emulate and handling the requests it makes differently. For simplicity, I am going to pretend that the Safari browser, which is used on iOS devices such as the iPhone, can't support the table layout in my application and that I need to work around this problem by using an alternative approach. I'll show you different ways of solving the problem, building up to the *display modes* feature, which is the most flexible and easiest to work with in complex applications.

Adapting Directly in the View

The most direct approach is to adapt the content you send to the client directly in the view. You can see how I have done this in Listing 7-14 using a Razor conditional statement.

Listing 7-14. Using Capabilities in the Index.cshtml File

```
@using Mobile.Models
@model Programmer[]
@{
    Layout = null;
}
<!DOCTYPE html>
<html>
<head>
    <meta name="viewport" content="width=device-width" />
    <title>Mobile Devices</title>
    <link href="~/Content/bootstrap.min.css" rel="stylesheet" />
    <link href="~/Content/bootstrap-theme.min.css" rel="stylesheet" />
```

```
    <style>
        body { padding-top: 10px; }
    </style>
</head>
<body>
    <div class="alert alert-success">
        This is the /Views/Home/Index.cshtml view
    </div>
    <div class="panel panel-primary">
        <div class="panel-heading">Programmers</div>
        @if (Request.Browser.IsBrowser("Safari")) {
            <div class="panel-body">
                <ul>
                    @foreach (Programmer prog in Model) {
                        <li>
                            @prog.FirstName @prog.LastName,
                            @prog.City (@prog.Language)
                        </li>
                    }
                </ul>
            </div>
        } else {
            <table class="table table-striped">
                <tr>
                    <th>First Name</th>
                    <th class="hidden-xs">Last Name</th>
                    <th class="hidden-xs">Title</th>
                    <th>City</th>
                    <th class="hidden-xs">Country</th>
                    <th>Language</th>
                </tr>
                @foreach (Programmer prog in Model) {
                    <tr>
                        <td>@prog.FirstName</td>
                        <td class="hidden-xs">@prog.LastName</td>
                        <td class="hidden-xs">@prog.Title</td>
                        <td>@prog.City</td>
                        <td class="hidden-xs">@prog.Country</td>
                        <td>@prog.Language</td>
                    </tr>
                }
            </table>
        }
    </div>
</body>
</html>
```

I check to see which browser has made the request using the HttpBrowserCapabilities.IsBrowser convenience method, which checks to see whether the browser matches the specified name. This method is useful because it respects the hierarchy of browser files, which simplifies the matching process and means you don't have to remember to synchronize your capabilities data with your conditional view statements. When I receive a request from the Safari browser, I generate a simple list of programmers rather than the table. You can see the result in Figure 7-11.

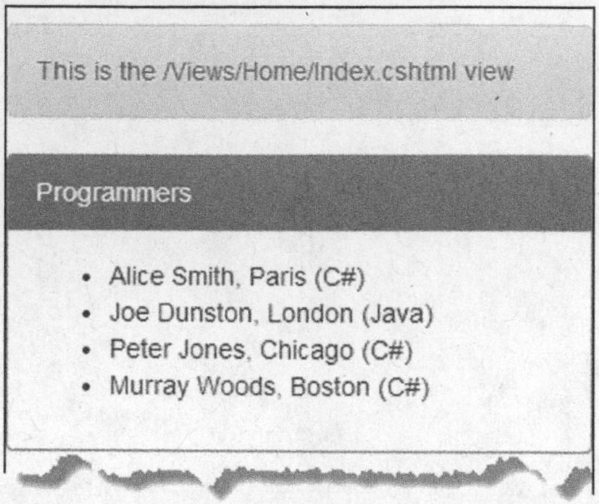

This is the /Views/Home/Index.cshtml view

Programmers

- Alice Smith, Paris (C#)
- Joe Dunston, London (Java)
- Peter Jones, Chicago (C#)
- Murray Woods, Boston (C#)

Figure 7-11. *Responding to device capabilities*

Using Partial Views

The problem with putting the conditional statements for browser capabilities into the view is that they quickly become unwieldy and difficult to maintain. A more elegant approach is to put the content for different browsers into partial views and select the one you need when the view is rendered. Small and simple views are easier to work with, and breaking out the browser-specific content makes it easy to keep changes isolated when the application enters testing and deployment. For my example application, I need to create two partial views. The first, which will be the default, is the `/Views/Home/Programmers.cshtml` file, the contents of which you can see in Listing 7-15.

Listing 7-15. The Contents of the Programmers.cshtml File

```
@using Mobile.Models
@model Programmer[]

<table class="table table-striped">
    <tr>
        <th>First Name</th>
        <th class="hidden-xs">Last Name</th>
        <th class="hidden-xs">Title</th>
        <th>City</th>
        <th class="hidden-xs">Country</th>
        <th>Language</th>
    </tr>
    @foreach (Programmer prog in Model) {
        <tr>
            <td>@prog.FirstName</td>
            <td class="hidden-xs">@prog.LastName</td>
            <td class="hidden-xs">@prog.Title</td>
            <td>@prog.City</td>
            <td class="hidden-xs">@prog.Country</td>
            <td>@prog.Language</td>
        </tr>
    }
</table>
```

This is the partial view that will be used for all requests that *don't* come from the Safari browser, and it contains the responsive table layout. I called the second partial view `Programmers.Safari.cshtml`, and you can see the contents in Listing 7-16. (Visual Studio won't let you create a view called `Programmers.Safari.cshtml` directly; first create a view called `Safari.cshtml` and then rename it in the Solution Explorer to `Programmers.Safari.cshtml`.)

Listing 7-16. The Contents of the Programmers.Safari.cshtml File

```
@using Mobile.Models
@model Programmer[]

<div class="panel-body">
    <ul>
        @foreach (Programmer prog in Model) {
            <li>
                @prog.FirstName @prog.LastName,
                @prog.City (@prog.Language)
            </li>
        }
    </ul>
</div>
```

■ **Tip** The naming of the partial views is slightly awkward, but it helps set the scene for the display modes feature, which I describe shortly.

This is the view that will be set to the Safari browser, and it contains the simpler list layout that I created in the previous section. In Listing 7-17, you can see how I updated the `Index.cshtml` file to use the new partial views.

Listing 7-17. Using the Partial Views in the Index.cshtml File

```
@using Mobile.Models
@model Programmer[]
@{
    Layout = null;
}
<!DOCTYPE html>
<html>
<head>
    <meta name="viewport" content="width=device-width" />
    <title>Mobile Devices</title>
    <link href="~/Content/bootstrap.min.css" rel="stylesheet" />
    <link href="~/Content/bootstrap-theme.min.css" rel="stylesheet" />
    <style>
        body { padding-top: 10px; }
    </style>
</head>
<body>
    <div class="alert alert-success">
        This is the /Views/Home/Index.cshtml view
    </div>
```

```
    <div class="panel panel-primary">
        <div class="panel-heading">Programmers</div>
        @Html.Partial(Request.Browser.IsBrowser("Safari")
            ? "Programmers.Safari" : "Programmers", Model)
    </div>
</body>
</html>
```

I use the Html.Partial helper to select one of the partial views based on the browser capability information. The result is a more maintainable approach than having the markup in a single view file.

Using Display Modes

The only problem with the approach in the previous section is that it requires the use of the Html.Partial helper method whenever an alternative view is required for the Safari browser. The final technique is the one that I have been building up in the previous steps: using *display modes*.

Display modes are not part of the ASP.NET platform, but I going to demonstrate their use here because they are usually applied in conjunction with the device capabilities feature. In short, display modes will automatically select alternative views when they exist based on a set of rules defined by the application. As a demonstration, Listing 7-18 shows how I created a display mode in the global application class.

Listing 7-18. Defining a Display Mode

```
using System;
using System.Collections.Generic;
using System.Linq;
using System.Web;
using System.Web.Configuration;
using System.Web.Mvc;
using System.Web.Routing;
using Mobile.Infrastructure;
using System.Web.WebPages;

namespace Mobile {
    public class MvcApplication : System.Web.HttpApplication {
        protected void Application_Start() {
            AreaRegistration.RegisterAllAreas();
            RouteConfig.RegisterRoutes(RouteTable.Routes);

            //HttpCapabilitiesBase.BrowserCapabilitiesProvider
            //      = new KindleCapabilities();

            DisplayModeProvider.Instance.Modes.Insert(0,
                new DefaultDisplayMode("Safari") {
                    ContextCondition = (ctx => ctx.Request.Browser.IsBrowser("Safari"))
            });
        }
    }
}
```

The support for display modes is built into the view engine, which is why the important classes are in the System.Web.WebPages namespace. The static DisplayModeProvider.Instance.Modes property returns a collection of objects that implement the IDisplayMode interface. Rather than work directly with this interface, it is easier to use the DefaultDisplayMode class, which takes a constructor argument that will be used to look for views and defines the ContextCondition property that is used to match requests.

The ContextCondition property is set using a lambda expression that receives an HttpContext object and returns true if the request matches the display mode condition. In the example, my condition is that the IsBrowser method matches the Safari browser. I used Safari as the constructor argument as well, and this means that when the ContextCondition expression returns true, the display mode will append Safari to the view name specified by the action method or HTML helper. For example, when I specify the Programmers view and the request is from the Safari browser, the display mode will instead cause the view engine to look for a Programmers.Safari view. If no such view exists, then the one originally specified will be used.

The collection of IDisplayMode implementation objects is applied in sequence, which is why I used the Insert method to place my display mode at the start of the list. There is a built-in display mode that uses the IsMobileDevice property and locates views that contain Mobile in the name, such as Programmers.Mobile.cshtml. You can use this view without any configuration, but you should be cautious about the broad range of devices that this display mode will be applied to if you use it.

In Listing 7-19, you can see how I removed the ternary statement from the Index.cshtml view so that the display mode in Listing 7-17 is responsible for selecting the view automatically.

Listing 7-19. Updating the Index.cshtml File to Rely on Display Modes

```
@using Mobile.Models
@model Programmer[]
@{
    Layout = null;
}
<!DOCTYPE html>
<html>
<head>
    <meta name="viewport" content="width=device-width" />
    <title>Mobile Devices</title>
    <link href="~/Content/bootstrap.min.css" rel="stylesheet" />
    <link href="~/Content/bootstrap-theme.min.css" rel="stylesheet" />
    <style>
        body { padding-top: 10px; }
    </style>
</head>
<body>
    <div class="alert alert-success">
        This is the /Views/Home/Index.cshtml view
    </div>
    <div class="panel panel-primary">
        <div class="panel-heading">Programmers</div>
        @Html.Partial("Programmers", Model)
    </div>
</body>
</html>
```

The Programmers partial view is always specified, and the display mode takes care of looking for the Programmers.Safari view when it is required. Display modes make working with device capabilities easy and consistent throughout an application, especially since they will fall back to using the default views when the special view isn't available.

Summary

In this chapter I explained the importance of device capabilities in supporting a wide range of browsers and devices. I demonstrated how to get capabilities data and how to extend the built-in data with custom browser files, providers, and third-party data. I showed you how to adapt an application to the capabilities of a client, directly using Razor and indirectly using partial views, HTML helpers, and, ultimately, display modes. In the next chapter, I show you can trace requests to get insight into how your application behaves.

CHAPTER 8

Tracing Requests

There will come a point where your web application doesn't behave the way you expect. Some problems manifest themselves in an obvious way—such as unexpected HTML content—and you need to figure out what goes wrong. Other problems are more complex and insubstantial, and you may have to dig deep into the application just to figure out what's happening, let alone apply a fix.

The Visual Studio debugger is useful for finding the first kind of problem, which is usually caused by the way that single requests are processed. The other kind—the more elusive problem—is often caused by interactions *between* requests, or deep configuration issues that cause problems only periodically. To find and resolve problems that span requests, you need to start building up a picture about the way that an application behaves over time. In this chapter, I'll show you different techniques for gaining insight into an application. Table 8-1 summarizes this chapter.

Table 8-1. *Chapter Summary*

Problem	Solution	Listing
Log details of requests.	Respond to the `LogRequest` event.	1–2
Combine logging information with additional details about the application and server.	Use the request tracing feature.	3–6
Generate additional information about requests.	Install the Glimpse package.	7

Preparing the Example Project

For this chapter I need a simple web application to inspect and monitor, so I am going to continue to use the Mobile project I created in Chapter 7 when I demonstrated how to detect and respond to device capabilities. No changes to the project are required.

Logging Requests

The simplest way to get insights into an application is to create a log of each request. In this section I explain how the ASP.NET request life cycle accommodates logging and show you how to capture logging information. Table 8-2 puts logging requests into context.

Table 8-2. Putting Request Logging in Context

Question	Answer
What is it?	Request logging is the process of capturing information about each request that ASP.NET receives and processes.
Why should I care?	Logging is the first step in understanding how your application behaves across multiple requests, which provides important information when tracking down complex problems.
How is it used by the MVC framework?	The MVC framework does not use the logging features.

Responding to the Logging Events

The ASP.NET request life cycle includes two events that are specifically related to the logging of requests: `LogRequest` and `PostLogRequest`. The first event is a signal to any logging functionality you have added to the application that the request has been processed and the content is about to be sent to the client. This is the perfect time to log details of the request and the way that it has been handled because there will be no further changes to the state of the request context objects. The `PostLogRequest` event is less useful, but it provides a signal that all of the handlers for the `LogRequest` event have been triggered.

■ **Tip** The `LogRequest` and `PostLogRequest` events are triggered even when the normal flow of events is interrupted by an unhandled exception and the `Error` event. See Chapter 6 for details of the error event flow.

To demonstrate custom logging, I added a class file called `LogModule.cs` to the `Infrastructure` folder and used it to define the module shown in Listing 8-1.

Listing 8-1. The Contents of the LogModule.cs File

```
using System;
using System.Diagnostics;
using System.IO;
using System.Web;

namespace Mobile.Infrastructure {
    public class LogModule : IHttpModule {
        private static int sharedCounter = 0;
        private int requestCounter;

        private static object lockObject = new object();
        private Exception requestException = null;

        public void Init(HttpApplication app) {
            app.BeginRequest += (src, args) => {
                requestCounter = ++sharedCounter;
            };
```

```
            app.Error += (src, args) => {
                requestException = HttpContext.Current.Error;
            };
            app.LogRequest += (src, args) => WriteLogMessage(HttpContext.Current);
        }

        private void WriteLogMessage(HttpContext ctx) {
            StringWriter sr = new StringWriter();
            sr.WriteLine("--------------");
            sr.WriteLine("Request: {0} for {1}", requestCounter, ctx.Request.RawUrl);
            if (ctx.Handler != null) {
                sr.WriteLine("Handler: {0}", ctx.Handler.GetType());
            }
            sr.WriteLine("Status Code: {0}, Message: {1}", ctx.Response.StatusCode,
                ctx.Response.StatusDescription);
            sr.WriteLine("Elapsed Time: {0} ms",
                DateTime.Now.Subtract(ctx.Timestamp).Milliseconds);
            if (requestException != null) {
                sr.WriteLine("Error: {0}", requestException.GetType());
            }
            lock (lockObject) {
                Debug.Write(sr.ToString());
            }
        }

        public void Dispose() {
            // do nothing
        }
    }
}
```

This module provides brief summaries of the requests that are received by the application to the Visual Studio Output window. This is the kind of logging that I find useful when I suspect there are inadvertent interactions between requests (through poorly protected shared data, a topic I describe in Chapter 10) or when I think that some requests for the same URL are taking too long to complete (which is usually caused by queuing for access to a shared resource somewhere in the application—often an external resource such as a database).

The request summary contains information about the order in which the request was received, the amount of time it took to process, the name of the handler class used to generate the content, the status code and message that will be sent to the client, and whether an unhandled exception was encountered.

There is nothing especially complex about this module, but there are two aspects of this kind of logging that require caution. First, it is important to remember that ASP.NET can process multiple concurrent requests, which means that synchronization is required to protect access to shared resources. In the example, I use the `lock` keyword to ensure that only one instance of my module will call the `System.Diagnostics.Debug.Write` method. Without this, requests that overlapped would cause the output from the module to be interleaved and rendered unreadable.

Second, any logging will slow down the application, especially when synchronization is required. There is always an overhead associated with logging because there are additional classes to create and C# statements to execute, but once synchronization is required, the problem can become more profound and choke points can form in the application where multiple requests have to queue up to gain exclusive access to a resource (such as the `Debug.Write` method in the example).

These aspects of logging rarely cause serious issues during the development phase of a web application because only the developer is making requests and there are not enough of them to highlight throughput problems—but in load testing and production environments, logging code can cause serious problems. Always minimize the amount of synchronization required and remember to disable unnecessary modules before you test and deploy the application. If the problem you are looking for is caused by an interaction between requests, the additional work and synchronization associated with logging can slow down and re-sequence request processing just enough to hide the problem, creating the dreaded "cannot reproduce" bug summary.

Returning to my example module, Listing 8-2 shows the additions I made to the `Web.config` file to register it with ASP.NET.

Listing 8-2. Registering the Module in the Web.config File

```
<?xml version="1.0" encoding="utf-8"?>
<configuration>
  <appSettings>
    <add key="webpages:Version" value="3.0.0.0" />
    <add key="webpages:Enabled" value="false" />
     <add key="ClientValidationEnabled" value="true" />
    <add key="UnobtrusiveJavaScriptEnabled" value="true" />
  </appSettings>
  <system.web>
    <compilation debug="true" targetFramework="4.5.1" />
    <httpRuntime targetFramework="4.5.1" />
  </system.web>
  <system.webServer>
    <modules>
      <add name="Log" type="Mobile.Infrastructure.LogModule"/>
    </modules>
  </system.webServer>
</configuration>
```

Simply start the application to test the logging module. The Visual Studio Output window will show messages similar to the following, although the exact output will depend on files your browser has cached from previous requests:

```
--------------
Request: 1 for /
Handler: System.Web.Mvc.MvcHandler
Status Code: 200, Message: OK
Elapsed Time: 2 ms
--------------
Request: 2 for /Content/bootstrap.min.css
Status Code: 200, Message: OK
Elapsed Time: 3 ms
--------------
Request: 3 for /Content/bootstrap-theme.min.css
Status Code: 200, Message: OK
Elapsed Time: 2 ms
```

Tracing Requests

ASP.NET includes a little used but incredibly helpful request tracing feature that provides information about the requests that an application receives. The tracing feature pre-dates the MVC framework, and there are some features that don't work outside of Web Forms applications, but there is still enough value in performing tracing that it should be a key part of your diagnostic toolkit. In the sections that follow, I'll show you how to enable, use, and customize the tracing process. Table 8-3 puts tracing requests into context.

Table 8-3. *Putting Request Tracing in Context*

Question	Answer
What is it?	Request tracing allows you to combine custom logging with the automatic capture of information about ASP.NET and the state of the application.
Why should I care?	Tracing means you can simplify your logging code and rely on ASP.NET to capture detailed information about requests.
How is it used by the MVC framework?	The MVC framework does not use the tracing features.

Enabling Request Tracing

Tracing is configured through the `Web.config` file, and in Listing 8-3 you can see the additions I made to set up request tracing.

Listing 8-3. Enabling Request Tracing in the Web.config File

```
<?xml version="1.0" encoding="utf-8"?>
<configuration>
  <appSettings>
    <add key="webpages:Version" value="3.0.0.0" />
    <add key="webpages:Enabled" value="false" />
     <add key="ClientValidationEnabled" value="true" />
    <add key="UnobtrusiveJavaScriptEnabled" value="true" />
  </appSettings>
  <system.web>
    <compilation debug="true" targetFramework="4.5.1" />
    <httpRuntime targetFramework="4.5.1" />
    <trace enabled="true" requestLimit="50" />
  </system.web>
  <system.webServer>
    <modules>
      <add name="Log" type="Mobile.Infrastructure.LogModule"/>
    </modules>
  </system.webServer>
</configuration>
```

The `trace` element is defined in the `system.web` section and controls the tracing feature. There are several attributes that can be used to fine-tune the way that tracing is performed, as described in Table 8-4. The configuration I have defined in the listing is a good starting point for most projects.

Table 8-4. The Attributes Defined by the trace Element

Name	Description
`enabled`	When set to `true`, the request tracing feature is enabled.
`localOnly`	When set to `true`, the trace viewer (which I describe in the next section) is accessible only when requested from the local machine. IIS Express, which is used to run ASP.ET applications during development, accepts only local requests by default, so enabling this option has no effect until the application is deployed.
`mostRecent`	Trace information is discarded when the number of requests received by the application exceeds the value of the `requestLimit` attribute. Setting this attribute to `true` discards the oldest requests, while `false` (the default value) discards newer requests.
`requestLimit`	Specifies the number of request traces that will be stored for viewing. The default value is 10.
`writeToDiagnosticsTrace`	When set to `true`, trace messages are written to the `System.Diagnostics.Trace` class. See the "Adding Custom Trace Messages" and the "Using Adding Trace Messages to Glimpse" sections for details.

■ **Tip** The `trace` element defines additional attributes beyond the ones I described in the table, but they either work only with Web Forms applications or are not especially useful in an MVC framework application.

View Request Traces

The request trace information is available through the special `/trace.axd` URL. To see the way that tracing works, start the application, request the `/Home/Browser` and `/Home/Index` URLs (the only two supported by the example application), and then request `/trace.axd`. You will see a summary of the requests received by the application, as shown by Figure 8-1.

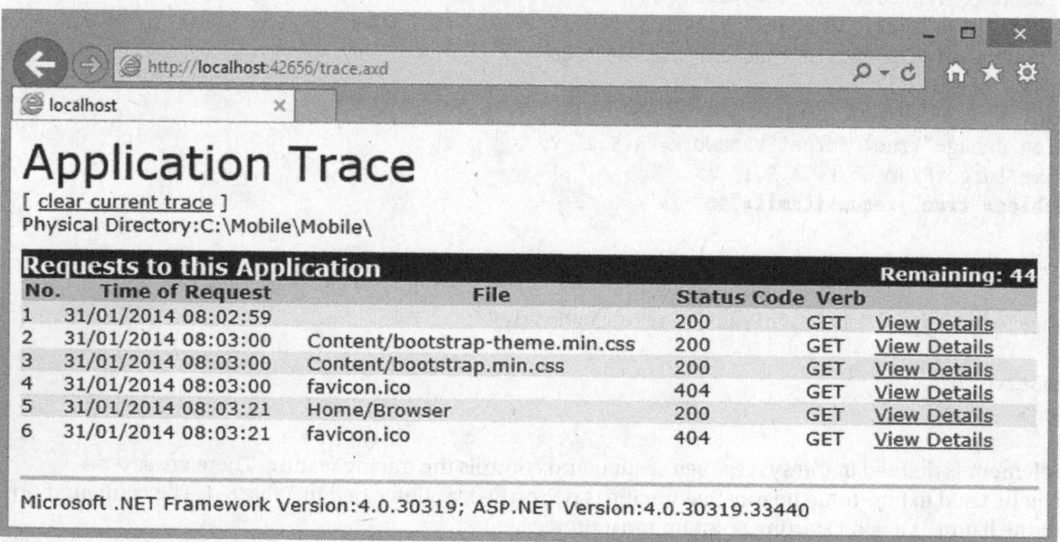

Figure 8-1. The summary of request traces

The list of requests that you see will, naturally, depend on which URLs you requested and which files your browser has cached. The summary shows the sequence in which requests have arrived, the URL that they requested (which is in the `File` column, a remnant from Web Forms), the request HTTP method, and the status code that was sent back to the client.

■ **Tip** Notice that some of the requests shown in the trace summary are for `favicon.ico`, which is the browser's attempt to obtain a favorite icon for the application. Wikipedia has a good summary of favorite icons and their use: `http://en.wikipedia.org/wiki/Favicon`.

You can inspect individual requests by clicking one of the View Details links. This displays the detailed trace data, as shown in Figure 8-2.

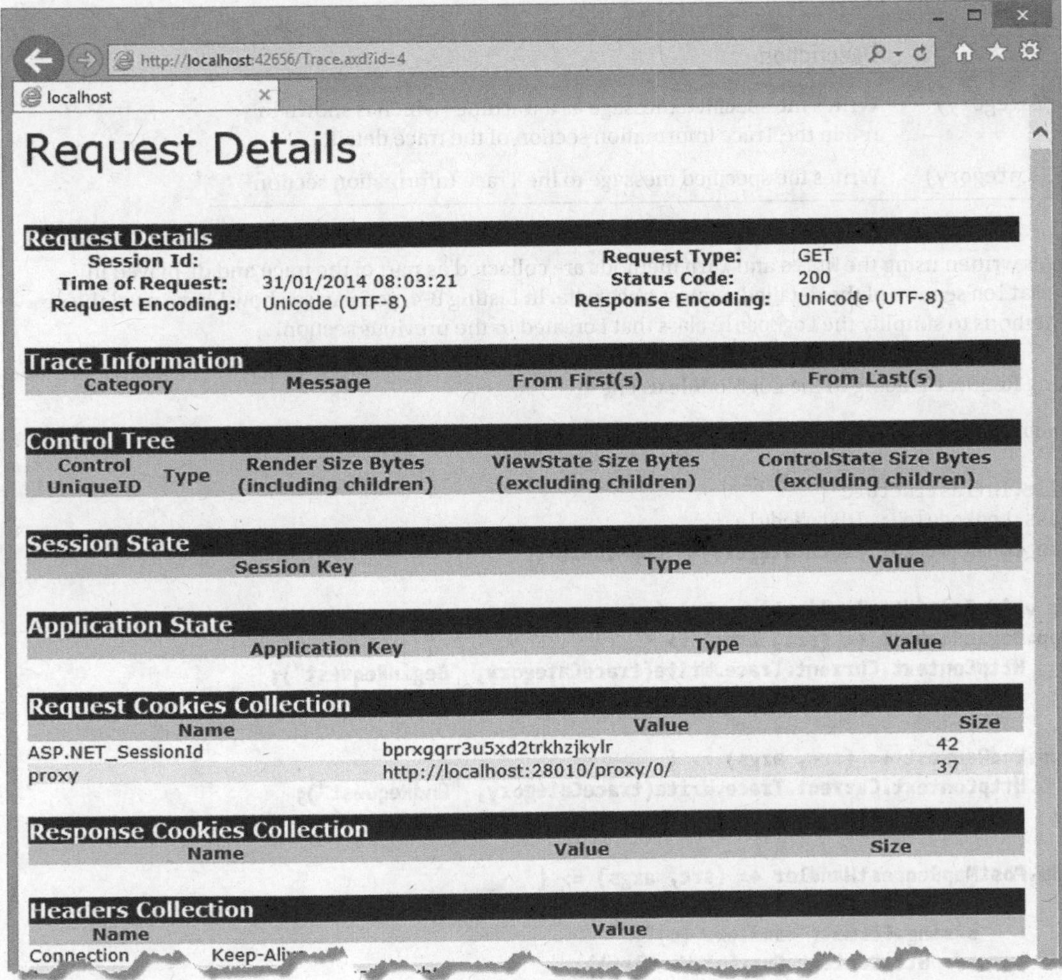

Figure 8-2. Detailed trace data

I have shown only part of the trace detail because there is so much information, covering every aspect of the request. Some sections, such as Session State and Application State, will be empty because they relate to features that I don't describe until Part 3. But even so, you can see a complete set of the request headers, cookies, and details of form and query string data. There are some holdovers from Web Forms, such as the Control Tree section, that has no bearing on an MVC framework, but most of the data is pertinent and can be helpful in understanding how multiple requests relate to one another.

Adding Custom Trace Messages

The default trace data can be useful, but it is generic to all applications and may not give you the insights that you are looking for. Fortunately, you can tailor the trace data by adding custom trace messages to your application, which is done through the `HttpContext.Trace` property, which returns a `TraceContext` object. The `TraceContext` class defines the methods shown in Table 8-5.

Table 8-5. *The Methods Defined by the TraceContext Class*

Name	Description
`Warn(message, category)`	Writes the specified message as a warning (which is shown in red in the Trace Information section of the trace detail)
`Write(message, category)`	Writes the specified message to the Trace Information section

The messages written using the `Write` and `Warn` methods are collected as part of the trace and displayed in the `Trace Information` section of the detailed request trace data. In Listing 8-4, you can see how I have used the `TraceContext` methods to simplify the `LogModule` class that I created in the previous section.

Listing 8-4. Using Request Tracing in the LogModule.cs File

```
using System.Web;

namespace Mobile.Infrastructure {
    public class LogModule : IHttpModule {
        private const string traceCategory = "LogModule";

        public void Init(HttpApplication app) {
            app.BeginRequest += (src, args) => {
                HttpContext.Current.Trace.Write(traceCategory, "BeginRequest");
            };

            app.EndRequest += (src, args) => {
                HttpContext.Current.Trace.Write(traceCategory, "EndRequest");
            };

            app.PostMapRequestHandler += (src, args) => {
                HttpContext.Current.Trace.Write(traceCategory,
                    string.Format("Handler: {0}",
                        HttpContext.Current.Handler));
            };
```

```
        app.Error += (src, args) => {
            HttpContext.Current.Trace.Warn(traceCategory, string.Format("Error: {0}",
                HttpContext.Current.Error.GetType().Name));
        };
    }

    public void Dispose() {
        // do nothing
    }
  }
}
```

My module has become simpler because I don't have to worry about working out relative timings or synchronizing access to shared data and resources—these tasks become the responsibility of the request tracing system. And, of course, generating trace messages isn't just for modules; you can instrument any part of the application, including the controllers and views. In Listing 8-5, you can see how I have added tracing to the Home controller.

Listing 8-5. Adding Tracing in the HomeController.cs File

```
using System.Web.Mvc;
using Mobile.Models;

namespace Mobile.Controllers {

    public class HomeController : Controller {

        private Programmer[] progs = {
            new Programmer("Alice", "Smith", "Lead Developer", "Paris", "France", "C#"),
            new Programmer("Joe", "Dunston", "Developer", "London", "UK", "Java"),
            new Programmer("Peter", "Jones", "Developer", "Chicago", "USA", "C#"),
            new Programmer("Murray", "Woods", "Jnr Developer", "Boston", "USA", "C#")
        };

        public ActionResult Index() {
            HttpContext.Trace.Write("HomeController", "Index Method Started");
            HttpContext.Trace.Write("HomeController",
                string.Format("There are {0} programmers", progs.Length));
            ActionResult result = View(progs);
            HttpContext.Trace.Write("HomeController", "Index Method Completed");
            return result;
        }

        public ActionResult Browser() {
            return View();
        }
    }
}
```

My example application isn't complex enough to need any real tracing, so I have added messages to report when the Index action method is invoked, the number of data items, and when the method has completed and only needs to return the result. (I have assigned the ActionResult returned from calling the View menu to a local variable so that I can insert a trace method between creating the result and returning it.)

It is also possible to add trace statements to views, although they make the views harder to read. As a consequence, I tend to limit my use of trace statements in views to just those I need to track down a complex layout problem (sadly, these are usually problems of the "duh" variety where I have mistyped a partial view name but can't see the error despite looking at the problem for quite a while). In Listing 8-6, you can see how I added a trace statement that reports on each data item as it is rendered.

■ **Tip** I have added the trace statement to the Programmers.cshtml partial view but not Programmer.Safari.cshtml. If you still have your browser configured to emulate the iPhone from the previous chapter, now is the time to return to using Internet Explorer or to disable Chrome device emulation.

Listing 8-6. Adding Trace Statements to the Programmers.cshtml File

```
@using Mobile.Models
@model Programmer[]

<table class="table table-striped">
    <tr>
        <th>First Name</th>
        <th class="hidden-xs">Last Name</th>
        <th class="hidden-xs">Title</th>
        <th>City</th>
        <th class="hidden-xs">Country</th>
        <th>Language</th>
    </tr>
    @foreach (Programmer prog in Model) {
        Context.Trace.Write("Programmers View",
            string.Format("Processing {0} {1}",
              prog.FirstName, prog.LastName));
        <tr>
            <td>@prog.FirstName</td>
            <td class="hidden-xs">@prog.LastName</td>
            <td class="hidden-xs">@prog.Title</td>
            <td>@prog.City</td>
            <td class="hidden-xs">@prog.Country</td>
            <td>@prog.Language</td>
        </tr>
    }
</table>
```

I don't like putting C# statements in view files, which is another reason why I use trace statements sparingly in views.

■ **Tip** I didn't need to prefix the call to the `Context.Trace.Write` method with an @ character in the listing because the statement appears inside the `foreach` block.

To see the custom trace messages, start the application, request the `/Home/Index` URL, and then request `/trace.axd`. Select the request for `/Home/Index`, and you will see the trace messages in the `Trace Information` section of the output, as shown in Figure 8-3.

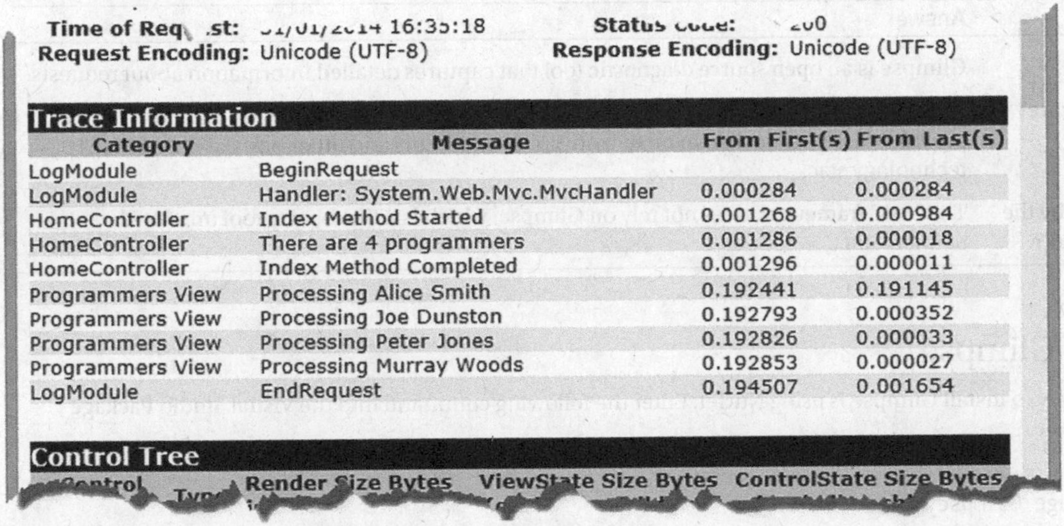

Time of Request: 31/01/2014 16:35:18 **Status Code:** 200
Request Encoding: Unicode (UTF-8) **Response Encoding:** Unicode (UTF-8)

Trace Information

Category	Message	From First(s)	From Last(s)
LogModule	BeginRequest		
LogModule	Handler: System.Web.Mvc.MvcHandler	0.000284	0.000284
HomeController	Index Method Started	0.001268	0.000984
HomeController	There are 4 programmers	0.001286	0.000018
HomeController	Index Method Completed	0.001296	0.000011
Programmers View	Processing Alice Smith	0.192441	0.191145
Programmers View	Processing Joe Dunston	0.192793	0.000352
Programmers View	Processing Peter Jones	0.192826	0.000033
Programmers View	Processing Murray Woods	0.192853	0.000027
LogModule	EndRequest	0.194507	0.001654

Control Tree

Control	Type	Render Size Bytes	ViewState Size Bytes	ControlState Size Bytes

Figure 8-3. Adding custom trace messages

The category information shows the flow of the request through the ASP.NET platform and the MVC framework, and individual messages provide detailed insights. The two columns of numbers provide timing information, which is always helpful in finding performance bottlenecks. The From First column shows the elapsed time since the first trace message, and the From Last column shows the elapsed time since the previous trace message. All times are expressed in seconds, and using the data in the figure, I can see that the elapsed time from the `BeginRequest` to the `EndRequest` method was 0.19 seconds and that most of that time passed from the point at which the action method returned its result, and I can see when the view rendering began.

■ **Tip** The timing information in the figure was for the first request after I started the application. There is a lot of startup preparation that is performed only when the first request is received, including preparing the routing system, generating a list of its controller classes, and compiling the view files into C# classes. This work isn't done for subsequent requests, which is why the elapsed time for the second request to the same URL took only 0.004 seconds on my development PC.

Using Glimpse

I use the custom tracing and logging approaches when I need to find a specific problem, but I use a tool called Glimpse when I don't know where to start looking or when I need to look at the overall behavior of the application. Glimpse is an open source diagnostics package that builds on the ASP.NET logging and tracing features and adds a lot of useful insight into how requests are handled within an application. In the sections that follow, I'll show you how to install and use Glimpse and explain why I find it so useful. Table 8-6 puts Glimpse into context.

Table 8-6. *Putting Glimpse in Context*

Question	Answer
What is it?	Glimpse is an open source diagnostic tool that captures detailed information about requests.
Why should I care?	Glimpse provides a level of detail that is beyond what the built-in tracing feature provides and is extensible to other software components and other parts of the ASP.NET technology stack.
How is it used by the MVC framework?	The MVC framework does not rely on Glimpse, which is a third-party tool unrelated to Microsoft.

Installing Glimpse

The simplest way to install Glimpse is using NuGet. Enter the following command into the Visual Studio Package Manager Console:

```
Install-Package Glimpse.MVC5
```

When you hit Enter, NuGet will download and install the Glimpse packages that support MVC framework applications. The package I have installed is for MVC5, but there are also packages for earlier MVC releases.

Once the installation is complete, start the application and navigate to the `/Glimpse.axd` URL. You will see the Glimpse configuration page, as shown in Figure 8-4.

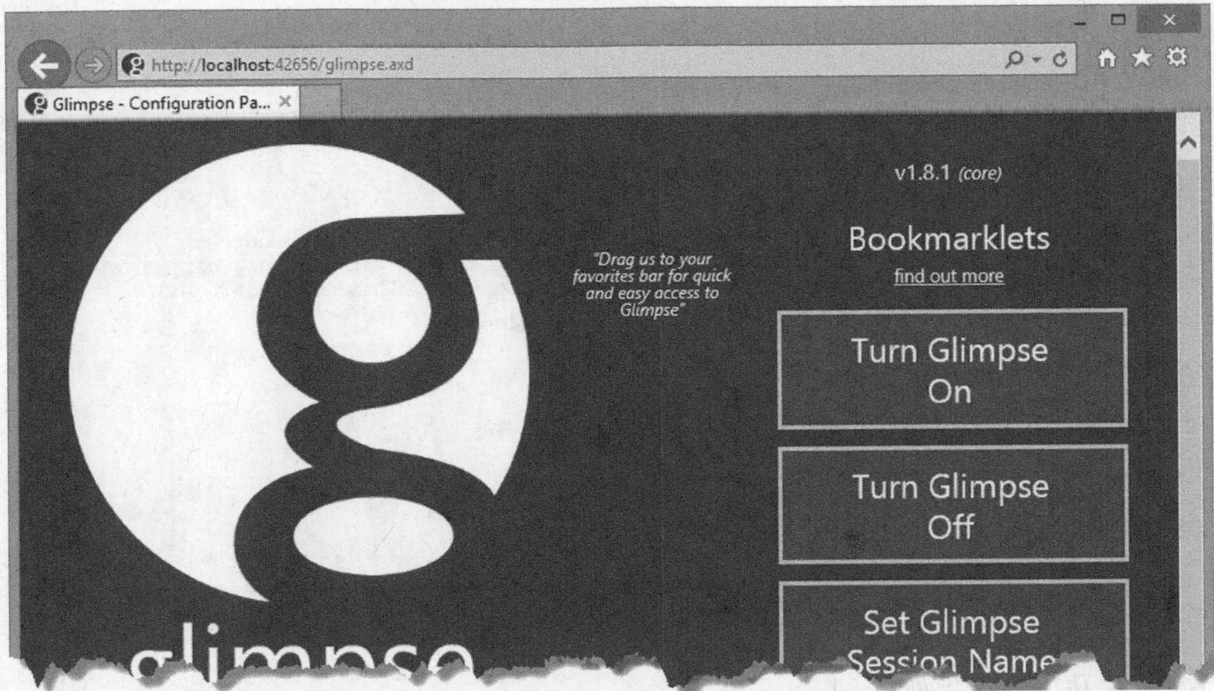

Figure 8-4. Configuring Glimpse

■ **Tip** Glimpse has a large catalog of extensions and packages that can be used to extend monitoring to other software components, including Entity Framework, and other parts of the ASP.NET technology stack, such as SignalR. See `http://getglimpse.com` for details.

Click the Turn Glimpse On button to enable Glimpse diagnostics. The `/glimpse.axd` page is also used to configure Glimpse, but the default configuration is suitable for most projects, and I don't need to make any configuration changes for this chapter.

Using Glimpse

Using Glimpse is as simple as requesting a URL from your application. Glimpse inserts a toolbar at the bottom of the screen that summarizes how the request has been handled, as shown in Figure 8-5.

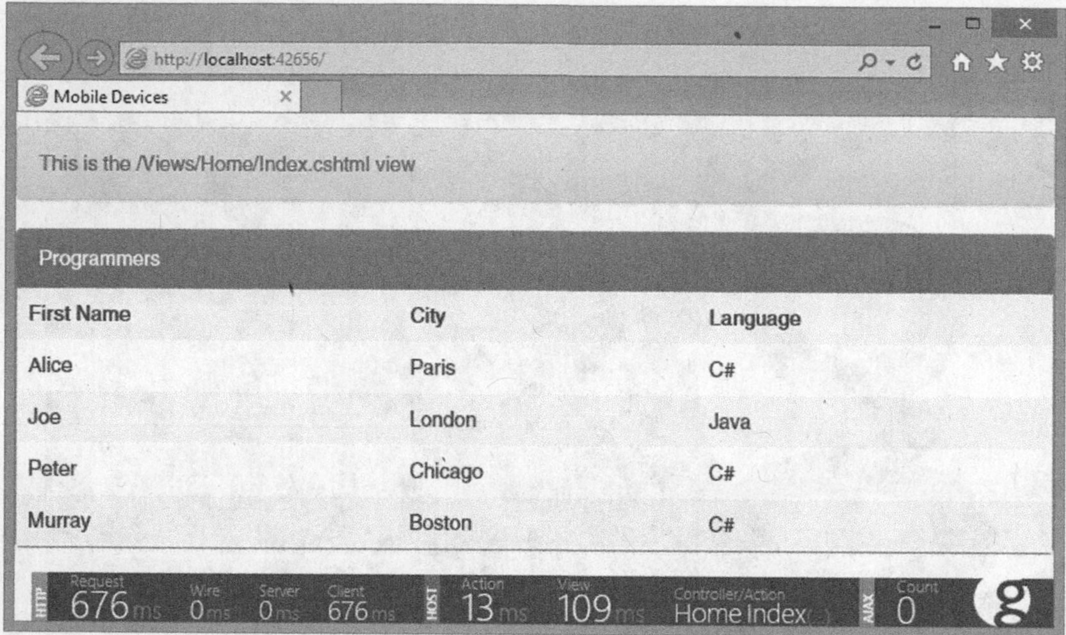

Figure 8-5. *The Glimpse toolbar*

It can be hard to make out the details of the toolbar from Figure 8-5, so I have increased the scale and broken the bar into sections in Figure 8-6 so you can see the details.

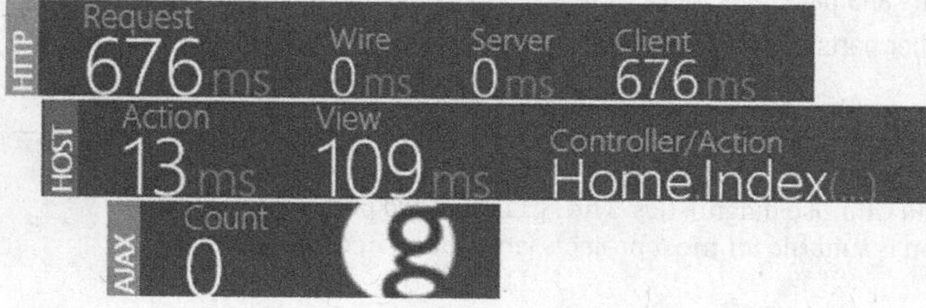

Figure 8-6. *A closer look at the Glimpse toolbar*

The summary is broken down into three sections. The HTTP section reports on the total amount of time elapsed from the moment that the request was started until the moment when the response was rendered and displayed to the user. The HOST section provides information about how long the action targeted by the request took to execute and how much time it took for the view be rendered. The final section, AJAX, summarizes the Ajax requests made by the content received from the server.

You can get more detailed information by moving the mouse over a section. Figure 8-7 shows the details of the HOST section, which is the one that you will most often be interested in when working with the ASP.NET platform.

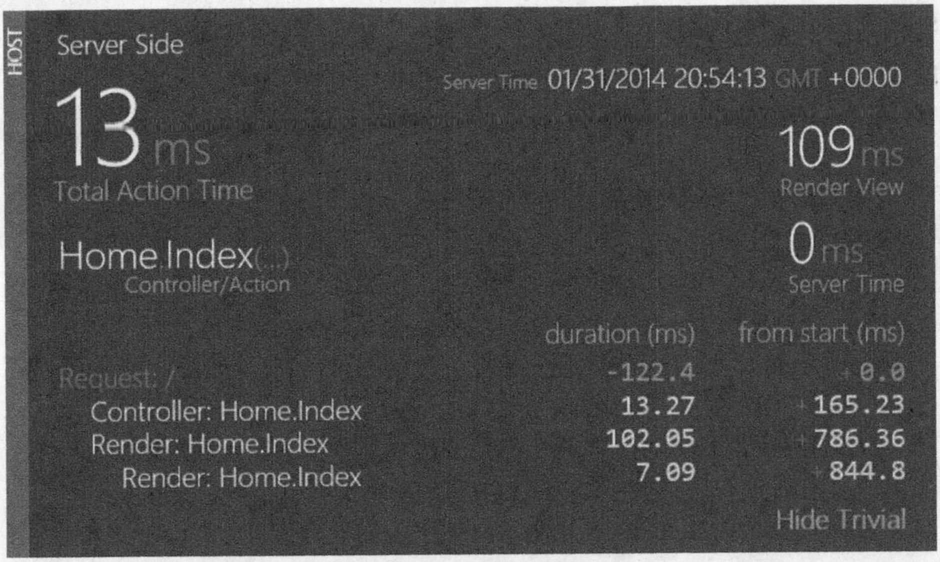

Figure 8-7. A more detailed view of the HOST section

Glimpse provides a lot more detail about requests when you click the G icon at the right edge of the toolbar. This opens a tabbed window that details every aspect of the request and how it was handled by the applications. There are tabs that detail the request, the configuration and environment of the server, state data (which I describe in Chapter 10), the routes that matched the request and much more. One of the most useful tabs is called Timeline, and it provides performance information about the way that the request was processed, as illustrated by Figure 8-8.

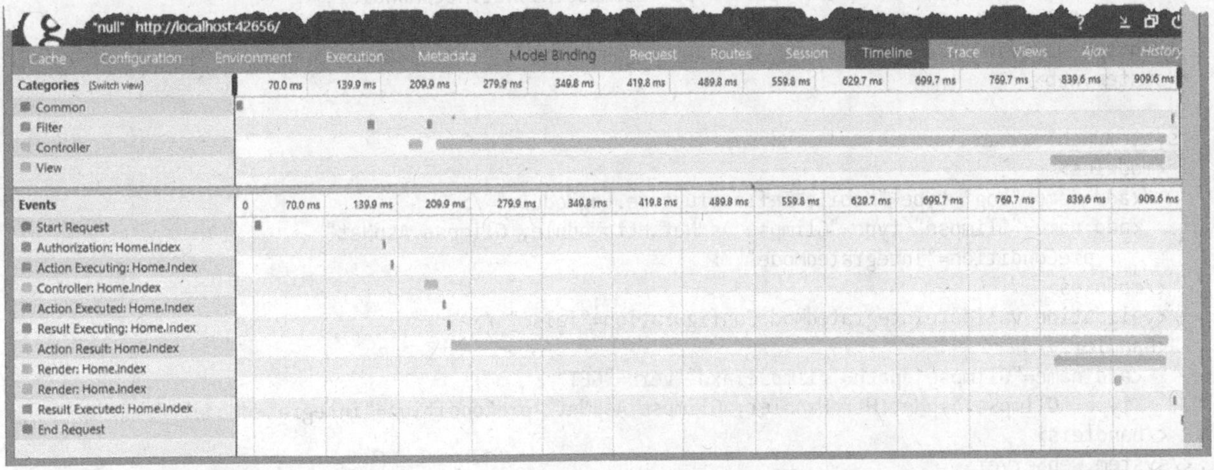

Figure 8-8. The Glimpse Timeline tab

The Timeline tab shows the amount of time the request spent in the ASP.NET platform and the amount of time the MVC framework spent executing controllers, filters, and views. There is also an end-to-end view that shows the flow of the request through the different components of the application, which can help identify those actions or views that are taking too long to complete. I am only touching on the surface of the information provided by Glimpse, but you can see that there is a lot of detail available, and I recommend that you take the time to explore it fully.

Adding Trace Messages to Glimpse

One of the tabs in the Glimpse detail view is Trace, but it doesn't capture the messages written through the `HttpContext.Trace` object unless you set `writeToDiagnosticsTrace` to `true` on the trace element in the `Web.config` file, as shown in Listing 8-7.

Listing 8-7. Forwarding Trace Messages So They Can Be Read by Glimpse

```
<?xml version="1.0" encoding="utf-8"?>
<configuration>
  <configSections>
    <section name="glimpse" type="Glimpse.Core.Configuration.Section, Glimpse.Core" />
  </configSections>

  <appSettings>
    <add key="webpages:Version" value="3.0.0.0" />
    <add key="webpages:Enabled" value="false" />
     <add key="ClientValidationEnabled" value="true" />
    <add key="UnobtrusiveJavaScriptEnabled" value="true" />
  </appSettings>
  <system.web>
    <compilation debug="true" targetFramework="4.5.1" />
    <httpRuntime targetFramework="4.5.1" />
    <trace enabled="true" requestLimit="50" writeToDiagnosticsTrace="true"/>
    <httpModules>
      <add name="Glimpse" type="Glimpse.AspNet.HttpModule, Glimpse.AspNet" />
    </httpModules>
    <httpHandlers>
      <add path="glimpse.axd" verb="GET" type="Glimpse.AspNet.HttpHandler,
          Glimpse.AspNet" />
    </httpHandlers>
  </system.web>

  <system.webServer>
    <modules>
      <add name="Log" type="Mobile.Infrastructure.LogModule" />
      <add name="Glimpse" type="Glimpse.AspNet.HttpModule, Glimpse.AspNet"
          preCondition="integratedMode" />
    </modules>
    <validation validateIntegratedModeConfiguration="false" />
    <handlers>
      <add name="Glimpse" path="glimpse.axd" verb="GET"
       type="Glimpse.AspNet.HttpHandler, Glimpse.AspNet" preCondition="integratedMode" />
    </handlers>
  </system.webServer>

  <glimpse defaultRuntimePolicy="On" endpointBaseUri="~/Glimpse.axd"></glimpse>
</configuration>
```

The additions to the `Web.config` file were added when Glimpse was installed. If you restart the application, open the Glimpse tabbed window, and move to the Trace tab, you will see the trace messages from the module, as shown in Figure 8-9.

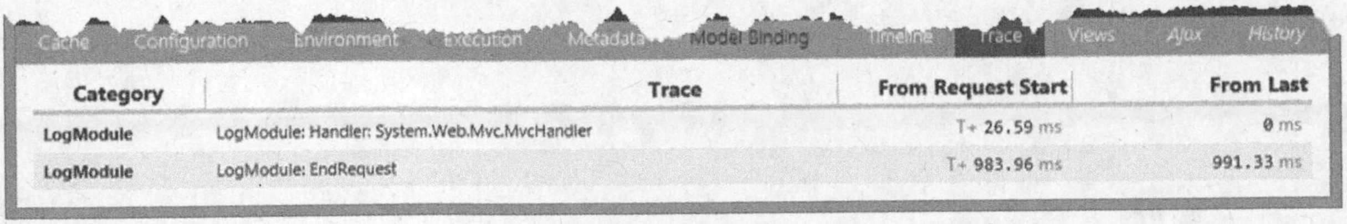
Cache
Configuration
Environment
Execution
Metadata
Model Binding
Timeline
Trace
Views
Ajax
History
Category
Trace
From Request Start
From Last
LogModule
LogModule: Handler: System.Web.Mvc.MvcHandler
T+ 26.59 ms
0 ms
LogModule
LogModule: EndRequest
T+ 983.96 ms
991.33 ms

Figure 8-9. *Trace information displayed by Glimpse*

Summary

In this chapter I showed you the facilities that ASP.NET provides for logging and tracing requests. I showed you how to handle the `LogRequest` method in the request life cycle and explained the use of the `TraceContext` class, instances of which are available through the `HttpContext.Trace` property. I demonstrated the built-in ASP.NET support for viewing trace information and finished the chapter by introducing Glimpse, which is an excellent open source diagnostics tool. In Part 3, I show you how ASP.NET builds on the foundation of handling features that described in this part of the book to provide useful services to web application developers.

PART 3

The ASP.NET Platform Services

CHAPTER 9

Configuration

The first service that the ASP.NET platform provides to applications is *configuration*. This may not seem like the most exciting topic, but the configuration feature is rich and flexible and helps avoid one of the pitfalls of complex software development: hard-coding behaviors into software components. As you will learn, the ASP.NET support for configuration can be adapted to suit all kinds of web applications and is worth taking the time to understand. Table 9-1 summarizes this chapter.

Table 9-1. *Chapter Summary*

Problem	Solution	Listing
Define simple configuration values.	Use application settings.	1–3
Read application settings.	Use the `WebConfigurationManager.AppSettings` property.	4–6
Define settings for connecting to remote services, such as databases.	Use connection strings.	7
Read connection strings.	Use the `WebConfigurationManager.ConnectionStrings` property.	8
Group related settings.	Define a configuration section.	9–12
Read configuration sections.	Use the `GetWebApplicationSection` method defined by the `WebConfigurationManager` class.	13, 19
Group a collection of similar settings together.	Define a collection configuration section.	14–18
Group sections together.	Define a collection section group.	20–21
Read section groups.	Use the `OpenWebConfiguration` method defined by the `WebConfigurationManager` class.	22
Override configuration settings.	Use the `location` element or create a folder-level configuration file.	23–27
Read the ASP.NET settings.	Use the handler classes in the `System.Configuration` namespace.	28

Preparing the Example Project

For this chapter I created a new project called ConfigFiles, following the same approach I used for earlier example applications. I used the Visual Studio ASP.NET Web Application template, selected the Empty option, and added the core MVC references. I'll be using Bootstrap again in this chapter, so enter the following command into the Package Manager Console:

```
Install-Package -version 3.0.3 bootstrap
```

I added a `Home` controller to the `Controllers` folder, the definition of which you can see in Listing 9-1. Throughout this chapter, I'll be displaying lists of configuration properties and their values, so the data that the `Index` action passes to the `View` method is a dictionary. So that I can test the application, I have defined some placeholder data in the controller.

Listing 9-1. The Contents of the HomeController.cs File

```
using System.Collections.Generic;
using System.Web.Mvc;

namespace ConfigFiles.Controllers {
    public class HomeController : Controller {

        public ActionResult Index() {
            Dictionary<string, string> configData = new Dictionary<string, string>();
            configData.Add("Placeholder Property", "Placeholder Value");
            return View(configData);
        }
    }
}
```

I created a view by right-clicking the `Index` action method in the code editor and selecting Add View from the pop-up menu. I called the view `Index.cshtml`, selected the Empty (without model) template, and unchecked all of the view option boxes. You can see the content I defined in the view in Listing 9-2.

Listing 9-2. The Contents of the Index.cshtml File

```
@model Dictionary<string, string>
@{ Layout = null; }
<!DOCTYPE html>
<html>
<head>
    <meta name="viewport" content="width=device-width" />
    <link href="~/Content/bootstrap.min.css" rel="stylesheet" />
    <link href="~/Content/bootstrap-theme.min.css" rel="stylesheet" />
    <style> body { padding-top: 10px; } </style>
    <title>Configuration</title>
</head>
<body class="container">
    <div class="panel panel-primary">
        <div class="panel-heading">Configuration Data</div>
        <table class="table table-striped">
```

```
        <thead>
            <tr><th>Property</th><th>Value</th></tr>
        </thead>
        <tbody>
            @foreach (string key in Model.Keys) {
                <tr><td>@key</td><td>@Model[key]</td></tr>
            }
        </tbody>
    </table>
  </div>
</body>
</html>
```

Start the application and navigate to the root URL or /Home/Index to see how the view is rendered, as shown in Figure 9-1.

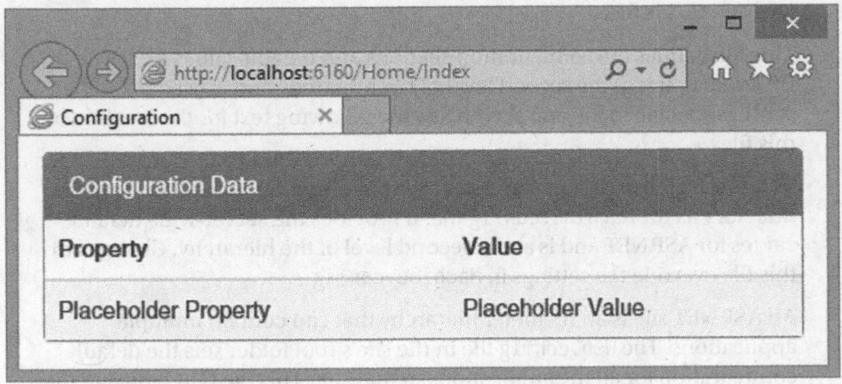

***Figure 9-1.** Testing the example application*

ASP.NET Configuration

Aside from a few standard additions to configure a database or enable debugging, most MVC framework developers don't give any thought to the Web.config file, which is a shame because it provides a useful set of features that configure ASP.NET *and* that can be consumed within application code. In the sections that follow, I describe how the Web.config file forms part of a larger configuration system and explain how you can use this system to control the behavior of your applications. Table 9-2 puts the ASP.NET configuration system into context.

***Table 9-2.** Putting the ASP.NET Configuration System in Context*

Question	Answer
What is it?	It's a flexible set of classes and files that control the behavior of the ASP.NET foundation and services, the MVC framework, and your web application code.
Why should I care?	Using the built-in configuration support is much easier than writing your own settings code, and there are some excellent features that ease application development.
How is it used by the MVC framework?	The MVC framework uses the configuration system extensively. The most visible use to the programmer is the web.config file in the Views folder, which is used to configure the Razor view engine.

Understanding the Configuration Hierarchy

Most MVC framework developers only need to edit the `Web.config` file in the top-level of the Visual Studio project, but this is just one of a hierarchy of configuration files that ASP.NET uses. When an application is started, ASP.NET starts at the top of the hierarchy and works its way down. Each level in the hierarchy has a slightly narrower scope, and the overall effect is to allow lower-level configuration files to override more general settings that have been previously defined. The application-level `Web.config` file—the one in the root folder of Visual Studio—is close to the bottom of the hierarchy and relies on dozens of settings that have been defined in higher-level files. Table 9-3 summarizes the configuration files and explains how they relate to one another.

Table 9-3. *The Hierarchy of Configuration Files*

Scope	Name	Description
Global	`Machine.config`	This is the top-level file in the hierarchy. Changes to this file affect every ASP.NET application running on the server. See the following text for the location of this file.
Global	`ApplicationHost.config`	This file defines the configuration sections and default values for IIS or IIS Express. It is at the second level of the hierarchy and is used to define settings specific to the app server. See the following text for the location of this file.
Global	`Web.config`	This is the global version of the `Web.config` file and is located in the same directory as the `Machine.config` file. It provides the server-wide default values for ASP.NET and is at the second level of the hierarchy. Changes to this file override the settings in `Machine.config`.
Site	`Web.config`	An ASP.NET site is an IIS folder hierarchy that can contain multiple applications. The `Web.config` file in the site's root folder sets the default configuration for all the applications in that site. This file is at level 3 in the hierarchy and is used to override settings in the global `Web.config` file.
App	`Web.config`	This is the application-level `Web.config` file found in the root folder of the application and is the one that developers most often use for configuration. It overrides the values specified in the site-level `Web.config`.
Folder	`location` elements	A `location` element in the app-level `Web.config` file specifies configuration settings for a URL specified by the `path` attribute. See the "Overriding Configuration Settings" section for details.
Folder	`Web.config`	This is a `Web.config` file added to a folder within the application and has the same effect as a `location` attribute in the app-level `Web.config` file. The MVC framework uses a `web.config` file in the `Views` folder to configure the view engine. See the "Overriding Configuration Settings" section for details.

■ **Tip** The MVC framework includes a file called `web.config` (with a lowercase `w`) in the `Views` folder. The file names are not case sensitive, and this is an example of a folder-level `Web.config` file as described in the table.

ASP.NET starts with the `Machine.config` file, which is at the top of the hierarchy to get the starting point for the configuration and then moves to the second-level of the hierarchy and processes the `ApplicationHost.config` and global `Web.config` files. New settings are added to form a *merged configuration,* and values for existing settings are replaced. This process continues down the hierarchy until the app-level `Web.config` file is reached, and elements are used to expand the merged configuration or replace existing configuration values. Finally, the `location` elements and the folder-level `Web.config` files are processed to create specific configurations for parts of the application. Figure 9-2 shows the hierarchy of files as they are processed.

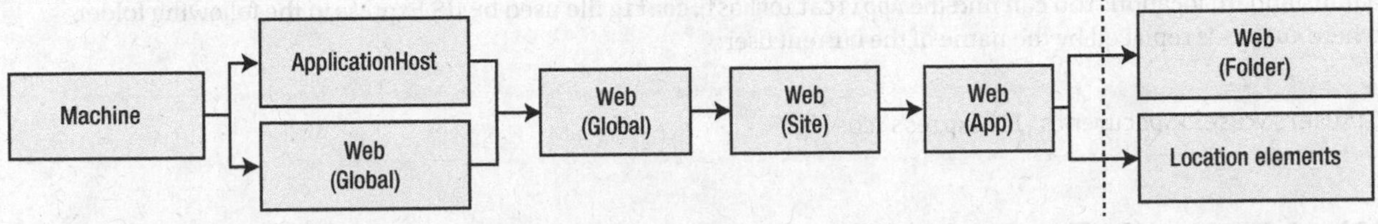

***Figure 9-2.** The hierarchy of ASP.NET configuration files*

■ **Tip** I have included the site-level `Web.config` file for completeness, but it is specific to IIS. IIS is still widely used, but there is a substantial shift toward cloud deployment and the use of other servers using the OWIN API. I recommend that you don't use IIS sites and that you install each application in isolation because it makes it easier to move between deployment models. Instead, use application-level `Web.config` files.

Although the configuration is spread throughout multiple files, the overall effect is a consistent configuration where settings are defined for every application at the global level and then progressively refined in the site, application, and folder-level files. This is why something as complex as an MVC framework application needs only a few lines of settings in the `Web.config` file: Hundreds of other settings are defined further up the hierarchy.

■ **Tip** If any of the files are missing, ASP.NET skips to the next level in the hierarchy. But, as you'll learn, the global files define the structure that later files use to define configuration settings as well as their default values.

One of the reasons that developers work with the application-level `Web.config` file is that the files higher up in the hierarchy cannot be edited, something that is almost always the case for hosting and cloud platforms and frequently true for IIS servers running in private data centers as well.

■ **Caution** The ASP.NET platform caches the configuration data after it processes the hierarchy of files to improve performance. However, the configuration files are monitored, and any changes cause the application to be restarted, which can cause any state data to be lost and interrupt service to users. For this reason, it is important you don't modify the configuration files for a production system while the application is running.

During development you will sometimes need to change the global configuration files to re-create the settings that you will encounter in production. You can find the Machine.config and global Web.config files in the following folder:

```
C:\Windows\Microsoft.NET\Framework\v4.0.30319\Config
```

You may have a slightly different path if you are using a later version of .NET or have installed Windows into a nonstandard location. You can find the ApplicationHost.config file used by IIS Express in the following folder, where <user> is replaced by the name of the current user:

```
C:\Users\<user>\Documents\IISExpress\config
```

Working with Basic Configuration Data

The configuration file system allows you to define settings for your application in different ways ranging from simple and generic key-value pairs to complex custom settings that are completely tailored to the needs of one application. In this section, I'll show you how to define different kinds of basic setting and explain how you access them programmatically. After all, there is no point in being able to define a configuration if you can't read it at runtime. Table 9-4 puts basic configuration data into context.

Table 9-4. *Putting the Basic ASP.NET Configuration Data in Context*

Question	Answer
What is it?	The basic configuration data consists of application settings and connection strings. Application settings are a set of key-value pairs, and connection strings contain information required to establish connections to external systems, such as databases.
Why should I care?	Application settings are the simplest way to define custom configuration information for an application. Connection strings are the standard mechanism for defining database connections and are widely used with ASP.NET.
How is it used by the MVC framework?	The MVC framework uses application settings to some of its own configuration data. Connection strings are not used directly but are relied on for persistence for application models.

Access to configuration data is provided through the WebConfigurationManager class, defined in the System.Web.Configuration namespace. The WebConfigurationManager class makes it easy to work with the configuration system—but there are some oddities, as I'll explain. There are several useful static members of the WebConfigurationManager class, as described in Table 9-5.

Table 9-5. The Most Useful Members Defined by the WebConfigurationManager Class

Name	Description
AppSettings	Returns a collection of key-value pairs used to define simple application-specific settings. See the "Using Application Settings" section for details.
ConnectionStrings	Returns a collection of ConnectionStringSettings objects that describe the connection strings. See the "Using Connection Strings" section for details.
GetWebApplicationSection(section)	Returns an object that can be used to get information about the specified configuration section at the application level. This method will ignore any folder-level configuration even if the current request targets such a folder. See the "Grouping Settings Together" section for details.
OpenWebConfiguration(path)	Returns a System.Configuration.Configuration object that reflects the complete configuration at the specified level. See the "Overriding Configuration Settings" section for details.

■ **Note** The classes that ASP.NET provides for obtaining configuration information also allow changes to be made to the configuration. I think this is a terrible idea; in fact, I think it is such a bad idea that I am not going to demonstrate how it is done. I sometimes come across projects that try to modify the configuration as the application is running and it always ends badly.

Using Application Settings

Application settings are simple key-value pairs and are the easiest way to extend the configuration to define values that are specific to an application. Listing 9-3 shows the application settings that I added to the application-level Web.config file (the one that is at the root level in the Visual Studio project).

Listing 9-3. Defining Application Settings in the Web.config File

```
<?xml version="1.0" encoding="utf-8"?>
<configuration>

  <appSettings>
    <add key="webpages:Version" value="3.0.0.0" />
    <add key="webpages:Enabled" value="false" />
    <add key="ClientValidationEnabled" value="true" />
    <add key="UnobtrusiveJavaScriptEnabled" value="true" />
    <add key="defaultCity" value="New York"/>
    <add key="defaultCountry" value="USA"/>
    <add key="defaultLanguage" value="English"/>
  </appSettings>
```

```
  <system.web>
    <compilation debug="true" targetFramework="4.5.1" />
    <httpRuntime targetFramework="4.5.1" />
  </system.web>
</configuration>
```

■ **Tip** The configuration examples in this chapter all follow a related theme, which is to express the default values that a new user account might require. This is one of the most common uses for configuration data in the projects that I see in development—and is often hard-coded into the application components.

The `Web.config` file that Visual Studio created for the project already has an `appSettings` element, which is defined within the top-level `configuration` element. There can be only one `appSettings` element in the configuration file (unless you are using a `location` element, which I describe later in this chapter), so I have added to the existing element to define some new settings.

■ **Tip** Don't confuse *application settings* with *application state*, which I describe in Chapter 10. Application *settings* are read-only values that are used to define custom configuration values, while *application state* is used for data values that can change as the application is running.

ASP.NET configuration files have a well-defined XML schema, which allows for some useful features. One such feature is that some configuration elements—including the `appSettings` element—are actually collections of properties and values. To control the content of the collection, you can use three different child elements within `appSettings`, as described in Table 9-6.

Table 9-6. *The Elements Used to Control the Contents of a Configuration Collection*

Name	Description
`add`	Defines a new application setting. The attributes supported by this element are `key` and `value`, which define the name of the setting and its value.
`clear`	Removes all of the application settings. No attributes are supported.
`remove`	Removes a single application setting, specified by the `key` attribute.

In Listing 9-3, I used the add element to define three new settings: `defaultCity`, `defaultCountry`, and `defaultLanguage`.

■ **Tip** You can get complete details of the XML schema used for configuration files from MSDN. See `http://msdn.microsoft.com/en-us/library/zeshe0eb(v=vs.100).aspx`.

Reading Application Settings

Reading application settings is done through the WebConfigurationManager.AppSettings property, which returns an instance of the NameValueCollection class, defined in the System.Collections.Specialized namespace. There are four useful properties for reading application settings, as described in Table 9-7.

Table 9-7. *The NameValueCollection Properties Useful for Reading Application Settings*

Name	Description
AllKeys	Returns a string array containing the application settings' names
Count	Returns the number of application settings
Item[index]	Returns the value of the application setting at the specified index
Item[key]	Returns the value of the application setting with the specified key

In Listing 9-4, you can see how I have updated the Index action in the Home controller to read application settings.

Listing 9-4. Reading Application Settings in the HomeController.cs File

```
using System.Collections.Generic;
using System.Web.Mvc;
using System.Web.Configuration;

namespace ConfigFiles.Controllers {
    public class HomeController : Controller {

        public ActionResult Index() {
            Dictionary<string, string> configData = new Dictionary<string, string>();
            foreach (string key in WebConfigurationManager.AppSettings) {
                configData.Add(key, WebConfigurationManager.AppSettings[key]);
            }
            return View(configData);
        }
    }
}
```

I have used a standard foreach loop to iterate through the set of application settings' names and add them—and the corresponding values—to the view model Dictionary. You can see the effect by starting the application and requesting the /Home/Index URL, as shown in Figure 9-3.

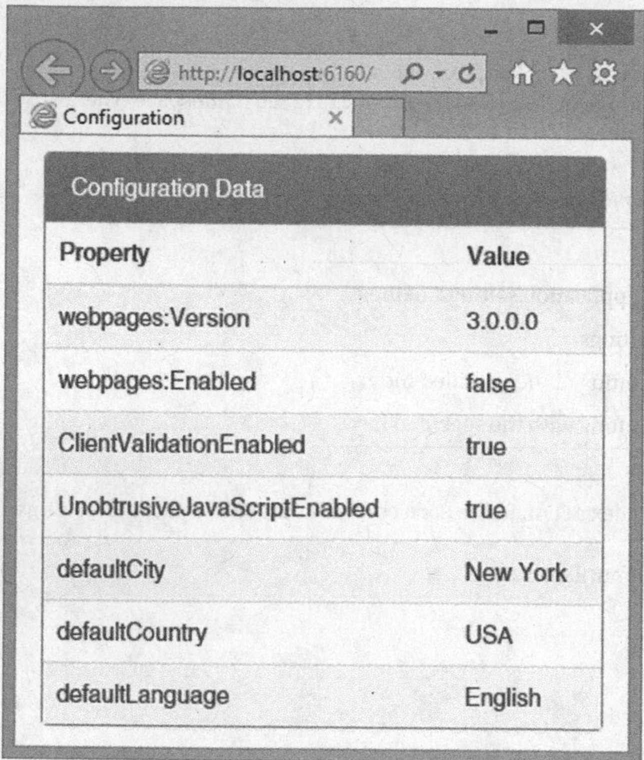

Figure 9-3. *Reading the application settings*

I enumerated all of the application settings, which is helpful to demonstrate how the configuration system works but isn't a realistic demonstration of how settings are usually consumed. In Listing 9-5, you can see that I have added a `DisplaySingle` action method to the `Home` controller, which uses an application setting to vary the model data sent to the view.

Listing 9-5. Adding an Action Method in the HomeController.cs File

```
using System.Collections.Generic;
using System.Web.Mvc;
using System.Web.Configuration;

namespace ConfigFiles.Controllers {
    public class HomeController : Controller {

        public ActionResult Index() {
            Dictionary<string, string> configData = new Dictionary<string, string>();
            foreach (string key in WebConfigurationManager.AppSettings) {
                configData.Add(key, WebConfigurationManager.AppSettings[key]);
            }
            return View(configData);
        }
```

```
        public ActionResult DisplaySingle() {
            return View((object)WebConfigurationManager.AppSettings["defaultLanguage"]);
        }
    }
}
```

In the new action method, I get the value of the `defaultLanguage` application setting and use it as the view model data. Listing 9-6 shows the view that I created for the action method.

Listing 9-6. The Contents of the DisplaySingle.cshtml File

```
@model string
@{
    Layout = null;
}
<!DOCTYPE html>
<html>
<head>
    <meta name="viewport" content="width=device-width" />
    <title>Single Config Value</title>
    <link href="~/Content/bootstrap.min.css" rel="stylesheet" />
    <link href="~/Content/bootstrap-theme.min.css" rel="stylesheet" />
    <style>body { padding-top: 10px; }</style>
</head>
<body class="container">
    <div class="alert alert-success">
        Value: @Model
    </div>
</body>
</html>
```

Defining simple settings in the configuration file has a number of benefits. First, settings are not hard-coded in the components of the application, such as models and views, and this means that making changes is simple and easy. Second, Visual Studio includes a useful feature that will automatically transform a configuration file for testing or deployment, which makes it easy to consistently change settings as an application moves out of development and toward production. Finally, using application settings makes it easy to ensure that all of the components that rely on a setting have the same value—something that is hard to do with hard-coded values. Start the application and request the `/Home/DisplaySingle` URL to see the effect of the new action method and its reliance on an application setting, as illustrated by Figure 9-4.

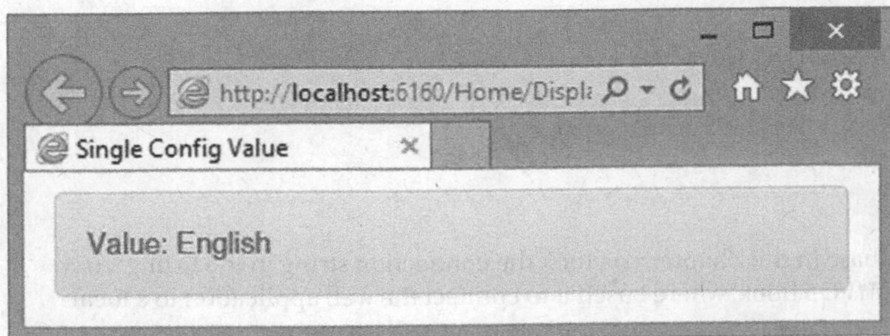

Figure 9-4. *Obtaining a single configuration value*

Using Connection Strings

The second type of setting that can be defined in a configuration file is a *connection string*. You have almost certainly defined connection strings in your MVC framework applications because they are most often used to define the connection details required for databases.

Although most connection strings are used to configure database connections, they actually represent a more flexible mechanism that can be used to describe any kind of connection to an external resource. There are two parts to a connection string: the name of the *provider* class that will be instantiated to establish the connection and the string that the provider will use to do its work. The format of the string isn't standardized because it has to make sense only to the provider, but in Listing 9-7 I have added a connection string to the application-level `Web.config` file that uses a format you may well recognize.

■ **Caution** The value for the `connectionString` attribute of the `add` element is too long to fit on the printed page, so it is shown wrapped on two lines. The configuration system can't cope with values that span two lines, so you must ensure that the complete string is on a single line in your project.

Listing 9-7. Adding a Connection String to the Web.config File

```
<?xml version="1.0" encoding="utf-8"?>
<configuration>

  <appSettings>
    <add key="webpages:Version" value="3.0.0.0" />
    <add key="webpages:Enabled" value="false" />
    <add key="ClientValidationEnabled" value="true" />
    <add key="UnobtrusiveJavaScriptEnabled" value="true" />
    <add key="defaultCity" value="New York"/>
    <add key="defaultCountry" value="USA"/>
    <add key="defaultLanguage" value="English"/>
  </appSettings>

  <connectionStrings>
    <add name="EFDbContext" connectionString="Data Source=(localdb)\v11.0;Initial
        Catalog=SportsStore;Integrated Security=True"
      providerName="System.Data.SqlClient"/>
  </connectionStrings>

  <system.web>
    <compilation debug="true" targetFramework="4.5.1" />
    <httpRuntime targetFramework="4.5.1" />
  </system.web>

</configuration>
```

I don't want to get into setting up a database in this chapter, so I took the connection string in the listing from the SportsStore example in my *Pro ASP.NET MVC 5* book, where I used it to connect the web application to a local database containing product data.

Connection strings are defined within the `configuration/connectionStrings` element, which, like `appSettings`, is expressed as a collection. That means new connection strings are defined using the add element and that connection strings can be changed using the `clear` and `remove` elements. When using the add element to define a connection string, there are three attributes that you may use, as described in Table 9-8.

Table 9-8. *The add Element Attributes for Defining Connection Strings*

Name	Description
`name`	The name with which the connection string will be referred to
`connectionString`	The string that tells the provider class how to connect to the external server or resource
`providerName`	The name of the provider class that will create and manage the connection

In the listing, my connection string uses the `providerName` attribute to specify that the `System.Data.SqlClient` class will be used as the provider, and the `connectionString` attribute specifies a string in a format that the `SqlClient` class can understand.

Reading Connection Strings

You won't usually need to read connection strings from the configuration unless you are writing a provider class or code that manages them, but in Listing 9-8 you can see how I have used the `WebConfigurationManager.ConnectionStrings` property to get the connection string details.

Listing 9-8. Reading a Connection String in the HomeController.cs File

```
using System.Collections.Generic;
using System.Web.Mvc;
using System.Web.Configuration;
using System.Configuration;

namespace ConfigFiles.Controllers {
  public class HomeController : Controller {

    public ActionResult Index() {
      Dictionary<string, string> configData = new Dictionary<string, string>();
      foreach (ConnectionStringSettings cs in
                WebConfigurationManager.ConnectionStrings) {
        configData.Add(cs.Name, cs.ProviderName + " " + cs.ConnectionString);
      }
      return View(configData);
    }

    public ActionResult DisplaySingle() {
      return View((object)WebConfigurationManager
          .ConnectionStrings["EFDbContext"].ConnectionString);
    }
  }
}
```

The ConnectionStrings property returns a collection of ConnectionStringSettings objects (defined in the System.Configuration namespace) that represent the configuration settings through the Name, ProviderName, and ConnectionString properties. In the listing, I enumerate all of the connection strings in the Index action and get the details of a connection string by name in the DisplaySingle action. Figure 9-5 shows the result of starting the application and requesting the /Home/Index URL.

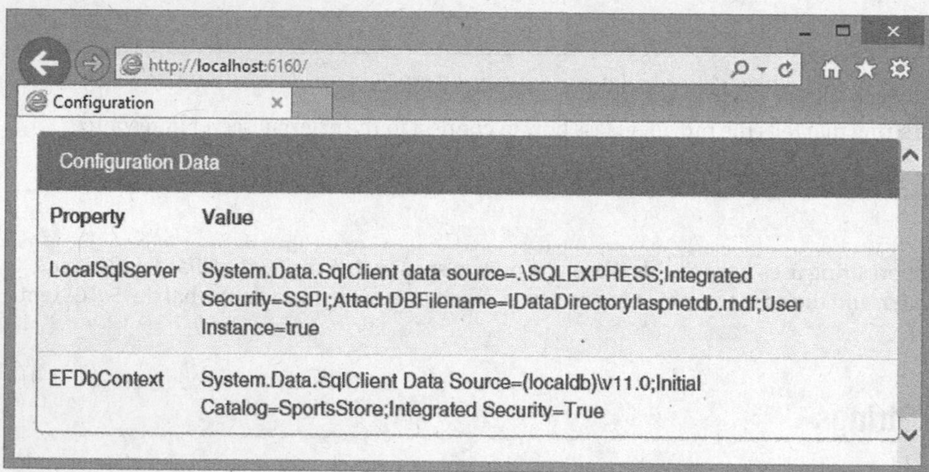

Figure 9-5. *Enumerating the connection strings*

There are two connection strings shown, even though I defined only one in Listing 9-7. When working with configuration data, it is important to remember that the data you are presented with is merged from the set of files I described in Table 9-3. In this example, the LocalSqlServer connection string is defined in the Machine.config file as a default connection string.

Grouping Settings Together

Application settings are useful for simple or self-contained settings, but for more complex configurations they quickly get out of hand because every setting is expressed as part of a flat list of key-value pairs.

ASP.NET uses odd terminology to describe the features that can be used to add structure to a configuration file by grouping related settings. *Configuration sections* are XML elements that have one or more attributes, and *configuration groups* are elements that contain one or more configuration sections. The application-level Web.config file contains a good example of both, as follows:

```
<?xml version="1.0" encoding="utf-8"?>
<configuration>

  <appSettings>
    <add key="webpages:Version" value="3.0.0.0" />
    <add key="webpages:Enabled" value="false" />
    <add key="ClientValidationEnabled" value="true" />
    <add key="UnobtrusiveJavaScriptEnabled" value="true" />
    <add key="defaultCity" value="New York"/>
    <add key="defaultCountry" value="USA"/>
    <add key="defaultLanguage" value="English"/>
  </appSettings>
```

```
<connectionStrings>
  <add name="EFDbContext" connectionString="Data Source=(localdb)\v11.0;
        Initial Catalog=SportsStore;Integrated Security=True"
    providerName="System.Data.SqlClient"/>
</connectionStrings>

<system.web>
  <compilation debug="true" targetFramework="4.5.1" />
  <httpRuntime targetFramework="4.5.1" />
</system.web>

</configuration>
```

The system.web element is a configuration group, and the compilation and httpRuntime elements are configuration sections. The configuration group brings together settings that define how the ASP.NET platform and the application behave. The configuration sections define related settings. For example, the compilation section has attributes that control whether debug mode is enabled and what version of .NET will be used. In the sections that follow, I'll show you how to read configuration sections in an application and explain how to create your own. Table 9-9 puts configuration sections into context.

Table 9-9. *Putting the Basic ASP.NET Configuration Sections in Context*

Question	Answer
What is it?	Configuration sections group related settings as attributes on a custom XML element.
Why should I care?	Configuration sections require more work than application settings, but they are less prone to typos and provide support for validating the values in configuration files.
How is it used by the MVC framework?	The MVC framework defines configuration sections in the Views/web.config file to configure view rendering.

Creating a Simple Configuration Section

To demonstrate how to create a configuration section, it is easier to show the process in reverse, starting with the configuration values and working back through the process of creating the section that defines them. In Listing 9-9, I have added a new configuration section to the Web.config file.

Listing 9-9. Adding a New Configuration Section to the Web.config File

```
<?xml version="1.0" encoding="utf-8"?>
<configuration>

  <appSettings>
    <add key="webpages:Version" value="3.0.0.0" />
    <add key="webpages:Enabled" value="false" />
    <add key="ClientValidationEnabled" value="true" />
    <add key="UnobtrusiveJavaScriptEnabled" value="true" />
    <add key="defaultCity" value="New York"/>
    <add key="defaultCountry" value="USA"/>
    <add key="defaultLanguage" value="English"/>
  </appSettings>
```

```
  <connectionStrings>
    <add name="EFDbContext" connectionString="Data Source=(localdb)\v11.0;
            Initial Catalog=SportsStore;Integrated Security=True"
        providerName="System.Data.SqlClient"/>
  </connectionStrings>

  <newUserDefaults city="Chicago" country="USA" language="English" regionCode="1"/>

  <system.web>
    <compilation debug="true" targetFramework="4.5.1" />
    <httpRuntime targetFramework="4.5.1" />
  </system.web>

</configuration>
```

The configuration section is represented by the `newUserDefaults` element, which defines `city`, `country`, `language`, and `regionCode` attributes. The first three attributes correspond to the application settings I defined earlier, and I added the `regionCode` attribute to demonstrate how configuration settings can be used to automatically parse numeric values. This may not seem like a significant improvement over using application settings, but you'll see that there are some advantages of taking the time to create custom configuration sections for your applications.

■ **Tip** You will see an error if you start the application at this point because all of the elements in a configuration file need to be supported by a *section definition* and *handler class*, both of which I create in the following sections.

Creating the Configuration Section Handler Class

Configuration sections are processed by a *handler class*, which is responsible for processing the information from the configuration file and presenting it to the application. Handler classes are derived from the `System.Configuration.ConfigurationSection` class and define properties that correspond to the attributes of the XML element they support. I created an `Infrastructure` folder in the example application and added to it a class file called `NewUserDefaultsSection.cs`, the contents of which can be seen in Listing 9-10.

Listing 9-10. The Contents of the NewUserDefaultsSection.cs File

```
using System.Configuration;

namespace ConfigFiles.Infrastructure {
    public class NewUserDefaultsSection : ConfigurationSection {

        [ConfigurationProperty("city", IsRequired = true)]
        public string City {
            get { return (string)this["city"]; }
            set { this["city"] = value; }
        }

        [ConfigurationProperty("country", DefaultValue = "USA")]
        public string Country {
            get { return (string)this["country"]; }
            set { this["country"] = value; }
        }
```

```
        [ConfigurationProperty("language")]
        public string Language {
            get { return (string)this["language"]; }
            set { this["language"] = value; }
        }

        [ConfigurationProperty("regionCode")]
        [IntegerValidator(MaxValue = 5, MinValue = 0)]
        public int Region {
            get { return (int)this["regionCode"]; }
            set { this["regionCode"] = value; }
        }
    }
}
```

The names of the properties usually match the attribute names with the first letter capitalized, although this is just a convention and property names should make it obvious which attributes they relate to. You can use any name for the properties; for example, the property that represents the `regionCode` attribute is called `Region` in the handler class.

The base for configuration sections is the `ConfigurationSection` class, which defines a `protected` collection used to store the configuration values. This collection is available through the `this` indexer, and I implement each property so that the `set` and `get` blocks assign and retrieve values from the `this` collection, like this:

```
...
public string City {
    get { return (string)this["city"]; }
    set { this["city"] = value; }
}
...
```

The next step is to apply the `ConfigurationProperty` attribute to each property. The first parameter is the name of the attribute in the configuration file that the property corresponds. There are some optional parameters that refine the property behavior, as shown in Table 9-10.

Table 9-10. *The Parameters Used with the ConfigurationProperty Attribute*

Name	Description
`DefaultValue`	This specifies the default value for the property if one is not set in the configuration file.
`IsDefaultCollection`	This is used when a configuration section manages a collection of elements.
`IsRequired`	When set to `true`, an exception will be thrown if a value is not defined in the hierarchy for this property.

The use of the attribute parameters is optional, but they help prevent configuration mistakes from causing unexpected behaviors when the application is running. The `DefaultValue` parameter ensures that there is a sensible fallback value when one is not supplied in the configuration files, and the `IsRequired` parameter allows ASP.NET to report a configuration exception rather than letting code fail when it tries to read the configuration property values. In the listing, I have used IsRequired on the City property and DefaultValue on the Country property, as follows:

```
...
[ConfigurationProperty("city", IsRequired = true)]
public string City {
    get { return (string)this["city"]; }
    set { this["city"] = value; }
}

[ConfigurationProperty("country", DefaultValue = "USA")]
public string Country {
    get { return (string)this["country"]; }
    set { this["country"] = value; }
}
...
```

When ASP.NET processes the configuration section, it instantiates the handler class and sets the properties using the values in the file. ASP.NET will report an error if it can't convert a value from the configuration file into the type of the handler class property, but it is possible to be more specific about the range of allowed values by applying a set of validation attributes, such as the IntegerValidator attribute that I applied to the Region property:

```
...
[ConfigurationProperty("regionCode")]
[IntegerValidator(MaxValue = 5, MinValue = 0)]
public int Region {
    get { return (int)this["regionCode"]; }
    set { this["regionCode"] = value; }
}
...
```

The MinValue and MaxValue parameters specify the range of acceptable values for this property, and the ASP.NET framework will report an error if the value specified in the configuration file is outside this range or cannot be parsed to an int value. Table 9-11 describes the full set of validation attributes, all of which are defined in the System.Configuration namespace.

Table 9-11. The Configuration Validation Attribtutes

Name	Description
CallbackValidator	Used to perform custom validation; see the text following the table.
IntegerValidator	Used to validate int values. By default, this attribute accepts values *within* the range defined by the MinValue and MaxValue parameters, but you can use the ExcludeRange parameter to true to exclude values in that range instead.
LongValidator	Used to validate long values. This defines the same parameters as the IntegerValidator.
RegexStringValidator	Used to ensure that a string value matches a regular expression. The expression is specified using the Regex parameter.

(*continued*)

Table 9-11. (*continued*)

Name	Description
StringValidator	Used to perform simple validations on string values. The MinLength and MaxLength parameters constrain the length of the value, and the InvalidCharacters parameter is used to exclude characters.
TimeSpanValidator	Used to validate time spans. The MinValueString and MaxValueString parameters restrict the range of values, expressed in the form 0:30:00. The MinValue and MaxValue parameters do the same thing but require TimeSpan values. When set to true, the ExcludeRange parameter excludes values that fall between the minimum and maximum values.

The validation attributes are easy to use, but the CallbackValidator allows you to specify a method that contains validation logic for custom configuration properties. Listing 9-11 shows the use of the CallbackValidator attribute applied to the NewUserDefaultsSection class.

Listing 9-11. Performing Custom Validation in the NewUserDefaultsSection.cs File

```
using System.Configuration;
using System;

namespace ConfigFiles.Infrastructure {
    public class NewUserDefaultsSection : ConfigurationSection {

        [ConfigurationProperty("city", IsRequired = true)]
        [CallbackValidator(CallbackMethodName = "ValidateCity",
            Type = typeof(NewUserDefaultsSection))]
        public string City {
            get { return (string)this["city"]; }
            set { this["city"] = value; }
        }

        // ...other properties omitted for brevity...

        public static void ValidateCity(object candidateValue) {
            if ((string)candidateValue == "Paris") {
                throw new Exception("Unsupported City Value");
            }
        }
    }
}
```

The parameters for the CallbackValidator attribute are CallbackMethodName and Type, which are used to specify the method that should be called when the configuration data is processed. The method must be public and static, take a single object argument, and not return a result—the method throws an exception if the value passed as the argument is not acceptable. In the listing, I throw an exception if the value is Paris. (I could have achieved the same effect using the RegexStringValidator attribute, but I wanted to demonstrate the CallbackValidator attribute, which can be a lot more flexible.)

Defining the Section

The next step is to associate the handler class with the configuration section, which requires an addition to the Web.config file. All configuration sections have to be defined somewhere, but the ones used by ASP.NET, such as compilation and httpRuntime, are defined in higher-level files, so you won't have seen the definition of them in the application-level Web.config file. Listing 9-12 shows the additions I made to the application-level Web.config file to define my custom configuration section.

Listing 9-12. Defining a Custom Configuration Section in the Web.config File

```
<?xml version="1.0" encoding="utf-8"?>
<configuration>

  <configSections>
    <section name="newUserDefaults"
        type="ConfigFiles.Infrastructure.NewUserDefaultsSection"/>
  </configSections>

  <!-- ...application settings and connection strings omitted for brevity... -->

  <newUserDefaults city="Chicago" country="USA" language="English" regionCode="1"/>

  <system.web>
    <compilation debug="true" targetFramework="4.5.1" />
    <httpRuntime targetFramework="4.5.1" />
  </system.web>

</configuration>
```

The configSections element is used to define new sections and section groups. I used the section element in the listing, which defines the attributes shown in Table 9-12.

Table 9-12. *The Attributes Defined by the configSections/section Element*

Name	Description
allowDefinition	Used to limit where the section can be defined. The values are Everywhere (the section can be defined anywhere in the configuration hierarchy), MachineToApplication (the section can be defined in the hierarchy from the Machine.config through to the app-level Web.config file), MachineToWebRoot (in the Machine.config or the global Web.config file), and MachineOnly (only in the Machine.config file). If the attribute is omitted, then the default value of Everywhere is used.
allowLocation	Specifies whether the section can be defined in location elements. The default is true. See the "Overriding Configuration Settings" section for details of location elements.
name	The name of the section.
Type	The name of the handler class.

Using the table, you can see I have defined my new section with the name newUserDefaults, specified the NewUserDefaultsSection handler class, and accepted the default values for the allowDefinition and allowLocation attributes.

Reading Configuration Sections

All that remains is to read the values from the custom configuration section, which is done through the WebConfigurationManager. Listing 9-13 shows the changes I made to the Home controller to read the settings in the newUserDefaults section.

Listing 9-13. Reading Values from a Configuration Section

```
using System.Collections.Generic;
using System.Web.Mvc;
using System.Web.Configuration;
using System.Configuration;
using ConfigFiles.Infrastructure;

namespace ConfigFiles.Controllers {
    public class HomeController : Controller {

        public ActionResult Index() {
            Dictionary<string, string> configData = new Dictionary<string, string>();

            NewUserDefaultsSection nuDefaults = WebConfigurationManager
                .GetWebApplicationSection("newUserDefaults") as NewUserDefaultsSection;
            if (nuDefaults != null) {
                configData.Add("City", nuDefaults.City);
                configData.Add("Country", nuDefaults.Country);
                configData.Add("Language", nuDefaults.Language);
                configData.Add("Region", nuDefaults.Region.ToString());
            };
            return View(configData);
        }

        public ActionResult DisplaySingle() {
            return View((object)WebConfigurationManager
                .ConnectionStrings["EFDbContext"].ConnectionString);
        }
    }
}
```

The WebConfigurationManager.GetWebApplicationSection method takes the name of the section as its argument and returns an instance of the handler class, which is NewUserDefaultsSection in this case. I can then use the properties defined by the handler class to read the configuration values. To see the result, start the application and request the /Home/Index URL, as shown in Figure 9-6.

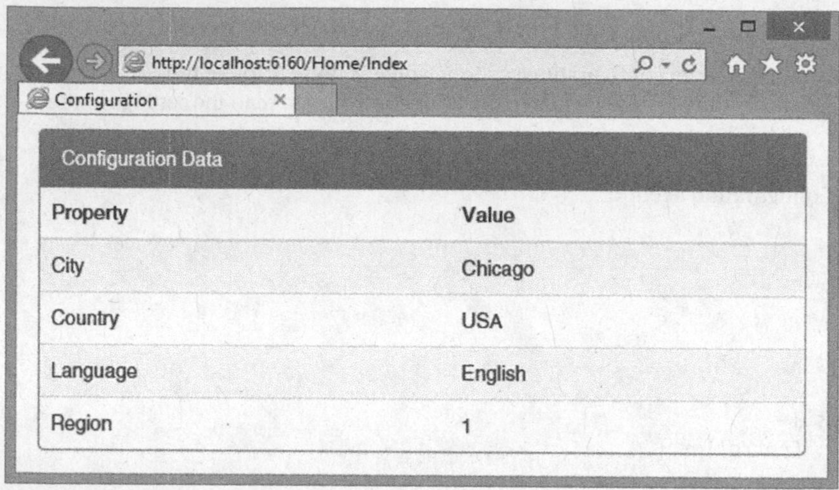

Figure 9-6. *Reading a configuration section*

Creating a Collection Configuration Section

Simple configuration sections are useful when you want to define a set of related values, such as the defaults for users in the previous section. If you want to define a set of repeating values, then you can define a *collection configuration section*, of which the appSettings and connectionStrings sections are examples. Configuration values are added to the collection with the add element and deleted from the collection using the remove element, and the collection is reset entirely with the clear element.

Once again, I am going to start by adding a configuration section to Web.config and then work back to define the supporting features. Listing 9-14 shows the addition of a custom collection configuration section to the application-level Web.config file.

Listing 9-14. Adding a Collection Configuration Section to the Web.config File

```
<?xml version="1.0" encoding="utf-8"?>
<configuration>

  <configSections>
    <section name="newUserDefaults"
        type="ConfigFiles.Infrastructure.NewUserDefaultsSection"/>
  </configSections>

  <!-- ...application settings and connection strings omitted for brevity... -->

  <newUserDefaults city="Chicago" country="USA" language="English" regionCode="1"/>

  <places default="LON">
    <add code="NYC" city="New York" country="USA" />
    <add code="LON" city="London" country="UK" />
    <add code="PAR" city="Paris" country="France" />
  </places>
```

```
  <system.web>
    <compilation debug="true" targetFramework="4.5.1" />
    <httpRuntime targetFramework="4.5.1" />
  </system.web>

</configuration>
```

Creating the Item Handler Class

The process for supporting this kind of configuration section is a little more complex than for a basic section. The first step is to create a class that will represent each of the items that the add element creates. To this end, I added a class file called `Place.cs` to the `Infrastructure` folder and used it to define the class shown in Listing 9-15.

Listing 9-15. The Contents of the Place.cs File

```
using System;
using System.Configuration;

namespace ConfigFiles.Infrastructure {

    public class Place : ConfigurationElement {

        [ConfigurationProperty("code", IsRequired = true)]
        public string Code {
            get { return (string)this["code"]; }
            set { this["code"] = value; }
        }

        [ConfigurationProperty("city", IsRequired = true)]
        public string City {
            get { return (string)this["city"]; }
            set { this["city"] = value; }
        }

        [ConfigurationProperty("country", IsRequired = true)]
        public String Country {
            get { return (string)this["country"]; }
            set { this["country"] = value; }
        }
    }
}
```

The handler class for individual collection items is derived from the `ConfigurationElement` class and defines properties that correspond to the attributes on the add element. The add element can define any attributes you need to represent the data, which is why the add element for, say, application settings has different attributes from the one used for connection strings. The class in Listing 9-15 has properties for `Code`, `City`, and `Country`, which I will use to define a set of cities. The properties in the handler class are decorated with the `ConfigurationProperty` attribute, which is used in the same way as the previous example.

Creating the Collection Handler Class

I also need to create a handler class for the overall collection of configuration elements. The job of the handler class is to override a series of methods that the ASP.NET platform will use to populate the collection. I added a class file called `PlaceCollection.cs` to the `Infrastructure` folder and used it to define the class shown in Listing 9-16.

Listing 9-16. The Contents of the PlaceCollection.cs File

```
using System.Configuration;

namespace ConfigFiles.Infrastructure {

    public class PlaceCollection : ConfigurationElementCollection {

        protected override ConfigurationElement CreateNewElement() {
            return new Place();
        }

        protected override object GetElementKey(ConfigurationElement element) {
            return ((Place)element).Code;
        }

        public new Place this[string key] {
            get { return (Place)BaseGet(key); }
        }
    }
}
```

The base class is `ConfigurationElementCollection`, which is integrated with the other classes in the `System.Configuration` namespace. My implementation has to override the `CreateNewElement` method to create instances of the item handler class (`Place` in this example) and has to override the `GetElementKey` method to return a key that will be used to store an item in the collection—I used the value of the `Code` property. I have also added an indexer so that I can request items directly by key; the base class already defines a `protected` indexer, so I had to apply the `new` keyword to hide the base implementation.

Creating the Configuration Section Handler Class

The last handler class is for the configuration section itself. I added a class file called `PlaceSection.cs` to the `Infrastructure` folder and used it to define the class shown in Listing 9-17.

Listing 9-17. The Contents of the PlaceSection.cs File

```
using System.Configuration;

namespace ConfigFiles.Infrastructure {

    public class PlaceSection : ConfigurationSection {
        [ConfigurationProperty("", IsDefaultCollection = true)]
        [ConfigurationCollection(typeof(PlaceCollection))]
        public PlaceCollection Places {
            get { return (PlaceCollection)base[""]; }
        }
```

```
    [ConfigurationProperty("default")]
    public string Default {
        get { return (string)base["default"]; }
        set { base["default"] = value; }
    }
  }
}
```

The complexity in managing the configuration section is contained in the other handler classes. For the section handler, all that I need to do is create a property that returns an instance of the collection handler class, which I have called Places, and apply two attributes to it.

The ConfigurationProperty attribute is applied with an empty string for name and the IsDefaultCollection parameter set to true. This tells the ASP.NET framework that the add, remove, and clear elements in the configuration section will be applied to this collection. The empty string is also used in the property getter and is a special incantation that sets up the collection. The ConfigurationCollection attribute tells the ASP.NET framework what collection class should be instantiated to hold the configuration items—in this example, the PlaceCollection class.

When I defined the configuration data in Listing 9-14, I included an attribute on the section element, like this:

```
...
<places default="LON">
  <add code="NYC" city="New York" country="USA" />
  <add code="LON" city="London" country="UK" />
  <add code="PAR" city="Paris" country="France" />
</places>
...
```

This is a common technique for collections, which define the range of allowable values and use an element to specify the default value if one has not otherwise been selected. In Listing 9-17, I added the Default property to provide access to the value of the default attribute, which I am able to obtain using the indexer provided by the base handler class.

Defining the Configuration Section

Now that the (many) handler classes are in place, I can define the collection configuration section in the Web.config file, which has the effect of associating the handlers with the XML element. Listing 9-18 shows the addition I made to the configSections element in the application-level Web.config file.

Listing 9-18. Adding a New Configuration Section to the Web.config File

```
...
<configSections>
  <section name="newUserDefaults"
        type="ConfigFiles.Infrastructure.NewUserDefaultsSection"/>
  <section name="places" type="ConfigFiles.Infrastructure.PlaceSection"/>
</configSections>
...
```

There are no special attributes required to define a collection section; the complexity of the collection is managed by the section handler class.

Reading Collection Configuration Sections

The process for reading collection configuration sections is similar to that for simple sections. Listing 9-19 shows the changes that I made to the Home controller to read the values for the places section.

Listing 9-19. Reading a Collection Configuration Section in the HomeController.cs File

```
using System.Collections.Generic;
using System.Web.Mvc;
using System.Web.Configuration;
using System.Configuration;
using ConfigFiles.Infrastructure;

namespace ConfigFiles.Controllers {
    public class HomeController : Controller {

        public ActionResult Index() {
            Dictionary<string, string> configData = new Dictionary<string, string>();
            PlaceSection section = WebConfigurationManager
                .GetWebApplicationSection("places") as PlaceSection;
            foreach (Place place in section.Places) {
                configData.Add(place.Code, string.Format("{0} ({1})",
                    place.City, place.Country));
            }
            return View(configData);
        }

        public ActionResult DisplaySingle() {
            PlaceSection section = WebConfigurationManager
                .GetWebApplicationSection("places") as PlaceSection;
            Place defaultPlace = section.Places[section.Default];
            return View((object)string.Format("The default place is: {0}",
                defaultPlace.City));
        }
    }
}
```

I have used the Index action method to enumerate all of the configuration items in the collection. I use the WebConfigurationManager.GetWebApplicationSection method to get an instance of the section handler class (PlaceSection) and read the value of the Places property to get an instance of the collection handler class (PlaceCollection). I use a foreach loop to obtain each item handler class (Place) and add the individual property values, which are obtained from the attributes of the add element, to the view data.

For the DisplaySingle action method, I read the value of the PlaceSection.Default property to get the value of the default attribute and use this as a key to retrieve the corresponding Place object. You can see the output from both action methods by starting the application and requesting the /Home/Index and /Home/DisplaySingle URLs, as illustrated by Figure 9-7.

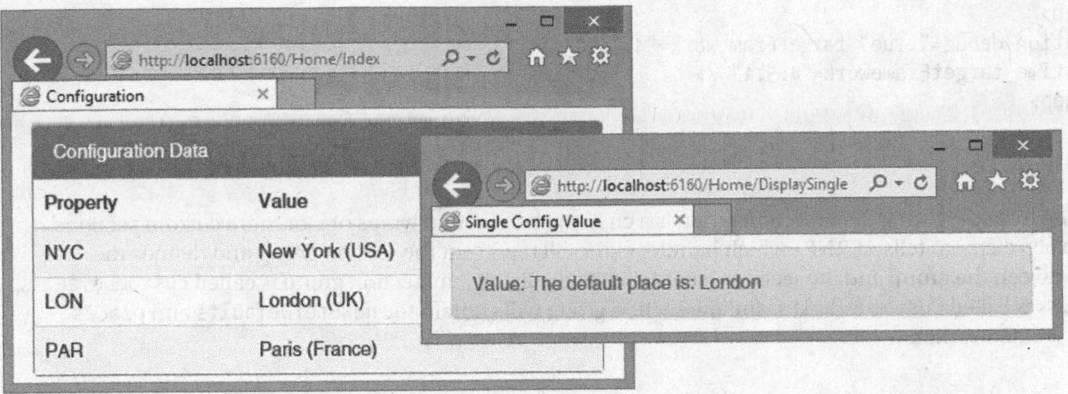

***Figure 9-7.** Reading a collection configuration section*

Creating Section Groups

A *section group*—as the name suggests—allows configuration sections to be grouped together. The main reason for using section groups is to add further structure to the data in the configuration files in order to make it clear that section groups are related to one another and affect related parts of the application. Listing 9-20 shows the addition of a section group to contain the `newUserDefaults` and `places` sections in the `Web.config` file. I have also added the definition of the section group in the `configSections` element.

***Listing 9-20.** Adding a Configuration Section Group to the Web.config File*

```
<?xml version="1.0" encoding="utf-8"?>
<configuration>

  <configSections>
    <sectionGroup name="customDefaults" type="ConfigFiles.Infrastructure.CustomDefaults">
      <section name="newUserDefaults"
          type="ConfigFiles.Infrastructure.NewUserDefaultsSection"/>
      <section name="places" type="ConfigFiles.Infrastructure.PlaceSection"/>
    </sectionGroup>
  </configSections>

  <!-- ...application settings and connection strings omitted for brevity... -->

  <customDefaults>
    <newUserDefaults city="Chicago" country="USA" language="English" regionCode="1"/>
    <places default="LON">
      <add code="NYC" city="New York" country="USA" />
      <add code="LON" city="London" country="UK" />
      <add code="PAR" city="Paris" country="France" />
    </places>
  </customDefaults>
```

```
  <system.web>
    <compilation debug="true" targetFramework="4.5.1" />
    <httpRuntime targetFramework="4.5.1" />
  </system.web>

</configuration>
```

You can see from the listing that a section group is a custom element that wraps one or more custom sections. The sectionGroup element tells ASP.NET which handler class will represent the section group and defines the relationship between the group and the sections it contains. In the listing, my section group is called customDefaults, the handler class is called CustomDefaults, and the section group will contain the newUserDefaults and places sections that I created earlier.

Creating the Section Group Handler Class

Section groups rely on handler classes, similar to the ones used for configuration sections. For my customDefaults section group, I added a class file called CustomDefaults.cs to the Infrastructure folder and used it to define the class shown in Listing 9-21.

Listing 9-21. The Contents of the CustomDefaults.cs File

```
using System.Configuration;

namespace ConfigFiles.Infrastructure {
    public class CustomDefaults : ConfigurationSectionGroup {

        public NewUserDefaultsSection NewUserDefaults {
            get { return (NewUserDefaultsSection)Sections["newUserDefaults"]; }
        }

        public PlaceSection Places {
            get { return (PlaceSection)Sections["places"]; }
        }
    }
}
```

The purpose of the section group handler class is to expose properties that access the configuration sections that the group element contains. Section group handler classes are derived from the ConfigurationSectionGroup class, which defines a Sections property through which instances of section handler classes can be obtained by name, like this:

```
...
get { return (PlaceSection)Sections["places"]; }
...
```

Reading Section Groups

Reading section groups is a little more complex than reading individual sections because there is no direct convenience method in the WebConfigurationManager class. Instead, I have to obtain a System.Configuration.Configuration object from WebConfigurationManager and then request the section group, as shown in Listing 9-22.

Listing 9-22. Reading a Section Group in the HomeController.cs File

```
using System.Collections.Generic;
using System.Web.Mvc;
using System.Web.Configuration;
using System.Configuration;
using ConfigFiles.Infrastructure;

namespace ConfigFiles.Controllers {
    public class HomeController : Controller {

        public ActionResult Index() {
            Dictionary<string, string> configData = new Dictionary<string, string>();

            CustomDefaults cDefaults
                = (CustomDefaults)WebConfigurationManager.OpenWebConfiguration("/")
                    .GetSectionGroup("customDefaults");

            foreach (Place place in cDefaults.Places.Places) {
                configData.Add(place.Code, string.Format("{0} ({1})",
                    place.City, place.Country));
            }
            return View(configData);
        }

        public ActionResult DisplaySingle() {
            PlaceSection section = WebConfigurationManager
                .GetWebApplicationSection("customDefaults/places") as PlaceSection;
            Place defaultPlace = section.Places[section.Default];
            return View((object)string.Format("The default place is: {0}",
                defaultPlace.City));
        }
    }
}
```

I have used the `WebConfigurationManager.OpenWebConfiguration` method in the `Index` action method to get the `Configuration` object, which allows me to call the `GetSectionGroup` method to get an instance of my handler class. The argument I have passed to the `OpenWebConfiguration` method specifies where in the configuration hierarchy the data will be read from, which I return to in the next section. Once I have obtained an instance of the section group handler class, I can access the properties it defines to get instances of the section handlers and read the configuration data.

You can see an alternative approach to dealing with section groups in the `DisplaySingle` action method, where I used the `WebConfigurationManager.GetWebApplicationSection` method and included the name of the section group along with the section, like this:

```
...
WebConfigurationManager.GetWebApplicationSection("customDefaults/places")
...
```

The configuration system is smart enough to navigate the elements in the configuration file and locate the correct section.

Overriding Configuration Settings

The ASP.NET platform provides a means to override configuration values within an application, allowing you to change the settings for specific requests. These features were originally designed to work with Web Forms, where the requested URL corresponds directly with the file that will be used to generate the response. They don't work quite as well with MVC framework applications, but I have included them in this chapter because I sometimes find them useful for applying quick patches to applications where an urgent fix is needed to buy time while a real solution is found and tested. Table 9-13 puts configuration overrides in context.

***Table 9-13.** Putting Configuration Overrides in Context*

Question	Answer
What is it?	Overriding configuration settings allows you to create different configurations for different parts of the application.
Why should I care?	Overriding configuration settings allows you to specify only the changes you require, rather than duplicating the entire configuration.
How is it used by the MVC framework?	The MVC framework uses the `Views/web.config` file to configure the Razor view engine separately from the configuration for the rest of the framework.

Using the Location Element

The `location` element allows you to create sections in configuration files that are used for requests with specific URLs. In Listing 9-23, I have added a `location` element to the application-level `Web.config` file.

***Listing 9-23.** Adding a location Element to the Web.config File*

```
<?xml version="1.0" encoding="utf-8"?>
<configuration>

  <configSections>
    <sectionGroup name="customDefaults" type="ConfigFiles.Infrastructure.CustomDefaults">
      <section name="newUserDefaults"
          type="ConfigFiles.Infrastructure.NewUserDefaultsSection"/>
      <section name="places" type="ConfigFiles.Infrastructure.PlaceSection"/>
    </sectionGroup>
  </configSections>

  <appSettings>
    <add key="webpages:Version" value="3.0.0.0" />
    <add key="webpages:Enabled" value="false" />
     <add key="ClientValidationEnabled" value="true" />
    <add key="UnobtrusiveJavaScriptEnabled" value="true" />
    <add key="defaultCity" value="New York"/>
    <add key="defaultCountry" value="USA"/>
    <add key="defaultLanguage" value="English"/>
  </appSettings>
```

```
<connectionStrings>
  <add name="EFDbContext" connectionString="Data Source=(localdb)\v11.0;Initial
       Catalog=SportsStore;Integrated Security=True"
     providerName="System.Data.SqlClient"/>
</connectionStrings>

<customDefaults>
  <newUserDefaults city="Chicago" country="USA" language="English" regionCode="1"/>
  <places default="LON">
    <add code="NYC" city="New York" country="USA" />
    <add code="LON" city="London" country="UK" />
    <add code="PAR" city="Paris" country="France" />
  </places>
</customDefaults>

<system.web>
  <compilation debug="true" targetFramework="4.5.1" />
  <httpRuntime targetFramework="4.5.1" />
</system.web>

<location path="Home/Index">
  <appSettings>
    <add key="defaultCity" value="London"/>
    <add key="defaultCountry" value="UK"/>
  </appSettings>
</location>

</configuration>
```

The location element defines the path attribute, which identifies the URL that the overridden configuration applies to. In this case, I have specified the Home/Index URL, which means that the location element will be applied to requests that target the Index action on the Home controller.

Within the location element, you can define the configuration settings that you want to override for requests that target the path URL. In the listing, I have used an appSettings element to change two of the application settings that I defined earlier. To demonstrate the effect, I have updated the Home controller to read the application settings, 3as shown in Listing 9-24.

Listing 9-24. Reading Application Settings in the HomeController.cs File

```
using System.Collections.Generic;
using System.Web.Configuration;
using System.Web.Mvc;

namespace ConfigFiles.Controllers {
  public class HomeController : Controller {

      public ActionResult Index() {
          Dictionary<string, string> configData = new Dictionary<string, string>();
          foreach (string key in WebConfigurationManager.AppSettings.AllKeys) {
              configData.Add(key, WebConfigurationManager.AppSettings[key]);
          }
          return View(configData);
      }
```

```
        public ActionResult OtherAction() {
            Dictionary<string, string> configData = new Dictionary<string, string>();
            foreach (string key in WebConfigurationManager.AppSettings.AllKeys) {
                configData.Add(key, WebConfigurationManager.AppSettings[key]);
            }
            return View("Index", configData);
        }
    }
}
```

As well as modifying the Index action method, I have replaced the DisplaySingle action with the OtherAction method that contains the same code as the Index action. Both the Index and OtherAction action methods read application settings, but the location element means that the DisplaySingle action method will be provided with a different set of values. To see the difference, start the application and request the /Home/Index and /Home/OtherAction URLs, as shown in Figure 9-8.

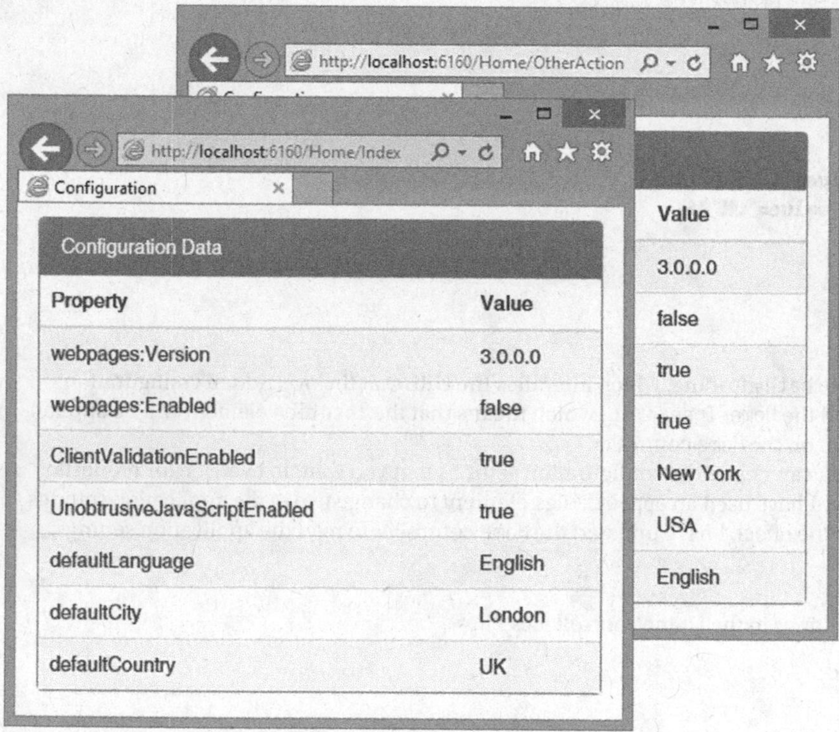

Figure 9-8. *The effect of using the location element*

Only the application settings that I included in the location element have changed. The other values are inherited, which means that when the WebConfigurationManager class is used, it merges the data in the hierarchy of files with the contents of the location element to present a unique view of the data to a single action method.

■ **Caution** The problem with this approach is that the value of the path attribute doesn't take into account the effect of the routing system, so changes to the routes in an application can render a location element ineffective. This isn't a problem in classic Web Forms projects but has the effect of limiting the use of the location element when routing is used, either with Web Forms or in the MVC framework.

Using Folder-Level Files

You can define Web.config files in individual folders and use them to extend the hierarchy of configuration files. This feature is a little harder to work with because you have to explicitly request the configuration file you want (and work with some different classes), but it does have the benefit of not being tied to the requested URL so it can be used in multiple controllers and action methods. To get started, I added a Web.config file to the Views/Home folder and defined the configuration elements shown in Listing 9-25.

Listing 9-25. The Contents of the Web.config File in the Views/Home Folder

```
<?xml version="1.0"?>
<configuration>
  <appSettings>
    <add key="defaultCity" value="Paris"/>
    <add key="defaultCountry" value="France"/>
  </appSettings>
</configuration>
```

I have used the appSettings element to define new values for the defaultCity and defaultCountry application settings. To read these values, I have updated the OtherAction method in the Home controller, as shown in Listing 9-26.

Listing 9-26. Reading a Folder-Level Configuration in the HomeController.cs File

```
using System.Collections.Generic;
using System.Configuration;
using System.Web.Configuration;
using System.Web.Mvc;

namespace ConfigFiles.Controllers {
    public class HomeController : Controller {

        public ActionResult Index() {
            Dictionary<string, string> configData = new Dictionary<string, string>();
            foreach (string key in WebConfigurationManager.AppSettings.AllKeys) {
                configData.Add(key, WebConfigurationManager.AppSettings[key]);
            }
            return View(configData);
        }

        public ActionResult OtherAction() {
            Dictionary<string, string> configData = new Dictionary<string, string>();
            AppSettingsSection appSettings =
                WebConfigurationManager.OpenWebConfiguration("~/Views/Home").AppSettings;
```

```
                foreach (string key in appSettings.Settings.AllKeys) {
                    configData.Add(key, appSettings.Settings[key].Value);
                }
                return View("Index", configData);
            }
        }
    }
```

I have called the WebConfigurationManager.OpenWebConfiguration method, which takes a path as its arguments. Paths are a central part of the Web Forms programming model, but in an MVC framework application they can be used to specify the location of the folder-level configuration file. The path must be prefixed with a tilde character (~) followed by the name of the folder that contains the Web.config file; in this case, I have specified Views/Home, which is the location of the file I created in Listing 9-25.

The OpenWebConfiguration method returns an instance of the Configuration class, which is defined in the System.Configuration namespace. The Configuration class provides access to all the features I described in this chapter but does it using a different set of methods and properties from the WebConfigurationManager class. (In fact, the WebConfigurationManager class relies on the System.Configuration namespace for its functionality, but with an emphasis on ease of use in web applications.)

■ **Caution** Don't create a folder hierarchy that matches the URLs that your application supports, such as a Home/Index folder. The routing configuration is set up to not route requests that correspond to folders on the disk, and you'll see an error. Instead, either define a separate top-level folder to contain your folder-level configuration files or use the Views folder, as I have done in the example.

The Configuration.AppSettings property returns an AppSettingsSection object, which exposes a collection of the application settings through its Settings property. I use this collection to enumerate the application settings and generate the view model data.

When you request a Configuration object through the OpenWebConfiguration method, the contents of the Web.config file in the folder that you specify are merged with the contents of the files higher in the hierarchy. This includes any folder-level files that exist in folders that are closer to the root of the project. I defined the Web.config file in Listing 9-25 in the Views/Home folder, but Visual Studio created a web.config file in the Views folder when the project was started. To show that all of the files in the hierarchy are used to create the configuration data, I added an application setting to the Views/web.config file, as shown in Listing 9-27.

■ **Tip** The name of the Web.config file is not case-sensitive. Web.config and web.config are both acceptable names for folder-level configuration files.

Listing 9-27. Adding an Application Setting to the web.config file in the Views Folder

```
<?xml version="1.0"?>

<configuration>
  <configSections>
    <sectionGroup name="system.web.webPages.razor"
        type="System.Web.WebPages.Razor.Configuration.RazorWebSectionGroup,
        System.Web.WebPages.Razor, Version=3.0.0.0, Culture=neutral,
```

```
        PublicKeyToken=31BF3856AD364E35">
      <section name="host" type="System.Web.WebPages.Razor.Configuration.HostSection,
        System.Web.WebPages.Razor, Version=3.0.0.0, Culture=neutral,
        PublicKeyToken=31BF3856AD364E35" requirePermission="false" />
      <section name="pages"
        type="System.Web.WebPages.Razor.Configuration.RazorPagesSection,
        System.Web.WebPages.Razor, Version=3.0.0.0, Culture=neutral,
        PublicKeyToken=31BF3856AD364E35" requirePermission="false" />
    </sectionGroup>
  </configSections>

  <system.web.webPages.razor>
    <host factoryType="System.Web.Mvc.MvcWebRazorHostFactory, System.Web.Mvc,
        Version=5.0.0.0, Culture=neutral, PublicKeyToken=31BF3856AD364E35" />
    <pages pageBaseType="System.Web.Mvc.WebViewPage">
      <namespaces>
        <add namespace="System.Web.Mvc" />
        <add namespace="System.Web.Mvc.Ajax" />
        <add namespace="System.Web.Mvc.Html" />
        <add namespace="System.Web.Routing" />
        <add namespace="ConfigFiles" />
      </namespaces>
    </pages>
  </system.web.webPages.razor>

  <appSettings>
    <add key="webpages:Enabled" value="false" />
    <add key="defaultLanguage" value="French"/>
  </appSettings>

  <system.webServer>
    <handlers>
      <remove name="BlockViewHandler"/>
      <add name="BlockViewHandler" path="*" verb="*"
          preCondition="integratedMode" type="System.Web.HttpNotFoundHandler" />
    </handlers>
  </system.webServer>
</configuration>
```

The Views/web.config file is used by the MVC framework to configure the Razor view engine, and you wouldn't usually add configuration elements for the application. But that's just convention, and you can see the effect of my addition by starting the application and requesting the /Home/OtherAction URL, as shown in Figure 9-9.

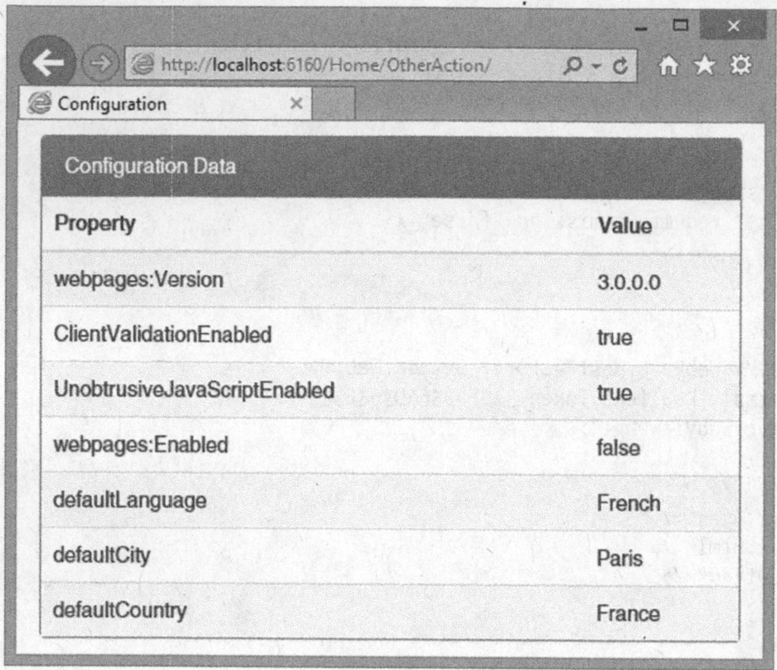

Figure 9-9. *Using a folder-level configuration file*

As the figure shows, the set of application settings consists of those defined by the application-level `Web.config` file, supplemented by those in the folder-level files in the `Views` and `Views/Home` folders.

Navigating the ASP.NET Configuration Elements

The examples so far in this chapter have been focused on defining configuration settings for an application, largely because that's the most common reason for using the configuration system. However, the settings that control the behavior of the ASP.NET platform and the MVC framework are also defined in the configuration files and are available to be read within an application. This isn't a common task—and I won't spend much time on it—but I find it useful when I suspect that a problem I am tracking down is caused by a configuration problem.

The ASP.NET configuration elements are contained in the `system.web` section, and the handler classes are defined in the `System.Web.Configuration` namespace. When you request a configuration section or section group through the `WebConfigurationManager` class, it will be represented by one of the classes in that namespace. I have listed the most commonly used handler classes in Table 9-14. There are others, but some of them are just for backward compatibility or have no bearing in an MVC framework application.

Table 9-14. *The Commonly Used Handler Classes to Represent ASP.NET Configuration Sections*

Name	Description
CacheSection	Represents the cache section, which controls content caching. See Chapters 11 and 12.
CompilationSection	Represents the compilation section, which controls how the application code is compiled. See the following text for details.
CustomErrorsSection	Represents the customErrors section, which controls the error handling policy. See *Pro ASP.NET MVC 5* for details.
GlobalizationSection	Represents the globalization section, which controls locale and culture settings for the application.
HttpRuntimeSection	Represents the httpRuntime section, which defines basic behavior for the application.
SessionStateSection	Represents the sessionState section, which I describe in Chapter 10.
SystemWebSectionGroup	Represents the system.Web section group, which contains the ASP.NET configuration sections.
TraceSection	Represents the trace section, which control request tracing. See Chapter 8.

To demonstrate reading the ASP.NET settings, I have modified the Home controller so that it displays details of the compilation section, as shown in Listing 9-28.

Listing 9-28. Reading ASP.NET Configuration Elements in the HomeController.cs File

```
using System.Collections.Generic;
using System.Configuration;
using System.Web.Configuration;
using System.Web.Mvc;

namespace ConfigFiles.Controllers {

    public class HomeController : Controller {

        public ActionResult Index() {
            Dictionary<string, string> configData = new Dictionary<string, string>();
            SystemWebSectionGroup sysWeb =
                (SystemWebSectionGroup)WebConfigurationManager.OpenWebConfiguration("/")
                    .GetSectionGroup("system.web");
            configData.Add("debug", sysWeb.Compilation.Debug.ToString());
            configData.Add("targetFramework", sysWeb.Compilation.TargetFramework);
            return View(configData);
        }
    }
}
```

I use the technique I described at the start of the chapter to get the handler for the system.Web section group, which defines properties for each of the sections it defines. The Compilation property returns the handler for the compilation section, which defines properties for the debug and targetFramework settings. You can see the result from reading the compilation settings by starting the application, as shown in Figure 9-10.

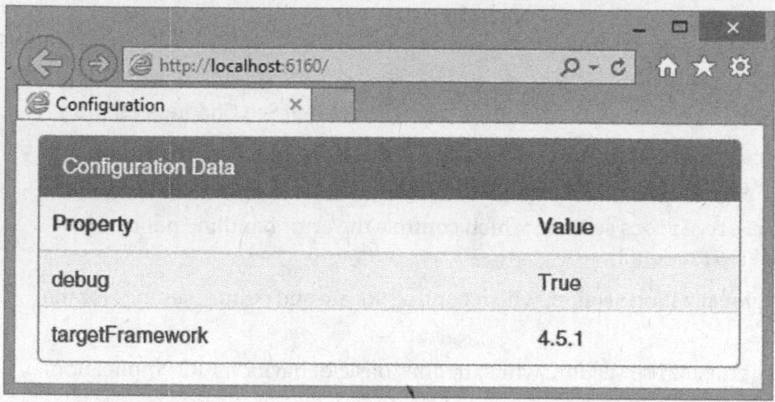

Figure 9-10. *Reading an ASP.NET configuration section*

Summary

In this chapter, I explained how the ASP.NET configuration system works. I introduced the hierarchy of configuration files and the way that the ASP.NET platform merges them to create a unified configuration. I explained how you can create simple custom configurations for your application using application settings and connection strings and, with a little more effort, create your own configuration sections and collections. In the next chapter, I introduce the ASP.NET platform services for state data: *application state* and *session state*.

CHAPTER 10

State Data

In this chapter, I describe the two services that the ASP.NET platform provides for creating stateful data: *application state* and *session state*. These features are easy to use, but they require forethought and caution to avoid serious performance penalties. I explain how each feature works and how to sidestep the pitfalls. Table 10-1 summarizes this chapter.

Table 10-1. *Chapter Summary*

Problem	Solution	Listing
Store data so that it is available to every component in the application.	Use the application state data feature.	1–4
Perform multiple read or write operations on application state data.	Use the `Lock` and `UnLock` methods defined by the `HttpApplicationState` class.	5, 6
Associate data with requests from the same client.	Use the session and session state features.	7–14
Prevent requests in the same session from being processed in sequence.	Use the `SessionState` attribute with the `Disabled` or `ReadOnly` argument.	15–17
Control how sessions are tracked.	Use the `cookieless` option in the `sessionState` configuration section.	18, 19
Change the storage mechanism for sessions.	Use the `mode` option in the `sessionState` configuration section to specify the state server or a SQL database.	20–21

Preparing the Example Project

For this chapter, I created a new project called StateData, following the same pattern that I have been using in earlier chapters. I used the Visual Studio ASP.NET Web Application template, selected the Empty option, and added the core MVC references. I'll be using Bootstrap again in this chapter, so enter the following command into the Package Manager Console:

```
Install-Package -version 3.0.3 bootstrap
```

Listing 10-1 shows the contents of the HomeController.cs file, which I used to define the default controller for the project in the Controllers folder.

Listing 10-1. The Contents of the HomeController.cs File

```
using System;
using System.Collections.Generic;
using System.Web.Configuration;
using System.Web.Mvc;

namespace StateData.Controllers {

    public class HomeController : Controller {

        public ActionResult Index() {
            Dictionary<string, object> data = new Dictionary<string, object>();
            data.Add("Placeholder Property", "Placeholder Value");
            return View(data);
        }
    }
}
```

The view model data in the Index action method is a dictionary collection that allows me to pass arbitrary key-value pairs to the view. I created the view by right-clicking the action method in the code editor and selecting Add View from the pop-up menu. I called the view Index.cshtml, selected the Empty (without model) template, and unchecked all of the View Option boxes. You can see the content I defined in the view in Listing 10-2.

Listing 10-2. The Contents of the Index.cshtml File

```
@model Dictionary<string, object>
@{ Layout = null; }
<!DOCTYPE html>
<html>
<head>
    <meta name="viewport" content="width=device-width" />
    <link href="~/Content/bootstrap.min.css" rel="stylesheet" />
    <link href="~/Content/bootstrap-theme.min.css" rel="stylesheet" />
    <style>
        body { padding-top: 10px; }
    </style>
    <title>State Data</title>
</head>
<body class="container">
    <div class="panel panel-primary">
        <div class="panel-heading">Data</div>
        <table class="table table-striped">
            <thead>
                <tr><th>Property</th><th>Value</th></tr>
            </thead>
```

```
            <tbody>
                @foreach (string key in Model.Keys) {
                    <tr><td>@key</td><td>@Model[key]</td></tr>
                }
            </tbody>
        </table>
    </div>
</body>
</html>
```

The layout generates a table that displays the contents of the collection, as shown in Figure 10-1.

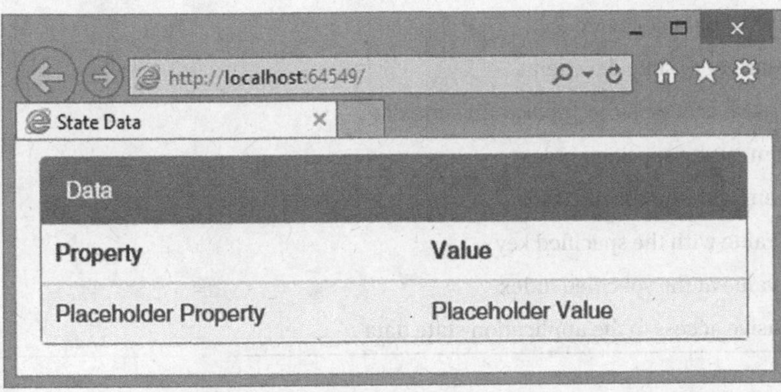

Figure 10-1. Testing the example application

Application State Data

Application state data is common to all components in the application and is shared between all requests. The main purpose of application state is to store data or objects that you need frequently and that are too resource-expensive or time-consuming to create for every use. Application state can improve the performance of an application, but it is easy to create the opposite effect and slow everything down instead. In this section, I'll demonstrate how application state data is created and used, point out the pitfalls, and show you how to avoid them. Table 10-2 puts application state into context.

Table 10-2. Putting the Appliction State in Context

Question	Answer
What is it?	Application state data allows small amounts of data to be shared throughout an application and is available to every component.
Why should I care?	Application state is a convenient way of ensuring that data values are used consistently throughout an application, albeit it works well when the data that is stored has some specific characteristics.
How is it used by the MVC framework?	This feature is not used directly by the MVC framework, but it is available for use in application components, including modules, controllers, and views.

Using Application State

Application state is implemented by the `HttpApplicationState` class, which is defined in the `System.Web` namespace. An instance of the `HttpApplicationState` class is available through the `HttpContext.Application` property. The `HttpApplicationState` class defines the properties and methods shown in Table 10-3.

***Table 10-3.** The Members Defined by the HttpApplicationState Class*

Name	Description
`Add(key, value)`	Adds a value to the state data collection with the specified key
`AllKeys`	Returns the collection keys as a string array
`Clear()`	Removes all the application state data
`Count`	Returns the number of state data items
`Lock()`	Acquires exclusive access to the application state data
`Item[index]`	Returns the item at the specified index
`Item[key]`	Returns the item with the specified key
`Remove(key)`	Removes the value with the specified key
`RemoveAt(index)`	Removes the value at the specified index
`UnLock()`	Releases exclusive access to the application state data

The `HttpApplicationState` class is a collection of key-value pairs stored in memory and shared across the application. The collection can be modified when the application is running, and the methods that it defines are thread-safe to prevent multiple updates from colliding when requests are being processed concurrently.

It can be hard to find good uses for application state data because of the way the `HttpApplicationState` class is implemented. The sweet spot is data that is resource-intensive or time-consuming to create, but also the data has to be the following:

- Can be re-created if the application is started (because the data is not persistent)
- Has a relatively small number of data items, all of which are equally important
- Is common for all users or requests
- Needs to be modified during the life of the application

If the data doesn't have all those characteristics, then there are better alternatives available than application state, such as session state (see the "Sessions and Session State Data" section), a data cache (see Chapter 11), or just a set of `static` variables. I'll show you an example of how the application state data feature is commonly used and then explain why it isn't always ideal.

WHY COVER APPLICATION STATE AT ALL?

You might be wondering why I have included application state at all, given its limitations. There are several reasons. First, even though I don't often come across data that fits every characteristic that suits application state, *your* application may be chock-full of it and the `HttpApplicationState` class may suit your needs perfectly. One of the most interesting aspects of talking with readers of my books is just how diverse web applications can be.

Second, I am describing the sweet spot for which application state is ideal, but you may be willing to compromise and exchange a little performance for a lot of convenience. The main advantage of the application state feature is that it is simple and easy to use, and that is not to be underestimated, especially when you compare application state to the data caching feature I describe in Chapter 11.

Third, I find application state data useful when I am debugging problems in a web application. Tools such as request tracing and Glimpse (see Chapter 8) are great for figuring out what has gone wrong in an application, but application state is helpful for quickly digging into the detail and prototyping a solution. I use it to short-circuit the separation of concerns in an application just to get a working solution before refactoring controllers and views to put a permanent fix in place. Like every web application developer, I spend a substantial amount of time tracking down and fixing bugs, and I will use any tool that helps me, however imperfect it is.

So, the application state data feature can be useful, even though it is flawed. You should understand its limitations but also be aware of where it is helpful and when it represents a reasonable compromise between performance and convenience.

I don't like to work directly with the `HttpApplicationState` class in controllers and views. Instead, I prefer to create a helper class that acts as an intermediary. I'll explain the reasons for this shortly, but to get started I created an `Infrastructure` folder in the example project and added to it a class file called `AppStateHelper.cs`, the contents of which are shown in Listing 10-3.

Listing 10-3. The Contents of the AppStateHelper.cs File

```
using System;
using System.Web;

namespace StateData.Infrastructure {

    public enum AppStateKeys {
        COUNTER
    };

    public static class AppStateHelper {

        public static object Get(AppStateKeys key, object defaultValue = null) {
            string keyString = Enum.GetName(typeof(AppStateKeys), key);
            if (HttpContext.Current.Application[keyString] == null
                    && defaultValue != null) {
                HttpContext.Current.Application[keyString] = defaultValue;
            }
            return HttpContext.Current.Application[keyString];
        }
```

```
        public static object Set(AppStateKeys key, object value) {
            return HttpContext.Current.Application[Enum.GetName(typeof(AppStateKeys),
                key)] = value;
        }
    }
}
```

The code in this class looks a little gnarly, and that's one of the reasons why I like to create a helper class. The data stored by the HttpApplicationState class can be modified while the application is running, and that means care must be taken to check that data values actually exist and have not been deleted by another request. For this reason, I have defined the Get method, which accepts a default value that will be used to set the state data when no value is found for the specified key, like this:

```
...
if (HttpContext.Current.Application[keyString] == null && defaultValue != null) {
    HttpContext.Current.Application[keyString] = defaultValue;
}
...
```

The argument used for the default value is optional, but its use means I don't have to check for null values wherever I use application state. Notice that the Get and Set methods accept values from the AppStateKeys enumeration as keys, rather than strings. The nature of application-wide state data means that its use is diffused across multiple components, which presents opportunities for bugs caused by mistyping the key name and maintenance problems when you need to locate and change the name of a key. To prevent this from happening, I use an enumeration to constrain and centralize the keys and use the static methods of the Enum class to convert from enumeration values to names, like this:

```
...
string keyString = Enum.GetName(typeof(AppStateKeys), key);
...
```

The final reason that I like to use a helper class is that it makes changes easier because all of the references to the HttpApplicationState class are contained in one place.

The key that I defined in the AppStateKeys enumeration is called COUNTER, and you can see how I have used it in Listing 10-4, which shows changes I made to the Home controller.

Listing 10-4. Using Application State Data in the HomeController.cs File

```
using System;
using System.Collections.Generic;
using System.Web.Configuration;
using System.Web.Mvc;
using StateData.Infrastructure;

namespace StateData.Controllers {

    public class HomeController : Controller {

        public ActionResult Index() {
            Dictionary<string, object> data = new Dictionary<string, object>();
            data.Add("Counter", AppStateHelper.Get(AppStateKeys.COUNTER, 0));
            return View(data);
        }
```

```
        public ActionResult Increment() {
            int currentValue = (int)AppStateHelper.Get(AppStateKeys.COUNTER, 0);
            AppStateHelper.Set(AppStateKeys.COUNTER, currentValue + 1);
            return RedirectToAction("Index");
        }
    }
}
```

I have changed the Index action method so that it obtains the COUNTER state variable using the helper class and adds it to the collection that is rendered by the view. I have added a new action method, called Increment, which gets the value of the COUNTER variable and increments it. Once the state data value has been incremented, the client is redirected to the Index action, which will display the new value. To test the changes, start the application and request the /Home/Index URL followed by /Home/Increment, as shown in Figure 10-2.

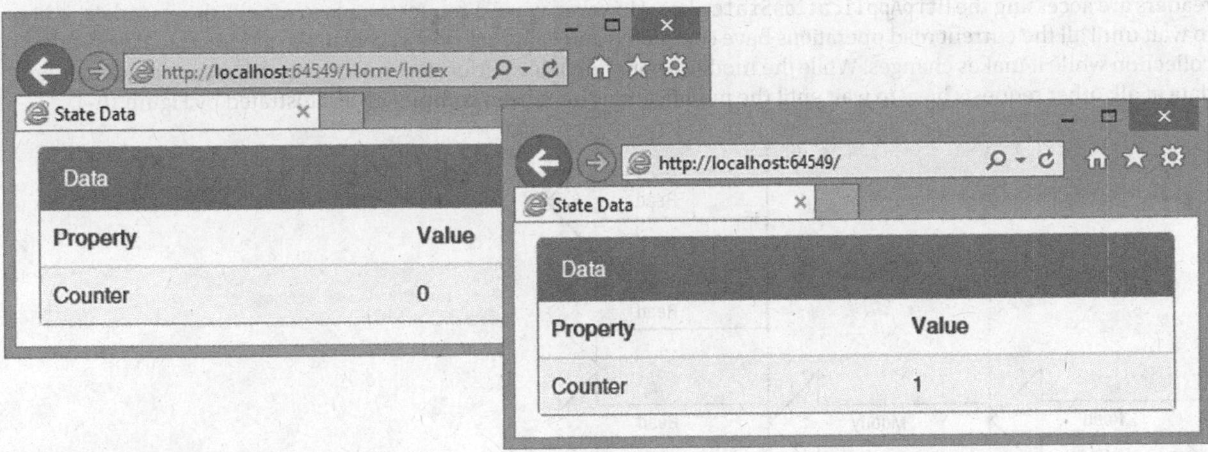

Figure 10-2. *Working with application state data*

Understanding the Synchronization Effect

This isn't the most compelling example, but it demonstrates an important aspect (and pitfall) of working with application state data. ASP.NET processes requests concurrently, and to ensure that one request isn't trying to read data that another is trying to simultaneously modify, the methods and properties of the HttpApplicationState class are synchronized.

The kind of synchronization used in the HttpApplicationState class means that when multiple requests are *reading* application state data, they can all access that data simultaneously, as shown in Figure 10-3.

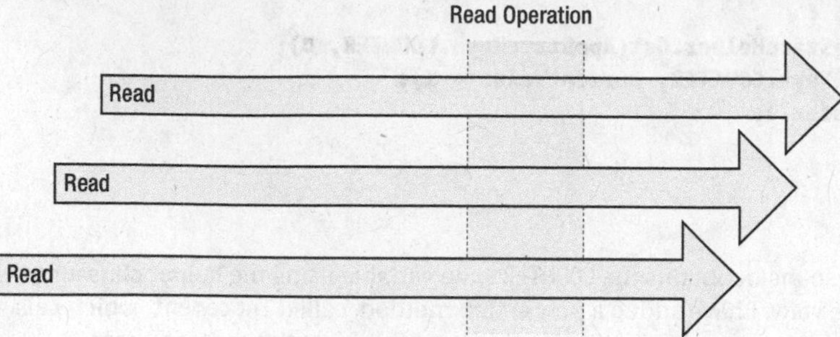

Figure 10-3. Multiple requests reading application state data

All of the requests can read the data without delay, aside from the small overhead required to make sure that only readers are accessing the HttpApplicationState class. However, when a request wants to *modify* the state data, it has to wait until all the current read operations have completed and gain exclusive access to the HttpApplicationState collection while it makes changes. While the modifications are being performed, no other request can access the state data at all; other requests have to wait until the modifications have been completed, as illustrated by Figure 10-4.

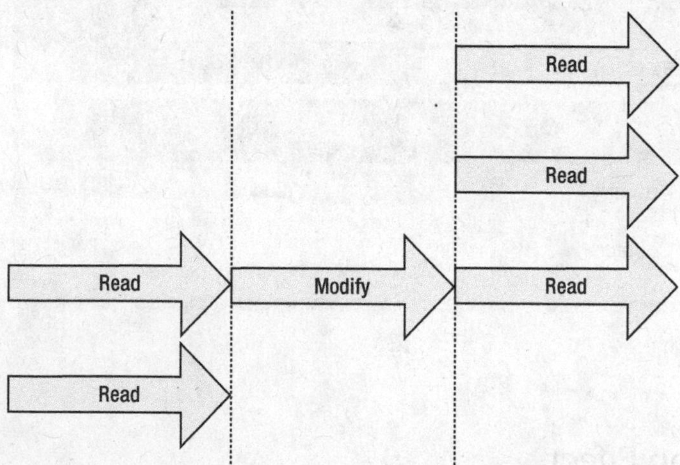

Figure 10-4. The effect of a request modifying application state data

A queue of requests forms each time that one of them wants to modify the data. At the head of the queue is the request that wants to make the modification, waiting for the current readers to complete the work. Following those are all of the other requests that want to access the state data, which have to wait until the modification is complete before they can proceed.

The queuing effect wouldn't be quite so bad if it applied to individual state data items, but it applies to the entire HttpApplicationState object, so a modification for *any* state data value causes a queue to form, even if the other requests want to access a different data item.

The impact of the synchronization on performance depends on the number of concurrent requests that the application processes, the ratio of reads to modifications, and the complexity of the operations being performed. For applications with simple state data items, a low volume of requests, and occasional modifications, the performance impact will be negligible. For an application at the other end of the spectrum, the impact is striking, and the application will essentially lock up for each modification. Most applications will fall somewhere between these extremes, and you will have to decide whether the convenience of being able to share data between components through the HttpApplicationState class is worth the performance penalty.

Performing Related Operations

A side effect of the way that the application state data collection is synchronized is that caution must be taken if you need to read or write multiple related values. The problem is that each read or modification operation is synchronized independently and the request goes to the back of the synchronization queue between operations, allowing another request to make a change and create an inconsistency in the data.

The Lock method defined by the HttpApplicationState class provides exclusive access to the state data collection until the UnLock method is called. To be sure that the state data is read or modified consistently, you must use the Lock method whenever multiple related operations are performed and remember to call the UnLock method when they are complete. In Listing 10-5, you can see how I have updated the AppStateHelper class so that there are two related state data variables and that I used the Lock and UnLock methods to ensure that they are read and modified together.

Listing 10-5. Gaining Exclusive Access to the Application State Data in the AppStateHelper.cs File

```
using System;
using System.Web;
using System.Collections.Generic;

namespace StateData.Infrastructure {

    public enum AppStateKeys {
        COUNTER,
        LAST_REQUEST_TIME,
        LAST_REQUEST_URL
    };

    public static class AppStateHelper {

        public static object Get(AppStateKeys key, object defaultValue = null) {
            string keyString = Enum.GetName(typeof(AppStateKeys), key);
            if (HttpContext.Current.Application[keyString] == null
                    && defaultValue != null) {
                HttpContext.Current.Application[keyString] = defaultValue;
            }
            return HttpContext.Current.Application[keyString];
        }

        public static object Set(AppStateKeys key, object value) {
            return HttpContext.Current.Application[Enum.GetName(typeof(AppStateKeys),
                key)] = value;
        }

        public static IDictionary<AppStateKeys, object>
            GetMultiple(params AppStateKeys[] keys) {

            Dictionary<AppStateKeys, object> results
                = new Dictionary<AppStateKeys, object>();
            HttpApplicationState appState = HttpContext.Current.Application;
            appState.Lock();
```

```
            foreach (AppStateKeys key in keys) {
                string keyString = Enum.GetName(typeof(AppStateKeys), key);
                results.Add(key, appState[keyString]);
            }
            appState.UnLock();
            return results;
        }

        public static void SetMultiple(IDictionary<AppStateKeys, object> data) {
            HttpApplicationState appState = HttpContext.Current.Application;
            appState.Lock();
            foreach (AppStateKeys key in data.Keys) {
                string keyString = Enum.GetName(typeof(AppStateKeys), key);
                appState[keyString] = data[key];
            }
            appState.UnLock();
        }
    }
}
```

I have added GetMultiple and SetMultiple methods to the helper class, and these methods operate on arbitrary numbers of application state data values, all of which are read or modified following a call to the Lock method, ensuring that no other request can read or modify the data until the UnLock method is called. In Listing 10-6, you can see how I have updated the Home controller to use the new helper methods.

Listing 10-6. Performing Related Operations in the HomeController.cs File

```
using System;
using System.Collections.Generic;
using System.Web.Configuration;
using System.Web.Mvc;
using StateData.Infrastructure;

namespace StateData.Controllers {

    public class HomeController : Controller {

        public ActionResult Index() {
            Dictionary<string, object> data = new Dictionary<string, object>();
            data.Add("Counter", AppStateHelper.Get(AppStateKeys.COUNTER, 0));
            IDictionary<AppStateKeys, object> stateData
                = AppStateHelper.GetMultiple(AppStateKeys.LAST_REQUEST_TIME,
                    AppStateKeys.LAST_REQUEST_URL);
            foreach (AppStateKeys key in stateData.Keys) {
                data.Add(Enum.GetName(typeof(AppStateKeys), key), stateData[key]);
            }
            return View(data);
        }
```

```
        public ActionResult Increment() {
            int currentValue = (int)AppStateHelper.Get(AppStateKeys.COUNTER, 0);
            AppStateHelper.Set(AppStateKeys.COUNTER, currentValue + 1);
            AppStateHelper.SetMultiple(new Dictionary<AppStateKeys, object> {
                { AppStateKeys.LAST_REQUEST_TIME, HttpContext.Timestamp},
                { AppStateKeys.LAST_REQUEST_URL, Request.RawUrl}
            });
            return RedirectToAction("Index");
        }
    }
}
```

To see the effect, start the application and request the /Home/Increment method, which will generate the output shown in Figure 10-5.

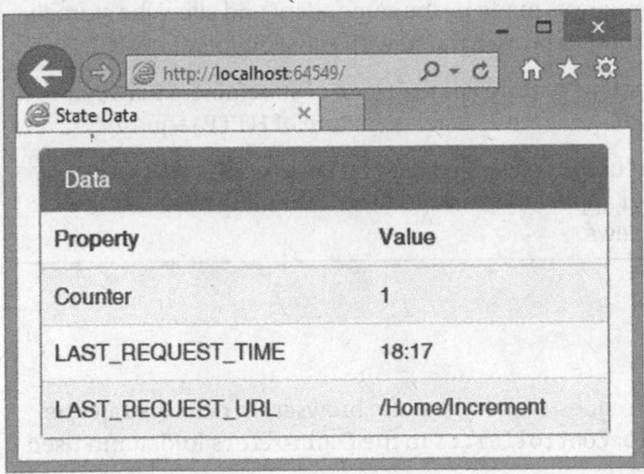

***Figure 10-5.** Reading and modifying multiple state data properties in a single operation*

Using the Lock and UnLock methods ensures that the state data is always consistent, but it does so by forcing each operation that uses them to execute in strict sequence. Each time that the Lock method is called, all of the other requests that use application state data will form a queue and wait until the UnLock method is called, in effect preventing requests from using the application state data concurrently.

WHAT ABOUT VIEW STATE?

You may encounter references to *view state* and wonder what it is. View state is a feature of Web Forms and tries to provide the stateful development experience that is common with desktop application work. View state isn't used in the MVC framework.

View state is part of the way that Web Forms abstracts away the details of HTTP and web browsers and works by including hidden form data that describes the state of the user interface presented via HTML, essentially allowing HTML elements to be represented by server-side components. The careless use of view state can result in large amounts of data being sent between the server and the browser and is one of the reasons that Web Forms has gained such a mixed reputation as a web application development platform. The MVC framework is designed to work in concert with HTTP requests and doesn't need a feature like view state.

Sessions and Session State Data

HTTP is a stateless protocol, but it is often important to be able to identify related requests in order to deliver continuity in a web application. To this end, the ASP.NET platform supports *sessions*, which allow requests from the same browser to be identified, and *session state*, which allows data to be stored for one request in a session and retrieved when subsequent requests are being processed.

In this section, I'll explain how sessions work and how to associate state data with a session. Along the way, I'll point out a performance issue similar to the one that I described for application state data in the previous section and explain and demonstrate different ways for storing state data. Table 10-4 puts sessions and session state data into context.

Table 10-4. *Putting Sessions and Session State Data in Context*

Question	Answer
What is it?	Sessions identify requests made by the same client and allow the storage of data in one request to be associated with subsequent requests.
Why should I care?	Almost all applications require some degree of statefulness between requests to compensate for the stateless nature of HTTP requests.
How is it used by the MVC framework?	This feature is not used directly by the MVC framework, but it is available for use in application components, including modules, controllers, and views.

Working with Session Data

Session data stores data and makes it available across multiple requests from the same browser. To demonstrate the use of session data, I have added a class file called `RegistrationController.cs` to the `Controllers` folder and used it to define the controller shown in Listing 10-7.

Listing 10-7. The Contents of the RegistrationController.cs File

```
using System.Web.Mvc;

namespace StateData.Controllers {
    public class RegistrationController : Controller {

        public ActionResult Index() {
            return View();
        }

        [HttpPost]
        public ActionResult ProcessFirstForm(string name) {
            System.Diagnostics.Debug.WriteLine("Name: {0}", (object)name);
            return View("SecondForm");
        }
        [HttpPost]
        public ActionResult CompleteForm(string country) {
            System.Diagnostics.Debug.WriteLine("Country: {0}", (object)country);
            // in a real application, this is where the call to create the
            // new user account would be
```

```
            ViewBag.Name = "<Unknown>";
            ViewBag.Country = country;
            return View();
        }
    }
}
```

This controller simulates a user registration process that spans two forms and a summary page. To keep the example simple, I collect only one item of data in each form and then display both data items in a summary view. To complete the example, I added three views to the `Views/Registration` folder. Listing 10-8 shows the markup for the first view, called `Index.cshtml`, returned by the `Index` action method and representing the start of the registration process.

Listing 10-8. The Contents of the Index.cshtml File in the Views/Registration Folder

```
@{ Layout = null; }
<!DOCTYPE html>
<html>
<head>
    <meta name="viewport" content="width=device-width" />
    <title>First Form</title>
    <link href="~/Content/bootstrap.min.css" rel="stylesheet" />
    <link href="~/Content/bootstrap-theme.min.css" rel="stylesheet" />
    <style>body { padding-top: 10px; }</style>
</head>
<body class="container">
    @using (Html.BeginForm("ProcessFirstForm", "Registration")) {
        <div class="form-group">
            <label for="name">Name</label>
            <input class="form-control" name="name" placeholder="Enter name">
        </div>
        <button class="btn btn-primary" type="submit">Submit</button>
    }
</body>
</html>
```

This is a simple form, styled with Bootstrap, which uses an `input` element to capture the user's name and post the result to the `ProcessFirstForm` action method in the `Registration` controller. The `ProcessFirstForm` action uses model binding to extract the name from the request and returns the content shown in Listing 10-9, which shows the `SecondForm.cshtml` file.

Listing 10-9. The Content of the SecondForm.cshtml File

```
@{ Layout = null; }
<!DOCTYPE html>
<html>
<head>
    <meta name="viewport" content="width=device-width" />
    <title>Second Form</title>
    <link href="~/Content/bootstrap.min.css" rel="stylesheet" />
    <link href="~/Content/bootstrap-theme.min.css" rel="stylesheet" />
    <style>body { padding-top: 10px; }</style>
</head>
```

```
<body class="container">
    @using (Html.BeginForm("CompleteForm", "Registration")) {
        <div class="form-group">
            <label for="country">Country</label>
            <input class="form-control" name="country" placeholder="Enter country">
        </div>
        <button class="btn btn-primary" type="submit">Submit</button>
    }
</body>
</html>
```

This form is similar to the first, except that it captures the user's country and posts the data to the `CompleteForm` action in the `Registration` controller. The `CompleteForm` action uses model binding to receive the country and renders the `CompleteForm.cshtml` view in response, which is shown in Listing 10-10.

Listing 10-10. The Contents of the CompleteForm.cshtml File

```
@{ Layout = null; }
<!DOCTYPE html>
<html>
<head>
    <meta name="viewport" content="width=device-width" />
    <title>Finished</title>
    <link href="~/Content/bootstrap.min.css" rel="stylesheet" />
    <link href="~/Content/bootstrap-theme.min.css" rel="stylesheet" />
    <style>body { padding-top: 10px; }</style>
</head>
<body class="container">
    <div class="panel panel-default">
        <div class="panel-heading">Registration Details</div>
        <table class="table table-striped">
            <tr><th>Name</th><td>@ViewBag.Name</td></tr>
            <tr><th>Country</th><td>@ViewBag.Country</td></tr>
        </table>
    </div>
</body>
</html>
```

This view contains a table that displays the name and country provided by the user. Start the application and request the `/Registration` URL to test the application. Enter your name and click the Submit button. Enter your country and click the Submit button. The browser will display the summary table, which will be similar to the one shown in Figure 10-6.

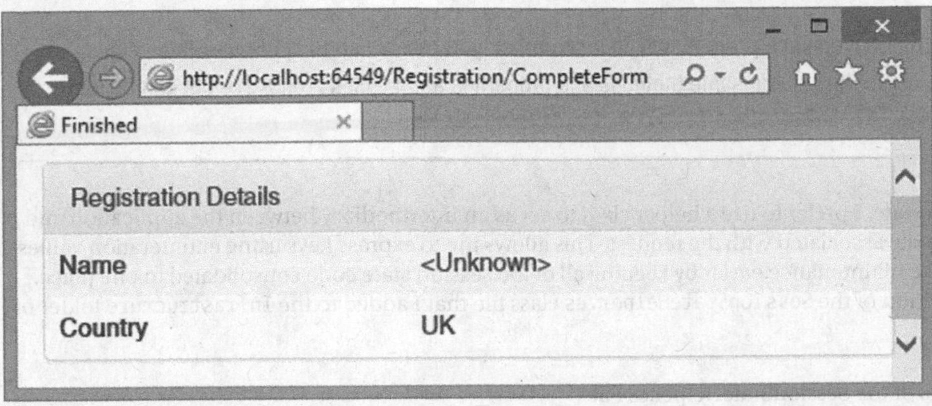

Figure 10-6. Displaying a summary of the registration data

Using Session State Data

HTTP requests are stateless, which is a problem when you need to create application functionality that spans multiple requests. In my example application, this problem can be seen in Figure 10-6, where there the value provided for the Name property isn't the value entered by the user. This is because the name was sent to the server in an earlier request and isn't included in the request through which the server receives the user's country. The session state feature will allow me to store the user's name in one request and then retrieve it in a subsequent request.

Session state data is accessed through the HttpContext.Session property, which returns an instance of the System.Web.SessionState.HttpSessionState class. This class is responsible for managing the session state data and the session itself. I return to session management later in this chapter, but Table 10-5 describes the members of the HttpSessionState class that support session state data. Within controllers and views, you can use the Session convenience property, without needing to go through the HttpContext object (although this is what is done for you behind the scenes).

Table 10-5. The HttpSessionState Members That Manage Session State Data

Name	Description
Count	Returns the number of session state data items.
IsReadyOnly	Returns true if the session state data cannot be modified. See the later "Understanding the Synchronization Effect" section.
IsSynchronized	Returns true if the session state data is synchronized.
Item[index]	Returns the state data item at the specified index.
Item[key]	Returns the state data item with the specified key.
Clear()	Removes all of the state data items.
Remove(key)	Removes the state data item with the specified key.
Remove(index)	Removes the state data item at the specified index.

■ **Tip** If you use the `Session` convenience property within a controller, you receive an `HttpContextBase` object, as I explained in Chapter 3. This object has all the same methods and properties as `HttpSessionState` but can be more readily used in unit testing.

Just as with application state, I prefer to use a helper class to act as an intermediary between the application and the `HttpSessionState` instance associated with the request. This allows me to express keys using enumeration values so as to avoid typos and make maintenance easier by keeping all of the session state code consolidated in one place. Listing 10-11 shows the addition of the `SessionStateHelper.cs` class file that I added to the `Infrastructure` folder of the example project.

Listing 10-11. The Contents of the SessionStateHelper.cs File

```
using System;
using System.Web;

namespace StateData.Infrastructure {

    public enum SessionStateKeys {
        NAME
    }

    public static class SessionStateHelper {

        public static object Get(SessionStateKeys key) {
            string keyString = Enum.GetName(typeof(SessionStateKeys), key);
            return HttpContext.Current.Session[keyString];
        }

        public static object Set(SessionStateKeys key, object value) {
            string keyString = Enum.GetName(typeof(SessionStateKeys), key);
            return HttpContext.Current.Session[keyString] = value;
        }
    }
}
```

The `SessionStateHelper` class follows the same basic approach that I used for the application state equivalent but is a little simpler because I make no effort to check to see whether values exist or set default values because session state data tends to be set as a result of user interactions and, as a consequence, default values are less useful. Listing 10-12 shows how I have applied session state data in the `Registration` controller through the helper class.

Listing 10-12. Using Session State Data in the RegistrationController.cs File

```
using System.Web.Mvc;
using StateData.Infrastructure;

namespace StateData.Controllers {
    public class RegistrationController : Controller {
```

```
        public ActionResult Index() {
            return View();
        }

        [HttpPost]
        public ActionResult ProcessFirstForm(string name) {
            SessionStateHelper.Set(SessionStateKeys.NAME, name);
            return View("SecondForm");
        }

        [HttpPost]
        public ActionResult CompleteForm(string country) {
            ViewBag.Name = SessionStateHelper.Get(SessionStateKeys.NAME);
            ViewBag.Country = country;
            return View();
        }
    }
}
```

When the user submits their name, the ProcessFirstForm action method stores the value as session state data, which is then retrieved by the CompleteForm action method when the user subsequently submits their country in the next request. This allows both form values to be used together, even though they were received by the server in two separate HTTP requests, as shown in Figure 10-7.

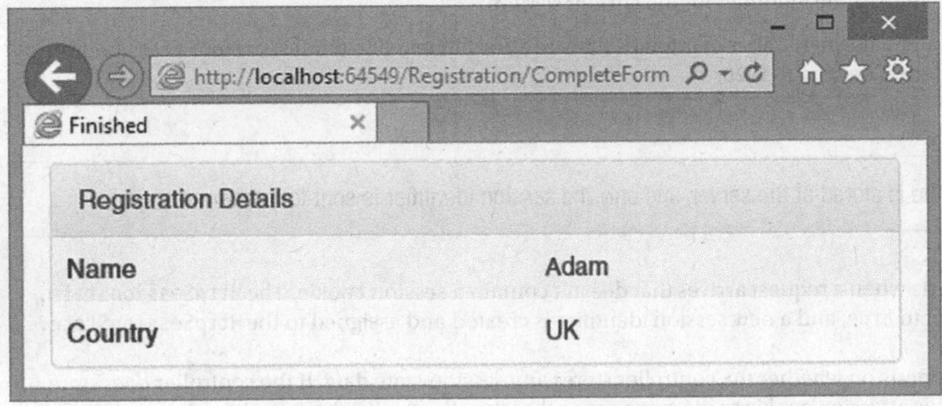

Figure 10-7. Using session state data

Understanding How Sessions Work

As the previous example demonstrated, using session state data is simple, but there is a lot of work that goes on behind the scenes, and understanding it is essential to creating an application that works and performs the way you want. The entry point into the sessions feature is a module called SessionStateModule, which handles the AcquireRequestState request life-cycle event and is responsible for associating session state data with the request.

The SessionStateModule looks for a session identifier in each request that is received by ASP.NET. The identifier is usually a cookie (although this can be changed, as I explain in the "Tracking Sessions Without Cookies" section), and it is used to load the state data into an HttpSessionState object that is attached to the HttpContext object associated with the request. This process, which is repeated for every request, allows session state to be used across requests from the same browser.

> ■ **Tip** You can receive notifications when sessions are created and destroyed by handling the events defined by the `SessionStateModule`. See Chapter 4 for details.

The `HttpSessionState` class defines methods and properties that describe and manage the session associated with a request, as described in Table 10-6. These are in addition to the state data members that I described in Table 10-5.

Table 10-6. *The HttpSessionState Members That Manage Sessions*

Name	Description
`Abandon()`	Terminates the current session.
`CookieMode`	Returns a value from the `HttpCookieMode` enumeration that describes how sessions are identified. This corresponds to the value of the `mode` setting in the `sessionState` configuration section; see the "Tracking Sessions Without Cookies" section.
`IsCookieless`	Returns `true` if identification is performed without cookies for this request; see the "Tracking Sessions Without Cookies" section.
`IsNewSession`	Returns `true` if the session has been created during the current request.
`Mode`	Returns a value from the `SessionStateMode` enumeration, which describes how session state data is stored; see the "Storing Session Data" section.
`SessionID`	Returns the identifier for the current session.
`Timeout`	Returns the number of minutes that are allowed between requests before a session times out. The default is 20.

> ■ **Tip** The session state data is stored at the server, and only the session identifier is sent to the browser.

The life of a session starts when a request arrives that doesn't contain a session cookie. The `HttpSessionState.IsNewSession` property is set to `true`, and a new session identifier is created and assigned to the `HttpSessionState.SessionID` property.

What happens next depends on whether the controller stores any session state data. If the controller *does* store state data, then ASP.NET adds a session cookie to the response so that the client will submit it with subsequent requests. The session and its state data remain active as long as the browser continues to make requests within the limit defined by the `Timeout` variable or until the `Abandon` method is called.

The ASP.NET platform does *not* add the session cookie to the response if no state data has been stored. This means that any subsequent requests from the browser won't have a session cookie and the process begins again. To demonstrate the life cycle of a session, I added a class file called `LifecycleController.cs` to the `Controllers` folder and used it to define the controller shown in Listing 10-13.

Listing 10-13. The Contents of the LifecycleController.cs File

```
using System.Web;
using System.Web.Mvc;
using StateData.Infrastructure;
```

```
namespace StateData.Controllers {
    public class LifecycleController : Controller {

        public ActionResult Index() {
            return View();
        }

        [HttpPost]
        public ActionResult Index(bool store = false, bool abandon = false) {
            if (store) {
                SessionStateHelper.Set(SessionStateKeys.NAME, "Adam");
            }
            if (abandon) {
                Session.Abandon();
            }
            return RedirectToAction("Index");
        }
    }
}
```

This controller contains two versions of an action called Index, one of which just renders the default view and the other that receives POST requests and manipulates the session or session state based on form values in the request. I created the /Views/Lifecycle/Index.cshtml view to display information about the session, which you can see in Listing 10-14.

Listing 10-14. The Contents of the Index.cshtml File in the /Views/Lifecycle Folder

```
@{ Layout = null; }

<!DOCTYPE html>
<html>
<head>
    <meta name="viewport" content="width=device-width" />
    <title>Session Lifecycle</title>
    <link href="~/Content/bootstrap.min.css" rel="stylesheet" />
    <link href="~/Content/bootstrap-theme.min.css" rel="stylesheet" />
    <style> body { padding-top: 10px; } </style>
</head>
<body class="container">
    <div class="panel panel-primary">
        <div class="panel-heading">Session</div>
        <table class="table">
            <tr><th>Session ID</th><td>@Session.SessionID</td></tr>
            <tr><th>Is New?</th><td>@Session.IsNewSession</td></tr>
            <tr><th>State Data Count</th><td>@Session.Count</td></tr>
        </table>
    </div>
    @using(Html.BeginForm()) {
        <div class="checkbox">
            <label>
            @Html.CheckBox("store") Store State Data</label>
        </div>
```

```
        <div class="checkbox">
            <label>
            @Html.CheckBox("abandon") Abandon Session</label>
        </div>
        <button class="btn btn-primary" type="submit">Submit</button>
    }
</body>
</html>
```

The view contains a table that provides some basic information about the session and its state data, as well as a form that drives the arguments to the POST version of the `Index` action method from Listing 10-13. To see the view rendered, start the application and navigate to the `/Lifecycle/Index` URL, as shown in Figure 10-8.

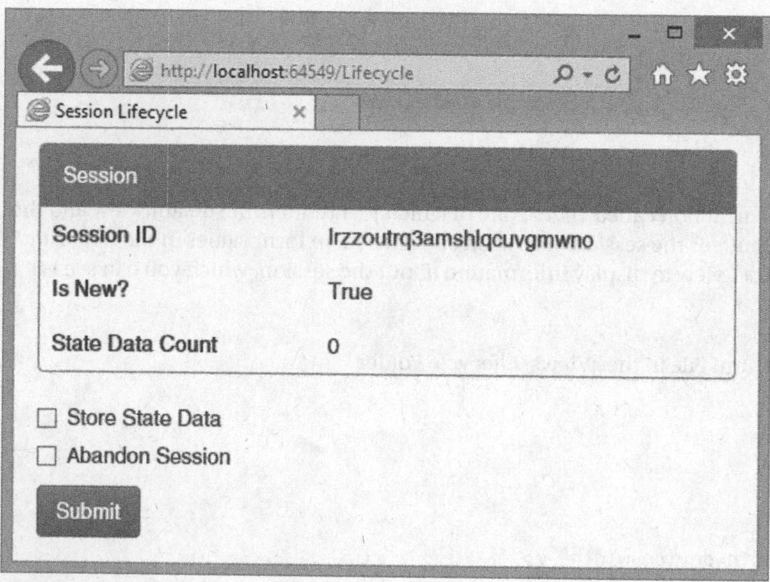

***Figure 10-8.** Querying and manipulating sessions*

When you first start the application, your browser will send its request to the server without a session cookie. The ASP.NET platform will respond by generating a session ID, which you can see in the output from the view, but it won't add the cookie to the response. The `IsNew` property is `true`, and a new session ID will be generated each time you reload or submit the page (because ASP.NET isn't adding the cookie to the response, the browser doesn't send any session information back for subsequent requests and the process begins afresh).

Now check the Store State Data box and click the Submit button. When the controller receives this request, it will set a state data item, as follows:

```
...
SessionStateHelper.Set(SessionStateKeys.NAME, "Adam");
...
```

The ASP.NET platform responds by adding a session cookie to the response so that subsequent requests from the browser will be associated with the saved state data. If you reload or resubmit the browser now, you will see that the session ID remains fixed and that the `IsNew` property is `false`.

■ **Caution** Browsers that offer tabbed windows generally share cookies between those tabs. That means requests to the ASP.NET server from different tabs in the same browser window will be associated with the same session.

Now check the Abandon Session box and submit the form. When the controller receives this request, it will forcefully terminate the session, as follows:

```
...
Session.Abandon();
...
```

This marks the session as expired and releases the state data that has been associated with it.

■ **Tip** The state data itself may not be deleted immediately, depending on how it has been stored, but it will no longer be associated with subsequent requests from the browser. See the "Storing Session Data" section for details of storage options.

When you reload or submit the browser now, you will see something slightly different. The number of state data items is zero, but the session ID won't change for each request, and the `IsNew` property is shown as `true` for the first request and then `false` thereafter. This happens because the session cookie isn't deleted when the session is abandoned. The browser is still sending a session cookie to the server with each request, and the ASP.NET platform responds by reusing it, rather than generating a new one.

■ **Tip** You have to restart the application to return to the point where a new session ID is generated for each request. This clears all the in-memory sessions and session data. In the "Storing Session Data" section I explain how to persistently store the session data.

Understanding the Synchronization Effect

ASP.NET processes multiple requests concurrently, and modern browsers can make multiple requests concurrently. That means it is possible that two requests from the same browser may try to modify the state data simultaneously, presenting the risk of data corruption or inconsistent.

To mitigate this risk, the ASP.NET platform does something that sounds sensible but actually causes lots of problems and even more confusion: It forces requests that are part of the same session to execute sequentially. Each new request is executed only if there are no other requests that are part of the same session currently being processed.

Queuing concurrent requests for the same session made more sense when the feature was implemented because it was a rare situation and protecting the integrity of the session state data was seen as being important. These days, however, browsers obtain content and data via Ajax, and, as you might expect, the browsers include the session cookie as part of these requests, causing Ajax operations to be queued up and processed sequentially, even when ASP.NET is perfectly capable of processing them concurrently. Worse, the queuing is applied even when a request doesn't access the session state data; all it takes is that the request contains the session cookie, and the ASP.NET platform will begin queuing requests.

■ **Note** To be clear, only requests that are part of the *same* session are queued. Requests for different sessions are processed concurrently as are those that are not associated with a session. The problem I describe here arises *only* if you make multiple concurrent requests from the same browser, something that generally happens when working with Ajax.

Demonstrating the Problem

To demonstrate the problem that session synchronization creates and the effect it has on performance, I added a new controller called SyncTest to the example application. Listing 10-15 shows the definition of the controller.

Listing 10-15. The Contents of the SyncTestController.cs File

```
using System.Web.Mvc;

namespace StateData.Controllers {
    public class SyncTestController : Controller {

        public ActionResult Index() {
            return View();
        }

        [OutputCache(NoStore = true, Duration = 0)]
        public string GetMessage(int id) {
            return string.Format("Message: {0}", id);
        }
    }
}
```

This controller consists of an Index action method that renders the default view and a GetMessage action method that I will target from the browser using Ajax requests. The GetMessage method returns a string that is generated from the method argument, which will be set using the built-in MVC framework model binding feature. This controller doesn't do anything useful, other than provide me with a target for Ajax requests.

■ **Tip** I have applied the OutputCache attribute to the GetMessage method to prevent the output strings from being stored in the ASP.NET content cache. I describe the cache and the effect of the attribute in Chapter 12.

I created a view for the Index action method by right-clicking the method in the Visual Studio code editor and selecting Add View from the pop-up menu. I set the name to Index, selected the Empty (without model) option for the template, and unchecked all of the view option boxes. When I clicked the Add button, Visual Studio created the Views/SyncTest/Index.cshtml file, to which I added the content shown in Listing 10-16.

Listing 10-16. The Contents of the Index.cshtml File in the Views/SyncTest Folder

```
@{ Layout = null;}

<!DOCTYPE html>
<html>
<head>
    <meta name="viewport" content="width=device-width" />
    <title>SyncTest</title>
    <script src="http://code.jquery.com/jquery-1.10.1.min.js"></script>
    <link href="~/Content/bootstrap.min.css" rel="stylesheet" />
    <link href="~/Content/bootstrap-theme.min.css" rel="stylesheet" />
    <style>
        body { padding-top: 10px; }
    </style>
    <script>
        $(document).ready(function () {
            var start = new Date();
            var counter = 10;
            for (var i = 0; i < 10; i++) {
                $.get("/SyncTest/GetMessage", { id: i }, function (data) {
                    $("#msgTable tbody").append("<tr><td>" + data + "</th></tr>");
                    counter--;
                    if (counter == 0) {
                        var time = new Date().getTime() - start.getTime();
                        $("#results").text("Time (ms): " + time);
                    }
                });
            }
        });
    </script>
</head>
<body class="container">
    <div id="results" class="alert alert-success"></div>
    <table id="msgTable" class="table table-bordered table-striped">
        <tr><th>Messages</th></tr>
    </table>
</body>
</html>
```

For this view, I have added a `script` element that imports the jQuery library from a content delivery network (CDN) and another that uses jQuery to make Ajax requests to the `GetMessage` action on the `SyncTest` controller. Ten requests are made in total, and the elapsed time is displayed when all of the requests have completed.

■ **Note** I am going to treat the jQuery script in this example as a black box that makes Ajax requests and reports on them. jQuery is an excellent client-side library, but it isn't part of the ASP.NET platform and is beyond the scope of this book. I describe jQuery in detail in my *Pro jQuery 2* book, and I describe client-side development for MVC framework applications in my forthcoming *Pro ASP.NET MVC Client Development* book.

To see how this works, start the application and request the /SyncTest/Index URL. The application will render the default view for the Index action, which includes the jQuery code that makes the Ajax requests. The view includes a table that is populated with messages as each Ajax requests. Reload the page a few times by pressing the F5 key to get a sense of how long it takes for all of the requests to complete, as shown in Figure 10-9.

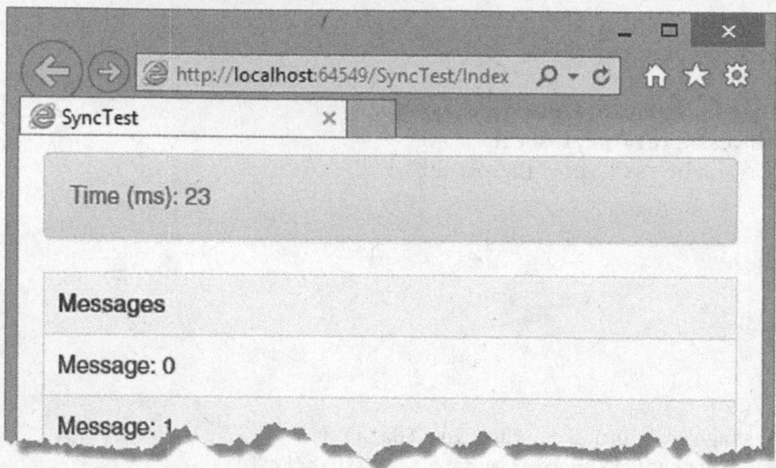

***Figure 10-9.** Measuring concurrent Ajax requests*

On my development desktop, the process takes about 20 to 25 milliseconds. These are short and simple requests to a server running on the same (powerful) machine, and I would expect them to be fast.

Leave the application running and navigate to the /Lifecycle/Index URL to see what happens when the Ajax requests are made as part of a session. Check the Store State Data box and click the Submit button and then navigate back to /SyncTest/Index. Now the Ajax requests will include a session cookie, so the ASP.NET will process them sequentially instead of concurrently. You can see the effect in Figure 10-10.

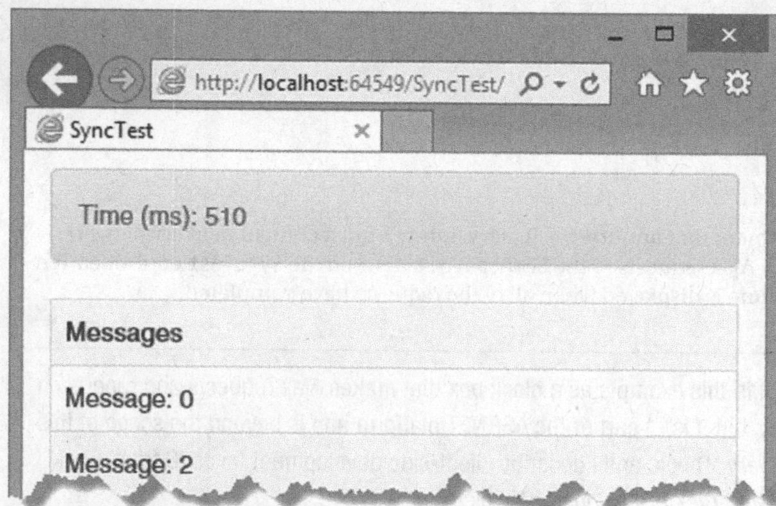

***Figure 10-10.** Measuring sequential Ajax requests*

On my development desktop, the requests now take about 500 milliseconds to complete, which is a striking difference given that the only difference is a session cookie. You may see different timings, but the difference should be loosely comparable.

Controlling Session State

The solution to this problem is to apply the `SessionState` attribute to control the use of the session state feature. Listing 10-17 shows the application of the attribute to the `SyncTest` controller.

Listing 10-17. Applying the SessionState Attribute in the SyncTestController.cs File

```
using System.Web.Mvc;
using System.Web.SessionState;

namespace StateData.Controllers {

    [SessionState(SessionStateBehavior.Disabled)]
    public class SyncTestController : Controller {

        public ActionResult Index() {
            return View();
        }

        [OutputCache(NoStore = true, Duration = 0)]
        public string GetMessage(int id) {
            return string.Format("Message: {0}", id);
        }
    }
}
```

The attribute is applied to the controller class and affects all of the action methods it contains. The attribute argument is a value from the `SessionStateBehavior` enumeration, which is defined in the `System.Web.SessionState` namespace. Table 10-7 describes the range of enumeration values.

Table 10-7. *The SessionStateBehavior Values*

Name	Description
`Default`	This is the standard ASP.NET behavior, in which the platform checks to see whether the `IHttpHandler` implementation that handles the request implements the `IRequiresSessionState` interface. If so, and the handler for the MVC Framework *does* implement the interface, then requests within a session will be processed sequentially, and all other requests will be processed concurrently.
`Disabled`	Session state is disabled for the controller, and requests that target the controller will be processed concurrently, even if they are made with the same session cookie. Attempting to access session state will result in an exception.
`ReadOnly`	The action methods in the controller will be able to read, but not modify, the session state data. Read-only requests within a session will be processed concurrently, but read-write requests will still acquire exclusive access to the state data and be processed sequentially (and delay any subsequent read-only requests until they have completed).
`Required`	The action methods in the controller have read-write access to the session state data and will cause other requests within the session to queue while they are processed. For the MVC framework, this is equivalent to the `Default` value.

As you can see from the listing, I specified the `Disabled` value, which ensures that my Ajax requests will be processed concurrently, even when they include a session cookie. However, that also means any attempt to access the session data will throw an exception.

■ **Tip** I could also have used the Web API technology stack to solve the problem for the example I created to demonstrate the problem. Web API is used to create web services and doesn't use the ASP.NET session state feature. Web API doesn't help, however, when you need to render views to generate fragments of HTML content for which the MVC framework and the `SessionState` should be used.

Configuring Sessions and Session State

The session feature is configured through the `sessionState` configuration section in the `Web.config` file (I described the ASP.NET configuration feature in Chapter 9). I have been using the default settings so far in this chapter, but a number of attributes can be applied to the `sessionState` element to control how sessions work and how session state data is stored. Table 10-8 describes the most useful configuration attributes available.

***Table 10-8.** The Most Useful Configuration Attributes for the sessionState Section*

Name	Description
`compressionEnabled`	When set to `true`, the session state data is compressed. The default value is `false`.
`cookieless`	This controls how cookies are used to identify sessions. See the "Tracking Sessions Without Cookies" section for details.
`cookieName`	This specifies the name of the cookie used to identify sessions. The default value is `ASP.NET_<id>`.
`mode`	This specifies where session IDs and state data are stored. See the "Storing Session Data" section for details.
`regenerateExpiredSessionId`	When set to `true` (the default value), expired session IDs will be reissued when used to make a request.
`customProvider`	This is used to define a custom storage system for session data. See the "Using a SQL Database" section later in this chapter for more details.
`timeout`	This specifies the number of minutes after which a session is expired if no requests have been received. The default value is 20.

Tracking Sessions Without Cookies

The ASP.NET platform identifies sessions with a cookie, relying on the browser to include it in the requests it sends to the server. Although all modern browsers support cookies, there are times when they cannot be used, either because cookies are disabled or because the device making the request doesn't support them (not all requests originate from browsers in the real world).

ASP.NET has a fallback technique when cookies cannot be used, which is to include the session ID in the URLs that are sent in the response to the client. The `cookieless` configuration setting determines how the ASP.NET platform decides when to use cookies and when to use query strings and can be set to the values shown in Table 10-9.

Table 10-9. *The Values for the Cookieless Configuration Setting*

Name	Description
AutoDetect	ASP.NET sends a 302 redirection response to the client that includes a cookie. If the cookie is present when the client follows the redirection, then ASP.NET knows that cookies are supported and enabled. Otherwise, cookies are assumed to be unavailable, and query strings are used instead.
UseCookies	This forces ASP.NET to use cookies, even for clients that may not support their use. This presents the possibility that the application may not work for all devices. This is the default value.
UseDeviceProfile	ASP.NET uses the device capabilities feature I described in Chapter 7 to determine whether the client supports cookies.
UseUri	This forces ASP.NET to use URLs to track sessions, even for clients that support cookies. This option ensures the widest possible device support.

Using URLs to track sessions ensures that devices that can't use cookies can still use an application, but it does so by creating ugly URLs. To demonstrate how the URL is used to hold the session ID, I have applied the `sessionState` configuration section to the application-level `Web.config` file and set `cookieless` to `UseUri`, as shown in Listing 10-18.

Listing 10-18. Setting the Cookie Tracking Mode in the Web.config File

```
<?xml version="1.0" encoding="utf-8"?>

<configuration>
  <appSettings>
    <add key="webpages:Version" value="3.0.0.0" />
    <add key="webpages:Enabled" value="false" />
     <add key="ClientValidationEnabled" value="true" />
    <add key="UnobtrusiveJavaScriptEnabled" value="true" />
  </appSettings>
  <system.web>
    <compilation debug="true" targetFramework="4.5.1" />
    <httpRuntime targetFramework="4.5.1" />
    <sessionState cookieless="UseUri" />
  </system.web>
</configuration>
```

I also modified the `Index.cshtml` file in the `Views/Lifecycle` folder to display more information about the session and include URLs generated through HTML and URL helper methods, as shown in Listing 10-19.

Listing 10-19. Adding More Session Information to the Index.cshtml File in the Views/Lifecycle File

```
@{ Layout = null; }

<!DOCTYPE html>
<html>
<head>
    <meta name="viewport" content="width=device-width" />
    <title>Session Lifecycle</title>
```

```
    <link href="~/Content/bootstrap.min.css" rel="stylesheet" />
    <link href="~/Content/bootstrap-theme.min.css" rel="stylesheet" />
    <style>
        body { padding-top: 10px; }
    </style>
</head>
<body class="container">
    <div class="panel panel-primary">
        <div class="panel-heading">Session</div>
        <table class="table">
            <tr><th>Session ID</th><td>@Session.SessionID</td></tr>
            <tr><th>Is New?</th><td>@Session.IsNewSession</td></tr>
            <tr><th>State Data Count</th><td>@Session.Count</td></tr>
            <tr><td>Mode</td><td>@Session.CookieMode</td></tr>
            <tr><td>Cookieless</td><td>@Session.IsCookieless</td></tr>
            <tr><td>URL</td><td>@Url.Action("Index")</td></tr>
            <tr><td>Link</td><td>@Html.ActionLink("Click Me", "Index")</td></tr>
        </table>
    </div>
    @using (Html.BeginForm()) {
        <div class="checkbox">
            <label>@Html.CheckBox("store") Store State Data</label>
        </div>
        <div class="checkbox">
            <label>@Html.CheckBox("abandon") Abandon Session</label>
        </div>
        <button class="btn btn-primary" type="submit">Submit</button>
    }
</body>
</html>
```

I have added rows to the table that display the value of the `HttpSessionState.CookieMode` property, which returns a value from the `HttpCookieMode` enumeration, whose values correspond to the configuration options I described in Table 10-9. I also included the value of the `IsCookieless` property, which returns `true` if ASP.NET uses the URL to track the session. Finally, I included the output from the `Url.Action` and `Html.ActionLink` helper methods to demonstrate how closely integrated session management is. To see the effect of these changes, start the application and navigate to the `/Lifecycle/Index` URL, as shown in Figure 10-11.

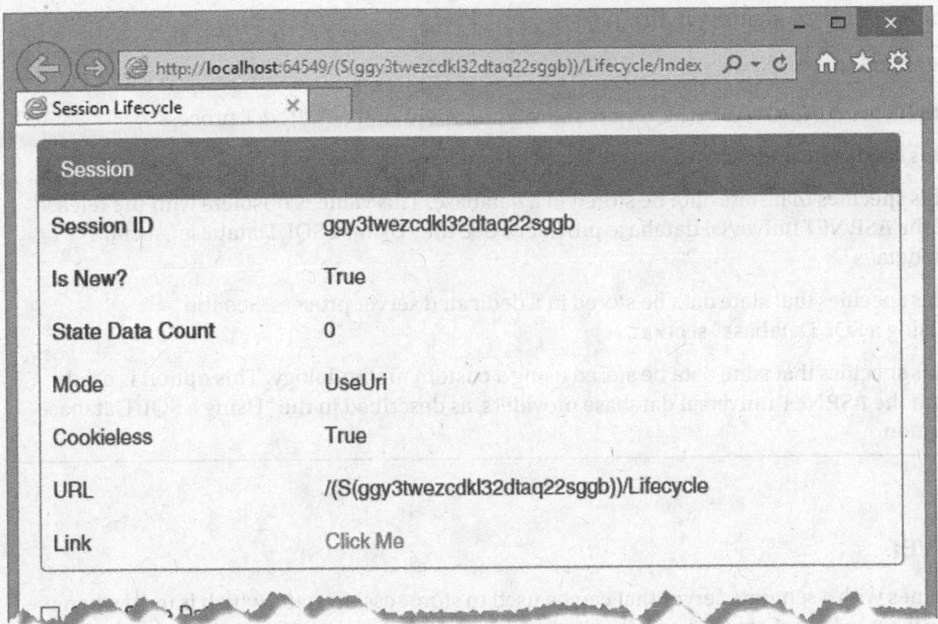

***Figure 10-11.** Using the URL to track sessions*

The first thing to notice is the URL displayed in the browser bar, which is as follows:

```
http://localhost:64549/(S(ggy3twezcdkl32dtaq22sggb))/Lifecycle/Index
```

You will see a different URL because the long sequence of digits is the session ID generated by ASP.NET. ASP.NET redirects the browser to this URL to begin tracking the session. The `CookieMode` and `IsCookieless` properties report the configuration of the session feature and the way that the current session is being tracked, and they can be used within the application to adapt to different devices (although this is something I have yet to find useful in a real application).

Finally, notice that the outgoing URLs that I generated with the helper methods automatically include the session ID. Sessions are tightly integrated into the ASP.NET platform, and this extends to the routing system, which is used to generate these URLs. This makes it easy to use sessions without cookies, but it does undermine the idea of clear and simple URLs that the routing system promotes.

Storing Session Data

By default, details of sessions and session state data are stored in memory within the ASP.NET process. This has the benefit of being fast and simple, but it means that sessions are lost when the server is restarted and that sessions can scale only to the limit of the system memory. ASP.NET supports two other storage options to help sessions scale better and survive application resets, controlled through the `mode` configuration attribute, which can be set to the values shown in Table 10-10. In the sections that follow, I'll show you how to configure and these alternative storage options.

Table 10-10. The Values for the mode Configuration Attribute

Name	Description
`InProc`	This is the default value, which stores session data within the ASP.NET process.
`Off`	This disables sessions for the entire application. Use with care.
`SQLServer`	This specifies that state data be stored in a database. This value is obsolete with the release of the ASP.NET universal database providers. See the "Using a SQL Database" section for details.
`StateServer`	This specifies that state data be stored in a dedicated server process. See the "Using a SQL Database" section.
`Custom`	This specifies that state data be stored using a custom methodology. This option is used with the ASP.NET universal database providers, as described in the "Using a SQL Database" section.

Using the State Server

The ASP.NET framework comes with a separate server that can be used to store session state, which is used when the `mode` configuration attribute is set to `StateServer`. The advantage of this approach is that you can host the session state server on a dedicated machine, which means that session data won't be lost when the application is stopped or restarted.

The session data is still stored in memory—just the memory of another process, potentially running on another server. Performance is not as good as when using the `InProc` option because the data has to be sent from one process to another, potentially across a network. Data stored in the state server is not persistent and will be lost when the state server process is stopped.

■ **Tip** When using the state server, you must ensure that all of your session data can be serialized. See `http://msdn.microsoft.com/en-gb/library/vstudio/ms233843.aspx` for details of making objects serializable. Built-in types, such as `int` and `string`, are already serializable and require no special action.

The state server is useful if you have a lot of state data and don't want to isolate it from the application process. The data in the state server will survive the ASP.NET application being restarted, but the data is not truly persistent since the state server can itself crash or restart.

The ASP.NET state server is a Windows service that is installed as part of the .NET Framework. To start the server, open the Services control panel, and locate and start the ASP.NET State Service, as shown in Figure 10-12.

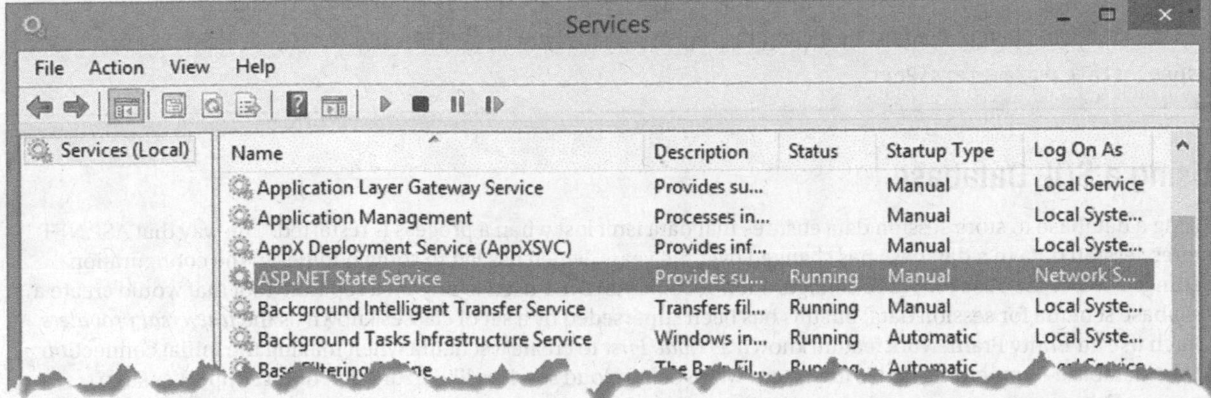

***Figure 10-12.** Starting the ASP.NET State Service*

■ **Tip** A couple of extra configuration steps are required if you want to run the state server on another machine. On the machine that will run the service, change the register property `HKLM\SYSTEM\CurrentControlSet\Services\aspnet_state\Parameters\AllowRemoteConnection` to `1` and add a firewall rule that allows incoming requests on port 42424. You can now start the service and specify the `stateConnectionString` attribute in your application as `tcpip=<servername>:42424`.

Listing 10-20 shows how I have updated the `Web.config` file to use the state server by setting the `mode` and `stateConnectionString` attributes on the `sessionState` configuration section element.

***Listing 10-20.** Configuring the State Server in the Web.config File*

```
<?xml version="1.0" encoding="utf-8"?>

<configuration>
  <appSettings>
    <add key="webpages:Version" value="3.0.0.0" />
    <add key="webpages:Enabled" value="false" />
     <add key="ClientValidationEnabled" value="true" />
    <add key="UnobtrusiveJavaScriptEnabled" value="true" />
  </appSettings>
  <system.web>
    <compilation debug="true" targetFramework="4.5.1" />
    <httpRuntime targetFramework="4.5.1" />
    <sessionState cookieless="UseCookies" mode="StateServer"
         stateConnectionString="tcpip=localhost:42424" />
  </system.web>
</configuration>
```

I set the `mode` attribute to `StateServer` and used the `stateConnetionString` to specify the name of the server and the port on which the state server is running, which is 42424 by default. There won't be a visible change to the way the application operates, but the session data won't be lost if you restart the application.

■ **Tip** You can change the port by editing the registry property `HKLM\SYSTEM\CurrentControlSet\Services\aspnet_state\Parameters\Port`.

Using a SQL Database

Using a database to store session data ensures that data isn't lost when a process is restarted. The way that ASP.NET stores session data in a database has changed over the years, which has led to some oddities in the configuration settings used in the `sessionState` configuration section. ASP.NET used to rely on a separate tool that would create a database schema for session data, but this has been superseded by a set of classes known as the *universal providers*, which use an Entity Framework feature known as *Code First* to create a schema when making the initial connection to the database—something that is important when using cloud services like Azure that don't support custom command-line tools.

■ **Note** The universal providers are not just for session data; they also store user details for the ASP.NET membership API. However, the membership API has been superseded by the Identity API, which I describe in Chapters 13 to 15. It can be hard to keep up with Microsoft's sudden changes in direction.

To get started, I need to create the database that ASP.NET will use to store the session information. I will be using the `localdb` feature, which is a simplified version of SQL Server included in Visual Studio that makes it easy for developers to create and manage databases. Select SQL Server Object Explorer from the Visual Studio View menu and right-click the SQL Server object in the window that appears. Select Add SQL Server from the pop-up menu, as shown in Figure 10-13.

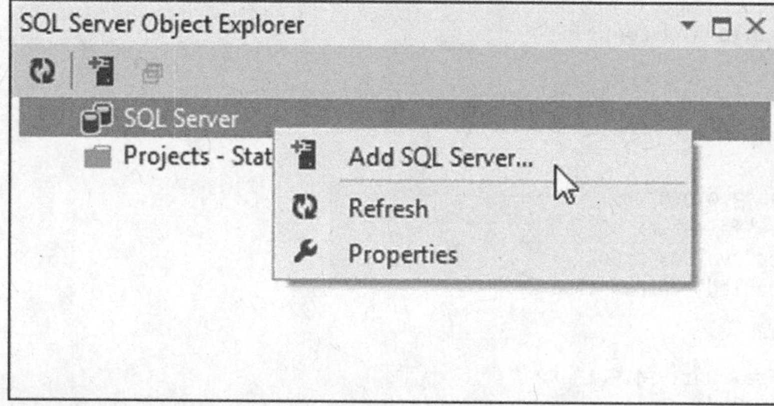

Figure 10-13. *Creating a new database connection*

Visual Studio will display the Connect to Server dialog window. Set the server name to be (localdb)\v11.0, select the Windows Authentication option, and click the Connect button. A connection to the database will be established and shown in the SQL Server Object Explorer window. Expand the new item, right-click Databases, and select Add New Database from the pop-up window, as shown in Figure 10-14.

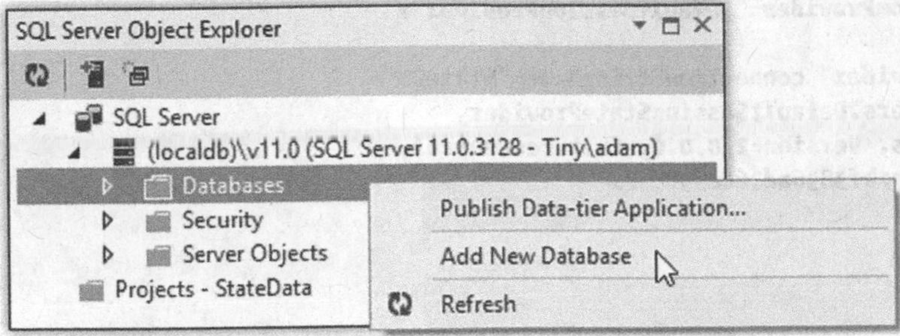

Figure 10-14. *Adding a new database*

Set the Database Name option to StateDb, leave the Database Location value unchanged, and click the OK button to create the database. The new database will be shown in the Databases section of the SQL connection in the SQL Server Object Explorer.

■ **Tip** There is no need to configure the schema for the new database. This will be done automatically the first time a connection is made with the universal provider.

The next step is to install the universal providers NuGet package by entering the following command into the Visual Studio Package Manager Console:

```
Install-Package -version 2.0.0 Microsoft.AspNet.Providers
```

NuGet installs the package and updates the `Web.config` file to configure the different databases that ASP.NET supports. Most of these are for the now-obsolete membership API, so I removed the unwanted additions, as shown in Listing 10-21.

Listing 10-21. Configuring the Universal Provider for Session Data in the Web.config File

```
<?xml version="1.0" encoding="utf-8"?>
<configuration>
  <connectionStrings>
    <add name="StateDb" providerName="System.Data.SqlClient"
        connectionString="Data Source=(localdb)\v11.0;Initial Catalog=StateDb;
            Integrated Security=True" />
  </connectionStrings>
  <appSettings>
    <add key="webpages:Version" value="3.0.0.0" />
    <add key="webpages:Enabled" value="false" />
    <add key="ClientValidationEnabled" value="true" />
    <add key="UnobtrusiveJavaScriptEnabled" value="true" />
  </appSettings>
  <system.web>
    <compilation debug="true" targetFramework="4.5.1" />
    <httpRuntime targetFramework="4.5.1" />
```

```
    <sessionState mode="Custom" customProvider="DefaultSessionProvider">
      <providers>
        <add name="DefaultSessionProvider" connectionStringName="StateDb"
             type="System.Web.Providers.DefaultSessionStateProvider,
                 System.Web.Providers, Version=2.0.0.0, Culture=neutral,
                     PublicKeyToken=31bf3856ad364e35"  />
      </providers>
    </sessionState>
  </system.web>
</configuration>
```

■ **Caution** I have had to split some of the strings in the listing across multiple lines to make them fit on the page. You must ensure that all of the text is on a single line when you edit the `Web.config` file. If in doubt, download the source code for this chapter from `www.apress.com`.

I defined a connection string called `StateDb` for the database I created. The changes to the `sessionState` configuration section don't make a lot of sense, but they are required verbatim to use the universal providers, and you should cut and paste them as required, making sure to change the `connectionStringName` attribute of the `providers/add` element to match the connection string that refers to the database you want to use, like this:

```
...
<sessionState mode="Custom" customProvider="DefaultSessionProvider">
  <providers>
    <add name="DefaultSessionProvider" connectionStringName="StateDb"
        type="System.Web.Providers.DefaultSessionStateProvider,
            System.Web.Providers, Version=2.0.0.0, Culture=neutral,
            PublicKeyToken=31bf3856ad364e35"  />
  </providers>
</sessionState>
...
```

To test the database, start the application, request the `/Lifecycle/Index` URL, and check the option Store State Data. A connection to the database will be established when you click the Submit button, and the schema for the database will be created so that the session data can be stored. The schema is created only when needed, and subsequent connections will reuse the schema.

Summary

In this chapter I described the two state data features that the ASP.NET platform provides: application and session state. I demonstrated their use, explained the pitfalls of synchronization, and showed you how they can be used to store data across the entire application or across a series of requests from the same client. In the next chapter, I describe a flexible—but more complicated—state data feature: the data cache.

CHAPTER 11

Caching Data

In this chapter, I describe the ASP.NET data caching feature, which is a state data service that actively manages the data it contains to limit the amount of memory that it occupies and to ensure that stale data isn't used by the application. Table 11-1 summarizes this chapter.

Table 11-1. *Chapter Summary*

Problem	Solution	Listing
Cache data for later use.	Use the `Cache` class, an instance of which can be obtained through the `HttpContext.Cache` property.	1–2
Configure the cache.	Use the `cache` configuration section within the `caching` section group.	3
Set a time at which an item will be ejected from the cache.	Use an absolute time expiration.	4
Set an interval after which an item will be ejected from the cache if it has not been requested.	Use a sliding time expiration.	5
Create a dependency that causes an item to be ejected from the cache when it changes.	Use the `CacheDependency` or `AggregateCacheDependency` class.	6, 7, 10
Create a custom cache dependency.	Derive from the `CacheDependency` class and call the `NotifyDependencyChanged` method to trigger cache ejection.	8, 9
Receive a notification when an item has been—or is about to be—ejected from the cache.	Pass method references to the `Cache.Add` or `Cache.Insert` method when adding an item to the cache.	11, 12

Preparing the Example Project

For this chapter, I am going to continue using the StateData project I created in Chapter 10. I'll be using Glimpse in this chapter, which provides information about the cache. Enter the following command into the Visual Studio Package Manager Console:

```
Install-Package Glimpse.MVC5
```

When you hit Enter, NuGet will download and install the Glimpse packages that support the MVC framework application. Once the installation is complete, start the application, navigate to the `/Glimpse.axd` URL, and click the Turn Glimpse On button to enable Glimpse diagnostics.

Adding the System.Net.Http Assembly

I'll be using an example that relies on the `System.Net.Http` assembly, which isn't added to MVC projects by default. Select Add Reference from the Visual Studio Project menu to open the Reference Manager window. Ensure that the Assemblies section is selected on the left side and locate and check the System.Net.Http item, as shown in Figure 11-1.

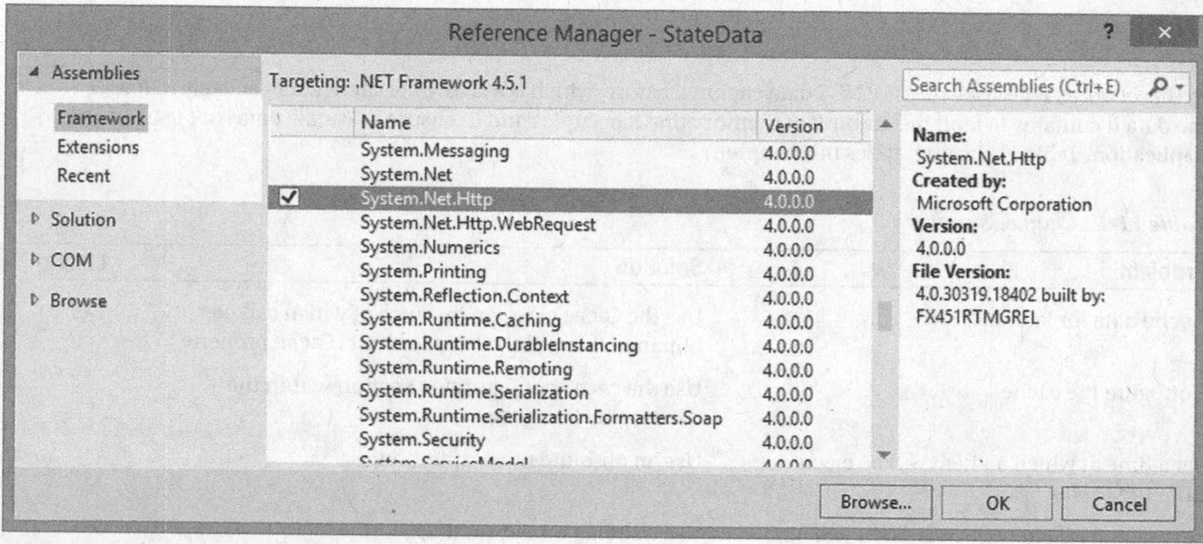

Figure 11-1. Adding an assembly to the project

■ **Tip** You will need to stop the application before you can add the assembly reference.

Caching Data

The difference between the cache and other state data services, such as application state and session state, is that the cache actively manages the data it receives and will remove data items that it judges are no longer required. The judgment the cache makes about which data items to remove isn't arbitrary; as you will learn, you can be specific about when a particular item of data is considered useful or not.

The cache stores its data in memory and is useful for data that is resource-intensive or time-consuming to generate, that you expect to need again in the future, and, critically, that you can re-create if it is removed from the cache or if the application is restarted. In the sections that follow, I'll show you the different ways in which to store and retrieve data in the cache and demonstrate how you can make the cache respond to the needs of your application. Table 11-2 puts the data cache feature into context.

Table 11-2. Putting the Data Cache in Context

Question	Answer
What is it?	Application data caching is a form of state data that is actively managed to ensure that stale or underused data is removed from use. This feature is also the foundation of the output cache, which I describe in Chapter 12.
Why should I care?	Caching can improve application performance while ensuring that only current data is used.
How is it used by the MVC framework?	The MVC framework does not use application caching directly, but the feature is available in application components such as controllers, views, and modules.

AVOIDING THE PREMATURE OPTIMIZATION PROBLEM

Caching is a form of optimization that can improve the performance of an application when used judiciously and sparingly—but like all forms of optimization, it can cause more problems than it solves if used carelessly.

Developers have a tendency to apply optimization too early in the project life cycle, in the mistaken belief that optimized code is more elegant and professional. In fact, over-eager optimization hides poorly designed code and makes it harder to test the application properly.

Don't optimize code until you know that you have a performance problem that breaks your application requirements. Focus on building the functionality of the application first and then, when you are confident that everything works properly, start to optimize. Remember that optimizations such as caching change the behavior of an application and make it harder to figure out what is happening when there is a problem, so make sure you arrange your application so that caching (and other optimizations) can be easily and simply disabled.

Above all, think about *why* you are optimizing your application. If you papering over the cracks caused by sloppily written code and bad design, then a feature such as caching will provide only temporary respite from your mistakes. You should only ever optimize a healthy application, not one that needs remedial attention.

Using Basic Caching

The cache is accessed through the `HttpContext.Cache` property, which returns an instance of the `Cache` class, defined in the `System.Web.Caching` namespace. The `Cache` class provides some useful members that make it easy to perform basic caching, which I have described in Table 11-3. Later in this chapter, I'll describe the facilities for creating more complex caching policies.

Table 11-3. The Basic Members of the Cache Class

Name	Description
`Item[key]`	Gets or sets the data item with the specified key
`Count`	Returns the number of data items stored in the cache

To demonstrate the basic caching technique, I added a controller called `Cache` to the example application, as shown in Listing 11-1.

Listing 11-1. Using the Cache in the CacheController.cs File

```
using System.Net.Http;
using System.Threading.Tasks;
using System.Web;
using System.Web.Mvc;

namespace StateData.Controllers {
    public class CacheController : Controller {

        public ActionResult Index() {
            return View((long?)(HttpContext.Cache["pageLength"]));
        }

        [HttpPost]
        public async Task<ActionResult> PopulateCache() {
            HttpResponseMessage result
                = await new HttpClient().GetAsync("http://apress.com");
            HttpContext.Cache["pageLength"] = result.Content.Headers.ContentLength;
            return RedirectToAction("Index");
        }
    }
}
```

■ **Tip** When I use the data cache in a project, I usually create a helper class like the ones that I used in Chapter 10 for the application and state data features. I have not created such a class in this chapter because a lot of the techniques I describe are about how to insert data into the cache to control its life cycle, and the handler class just makes all of the examples a little more complex because I would have to adjust the controller and the helper class for each example. I recommend you use a helper class once you have decided on how you are going to use the cache.

This controller uses the cache to store the length of the content returned from the Apress web site. The `Index` action method retrieves the data item from the cache with the key `pageLength` and passes it to the view. I cast the cached data value to a nullable long (`long?`) value so that I can differentiate between a cached value of zero and the null value that is returned from the cache when a nonexistent key is requested. The `PopulateCache` method uses the `HttpClient` class from the `System.Net.Http` namespace to get the contents of the Apress home page and cache the numeric value of the `ContentLength` header before redirecting the client to the `Index` action to see the effect.

■ **Tip** The data in the example is well-suited to demonstrate caching. It takes time to generate because establishing a connection to Apress.com and getting its content can take a few seconds—something that you wouldn't want to repeat for every request. Further, the data has a finite life because Apress often changes its site for new books and promotions, meaning that obtaining the data doesn't give a value that can be used forever. Finally, the data can be created again if need be—something that becomes important when the cache starts actively managing its content, as I explain later in this chapter.

I created a view for the Index action by right-clicking the method in the code editor and selecting Add View from the pop-up menu. I set View Name to Index, set Template to Empty (without model), and unchecked the View Option boxes. When I clicked the Add button, Visual Studio created the `Views/Cache/Index.cshtml` file, which I edited with the content shown in Listing 11-2.

Listing 11-2. The Contents of the Index.cshtml File in the Views/Cache Folder

```
@model long?
@{Layout = null;}
<!DOCTYPE html>
<html>
<head>
    <meta name="viewport" content="width=device-width" />
    <title>Data Cache</title>
    <link href="~/Content/bootstrap.min.css" rel="stylesheet" />
    <link href="~/Content/bootstrap-theme.min.css" rel="stylesheet" />
    <style>body { padding-top: 10px; }</style>
</head>
<body class="container">
    <div class="alert alert-info">
        @if (Model.HasValue) {
            @: Cached Data: @Model bytes
        } else {
            @: No Cached Data
        }
    </div>
    @using (Html.BeginForm("PopulateCache", "Cache")) {
        <button class="btn btn-primary">Populate Cache</button>
    }
</body>
</html>
```

The view contains a message that either displays the cached value or reports that there is no cached data for the `pageLength` key. I used the `Html.BeginForm` helper method to create a form that will invoke the `PopulateCache` action method when the `button` element is clicked, making it easy to see the cache in action.

■ **Tip** The individual methods defined by the `Cache` class are thread-safe to protect against concurrent access, but there is no built-in locking feature for performing multiple related operations. See Chapter 10 to understand the contrast against the application state and session state features.

To see the effect, start the application and request the `/Cache/Index` URL. The message will initially show that there is no cached data. Click the Populate Cache button; after the request to the Apress web site has completed, the length of the response will be shown, as illustrated by Figure 11-2. (You may see a different result because the Apress home page changes regularly.)

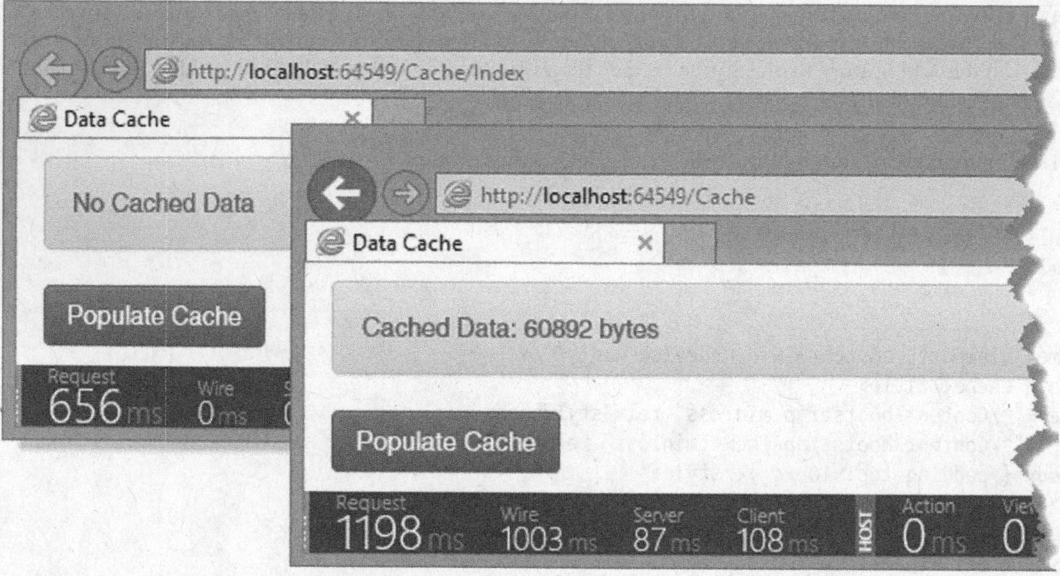

***Figure 11-2.** Using the cache*

The reason that I installed Glimpse at the start of the chapter is because it provides useful information about the cache. Click the G logo at the right edge of the Glimpse ribbon and select the Cache tab, and you will see the contents of the cache and some basic configuration information, as shown in Figure 11-3.

Cache | Configuration | Environment | Execution | Metadata | Model Binding | Reque: | Ajax | History | Session

Configuration

Key	Value
Effective Percentage Physical Memory Limit	99
Effective Private Bytes Limit	-1

Cache Items

Key	Value	Created On	Expires On	Sliding Expiration
_AppStartPage__~/_appstart.cshtml	~/_appstart.cshtml	02/13/2014 09:42:32	--	0
pageLength	60892	02/13/2014 09:42:55	--	0
_AppStartPage__~/_appstart.vbhtml	~/_appstart.vbhtml	02/13/2014 09:42:32	--	0

***Figure 11-3.** The Glimpse Cache tab*

The Cache Items section details the contents of the cache. There are three items shown, two of which were added by the ASP.NET platform and one is the `pageLength` item that is added by the `Cache` controller.

Configuring the Cache

The Configuration section of the Glimpse Cache tab shows the value of two properties defined by the Cache class that relate to the cache configuration, as described in Table 11-4.

Table 11-4. *The Cache Configuration Properties*

Name	Description
`EffectivePercentagePhysicalMemoryLimit`	Returns the percentage of system memory that can be used to store data items before the Cache class starts to remove them. The default value is 90, meaning that the cache can occupy 90 percent of the available memory.
`EffectivePrivateBytesLimit`	Returns the total number of bytes available for storing data in the cache. The default value is 0, meaning that ASP.NET will use its own policy for ejecting items when memory is under pressure.

By default, items are removed only when the cache starts to fill up and the limits of the cache size are controlled by the values of the properties shown in the table. These values are set in the `Web.config` file, as shown in Listing 11-3. (I have tidied up the Glimpse additions to the `Web.config` file to make it easier to read.)

Listing 11-3. Configuring the Cache in the Web.config File

```
<?xml version="1.0" encoding="utf-8"?>
<configuration>

  <configSections>
        <section name="glimpse" type="Glimpse.Core.Configuration.Section,
            Glimpse.Core" />
    </configSections>

  <glimpse defaultRuntimePolicy="On" endpointBaseUri="~/Glimpse.axd" />

  <connectionStrings>
    <add name="StateDb" providerName="System.Data.SqlClient"
        connectionString="Data Source=(localdb)\v11.0;Initial Catalog=StateDb;
            Integrated Security=True" />
  </connectionStrings>
  <appSettings>
    <add key="webpages:Version" value="3.0.0.0" />
    <add key="webpages:Enabled" value="false" />
    <add key="ClientValidationEnabled" value="true" />
    <add key="UnobtrusiveJavaScriptEnabled" value="true" />
  </appSettings>
  <system.web>
    <compilation debug="true" targetFramework="4.5.1" />
    <httpRuntime targetFramework="4.5.1" />
    <sessionState mode="Custom" customProvider="DefaultSessionProvider">
      <providers>
        <add name="DefaultSessionProvider" connectionStringName="StateDb"
           type="System.Web.Providers.DefaultSessionStateProvider,
```

```
                System.Web.Providers, Version=2.0.0.0, Culture=neutral,
                    PublicKeyToken=31bf3856ad364e35" />
        </providers>
    </sessionState>
    <caching>
      <cache percentagePhysicalMemoryUsedLimit="10" />
    </caching>
  </system.web>
  <system.webServer>
      <validation validateIntegratedModeConfiguration="false" />
      <modules>
          <add name="Glimpse" type="Glimpse.AspNet.HttpModule, Glimpse.AspNet"
              preCondition="integratedMode" />.
      </modules>
      <handlers>
          <add name="Glimpse" path="glimpse.axd" verb="GET"
              type="Glimpse.AspNet.HttpHandler, Glimpse.AspNet"
                  preCondition="integratedMode" />
      </handlers>
  </system.webServer>
</configuration>
```

Configuring the Cache class is performed through the cache configuration section, which in turn is part of the caching configuration group (I explained configuration sections and groups in Chapter 9). In the listing, I set the percentage of the memory that the cache can occupy to 10 percent. Table 11-5 lists all the settings available in the cache configuration section and describes their effect.

***Table 11-5.** The Settings in the cache Configuration Section*

Name	Description
disableMemoryCollection	Sets whether the cache will automatically eject items when the available free memory is limited. The default value is false, meaning that items will be ejected. Use with caution.
disableExpiration	Sets whether items are ejected when they expire. The default value is false, meaning that items will expire. See the "Using Advanced Caching" section for details of item expiry. Use with caution.
privateBytesLimit	Sets the limit (in bytes) of the cache size before items are ejected to free up memory. The default value is 0, which tells ASP.NET to use its own policy for memory management.
percentagePhysicalMemoryUsedLimit	Sets the percentage of the system memory that the cache can occupy before items are ejected to free up space. The default value is 90, meaning that the cache will occupy up to 90 percent of the available memory.
privateBytesPollTime	Sets the interval at which the size of the cache is checked to ensure that it is within the limit defined by the privateBytesLimit setting. The default value is 00:02:00, which corresponds to two minutes.

■ **Tip** Don't configure the cache until you have a sense of how it is affected by real user loads. Limiting the cache too low will cause items to be ejected too aggressively and undermine the optimization effect of the cache, but setting the limits too high will cause the cache to grow indefinitely and ultimately disrupt the ASP.NET application's performance. When working on a new application, start with the default settings and use the per-item configuration techniques that I describe in the "Using Advanced Caching" section.

The settings that control the size of the cache are most important when using the basic cache features demonstrated by Listing 11-1 because data items added via the indexer will be removed only when the cache grows too large. The `disableExpiration` setting affects items that are added to the cache with an expiration policy (which I explain in the next section), and setting the configuration to `true` will prevent items from being ejected when they expire.

Using Advanced Caching

Basic caching can be useful if the data items you are working with are all of equal importance and should be ejected from the cache only when the amount of available memory is under pressure. If you want more control over the life of your data items or you want to express relative importance so that the cache will eject some before others, then you can take advantage of the advanced features that the ASP.NET cache offers, which are available through the `Add` and `Insert` methods defined by the `Cache` class. Table 11-6 describes these methods and their overloads.

Table 11-6. *The Cache Methods for Advanced Caching*

Name	Description
`Insert(key, data)`	Inserts the data into the cache using the specified key. This is equivalent to using the `Cache` indexer, as demonstrated by Listing 11-1.
`Insert(key, data, dependency)`	Inserts the data into the cache using the specified key with an external dependency (see the "Using Cache Dependency" section for details).
`Insert(key, data, dependency, time, duration)`	Like the previous method, but the object will be removed from the cache at the `DateTime` specified by the `time` argument or after the `TimeSpan` specified by the `duration` argument.
`Insert(key, data, dependency, time, duration, callback)`	Like the previous method, but the callback will be used to send a notification when the item is removed from the cache. See the "Receiving Dependency Notifications" section for details of cache notifications.
`Insert(key, data, dependency, time, duration, priority, callback)`	Caches the data item with the dependency, time, and duration restrictions but also specifies a priority that is used when the cache is ejecting items to release memory. The callback is used to send a notification when the item is removed from the cache—see the "Receiving Dependency Notifications" section for details of cache notifications.
`Add(key, data, dependency, time, duration,priority, callback)`	Like the previous method, but throws an exception if the cache already contains a data object with the same key.

I tend not to use the `Add` method because I rarely want to receive an exception if there is already a data item with the same key, but the range of options available for both the `Add` and `Insert` methods allows you to be as specific as you need about when an item should be ejected from the cache. I explain each of the constraints in the sections that follow.

Using Absolute Time Expiration

The simplest way to control the life of a cached data item is to specify the time after which the data is invalid. This is most useful for data that becomes misleading to the user as it becomes stale, such as stock prices. Listing 11-4 shows how I modified the Cache controller so that the example cache item is removed after 30 seconds—this is an extremely short period, but it makes it possible to follow the example without having to wait hours to see the effect.

Listing 11-4. Expiring Cache Items in the CacheController.cs File

```
using System;
using System.Net.Http;
using System.Threading.Tasks;
using System.Web;
using System.Web.Mvc;
using System.Web.Caching;

namespace StateData.Controllers {
    public class CacheController : Controller {

        public ActionResult Index() {
            return View((long?)(HttpContext.Cache["pageLength"]));
        }

        [HttpPost]
        public async Task<ActionResult> PopulateCache() {
            HttpResponseMessage result
                = await new HttpClient().GetAsync("http://apress.com");
            long? data = result.Content.Headers.ContentLength;
            DateTime expiryTime = DateTime.Now.AddSeconds(30);
            HttpContext.Cache.Insert("pageLength", data, null, expiryTime,
                Cache.NoSlidingExpiration);
            return RedirectToAction("Index");
        }
    }
}
```

Cache expiration times are expressed using `System.DateTime` objects and passed as an argument to the `Cache.Insert` method. There are two time-related options for controlling cache ejection: absolute expiration and sliding expiration (which I describe in the next section). When you use one, you must set the other argument to a static value defined by the Cache class. In the listing, I am using an absolute time, which means I have to set the argument for the sliding expiration like this:

```
...
HttpContext.Cache.Insert("pageLength", data, null, expiryTime,
    Cache.NoSlidingExpiration);
...
```

■ **Tip** You will notice that the dependency argument for the Insert method is null in the listing. This indicates to the cache that I have not specified a dependency and that the cached data should be expired only based on the specified time or when the cache is short of memory. I show you how to specify dependencies in the "Using Cache Dependencies" section later in this chapter.

The NoSlidingExpiration property must be used for the duration argument when specifying an absolute time. To see the effect of the cache expiration, start the application, request the /Cache/Index URL, and click the Populate Cache button. If you look at the Glimpse Cache tab, you will see the time at which the item will expire. Wait 30 seconds and reload the web page by pressing the F5 key, and you will see that the cache is empty.

Using Sliding Time Expirations

Sliding time expirations remove an item from the cache if it hasn't been accessed for a period of time. This is useful when you want the cache to prune items that are not needed by users, while retaining those that remain in demand. In Listing 11-5, you can see how I have modified the Cache controller to use a sliding expiration.

Listing 11-5. Using a Sliding Expiration in the CacheController.cs File

```
using System;
using System.Net.Http;
using System.Threading.Tasks;
using System.Web;
using System.Web.Caching;
using System.Web.Mvc;

namespace StateData.Controllers {
    public class CacheController : Controller {

        public ActionResult Index() {
            return View((long?)(HttpContext.Cache["pageLength"]));
        }

        [HttpPost]
        public async Task<ActionResult> PopulateCache() {
            HttpResponseMessage result
                = await new HttpClient().GetAsync("http://apress.com");
            long? data = result.Content.Headers.ContentLength;
            TimeSpan idleDuration = new TimeSpan(0, 0, 30);
            HttpContext.Cache.Insert("pageLength", data, null,
                Cache.NoAbsoluteExpiration, idleDuration);
            return RedirectToAction("Index");
        }
    }
}
```

Sliding expirations are expressed using a TimeSpan, and in the listing, I created a TimeSpan instance for 30 seconds, which I passed to the Cache.Insert method. When using a sliding expiration, the time argument (as described in Table 11-6) must be set like this:

```
...
HttpContext.Cache.Insert("pageLength", data, null,
    Cache.NoAbsoluteExpiration, idleDuration);
...
```

The NoAbsoluteExpiration property must be used for the time argument when specifying a sliding expiration. To see the effect of a sliding expiration, start the application, request the /Cache/Index URL, and click the Populate Cache button.

You can see details of the cached item's expiration on the Glimpse Cache tab. Reload the page by pressing the F5 key, and you will see that the expiration time is extended each time the item is read for the cache. Wait 30 seconds and then press F5, and you will see that the cache is empty because the item was not accessed before it expired.

Specifying Scavenging Prioritization

Specifying absolute or sliding expirations will cause items to be removed from the cache when they are stale, but it is still possible for the cache to fill up. When this happens, the cache will eject items from the cache to manage its memory footprint—a process known as *scavenging*. The scavenging process is usually triggered when the cache is being used to store data for every user and there is a sudden spike in application utilization. (If this happens to you, then you should consider whether session state data would be more appropriate given that it can be stored in a database.)

Not all data is equally important, and you can provide the cache with instructions about the data you want ejected first when scavenging begins. The Add method and one of the Insert method overloads take a value from the CacheItemPriority enumeration, which defines the values listed in Table 11-7.

Table 11-7. *The Values Defined by the CacheItemPriority Enumeration*

Name	Description
Low	Items given this priority will be removed first.
BelowNormal	Items given this priority will be removed if scavenging the Low priority items has not released enough memory.
Normal	Items given this priority will be removed if scavenging the Low and BelowNormal priority items has not released enough memory. This is the default priority for the Insert method overloads that don't take a CacheItemPriority value.
AboveNormal	Items given this priority will be removed if scavenging the Low, BelowNormal, and Normal priority items has not released enough memory.
High	Items given this priority will be removed if scavenging the Low, BelowNormal, Normal, and AboveNormal priority items has not released enough memory.
NotRemovable	Items with this priority will not be removed during scavenging—although they *will* be removed if absolute or sliding expirations are used.
Default	This is equivalent to the Normal value.

I have not included a demonstration of using cache priorities because it is difficult to simulate exhausting the system memory—ASP.NET and the .NET Framework both have aggressive memory management techniques that are applied to prevent scavenging being necessary.

■ **Caution** Use the `NotRemovable` value with caution, especially if you are using it for data items that are cached without an absolute or sliding expiry.

Using Cache Dependencies

Absolute and sliding expiries are suitable for most cached data, but if you need more control over when an item expired, you can use a *dependency*. A dependency creates a relationship between the cached data and another object, and the data is removed from the cache when the object changes. There are built-in classes to create dependencies on files and other items in the cache. You can also create dependencies on multiple objects and even implement custom dependencies. I explain each option in the sections that follow.

Creating a File Dependency

The most basic dependency removes an item from the cache when a file changes. This kind of dependency is useful when you are populating the cache with data from a file to improve performance, but caution is required because this means storing files that will change on the ASP.NET server—something that is rarely a good idea in a production environment and usually impossible in a cloud deployment.

I am going to use a simple text file to demonstrate this kind of dependency. Right-click the StateData item in the Solution Explorer and select Add ➤ New Item from the pop-up menu. Select the Text File template from the Visual C# ➤ General section, set the name to `data.txt`, and click the Add button to create the file. Listing 11-6 shows how I created a dependency on the `data.txt` file.

Listing 11-6. Creating a File Dependency in the CacheController.cs File

```
using System;
using System.Net.Http;
using System.Threading.Tasks;
using System.Web;
using System.Web.Caching;
using System.Web.Mvc;

namespace StateData.Controllers {
    public class CacheController : Controller {

        public ActionResult Index() {
            return View((long?)(HttpContext.Cache["pageLength"]));
        }

        [HttpPost]
        public async Task<ActionResult> PopulateCache() {
            HttpResponseMessage result
                = await new HttpClient().GetAsync("http://apress.com");
            long? data = result.Content.Headers.ContentLength;
```

```
            CacheDependency dependency = new
                CacheDependency(Request.MapPath("~/data.txt"));
            HttpContext.Cache.Insert("pageLength", data, dependency);
            return RedirectToAction("Index");
        }
    }
}
```

■ **Tip** The contents of the data.txt file don't matter; all that counts is that the file will change, and this change will be detected and used to modify the contents of the cache.

The CacheDependency class takes a file path as its constructor argument. I used the HttpRequest.MapPath method to translate a local path into an absolute one, which is what the CacheDependency class operates on. I pass the CacheDependency object as the dependency argument to the Cache.Insert method. I have used the simplest of the CacheDependency constructors that depend on files, but you can see a complete list in Table 11-8.

Table 11-8. *The CacheDependency Constructors That Create Dependencies on Files*

Constructor	Description
CacheDependency(path)	Creates a dependency on a single path, which can be a file or a directory. Paths must be absolute. You can use the HttpRequest.MapPath method to translate a path relative to the root of the application to an absolute path.
CacheDependency(path[])	Creates a dependency on multiple paths. A change in any of the paths will invalidate the associated cached data.
CacheDependency(path, start)	Creates a dependency on the specified path but will invalidate the cached data only if the last modification time of the path is later than the start argument, which is a DateTime object.
CacheDependency(path[], start)	Like the previous constructor, but monitors an array of paths.

The result is that the data will remain in the cache until the data.txt file is modified or the cache scavenges the item to free up memory. To see the effect of the file modification, start the application, request the /Cache/Index URL, and click the Populate Cache button. If you look at the Glimpse Cache tab, you will see that the cached data has no expiry time. Edit the data.txt file, and when you save the changes, you will see that the data is removed from the cache when you reload the web page.

■ **Tip** You can create a dependency on a SQL database by using the SqlCacheDependency class, which is also in the System.Web.Caching namespace. I don't like this class because it relies on polling the database or reconfiguring the database to issue its own notification. I prefer to create custom notifications that work in a way that is consistent with the data abstractions I use—which usually means the Entity Framework. See http://msdn.microsoft.com/en-us/library/system.web.caching.sqlcachedependency.aspx for details of the SqlCacheDependency class if you are not deterred by direct dependence on databases, and see the "Creating Custom Dependencies" section later in this chapter for details of how to create custom dependencies for your cached data.

Depending on Another Cached Item

The CacheDependency class can also be used to create dependencies on other items in the cache. To demonstrate how this works, I have added a new action method to the Cache controller, as shown in Listing 11-7.

Listing 11-7. Adding a New Action Method to the CacheController.cs File

```
using System;
using System.Net.Http;
using System.Threading.Tasks;
using System.Web;
using System.Web.Caching;
using System.Web.Mvc;

namespace StateData.Controllers {
    public class CacheController : Controller {

        public ActionResult Index() {
            return View((long?)(HttpContext.Cache["pageLength"]));
        }

        [HttpPost]
        public async Task<ActionResult> PopulateCache() {
            HttpResponseMessage result
                = await new HttpClient().GetAsync("http://apress.com");

            long? data = result.Content.Headers.ContentLength;
            CacheDependency dependency = new
                CacheDependency(Request.MapPath("~/data.txt"));
            HttpContext.Cache.Insert("pageLength", data, dependency);

            DateTime timestamp = DateTime.Now;
            CacheDependency timesStampDependency
                = new CacheDependency(null, new string[] { "pageLength" });
            HttpContext.Cache.Insert("pageTimestamp", timestamp, timesStampDependency);

            return RedirectToAction("Index");
        }
    }
}
```

I added a second data item to the cache to record the timestamp for the content length data. When I created the CacheDependency object, I used the constructor form that takes an array of path names *and* an array of cache key names to monitor. I set the first argument to null to indicate that I am not interested in paths and specified the pageLength key in the second argument. The result is that the new cached item, pageTimestamp, will remain in the cache until the pageLength item changes or is ejected from the cache. To see the effect, repeat the steps from the previous example and modify the data.txt file. This will invalidate the pageLength item and will, in turn, cause the pageTimestamp item to be removed. Table 11-9 shows the CacheDependency constructors that can be used to create dependencies on other cached items.

Table 11-9. *The CacheDependency Constructors That Create Dependencies on Other Cached Items*

Constructor	Description
`CacheDependency(path[], keys[])`	Creates a dependency on multiple paths and multiple cache keys. Use `null` for the first argument if you want to work with just keys.
`CacheDependency(path[], keys[], start)`	Like the previous constructor, but with a `DateTime` object against which the modification date of the paths and the cache keys will be checked.
`CacheDependency(path[], keys[], start, dependency)`	Like the previous constructor, but with a `CacheDependency` object that, if invalidated, will also invalidate the `CacheDependency` instance created by the constructor.

■ **Tip** You can see from this example that it is possible to create chains of updates and ejections in the cache. This can be a useful feature, but don't get carried away with the complexity of your cache because it is easy to lose track of the relationships between data items and start ejecting items unexpectedly.

Creating Custom Dependencies

Custom dependencies allow items to be ejected from the cache when something other than a file or other cached item changes, which allows you to tailor the caching behavior to fit the needs of the application.

To demonstrate creating a custom dependency, I am going to create a class that acts as a wrapper around a data value and the dependency for that data value. When the data value has been requested a certain number of times, the dependency will cause the cache to eject the value from the cache, creating a data object that can be accessed only a limited number of times.

This isn't an especially realistic example because the data item will step closer to expiry each time it is read, which is not something you would usually do in an example without paying more attention to *why* the data is being used, but it allows me to keep the example simple and demonstrate a custom dependency without having to set up some external source of change events. Listing 11-8 shows the contents of the `SelfExpiringData.cs` file that I added to the `Infrastructure` folder of the example project.

Listing 11-8. The Contents of the SelfExpiringData.cs File

```
using System;
using System.Web.Caching;

namespace StateData.Infrastructure {
    public class SelfExpiringData<T> : CacheDependency {
        private T dataValue;
        private int requestCount = 0;
        private int requestLimit;

        public T Value {
            get {
                if (requestCount++ >= requestLimit) {
                    NotifyDependencyChanged(this, EventArgs.Empty);
                }
```

```
                return dataValue;
            }
        }

        public SelfExpiringData(T data, int limit) {
            dataValue = data;
            requestLimit = limit;
        }
    }
}
```

I have created a strongly typed class that accepts a data value and a request limit in its constructor and exposes the data value through a property called Value. Each time the getter for the Value property is used, I increment a counter and check to see whether the use limit has been reached.

If it has, then I call the `NotifyDependencyChanged` method, which is inherited from the CacheDependency class, which is the base used for custom dependencies. Calling the `NotifyDependencyChanged` method tells the cache that the dependency has changed and ejects the data item from the cache. Listing 11-9 shows how I applied the `SelfExpiringData` class in the Cache controller.

Listing 11-9. Applying the Self-expiring Cache Dependency in the CacheController.cs File

```
using System;
using System.Net.Http;
using System.Threading.Tasks;
using System.Web;
using System.Web.Caching;
using System.Web.Mvc;
using StateData.Infrastructure;

namespace StateData.Controllers {
    public class CacheController : Controller {

        public ActionResult Index() {

            SelfExpiringData<long?> seData =
                (SelfExpiringData<long?>)HttpContext.Cache["pageLength"];
            return View(seData == null ? null : seData.Value);
        }

        [HttpPost]
        public async Task<ActionResult> PopulateCache() {
            HttpResponseMessage result
                = await new HttpClient().GetAsync("http://apress.com");
            long? data = result.Content.Headers.ContentLength;
            SelfExpiringData<long?> seData = new SelfExpiringData<long?>(data, 3);
            HttpContext.Cache.Insert("pageLength", seData, seData);
            return RedirectToAction("Index");
        }
    }
}
```

Notice that I use the SelfExpiringData object twice when calling the Cache.Insert method, both as the data item and as the dependency. This allows me to track the number of times that the data value is read and to trigger the dependency change notification.

To test the custom dependency, start the application, request the /Cache/Index URL, and click the PopulateCache button. Now start reloading the browser page by pressing the F5 key—each time you reload the content, the Index action in the Cache controller will read the data value, and once the limit has been reached, the data item will be ejected from the cache.

Creating Aggregate Dependencies

You can get a sense from the constructors shown in Table 11-9 that it is possible to create chains of dependencies, such that one CacheDependency instance will eject its data item when another CacheDependency changes. An alternative approach of combining dependencies is to use an *aggregate dependency*, which allows multiple dependencies to be combined without the need to create chains. The cache item associated with an aggregate dependency will be removed from the cache when any one of the individual dependencies changes.

The AggregateCacheDependency class manages a collection of dependencies, which is populated through the Add method. Listing 11-10 shows the use of this class in the Cache controller.

Listing 11-10. Creating an Aggregate Dependency in the CacheController.cs File

```
using System;
using System.Net.Http;
using System.Threading.Tasks;
using System.Web;
using System.Web.Caching;
using System.Web.Mvc;
using StateData.Infrastructure;

namespace StateData.Controllers {
    public class CacheController : Controller {

        public ActionResult Index() {

            SelfExpiringData<long?> seData =
                (SelfExpiringData<long?>)HttpContext.Cache["pageLength"];
            return View(seData == null ? null : seData.Value);
        }

        [HttpPost]
        public async Task<ActionResult> PopulateCache() {
            HttpResponseMessage result
                = await new HttpClient().GetAsync("http://apress.com");
            long? data = result.Content.Headers.ContentLength;
            SelfExpiringData<long?> seData = new SelfExpiringData<long?>(data, 3);
            CacheDependency fileDep = new CacheDependency(Request.MapPath("~/data.txt"));
            AggregateCacheDependency aggDep = new AggregateCacheDependency();
            aggDep.Add(seData, fileDep);
            HttpContext.Cache.Insert("pageLength", seData, aggDep);
            return RedirectToAction("Index");
        }
    }
}
```

I used the AggregateCacheDependency class to combine two CacheDependency instances, one of which is an instance of my SelfExpiringData class and the other is a CacheDependency object that monitors the data.txt file for changes. The effect is that the data item will be removed from the cache when the data value has been read three times or the data.txt file changes, whichever happens first.

Receiving Dependency Notifications

When I created the SelfExpiringData class in the "Creating Custom Dependencies" section, I signaled that the dependency had changed by calling the NotifyDependencyChanged method.

The Cache class uses this notification to manage the contents of the class, but you can pass a notification handler to the Cache.Insert or Cache.Add method to be notified as well. Listing 11-11 shows how I receive and handle such a notification in the Cache controller.

Listing 11-11. Receiving Dependency Notifications in the CacheController.cs File

```
using System;
using System.Net.Http;
using System.Threading.Tasks;
using System.Web;
using System.Web.Caching;
using System.Web.Mvc;
using StateData.Infrastructure;

namespace StateData.Controllers {
    public class CacheController : Controller {

        public ActionResult Index() {

            SelfExpiringData<long?> seData =
                (SelfExpiringData<long?>)HttpContext.Cache["pageLength"];
            return View(seData == null ? null : seData.Value);
        }

        [HttpPost]
        public async Task<ActionResult> PopulateCache() {
            HttpResponseMessage result
                = await new HttpClient().GetAsync("http://apress.com");
            long? data = result.Content.Headers.ContentLength;
            SelfExpiringData<long?> seData = new SelfExpiringData<long?>(data, 3);
            HttpContext.Cache.Insert("pageLength", seData, seData,
                Cache.NoAbsoluteExpiration, Cache.NoSlidingExpiration,
                    CacheItemPriority.Normal, HandleNotification);
            return RedirectToAction("Index");
        }

        private void HandleNotification(string key, object data,
                CacheItemRemovedReason reason) {
            System.Diagnostics.Debug.WriteLine("Item {0} removed. ({1})",
                key, Enum.GetName(typeof(CacheItemRemovedReason), reason));
        }
    }
}
```

The method that handles the notification has to receive three arguments: the key of the item that the notification relates to, the value of the item, and a value from the `CacheItemRemovedReason` that explains why the item was removed. The `CacheItemRemovedReason` enumeration defines the values shown in Table 11-10.

Table 11-10. *The Values Defined by the CacheItemRemovedReason Enumeration*

Name	Description
`Removed`	Used when the item has been removed from the cache using the Remove method or when an item with the same key is cached with the `Insert` method.
`Expired`	Used when the item has expired. This value is used for both absolute and sliding expirations.
`Underused`	Used when the item has been removed by the cache scavenging process.
`DependencyChanged`	Used when a dependency that the item relies on has changed.

In the listing, I handle the notification by calling the `System.Diagnostics.Debug.WriteLine` method, which will produce a message in the Visual Studio Output window. To see the effect, start the application, navigate to `/Cache/Item`, and click the Populate Cache button. Repeatedly refresh the page using the F5 key until the item is removed from the cache and the following message is shown in the Output window:

```
Item pageLength removed. (DependencyChanged)
```

Using Notifications to Prevent Cache Ejection

The problem with the notifications in the previous section is that they are sent after the item has been removed from the cache. This is useful for tracking when data has expired but doesn't allow you to adjust the cache behavior. Fortunately, there is another kind of notification that is sent before an item is ejected and that can be used to keep the item in the cache. This kind of notification can be received only when using this version of the `Cache.Insert` method:

```
...
Insert(key, data, dependency, time, duration, callback)
...
```

This is the overload that requires expiration values but doesn't take a cache priority value. In Listing 11-12, you can see how I have updated the `Cache` controller to handle this kind of notification.

Listing 11-12. Receiving Pre-ejection Cache Notifications in the CacheController.cs File

```
using System;
using System.Net.Http;
using System.Threading.Tasks;
using System.Web;
using System.Web.Caching;
using System.Web.Mvc;
using StateData.Infrastructure;
```

```
namespace StateData.Controllers {
    public class CacheController : Controller {

        public ActionResult Index() {
            SelfExpiringData<long?> seData
                = (SelfExpiringData<long?>)HttpContext.Cache["pageLength"];
            return View(seData == null ? null : seData.Value);
        }

        [HttpPost]
        public async Task<ActionResult> PopulateCache() {
            HttpResponseMessage result
                = await new HttpClient().GetAsync("http://apress.com");
            long? data = result.Content.Headers.ContentLength;
            SelfExpiringData<long?> seData = new SelfExpiringData<long?>(data, 3);
            HttpContext.Cache.Insert("pageLength", seData, seData,
                Cache.NoAbsoluteExpiration, Cache.NoSlidingExpiration,
                    HandleNotification);
            return RedirectToAction("Index");
        }

        private void HandleNotification(string key,
            CacheItemUpdateReason reason,
            out object data,
            out CacheDependency dependency,
            out DateTime absoluteExpiry,
            out TimeSpan slidingExpiry) {

            System.Diagnostics.Debug.WriteLine("Item {0} removed. ({1})",
                key, Enum.GetName(typeof(CacheItemUpdateReason), reason));

            data = dependency
                = new SelfExpiringData<long?>(GetData(false).Result, 3);

            slidingExpiry = Cache.NoSlidingExpiration;
            absoluteExpiry = Cache.NoAbsoluteExpiration;
        }

        private async Task<long?> GetData(bool awaitCon = true) {
            HttpResponseMessage response = await new
                HttpClient().GetAsync("http://apress.com").ConfigureAwait(awaitCon);
            return response.Content.Headers.ContentLength;
        }
    }
}
```

The handler method for this kind of notification must define the arguments shown in Table 11-11, in the order in which they are listed. As the listing shows, many of these arguments are decorated with the out keyword, which means that the handler method must assign a value to the argument before the method returns.

Table 11-11. The Arguments Required for an Update Callback Handler Method

Type	Description
`string`	The key for the data item that is about to be ejected from the cache.
`CacheItemUpdateReason`	The reason that the data is about to be ejected. This is a different enumeration than the one used for ejection notifications—see the text after the table for details.
`object`	Set this `out` parameter to the updated data that will be inserted into the cache. Set to `null` to allow the item to be ejected.
`CacheDependency`	Set this `out` parameter to define the dependency for the updated item. Set to `null` for no dependency.
`DateTime`	Set this `out` parameter to define the absolute expiry. Use the `Cache.NoAbsoluteExpiration` property for no expiration.
`TimeSpan`	Set this `out` parameter to define the sliding expiration. Use the `Cache.NoSlidingExpiration` property for no expiration.

■ **Tip** You will notice that I call the `ConfigureAwait` method on the `Task` returned by the `HttpClient.GetAsync` method. This method prevents a deadlock when the asynchronous task is invoked from a method that has not been decorated with the `async` keyword.

The reason that the item is going to be removed from the cache is expressed using a value from the `CacheItemUpdateReason` enumeration, which defines the values shown in Table 11-12.

Table 11-12. The Values Defined by the CacheItemUpdateReason Enumeration

Name	Description
`Expired`	Used when the item has expired. This value is used for both absolute and sliding expirations.
`DependencyChanged`	Used when a dependency that the item relies on has changed.

This kind of notification isn't made when the cache ejects an item because it is scavenging for memory or when the `Cache.Remove` method is used. This is because the notification is an opportunity to update a cached item, something that doesn't make sense when it has been explicitly removed or when the cache is trying to free up memory.

The handler method parameters that are annotated with the `out` keyword provide the mechanism for updating the cache item, and you must assign a value to each of them before the method returns. If you don't want to update the cache item, set the object argument to `null`; otherwise, set it to the updated value and use the other parameters to configure the updated cache item. In the listing, I take the opportunity to update the data and extend its life by creating a new cache dependency.

Summary

In this chapter, I described the data caching feature, which actively manages data to improve application performance. Like all state data features, the data cache should be used with caution, not least because it can mask design or coding flaws in the application, which will then manifest when the application is in production. In the next chapter, I describe the output cache, which allows the content generated by views to be cached and reused by the ASP.NET platform.

CHAPTER 12

Caching Content

Caching content is a natural extension of caching data, which I described in the previous chapter. Caching data allows you to generate content without having to calculate or load the data that a controller and view requires, which can be a good thing—but if the data hasn't changed, then often the content produced by rendering the view won't have changed either. And yet, the ASP.NET platform has to go through the entire request's life cycle, which involves the MVC framework locating controllers, executing action methods, and rendering views—only to produce the same output as for the last request.

The ASP.NET platform provides a content caching feature that controls caching in several ways, including a server-side cache that is used to service requests and setting headers in responses to direct the client to cache content. In a complex, high-volume web application, reusing content generated for earlier requests can reduce the load on the application servers and, when the content is cached by the client, the amount of network capacity required. Table 12-1 summarizes this chapter.

Table 12-1. *Chapter Summary*

Problem	Solution	Listing
Cache content generated by an action method.	Apply the `OutputCache` attribute to the action method or the controller that contains it.	1-4
Cache content at the server.	Set the `OutputCache.Location` property to `Server`.	5
Cache variations of the content generated by an action method.	Use caching variations.	6-9
Define caching policies that can be used throughout an application.	Create cache profiles in the `Web.config` file.	10, 11
Cache the output from a child action.	Apply the `OutputCache` to the child action method.	12-14
Adapt caching policy for individual requests.	Control caching using C# statements inside the action method.	15
Validate cached content before it is used.	Define a validation callback method and use the `HttpCachePolicy.AddValidationCallback` method.	16

Preparing the Example Project

For this chapter, I created a new project called ContentCache, following the pattern I have been using in earlier chapters. I used the Visual Studio ASP.NET Web Application template, selected the Empty option, and added the core MVC references. I'll be using Bootstrap in this chapter, so enter the following command into the Package Manager Console:

```
Install-Package -version 3.0.3 bootstrap
```

I am going to use simple counters to illustrate when a request is served with cached content, and I will store the counters as application state data. As I explained in Chapter 10, I prefer to work with the application state feature through a helper class. I created a folder called `Infrastructure` and added to it a class file called `AppStateHelper.cs`, the contents of which are shown in Listing 12-1.

Listing 12-1. The Contents of the AppStateHelper.cs File

```
using System;
using System.Web;
using System.Web.SessionState;

namespace ContentCache.Infrastructure {

    public enum AppStateKeys {
        INDEX_COUNTER
    }

    public static class AppStateHelper {

        public static int IncrementAndGet(AppStateKeys key) {
            string keyString = Enum.GetName(typeof(AppStateKeys), key);
            HttpApplicationState state = HttpContext.Current.Application;
            return (int)(state[keyString] = ((int)(state[keyString] ?? 0) + 1));
        }
    }
}
```

The helper class contains a method called `IncrementAndGet`, which retrieves an `int` value from the application state collection and increments it. If there is no stored value, then one is created.

I added a controller called `Home` to the project, the definition of which is shown in Listing 12-2.

Listing 12-2. The Contents of the HomeController.cs File

```
using System.Diagnostics;
using System.Threading;
using System.Web.Mvc;
using System.Web.UI;
using ContentCache.Infrastructure;

namespace ContentCache.Controllers {
    public class HomeController : Controller {
```

```
        public ActionResult Index() {
            Thread.Sleep(1000);
            int counterValue = AppStateHelper.IncrementAndGet(
                AppStateKeys.INDEX_COUNTER);
            Debug.WriteLine(string.Format("INDEX_COUNTER: {0}", counterValue));
            return View(counterValue);
        }
    }
}
```

The controller defines the Index action method, which uses the helper class to increment and retrieve a counter called INDEX_COUNTER and passes it to the View method so that it is available as the model data in the view. The action method also writes a message to the Visual Studio Output window using the System.Diagnostics.Debug class to display the value of the counter.

You will notice that the first statement in the Index action method is a call to the Thread.Sleep method, which adds a one-second delay to processing the request. In many of the examples in this chapter, it is important to know when the action method is being executed and when cached content is being used, and a delay helps make this more obvious.

■ **Caution** Do not add deliberate delays to real ASP.NET projects. I have only called the Thread.Sleep method to make the effect of caching more obvious.

To create the view, I right-clicked the Index action method in the Visual Studio code editor and selected Add View from the pop-up menu. I set View Name to be Index, selected Empty (without model) for the Template option, and unchecked the View Options boxes. When I clicked the Add button, Visual Studio created the Views/Home/Index.cshtml file, which I edited with the content shown in Listing 12-3.

Listing 12-3. The Contents of the Index.cshtml File

```
@model int
@{ Layout = null; }
<!DOCTYPE html>
<html>
<head>
    <meta name="viewport" content="width=device-width" />
    <title>Output Caching</title>
    <link href="~/Content/bootstrap.min.css" rel="stylesheet" />
    <link href="~/Content/bootstrap-theme.min.css" rel="stylesheet" />
    <style>
        body { padding-top: 10px; }
    </style>
</head>
<body class="container">
    <div class="alert alert-info">
        The counter value: @Model
    </div>
    @Html.ActionLink("Update", "Index", null, new { @class = "btn btn-primary" })
</body>
</html>
```

The view displays the value of the counter. Start the application, and when you refresh the page or click the Update button, the counter is incremented, as shown in Figure 12-1.

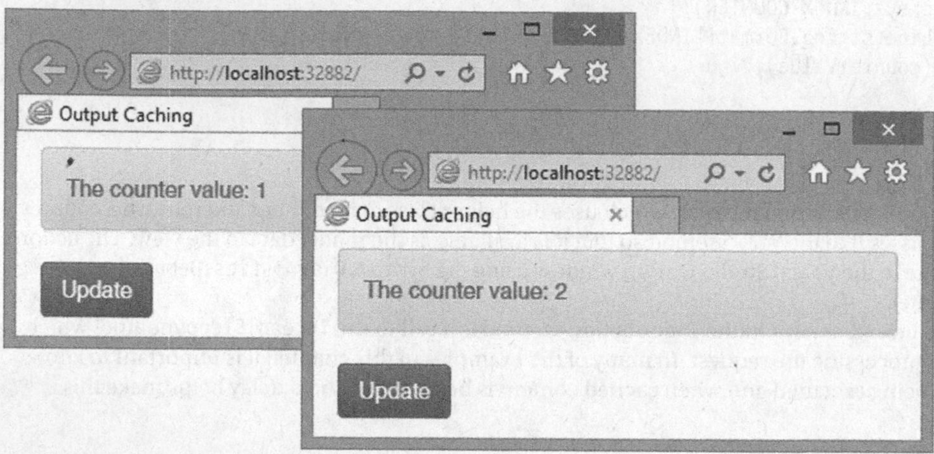

Figure 12-1. *Incrementing the counter when refreshing the page*

A good way to get insight into the effect of content caching is to use the browser F12 tools, which can capture information about the requests sent to the server and the responses they generate. To get a baseline without caching, press the F12 key to open the tools window, select the Network tab, and click the green arrow button; then reload the browser page. The request I am interested in is the first one in the list, which will be for the `/`, `/Home`, or `/Home/Index` URL, depending on what you asked the browser to display, as shown in Figure 12-2.

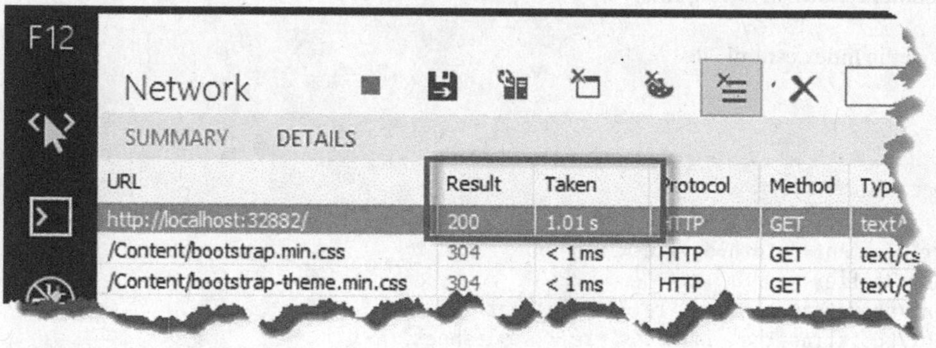

Figure 12-2. *The baseline request displayed in the F12 browser tools*

I have reordered the columns in the F12 window to make it easier to see the details in which I am most interested for this chapter, namely, the `Result` column, which shows the HTTP status code returned from the server, and the `Taken` column, which shows how long the request took.

■ **Tip** Tracing tools such as Glimpse are not especially helpful when it comes to studying the effect of content caching. Glimpse can only report on the request that the server receives and executes, but, as you will learn, a big part of content caching is to help the browser avoid making requests at all.

Using the Content Caching Attribute

There are two ways to control content caching. The first—and simplest—is to apply an attribute to action methods or controllers. This is the technique I describe in this section. Table 12-2 puts content caching into context.

***Table 12-2.** Putting Content Caching by Attribute in Context*

Question	Answer
What is it?	Applying the `OutputCache` attribute to action methods and controllers sets the caching policy, both in the ASP.NET server and in the HTTP clients, such as browsers and proxies.
Why should I care?	A careful caching policy can significantly reduce the amount of work required to service requests, allowing you to increase the throughput of your ASP.NET servers.
How is it used by the MVC framework?	The content cache isn't used directly by the MVC framework, but the feature is available for use in controllers and action methods.

■ **Note** Later in the chapter, I describe a second approach, which is to configure the caching programmatically from within an action method, which allows the action to adapt the way that content is cached based on the current request. This is more flexible and provides support for fine-grain control over caching options, but it is more complicated and requires careful testing to ensure that everything works as expected. I recommend you start with the attribute in your projects because it is simpler to work with and creates a consistent effect. Use the programmatic effect only if you need to cache the same content in different ways.

The easiest way to cache content is to apply the `OutputCache` attribute to a controller or to individual action methods. Applying the attribute to the controller allows you to specify a single cache policy for all of the action methods it contains, while applying the attribute to individual action methods allows you to vary the caching configuration for each one. The `OutputCache` attribute defines the properties described in Table 12-3.

Table 12-3. *The Properties Defined by the OutputCache Attribute*

Name	Description
`CacheProfile`	This specifies a predefined caching configuration. See the "Creating Cache Profiles" section.
`Duration`	This specifies the number of seconds that the content will be cached for. See the following text for an example. A value for this property must be specified.
`Location`	This specifies where the content can be cached. See the "Controlling the Cache Location" section.
`NoStore`	When set to `true`, the response will set the `no-store` flag on the `Cache-Control` HTTP header. This asks clients and proxies to avoid storing the content on persistent media, such as disks.
`SqlDependency`	This specifies a dependency between the cached content and a SQL database table. This property doesn't fit well with most MVC framework applications, whose models are typically defined through an intermediate layer such as the Entity Framework.
`VaryByCustom`	This specifies a custom value by which different versions of the content will be cached. See the "Creating Custom Cache Variations" section.
`VaryByHeader`	This specifies the set of HTTP headers by which different versions of the content will be cached. See the "Varying Caching Using Headers" section.
`VaryByParam`	This specifies the set of form and query string values by which different versions of the content will be cached. See the "Varying Caching Using Form or Query String Data" section.

Controlling the Cache Location

The only sensible place to cache *application data* is at the server, as demonstrated in Chapter 11. Raw data doesn't become useful outside the server until it is processed and rendered by a view. There is no point sending cached application data to the browser, for example, because it doesn't know anything about how your application transforms the data into content that can be displayed to the user.

Caching *content*, the topic of this chapter, is different because it is the finished product, produced in a format that is understood by the browser and that can be displayed to a user. If a browser has a cached copy of the content it requires, it doesn't need to send a request to the server.

The ASP.NET content caching feature includes a server-side memory cache but can also be used to control the caching by clients and proxies through the use of HTTP headers.

The `OutputCache` attribute defines the `Location` property, which specifies where the output from an action method can be cached. Listing 12-4 shows the `OuputCache` applied to the `Home` controller.

Listing 12-4. Adding Content Caching to the HomeController.cs File

```
using System.Diagnostics;
using System.Threading;
using System.Web.Mvc;
using System.Web.UI;
using ContentCache.Infrastructure;

namespace ContentCache.Controllers {
    public class HomeController : Controller {

        [OutputCache(Duration = 30, Location = OutputCacheLocation.Downstream)]
        public ActionResult Index() {
            Thread.Sleep(1000);
```

```
            int counterValue = AppStateHelper.IncrementAndGet(
                AppStateKeys.INDEX_COUNTER);
            Debug.WriteLine(string.Format("INDEX_COUNTER: {0}", counterValue));
            return View(counterValue);
        }
    }
}
```

■ **Tip** The Duration property must always be set when using the OutputCache attribute. I have set the cache duration to 30 seconds, which is too short for most real-life applications but makes it easy to test the examples without having to wait too long to see the effect of a change.

The Location property is set to one of the values from the OutputCacheLocation enumeration, which I have described in Table 12-4.

Table 12-4. *The Values Defined by the OutputCacheLocation Enumeration*

Name	Description
Any	The Cache-Control header is set to public, meaning that the content is cacheable by clients and proxy servers. The content will also be cached using the ASP.NET output cache at the server.
Client	The Cache-Control header is set to private, meaning that the content is cacheable by clients but not proxy servers. The content will also be cached using the ASP.NET output cache at the server.
Downstream	The Cache-Control header is set to public, meaning that the content is cacheable by clients and proxy servers. The content will not be cached using the ASP.NET output cache.
None	The Cache-Control header is set to no-cache, meaning that the content is not cacheable by clients and proxy servers. The ASP.NET output cache will not be used.
Server	The Cache-Control header is set to no-cache, but the content will be cached using the ASP.NET output cache.
ServerAndClient	The Cache-Control header is set to private, meaning that the content is cacheable by clients but not proxy servers. The content will also be cached using the ASP.NET output cache.

I specified the Downstream value in the listing, which means that the Cache-Control response HTTP header is used tell the browser (and any caching proxies) how to cache the data. The Downstream value doesn't put the content from the Index method in the server-side cache, which means that the action method will be executed if a request is made by the browser.

To see the effect of the OutputCache attribute, start the application, make a note of the counter value displayed, and then click the Update button. The counter value will not change as long as you clicked the button within 30 seconds of the original request. Wait 30 seconds and then click the Update button again, and the counter will be incremented.

You can see what is happening by using the F12 tools to record the network requests and looking at the response headers. The first time that the browser requests the content from the Index action method, ASP.NET adds the Cache-Control header to the response, like this:

```
...
Cache-Control:    public, max-age=30
...
```

This tells the browser that it should cache the content for 30 seconds. The public value indicates that intermediaries between the client and server, such as proxies, can also cache the data. If you look at the timings on the F12 Network tab, you will see results similar to those in Figure 12-3.

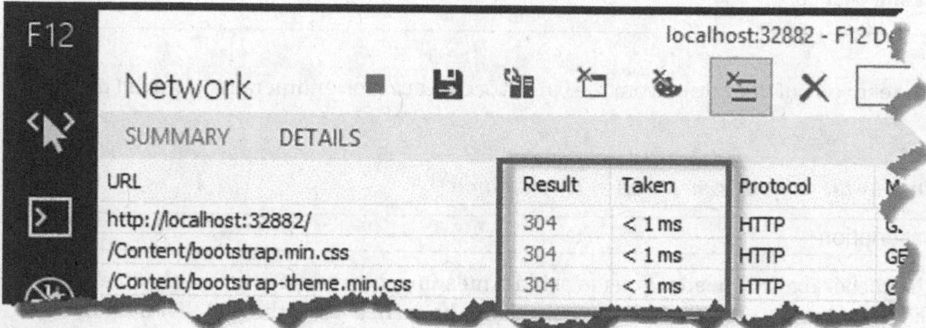

***Figure 12-3.** Caching content in the browser*

■ **Tip** If you don't see the results shown in the figure, make sure that the Always Refresh from Server option on the F12 Network tab isn't enabled. When enabled, the browser ignores caching instructions and sends requests to the server every time.

Internet Explorer shows that the result code for the request is 304, meaning that the content hasn't changed since it was last obtained. This is misleading because it implies that the server sent the 304 code; however, IE obtained the content from its local cache. The effect is that clicking the Update button causes the browser to display the cached data without making a server request at all.

■ **Tip** Other browsers, including Google Chrome, make it more obvious when content has been retrieved from the browser cache. If you want to be sure that Internet Explorer isn't sending requests to the server, then I recommend using Fiddler, which allows you to track all of the network activity on a machine. Fiddler is available without charge from www.telerik.com/fiddler.

Having content cached by the browser can improve performance for an individual user, but it has only a modest impact on the overall application because each user's browser has to make an initial request to the server in order to get the content to cache.

A further limitation of client caching is that the browser has no insight into how the web application is structured, and that means that even the slightest variation in URL can cause the browser to bypass its cached data and make a request to the server. In the example application, the URLs `/`, `/Home`, and `/Home/Index` all target the `Index` action method on the `Home` controller, but the browser has no way of knowing this is the case and will not use cached data from one URL for another. For this reason, you should ensure that the URLs that your application generates are consistent, which is done most readily by using the URL helper methods to create URLs using an application's routing policy.

Caching at the Server

The ASP.NET server has to perform a lot of work to generate content for a request, including locating the controller and action method and rendering the view to produce the content that will be sent to the client.

Caching the content at the server allows the ASP.NET platform to use content generated by earlier requests without having to go through the normal generation process, allowing the work performed for one request to be amortized across several. Listing 12-5 shows how I enabled server content caching in the `Home` controller.

Listing 12-5. Enabling Server Content Caching in the HomeController.cs File

```
using System.Diagnostics;
using System.Threading;
using System.Web.Mvc;
using System.Web.UI;
using ContentCache.Infrastructure;

namespace ContentCache.Controllers {
    public class HomeController : Controller {

        [OutputCache(Duration = 30, Location = OutputCacheLocation.Server)]
        public ActionResult Index() {
            Thread.Sleep(1000);
            int counterValue = AppStateHelper.IncrementAndGet(
                AppStateKeys.INDEX_COUNTER);
            Debug.WriteLine(string.Format("INDEX_COUNTER: {0}", counterValue));
            return View(counterValue);
        }
    }
}
```

I have changed the value of the `Location` property to `Server`. This disables the browser caching but enables the server cache. To see the effect, start the application, start monitoring the network requests with the F12 tools, and then click the Refresh button.

If you look at the response headers from the server, you will see that the `Cache-Control` header is set as follows:

```
...
Cache-Control:   no-cache
...
```

This tells the browser not to cache the content and to request it fresh from the server every time. In the summary view, you will see the results illustrated by Figure 12-4.

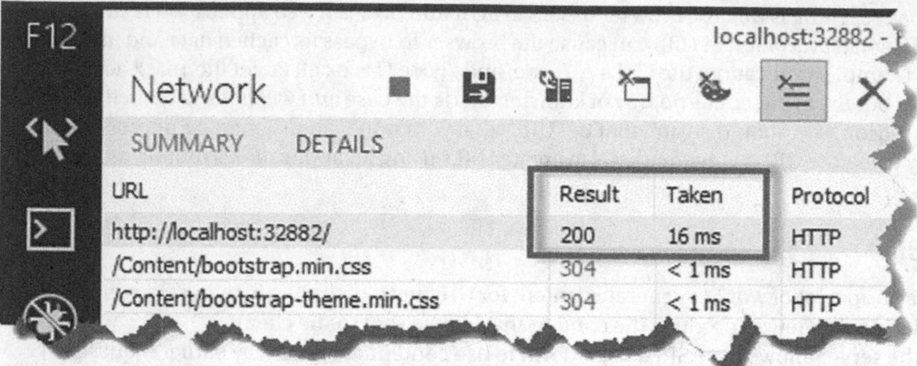

Figure 12-4. *The effect of server content caching*

The 200 status code shows that the content was requested from the server, but the time taken for the request is only 16 milliseconds, which indicates that the action method was not executed (because, as you will recall, it contains a one-second delay).

Server caching is implemented by a module defined in the `OutputCacheModule` class from the `System.Web.Caching` namespace. This module listens for the `UpdateRequestCache` event and uses it to populate its cache with content. The module listens for the `ResolveRequestCache` event and handles it by using its cached content as the response and terminates the request life cycle. (I described the life-cycle events in Chapter 3, modules in Chapter 4, and terminating the request handling process in Chapter 6.)

The result is that the ASP.NET platform is able to respond to requests engaging the MVC framework, avoiding all of the work required to execute an action and render a view—and that's why the duration shown in Figure 12-4 is so much shorter than when the MVC framework produced the content originally.

REAL-WORLD CACHE SETTINGS

In the previous examples, I showed you the `Downstream` and `Server` caching modes because they allowed me to isolate the way that ASP.NET implements client and server caching. Most real web applications, however, require only two caching settings: `Any` and `None`.

The `Any` setting enables caching at the client and the server and offers the best performance. The `None` setting disables all caching options and requires the client to make requests for the content, which in turn are always passed on to the controller, action method, and view.

When using the `Any` setting, make sure you understand what the impact of caching will be on the liveliness of your application. If you set the caching period to be too long, then your users will be working with stale data. If you set the caching period to be too short, then it is possible that users won't be requesting the data often enough to benefit from the cached content. I recommend disabling caching until you understand the performance profile of your application and are in a position to perform solid testing of the impact—both positive, in terms of reduced server load, and negative, in terms of liveliness.

The `None` setting is useful when the content must be generated fresh for every request. Applications that generate this content are few and far between, so the first thing to check before you apply the `None` setting is to make sure you are not trying to paper over a design or implementation issue in the application. If you find that you have a real need to disable caching, make sure you scale up your server infrastructure so that it can cope with clients always making requests to the server.

Managing Data Caching

The previous examples treated all requests as being equal, meaning that all requests for /Home/Index, for example, will receive the same cached content. You can also cache multiple versions of content and ASP.NET will match the cached content to the request using a *caching variation*, such as a request header or form data values.

Caching variations allow you to increase the flexibility of your application by generating cached content for a range of requests for the same URL, getting the performance increase that caching offers without being tied to a single version of the cached content for all requests. I'll demonstrate the way that you can vary caching in the sections that follow. Table 12-5 puts caching variations in context.

Table 12-5. *Putting Caching Variations in Context*

Question	Answer
What is it?	Caching variations allow caching of multiple copies of the content produced by an action method. The ASP.NET platform will match a request to the variations and deliver the right version of the content.
Why should I care?	Caching variations increase the flexibility of the content cache, allowing it to be useful in a wider range of applications.
How is it used by the MVC framework?	This feature is not used directly by the MVC framework, but it is available for use in controllers and action methods.

Varying Caching Using Headers

The simplest form of caching variation is to deliver different versions of cached content based on the headers in the HTTP request. To demonstrate how this works, I have modified configuration of the OutputCache applied to the Index action method on the Home controller, as shown in Listing 12-6.

Listing 12-6. Varying Cached Content Based on Headers in the HomeController.cs File

```
using System.Diagnostics;
using System.Threading;
using System.Web.Mvc;
using System.Web.UI;
using ContentCache.Infrastructure;

namespace ContentCache.Controllers {
    public class HomeController : Controller {

        [OutputCache(Duration = 30, VaryByHeader="user-agent",
            Location = OutputCacheLocation.Any)]
        public ActionResult Index() {
            Thread.Sleep(1000);
            int counterValue = AppStateHelper.IncrementAndGet(
                AppStateKeys.INDEX_COUNTER);
            Debug.WriteLine(string.Format("INDEX_COUNTER: {0}", counterValue));
            return View(counterValue);
        }
    }
}
```

The VaryByHeader property of the OutputCache attribute allows me to specify one or more headers that will be used to differentiate between requests. I selected the easiest header to test, which is User-Agent, used to identify the browser (and which is used by the browser capabilities feature that I described in Chapter 7).

The ASP.NET platform will execute the Index action method and cache the result for every different user-agent header value that it receives. Subsequent requests that contain the same user-agent header within the caching direction will receive the appropriate cached version.

You will need two different browsers to be able to test this example, such as Internet Explorer and Google Chrome. Start the application and navigate to /Home/Index with both browsers. You will see a different counter value for each browser, which reflects the fact that different content has been cached for each user-agent value.

Varying Caching Using Form or Query String Data

A similar approach can be taken to generate and cache content for different permutations of form or query string data. Of all the techniques I describe in the chapter, this is the one that requires the most caution and causes the most trouble. In most web applications, it is important that data sent from the user is processed and used to update the model, advancing the user through the application flows and features. Caching content based on form data can mean that user interactions don't target the action methods in the application, which means that user input is lost. That said, this technique can be useful if you have action methods that generate content without updating the model—although if this is the case, static HTML can often be a better alternative than caching content generated by an action method. Listing 12-7 shows how I have updated the Home controller so that the content generated from the Index action method is varied based on user data values.

Listing 12-7. Varying Cached Content Based on User Data in the HomeController.cs File

```
using System.Diagnostics;
using System.Threading;
using System.Web.Mvc;
using System.Web.UI;
using ContentCache.Infrastructure;

namespace ContentCache.Controllers {
    public class HomeController : Controller {

        [OutputCache(Duration = 30, VaryByHeader="user-agent",
            VaryByParam="name;city", Location = OutputCacheLocation.Any)]
        public ActionResult Index() {
            Thread.Sleep(1000);
            int counterValue = AppStateHelper.IncrementAndGet(
                AppStateKeys.INDEX_COUNTER);
            Debug.WriteLine(string.Format("INDEX_COUNTER: {0}", counterValue));
            return View(counterValue);
        }
    }
}
```

The VaryByParam property is used to specify one or more query string or form data parameter names. For each permutation of values of these parameters, ASP.NET will cache a version of the content generated by the action method and use it to satisfy subsequent requests made with the same values.

To see the effect, start the application and navigate to the following URL, which contains query string values for the parameters specified for the VaryByParam property:

```
/Home/Index?name=Adam&city=London
```

Open a second instance of the same browser and request the same URL, and you will receive the cached content from the previous request. If you specify a different name or city, then a new version of the content will be generated and cached.

■ **Tip** You can specify an asterisk (the * character) as the value for the VaryByParam property, which will cause different versions of the content to be cached for every permutation of every query string or form parameter. Use this with caution because it can effectively disable caching in most applications.

In Listing 12-7, I left the VaryByHeader property set, which means that different versions of the content will be cached for every permutation of query string values and user agents that ASP.NET receives requests for. This means that requesting the URL shown earlier from Internet Explorer and Google Chrome, for example, will generate different versions of the cached content, even though the query string values are the same.

■ **Tip** The best way to think about cache variations is to consider the combination of query string and headers as a key. The cache will be populated with content for each unique key for which a request is made, and requests for which the cache already contain a match for the key will receive that version of the cached content.

Creating Custom Cache Variations

You can create custom caching variations if headers and user data are not enough to differentiate between the requests that your application receives. The OutputCache.VaryByCustom property is used to specify an argument that is passed to a method in the global application class, which is called when requests are received to generate a cache key. Listing 12-8 shows the application of this property in the Home controller.

Listing 12-8. Using a Custom Cache Variation in the HomeController.cs File

```
using System.Diagnostics;
using System.Threading;
using System.Web.Mvc;
using System.Web.UI;
using ContentCache.Infrastructure;

namespace ContentCache.Controllers {
    public class HomeController : Controller {

        [OutputCache(Duration = 30,
            VaryByHeader="user-agent",
            VaryByParam="name;city",
            VaryByCustom="mobile",
            Location = OutputCacheLocation.Any)]
```

```
        public ActionResult Index() {
            Thread.Sleep(1000);
            int counterValue = AppStateHelper.IncrementAndGet(
                AppStateKeys.INDEX_COUNTER);
            Debug.WriteLine(string.Format("INDEX_COUNTER: {0}", counterValue));
            return View(counterValue);
        }
    }
}
```

I specified the value mobile, which I'll use to identify mobile devices using the capabilities detection feature that I described in Chapter 7. As I explained in Chapter 7, there are some serious hazards when it comes to detecting mobile devices because the term is so nebulous and the data quality is so low, but it is good enough for my purposes in this chapter. Listing 12-9 shows how I have added support for the mobile cache variation in the global application class.

Listing 12-9. Adding a Custom Cache Variation to the Global.asax.cs File

```
using System.Web;
using System.Web.Mvc;
using System.Web.Routing;

namespace ContentCache {

    public class MvcApplication : System.Web.HttpApplication {

        protected void Application_Start() {
            AreaRegistration.RegisterAllAreas();
            RouteConfig.RegisterRoutes(RouteTable.Routes);
        }

        public override string GetVaryByCustomString(HttpContext ctx, string custom) {
            if (custom == "mobile") {
                return Request.Browser.IsMobileDevice.ToString();
            } else {
                return base.GetVaryByCustomString(ctx, custom);
            }
        }
    }
}
```

HttpApplication, which is the base for the global application class, defines the GetVaryByCustomString method. To add support for a custom cache variation, I override this method and check the value of the custom argument. When this argument is mobile, I am being asked to generate my custom cache key from the request, which I do by returning the value of the HttpRequest.Browser.IsMobileDevice property. This means I will cause two variations of the data in the cache—one for devices that cause the IsMobileDevice property to return true and one for those that return false. I call the base implementation of the method for all other values of the custom argument, without which the other variation features won't work.

■ **Tip** To see the effect of the custom variation in Listing 12-9, you can use the device emulation feature that Google Chrome provides to simulate requests from a smartphone or tablet. See Chapter 7 for details.

Creating Cache Profiles

As Listing 12-8 shows, the configuration of the OutputCache attribute can be verbose and is required for any action method or controller class for which caching is required. To help reduce duplication and to ensure consistent caching policies, the ASP.NET platform supports *cache profiles*. A cache profile is a particular caching configuration defined in the Web.config file that can be applied anywhere in the application by name. Listing 12-10 shows how I created a cache profile for the example application.

Listing 12-10. Creating Cache Profiles in the Web.config File

```
<?xml version="1.0" encoding="utf-8"?>
<configuration>
  <appSettings>
    <add key="webpages:Version" value="3.0.0.0" />
    <add key="webpages:Enabled" value="false" />
     <add key="ClientValidationEnabled" value="true" />
    <add key="UnobtrusiveJavaScriptEnabled" value="true" />
  </appSettings>
  <system.web>
    <compilation debug="true" targetFramework="4.5.1" />
    <httpRuntime targetFramework="4.5.1" />
    <caching>
      <outputCacheSettings>
        <outputCacheProfiles>
          <add name="cp1" duration="30" location="Any"
               varyByHeader="user-agent" varyByParam="name;city" varyByCustom="mobile"/>
        </outputCacheProfiles>
      </outputCacheSettings>
    </caching>
  </system.web>
</configuration>
```

The outputCacheProfiles collection configuration section is used to define cache profiles and is applied within the caching/outputCacheSettings section group. The add element is used to create new profiles, and the attributes on the element correspond to the OutputCache properties that I listed in Table 12-3. In Listing 12-10, I defined a cache profile called cp1, which reproduces the configuration of the OutputCache attribute from Listing 12-8. Listing 12-11 shows the application of the profile to the Home controller.

Listing 12-11. Applying a Cache Profile in the HomeController.cs File

```
using System.Diagnostics;
using System.Threading;
using System.Web.Mvc;
using System.Web.UI;
using ContentCache.Infrastructure;

namespace ContentCache.Controllers {
    public class HomeController : Controller {

        [OutputCache(CacheProfile="cp1")]
        public ActionResult Index() {
            Thread.Sleep(1000);
```

```
            int counterValue = AppStateHelper.IncrementAndGet(
                AppStateKeys.INDEX_COUNTER);
            Debug.WriteLine(string.Format("INDEX_COUNTER: {0}", counterValue));
            return View(counterValue);
        }
    }
}
```

As the listing shows, the individual configuration properties are replaced with CacheProfile, which is set to the name of the profile in the Web.config file. Not only does this tidy up the code, but it allows a consistent caching policy to be applied throughout the application and makes it easy to change that policy without having to locate and modify every instance of the OutputCache attribute.

Caching Child Action Output

The OutputCache attribute can be applied to any action method, including those that are used only as child actions. This means you can specify different caching policies when using the MVC framework to compose content from child actions. To demonstrate how this works, I have added a child action method to the Home controller and applied the OutputCache attribute to it, as shown in Listing 12-12.

Listing 12-12. Adding a Child Action to the HomeController.cs File

```
using System.Diagnostics;
using System.Threading;
using System.Web.Mvc;
using System.Web.UI;
using ContentCache.Infrastructure;
using System;

namespace ContentCache.Controllers {
    public class HomeController : Controller {

        [OutputCache(CacheProfile = "cp1")]
        public ActionResult Index() {
            Thread.Sleep(1000);
            int counterValue = AppStateHelper.IncrementAndGet(
                AppStateKeys.INDEX_COUNTER);
            Debug.WriteLine(string.Format("INDEX_COUNTER: {0}", counterValue));
            return View(counterValue);
        }

        [ChildActionOnly]
        [OutputCache(Duration=60)]
        public PartialViewResult GetTime() {
            return PartialView((object)DateTime.Now.ToShortTimeString());
        }
    }
}
```

You can use the Duration, VaryByCustom, and VaryByParam properties only when applying the OutputCache attribute to child actions. I have set the Duration property for the child action to be 60 seconds, which is longer than the duration for the Index action method. The effect will be that the output from the GetTime child action will be stored in the cache, even when cached output from the Index action is refreshed.

■ **Tip** Specifying a shorter caching duration for a child action than its parent has no effect, and the caching policy for the parent action will be used. This is equivalent to not applying the OutputCache attribute to the child at all.

To create the partial view for the child action, I right-clicked the GetTime method in the code editor and selected Add View from the pop-up menu. I set View Name to be GetTime, set Template to Empty (without model), and checked the Create as a Partial View option. When I clicked the Add button, Visual Studio created the Views/Home/GetTime.cshtml file, which I edited as shown in Listing 12-13.

Listing 12-13. The Contents of the GetTime.cshtml File

```
@model string
<div class="alert alert-info">
    The time is: @Model
</div>
```

Finally, I updated the Index.cshtml file to invoke the child action, as shown in Listing 12-14.

Listing 12-14. Invoking a Child Action in the Index.cshtml File

```
@model int
@{ Layout = null; }
<!DOCTYPE html>
<html>
<head>
    <meta name="viewport" content="width=device-width" />
    <title>Output Caching</title>
    <link href="~/Content/bootstrap.min.css" rel="stylesheet" />
    <link href="~/Content/bootstrap-theme.min.css" rel="stylesheet" />
    <style>
        body { padding-top: 10px; }
    </style>
</head>
<body class="container">
    <div class="alert alert-info">
        The counter value: @Model
    </div>
    @Html.Action("GetTime")
    @Html.ActionLink("Update", "Index", null, new { @class = "btn btn-primary" })
</body>
</html>
```

To see the effect, start the application and periodically click the Update button. The counter value produced by the Index action method will update after 30 seconds, but the same time value from the GetTime child action will be used for a further 30 seconds.

DONUT AND DONUT-HOLE CACHING

There is a technique called *donut caching*, which is where the content from an action method is cached by the server and supplemented by calls to action methods in every request. The name arises because the part that is cached (the donut) entirely surrounds the parts that are not (the donut holes). The donut is the content from the action method, and the donut holes are the content from the child actions.

Donut caching can be useful when the skeletal structure of the content is static and needs to be blended with fragments of dynamic content. The ASP.NET platform doesn't support donut caching for MVC framework applications, but there is an open source package that provides this functionality. See `https://github.com/moonpyk/mvcdonutcaching` for details.

ASP.NET *does* support a related technique, called *donut-hole caching*. If you apply the `OutputCache` attribute to a child action but not its parent, you create an effect where the donut hole (the child action output) is cached while the donut (the content from the action method) is not. This is useful for caching relatively static content, such as navigation controls, while leaving other content to be generated for each and every request.

Controlling Caching with Code

The strength of the `OutputCache` attribute is that it allows consistent caching to be applied to the content generated by action methods, but this can also be a drawback if you want to dynamically alter the caching policy based on the request. In this section, I'll show you how to take control of the caching using C# statements inside of action methods. Table 12-6 puts code-based cache policy in context.

Table 12-6. *Putting Code-Based Caching Policy in Context*

Question	Answer
What is it?	Controlling caching with C# statements allows an action method to tailor the cached content on a per-request basis.
Why should I care?	Although more complicated than using the attribute, controlling the cache policy by code allows you to tightly integrate content caching into a controller.
How is it used by the MVC framework?	This feature is not used by the MVC framework but is available for use within action methods.

The caching policy for a response is set through the `HttpResponse.Cache` property, which returns an instance of the `HttpCachePolicy` class from the `System.Web` namespace. Table 12-7 describes the most useful properties and methods defined by the `HttpCachePolicy` class.

Table 12-7. The Members Defined by the HttpCachePolicy

Name	Description
AddValidationCallback(handler, data)	Specifies a callback handler that will validate that the cached content is still valid. See the "Validating Cached Content" section.
SetCacheability(policy)	Sets the Cache-Control response header using one of the values defined by the HttpCacheability enumeration. See the "Dynamically Setting Cache Policy" section.
SetExpires(time)	Sets the Expires response header using a DateTime value.
SetLastModified(time)	Sets the Last-Modified header using a DateTime value.
SetMaxAge(period)	Sets the max-age flag of the Cache-Control response header using a TimeSpan.
SetNoServerCaching()	Disables server caching for the current response.
SetNoStore()	Adds the no-store flag to the Cache-Control response header.
SetNoTransforms()	Adds the no-transform flag to the Cache-Control response header.
SetProxyMaxAge(period)	Sets the s-maxage flag of the Cache-Control response header using a TimeSpan.
SetVaryByCustom(name)	Sets the argument that will be passed to the global application class GetVaryByCustomString method. See the "Creating Custom Cache Variation" section.
VaryByHeaders	Specifies the headers that will be used to vary the cached content. See the "Varying Caching Using Headers" section.
VaryByParams	Specifies the query string or form parameters that will be used to vary the cache content. See the "Varying Caching Using Form or Query String Data" section.

■ **Note** Many of the methods defined by the HttpCachePolicy class relate to the Cache-Control header, which used to issue direction to clients and intermediate devices such as proxies. I am not going to detail the Cache-Control header here, in part because it is implemented as part of HTTP rather than as an ASP.NET feature and partly because there the HTTP specification already contains all the information you could possibly want about the header. See www.w3.org/Protocols/rfc2616/rfc2616-sec14.html#sec14.9 for details.

Dynamically Setting Cache Policy

The benefit of working with the HttpCachePolicy class is that you can inspect the request from within the action method and adapt the caching policy dynamically. Listing 12-15 shows how I updated the Home controller to use the HttpCachePolicy class to change the caching policy based on the URL that was used to target the Index action method.

Listing 12-15. Setting Cache Policy in the HomeController.cs File

```
using System.Diagnostics;
using System.Threading;
using System.Web.Mvc;
using System.Web.UI;
using ContentCache.Infrastructure;
using System;
using System.Web;

namespace ContentCache.Controllers {
    public class HomeController : Controller {

        public ActionResult Index() {
            if (Request.RawUrl == "/Home/Index") {
                Response.Cache.SetNoServerCaching();
                Response.Cache.SetCacheability(HttpCacheability.NoCache);
            } else {
                Response.Cache.SetExpires(DateTime.Now.AddSeconds(30));
                Response.Cache.SetCacheability(HttpCacheability.Public);
            }
            Thread.Sleep(1000);
            int counterValue = AppStateHelper.IncrementAndGet(
                AppStateKeys.INDEX_COUNTER);
            Debug.WriteLine(string.Format("INDEX_COUNTER: {0}", counterValue));
            return View(counterValue);
        }

        [ChildActionOnly]
        [OutputCache(Duration = 60)]
        public PartialViewResult GetTime() {
            return PartialView((object)DateTime.Now.ToShortTimeString());
        }
    }
}
```

■ **Tip** Be careful of using the Update button for this example because the URL it requests will always be `/`. When checking to see whether the `/Home/Index` URL is cached, use the F5 key to refresh the browser instead.

I use the `HttpRequest.RawUrl` property to set the caching policy for the content generated by the `Index` action method. If the action method has been targeted by the `/Home/Index` URL, then I disable server caching and use the `SetCacheability` method to disable browser caching. The argument to the `SetCacheability` method is a value from the `HttpCacheability` enumeration, which defines the values shown in Table 12-8. If the action method has been targeted by any other URL, then I set the cache duration to 30 seconds and use the `SetCacheability` method to enable browser caching.

Table 12-8. *The Values Defined by the HttpCacheability Enumeration*

Name	Description
NoCache	This sets the Cache-Control header to no-cache, which prevents content from being cached by clients and proxies. This is equivalent to setting the OutputCache.Location property to None.
Private	The Cache-Control header is set to private, meaning that the content is cacheable by clients but not proxy servers. This is equivalent to setting the OutputCache.Location property to Client.
Public	The Cache-Control header is set to public, meaning that the content is cacheable by clients and proxy servers. This is equivalent to setting the OutputCache.Location property to Downstream.
Server	The Cache-Control header is set to no-cache, but the content will be cached using the ASP.NET output cache. This is equivalent to setting the OutputCache.Location property to Downstream.
ServerAndNoCache	This combines the Server and NoCache settings.
ServerAndPrivate	This combines the Server and Private settings.

To test the effect of the changes I made to the Home controller, start the application and request the root URL for the application (/). When you click the Update button, you will see that the content is cached for 30 seconds. Navigate to the /Home/Index URL and use the F5 key to refresh the page, and you will see that the browser requests the content from the server every time—and if you look at the Visual Studio Output window, you will see that the request is passed to the Home controller for every request.

Validating Cached Content

The HttpCachePolicy.AddValidationCallback method takes a method that is called to validate whether a cached data item is valid before it is returned to the client. This allows for custom management of the content cache, beyond the duration and location-based configuration. Listing 12-16 shows how I have added a validation callback to the Home controller.

Listing 12-16. Using a Cache Validation Callback to the HomeController.cs File

```
using System.Diagnostics;
using System.Threading;
using System.Web.Mvc;
using System.Web.UI;
using ContentCache.Infrastructure;
using System;
using System.Web;

namespace ContentCache.Controllers {
    public class HomeController : Controller {
```

```
        public ActionResult Index() {

            Response.Cache.SetExpires(DateTime.Now.AddSeconds(30));
            Response.Cache.SetCacheability(HttpCacheability.Server);
            Response.Cache.AddValidationCallback(CheckCachedItem, Request.UserAgent);

            Thread.Sleep(1000);
            int counterValue = AppStateHelper.IncrementAndGet(
                AppStateKeys.INDEX_COUNTER);
            Debug.WriteLine(string.Format("INDEX_COUNTER: {0}", counterValue));
            return View(counterValue);
        }

        [ChildActionOnly]
        [OutputCache(Duration = 60)]
        public PartialViewResult GetTime() {
            return PartialView((object)DateTime.Now.ToShortTimeString());
        }

        public void CheckCachedItem(HttpContext ctx, object data,
            ref HttpValidationStatus status) {

            status = data.ToString() == ctx.Request.UserAgent ?
                HttpValidationStatus.Valid : HttpValidationStatus.Invalid;
            Debug.WriteLine("Cache Status: " + status);
        }
    }
}
```

The AddValidationCallback method takes two arguments. The first is the method that will be called to validate the cached content, and the second is an object that can be used to identify the cached content in order to decide whether it is valid. In the example, I specified the CheckCachedItem method and selected the user-agent string for the object argument.

The callback method must take a specific set of arguments: an HttpContext object, the object argument from the call to the AddValidationCallback method, and an HttpValidationStatus value, which is marked with the ref keyword. The job of the callback method is to use the context to examine the request and set the value of the HttpValidationStatus argument in order to tell the ASP.NET platform whether the content is still valid. Table 12-9 shows the set of values defined by the HttpValidatonStatus enumeration. In the listing, I invalidate the cached content if the user-agent string doesn't match the one used when the content was cached.

Table 12-9. *The Values Defined by the HttpValidationStatus Enumeration*

Name	Description
Valid	The cached content is still valid.
Invalid	The content is no longer valid and should be ejected from the cache. The request is passed to the action method.
IgnoreThisRequest	The request is passed to the action method, but the value in the cache is not ejected.

■ **Tip** You must set an expiry date and ensure that the content is cached at the server when using the `AddValidationCallback` method, just as I did in the listing. If you do not do this, then the callback method won't be used because the content won't be cached in the right place.

Summary

In this chapter, I described the content cache, which can be used to enable server caching of content produced by action methods and set the response headers used by HTTP clients such as browsers and proxies. I demonstrated how you can use an attribute or C# statements to control caching and showed you how to manage the cache and its contents. In the next chapter, I show you how to set up and use the ASP.NET Identity system, which is used to manage user accounts.

CHAPTER 13

Getting Started with Identity

Identity is a new API from Microsoft to manage users in ASP.NET applications. The mainstay for user management in recent years has been ASP.NET Membership, which has suffered from design choices that were reasonable when it was introduced in 2005 but that have aged badly. The biggest limitation is that the schema used to store the data worked only with SQL Server and was difficult to extend without re-implementing a lot of provider classes. The schema itself was overly complex, which made it harder to implement changes than it should have been.

Microsoft made a couple of attempts to improve Membership prior to releasing Identity. The first was known as *simple membership*, which reduced the complexity of the schema and made it easier to customize user data but still needed a relational storage model. The second attempt was the ASP.NET *universal providers*, which I used in Chapter 10 when I set up SQL Server storage for session data. The advantage of the universal providers is that they use the Entity Framework Code First feature to automatically create the database schema, which made it possible to create databases where access to schema management tools wasn't possible, such as the Azure cloud service. But even with the improvements, the fundamental issues of depending on relational data and difficult customizations remained.

To address both problems and to provide a more modern user management platform, Microsoft has replaced Membership with Identity. As you'll learn in this chapter and Chapters 14 and 15, ASP.NET Identity is flexible and extensible, but it is immature, and features that you might take for granted in a more mature system can require a surprising amount of work.

Microsoft has over-compensated for the inflexibility of Membership and made Identity so open and so adaptable that it can be used in just about any way—just as long as you have the time and energy to implement what you require.

In this chapter, I demonstrate the process of setting up ASP.NET Identity and creating a simple user administration tool that manages individual user accounts that are stored in a database.

ASP.NET Identity supports other kinds of user accounts, such as those stored using Active Directory, but I don't describe them since they are not used that often outside corporations (where Active Directive implementations tend to be so convoluted that it would be difficult for me to provide useful general examples).

In Chapter 14, I show you how to perform authentication and authorization using those user accounts, and in Chapter 15, I show you how to move beyond the basics and apply some advanced techniques. Table 13-1 summarizes this chapter.

Table 13-1. *Chapter Summary*

Problem	Solution	Listing
Install ASP.NET Identity.	Add the NuGet packages and define a connection string and an OWIN start class in the `Web.config` file.	1–4
Prepare to use ASP.NET Identity.	Create classes that represent the user, the user manager, the database context, and the OWIN start class.	5–8
Enumerate user accounts.	Use the `Users` property defined by the user manager class.	9, 10
Create user accounts.	Use the `CreateAsync` method defined by the user manager class.	11–13
Enforce a password policy.	Set the `PasswordValidator` property defined by the user manager class, either using the built-in `PasswordValidator` class or using a custom derivation.	14–16
Validate new user accounts.	Set the `UserValidator` property defined by the user manager class, either using the built-in `UserValidator` class or using a custom derivation.	17–19
Delete user accounts.	Use the `DeleteAsync` method defined by the user manager class.	20–22
Modify user accounts.	Use the `UpdateAsync` method defined by the user manager class.	23–24

Preparing the Example Project

I created a project called Users for this chapter, following the same steps I have used throughout this book. I selected the Empty template and checked the option to add the folders and references required for an MVC application. I will be using Bootstrap to style the views in this chapter, so enter the following command into the Visual Studio Package Manager Console and press Enter to download and install the NuGet package:

```
Install-Package -version 3.0.3 bootstrap
```

I created a `Home` controller to act as the focal point for the examples in this chapter. The definition of the controller is shown in Listing 13-1. I'll be using this controller to describe details of user accounts and data, and the `Index` action method passes a dictionary of values to the default view via the `View` method.

Listing 13-1. The Contents of the HomeController.cs File

```
using System.Web.Mvc;
using System.Collections.Generic;

namespace Users.Controllers {

    public class HomeController : Controller {

        public ActionResult Index() {
            Dictionary<string, object> data
                = new Dictionary<string, object>();
            data.Add("Placeholder", "Placeholder");
            return View(data);
        }
    }
}
```

I created a view by right-clicking the Index action method and selecting Add View from the pop-up menu. I set View Name to Index and set Template to Empty (without model). Unlike the examples in previous chapters, I want to use a common layout for this chapter, so I checked the Use a Layout Page option. When I clicked the Add button, Visual Studio created the Views/Shared/_Layout.cshtml and Views/Home/Index.cshtml files. Listing 13-2 shows the contents of the _Layout.cshtml file.

Listing 13-2. The Contents of the _Layout.cshtml File

```
<!DOCTYPE html>
<html>
<head>
    <meta name="viewport" content="width=device-width" />
    <title>@ViewBag.Title</title>
    <link href="~/Content/bootstrap.min.css" rel="stylesheet" />
    <link href="~/Content/bootstrap-theme.min.css" rel="stylesheet" />
    <style>
        .container {  padding-top: 10px; }
        .validation-summary-errors { color: #f00; }
    </style>
</head>
<body class="container">
    <div class="container">
        @RenderBody()
    </div>
</body>
</html>
```

Listing 13-3 shows the contents of the Index.cshtml file.

Listing 13-3. The Contents of the Index.cshtml File

```
@{
    ViewBag.Title = "Index";
}

<div class="panel panel-primary">
    <div class="panel-heading">User Details</div>
    <table class="table table-striped">
        @foreach (string key in Model.Keys) {
            <tr>
                <th>@key</th>
                <td>@Model[key]</td>
            </tr>
        }
    </table>
</div>
```

To test that the example application is working, select Start Debugging from the Visual Studio Debug menu and navigate to the /Home/Index URL. You should see the result illustrated by Figure 13-1.

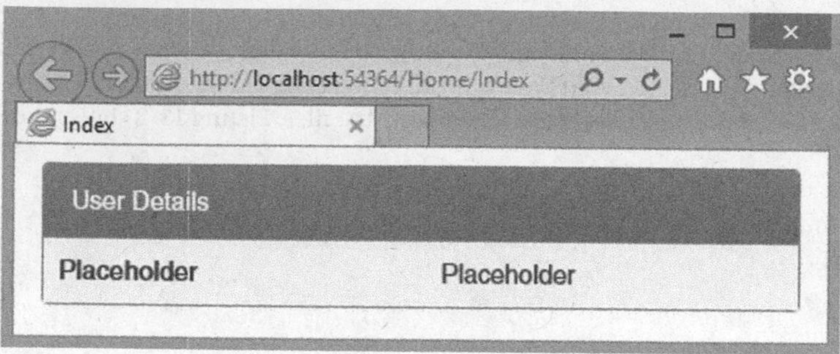

***Figure 13-1.** Testing the example application*

Setting Up ASP.NET Identity

For most ASP.NET developers, Identity will be the first exposure to the Open Web Interface for .NET (OWIN). OWIN is an abstraction layer that isolates a web application from the environment that hosts it. The idea is that the abstraction will allow for greater innovation in the ASP.NET technology stack, more flexibility in the environments that can host ASP.NET applications, and a lighter-weight server infrastructure.

OWIN is an open standard (which you can read at `http://owin.org/spec/owin-1.0.0.html`). Microsoft has created Project Katana, its implementation of the OWIN standard and a set of components that provide the functionality that web applications require. The attraction to Microsoft is that OWIN/Katana isolates the ASP.NET technology stack from the rest of the .NET Framework, which allows a greater rate of change.

OWIN developers select the services that they require for their application, rather than consuming an entire platform as happens now with ASP.NET. Individual services—known as *middleware* in the OWIN terminology—can be developed at different rates, and developers will be able to choose between providers for different services, rather than being tied to a Microsoft implementation.

There is a lot to like about the direction that OWIN and Katana are heading in, but it is in the early days, and it will be some time before it becomes a complete platform for ASP.NET applications. As I write this, it is possible to build Web API and SignalR applications without needing the `System.Web` namespace or IIS to process requests, but that's about all. The MVC framework requires the standard ASP.NET platform and will continue to do so for some time to come.

The ASP.NET platform and IIS are not going away. Microsoft has been clear that it sees one of the most attractive aspects of OWIN as allowing developers more flexibility in which middleware components are hosted by IIS, and Project Katana already has support for the `System.Web` namespaces. OWIN and Katana are not the end of ASP.NET—rather, they represent an evolution where Microsoft allows developers more flexibility in how ASP.NET applications are assembled and executed.

■ **Tip** Identity is the first major ASP.NET component to be delivered as OWIN middleware, but it won't be the last. Microsoft has made sure that the latest versions of Web API and SignalR don't depend on the `System.Web` namespaces, and that means that any component intended for use across the ASP.NET family of technologies has to be delivered via OWIN. I get into more detail about OWIN in my *Expert ASP.NET Web API 2 for MVC Developers* book, which will be published by Apress in 2014.

OWIN and Katana won't have a major impact on MVC framework developers for some time, but changes are already taking effect—and one of these is that ASP.NET Identity is implemented as an OWIN middleware component. This isn't ideal because it means that MVC framework applications have to mix OWIN and traditional ASP.NET platform techniques to use Identity, but it isn't too burdensome once you understand the basics and know how to get OWIN set up, which I demonstrate in the sections that follow.

Creating the ASP.NET Identity Database

ASP.NET Identity isn't tied to a SQL Server schema in the same way that Membership was, but relational storage is still the default—and simplest—option, and it is the one that I will be using in this chapter. Although the NoSQL movement has gained momentum in recent years, relational databases are still the mainstream storage choice and are well-understood in most development teams.

ASP.NET Identity uses the Entity Framework Code First feature to automatically create its schema, but I still need to create the database into which that schema—and the user data—will be placed, just as I did in Chapter 10 when I created the database for session state data (the universal provider that I used to manage the database uses the same Code First feature).

■ **Tip** You don't need to understand how Entity Framework or the Code First feature works to use ASP.NET Identity.

As in Chapter 10, I will be using the `localdb` feature to create my database. As a reminder, `localdb` is included in Visual Studio and is a cut-down version of SQL Server that allows developers to easily create and work with databases.

Select SQL Server Object Explorer from the Visual Studio View menu and right-click the SQL Server object in the window that appears. Select Add SQL Server from the pop-up menu, as shown in Figure 13-2.

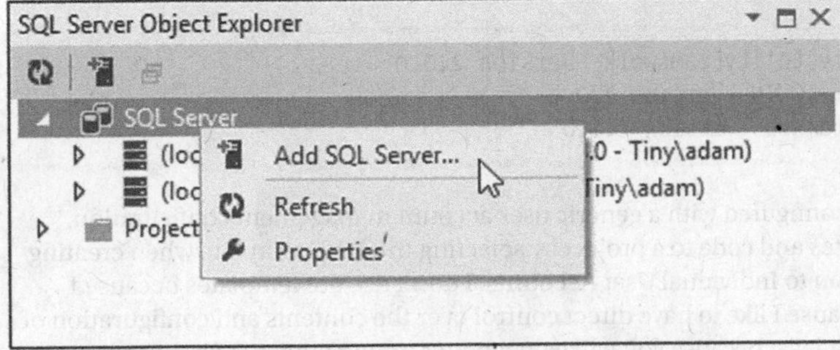

***Figure 13-2.** Creating a new database connection*

Visual Studio will display the Connect to Server dialog. Set the server name to (localdb)\v11.0, select the Windows Authentication option, and click the Connect button. A connection to the database will be established and shown in the SQL Server Object Explorer window. Expand the new item, right-click Databases, and select Add New Database from the pop-up window, as shown in Figure 13-3.

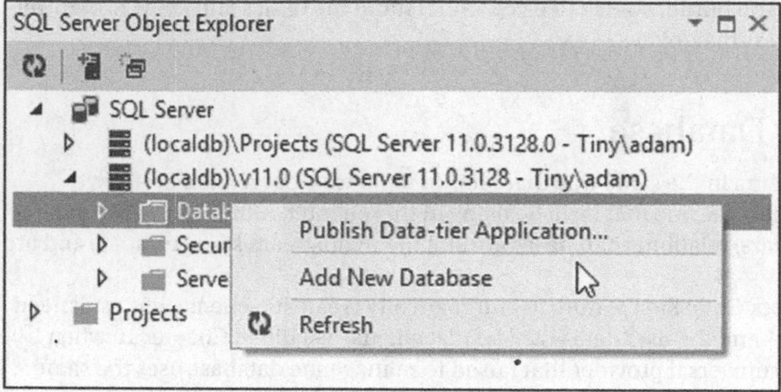

Figure 13-3. Adding a new database

Set the Database Name option to IdentityDb, leave the Database Location value unchanged, and click the OK button to create the database. The new database will be shown in the Databases section of the SQL connection in the SQL Server Object Explorer.

Adding the Identity Packages

Identity is published as a set of NuGet packages, which makes it easy to install them into any project. Enter the following commands into the Package Manager Console:

```
Install-Package Microsoft.AspNet.Identity.EntityFramework -Version 2.0.0
Install-Package Microsoft.AspNet.Identity.OWIN -Version 2.0.0
Install-Package Microsoft.Owin.Host.SystemWeb -Version 2.1.0
```

Visual Studio can create projects that are configured with a generic user account management configuration, using the Identity API. You can add the templates and code to a project by selecting the MVC template when creating the project and setting the Authentication option to Individual User Accounts. I don't use the templates because I find them too general and too verbose and because I like to have direct control over the contents and configuration of my projects. I recommend you do the same, not least because you will gain a better understanding of how important features work, but it can be interesting to look at the templates to see how common tasks are performed.

Updating the Web.config File

Two changes are required to the `Web.config` file to prepare a project for ASP.NET Identity. The first is a connection string that describes the database I created in the previous section. The second change is to define an application setting that names the class that initializes OWIN middleware and that is used to configure Identity. Listing 13-4 shows the changes I made to the `Web.config` file. (I explained how connection strings and application settings work in Chapter 9.)

Listing 13-4. Preparing the Web.config File for ASP.NET Identity

```
<?xml version="1.0" encoding="utf-8"?>
<configuration>
```

```
  <configSections>
    <section name="entityFramework"
        type="System.Data.Entity.Internal.ConfigFile.EntityFrameworkSection,
        EntityFramework, Version=6.0.0.0, Culture=neutral,
        PublicKeyToken=b77a5c561934e089" requirePermission="false" />
  </configSections>

  <connectionStrings>
    <add name="IdentityDb" providerName="System.Data.SqlClient"
        connectionString="Data Source=(localdb)\v11.0;Initial
            Catalog=IdentityDb;Integrated Security=True;Connect
            Timeout=15;Encrypt=False;TrustServerCertificate=False;
            MultipleActiveResultSets=True"/>
  </connectionStrings>

  <appSettings>
    <add key="webpages:Version" value="3.0.0.0" />
    <add key="webpages:Enabled" value="false" />
    <add key="ClientValidationEnabled" value="true" />
    <add key="UnobtrusiveJavaScriptEnabled" value="true" />
    <add key="owin:AppStartup" value="Users.IdentityConfig" />
  </appSettings>
  <system.web>
    <compilation debug="true" targetFramework="4.5.1" />
    <httpRuntime targetFramework="4.5.1" />
  </system.web>
  <entityFramework>
    <defaultConnectionFactory
        type="System.Data.Entity.Infrastructure.LocalDbConnectionFactory,
            EntityFramework">
      <parameters>
        <parameter value="v11.0" />
      </parameters>
    </defaultConnectionFactory>
    <providers>
      <provider invariantName="System.Data.SqlClient"
        type="System.Data.Entity.SqlServer.SqlProviderServices,
            EntityFramework.SqlServer" />
    </providers>
  </entityFramework>
</configuration>
```

■ **Caution** Make sure you put the `connectionString` value on a single line. I had to break it over several lines to make the listing fit on the page, but ASP.NET expects a single, unbroken string. If in doubt, download the source code that accompanies this book, which is freely available from `www.apress.com`.

OWIN defines its own application startup model, which is separate from the global application class that I described in Chapter 3. The application setting, called `owin:AppStartup`, specifies a class that OWIN will instantiate when the application starts in order to receive its configuration.

■ **Tip** Notice that I have set the `MultipleActiveResultSets` property to `true` in the connection string. This allows the results from multiple queries to be read simultaneously, which I rely on in Chapter 14 when I show you how to authorize access to action methods based on role membership.

Creating the Entity Framework Classes

If you have used Membership in projects, you may be surprised by just how much initial preparation is required for ASP.NET Identity. The extensibility that Membership lacked is readily available in ASP.NET Identity, but it comes with a price of having to create a set of implementation classes that the Entity Framework uses to manage the database. In the sections that follow, I'll show you how to create the classes needed to get Entity Framework to act as the storage system for ASP.NET Identity.

Creating the User Class

The first class to define is the one that represents a user, which I will refer to as the *user class*. The user class is derived from `IdentityUser`, which is defined in the `Microsoft.AspNet.Identity.EntityFramework` namespace. `IdentityUser` provides the basic user representation, which can be extended by adding properties to the derived class, which I describe in Chapter 15. Table 13-2 shows the built-in properties that `IdentityUser` defines, which are the ones I will be using in this chapter.

Table 13-2. *The Properties Defined by the IdentityUser Class*

Name	Description
`Claims`	Returns the collection of claims for the user, which I describe in Chapter 15
`Email`	Returns the user's e-mail address
`Id`	Returns the unique ID for the user
`Logins`	Returns a collection of logins for the user, which I use in Chapter 15
`PasswordHash`	Returns a hashed form of the user password, which I use in the "Implementing the Edit Feature" section
`Roles`	Returns the collection of roles that the user belongs to, which I describe in Chapter 14
`PhoneNumber`	Returns the user's phone number
`SecurityStamp`	Returns a value that is changed when the user identity is altered, such as by a password change
`UserName`	Returns the username

■ **Tip** The classes in the `Microsoft.AspNet.Identity.EntityFramework` namespace are the Entity Framework–specific concrete implementations of interfaces defined in the `Microsoft.AspNet.Identity` namespace. `IdentityUser`, for example, is the implementation of the `IUser` interface. I am working with the concrete classes because I am relying on the Entity Framework to store my user data in a database, but as ASP.NET Identity matures, you can expect to see alternative implementations of the interfaces that use different storage mechanisms (although most projects will still use the Entity Framework since it comes from Microsoft).

What is important at the moment is that the `IdentityUser` class provides access only to the basic information about a user: the user's name, e-mail, phone, password hash, role memberships, and so on. If I want to store any additional information about the user, I have to add properties to the class that I derive from `IdentityUser` and that will be used to represent users in my application. I demonstrate how to do this in Chapter 15.

To create the user class for my application, I created a class file called `AppUserModels.cs` in the `Models` folder and used it to create the `AppUser` class, which is shown in Listing 13-5.

Listing 13-5. The Contents of the AppUser.cs File

```
using System;
using Microsoft.AspNet.Identity.EntityFramework;

namespace Users.Models {
    public class AppUser : IdentityUser {
        // additional properties will go here
    }
}
```

That's all I have to do at the moment, although I'll return to this class in Chapter 15, when I show you how to add application-specific user data properties.

Creating the Database Context Class

The next step is to create an Entity Framework database context that operates on the `AppUser` class. This will allow the Code First feature to create and manage the schema for the database and provide access to the data it stores. The context class is derived from `IdentityDbContext<T>`, where `T` is the user class (`AppUser` in the example). I created a folder called `Infrastructure` in the project and added to it a class file called `AppIdentityDbContext.cs`, the contents of which are shown in Listing 13-6.

Listing 13-6. The Contents of the AppIdentityDbContext.cs File

```
using System.Data.Entity;
using Microsoft.AspNet.Identity.EntityFramework;
using Users.Models;

namespace Users.Infrastructure {
    public class AppIdentityDbContext : IdentityDbContext<AppUser> {

        public AppIdentityDbContext() : base("IdentityDb") { }
```

```
        static AppIdentityDbContext() {
            Database.SetInitializer<AppIdentityDbContext>(new IdentityDbInit());
        }

        public static AppIdentityDbContext Create() {
            return new AppIdentityDbContext();
        }
    }

    public class IdentityDbInit
            : DropCreateDatabaseIfModelChanges<AppIdentityDbContext> {

        protected override void Seed(AppIdentityDbContext context) {
            PerformInitialSetup(context);
            base.Seed(context);
        }

        public void PerformInitialSetup(AppIdentityDbContext context) {
            // initial configuration will go here
        }
    }
}
```

The constructor for the AppIdentityDbContext class calls its base with the name of the connection string that will be used to connect to the database, which is IdentityDb in this example. This is how I associate the connection string I defined in Listing 13-4 with ASP.NET Identity.

The AppIdentityDbContext class also defines a static constructor, which uses the Database.SetInitializer method to specify a class that will seed the database when the schema is first created through the Entity Framework Code First feature. My seed class is called IdentityDbInit, and I have provided just enough of a class to create a placeholder so that I can return to seeding the database later by adding statements to the PerformInitialSetup method. I show you how to seed the database in Chapter 14.

Finally, the AppIdentityDbContext class defines a Create method. This is how instances of the class will be created when needed by the OWIN, using the class I describe in the "Creating the Start Class" section.

■ **Note** Don't worry if the role of these classes doesn't make sense. If you are unfamiliar with the Entity Framework, then I suggest you treat it as something of a black box. Once the basic building blocks are in place—and you can copy the ones into your chapter to get things working—then you will rarely need to edit them.

Creating the User Manager Class

One of the most important Identity classes is the *user manager*, which manages instances of the user class. The user manager class must be derived from UserManager<T>, where T is the user class. The UserManager<T> class isn't specific to the Entity Framework and provides more general features for creating and operating on user data. Table 13-3 shows the basic methods and properties defined by the UserManager<T> class for managing users. There are others, but rather than list them all here, I'll describe them in context when I describe the different ways in which user data can be managed.

Table 13-3. *The Basic Methods and Properties Defined by the UserManager<T> Class*

Name	Description
`ChangePasswordAsync(id, old, new)`	Changes the password for the specified user.
`CreateAsync(user)`	Creates a new user without a password. See Chapter 15 for an example.
`CreateAsync(user, pass)`	Creates a new user with the specified password. See the "Creating Users" section.
`DeleteAsync(user)`	Deletes the specified user. See the "Implementing the Delete Feature" section.
`FindAsync(user, pass)`	Finds the object that represents the user and authenticates their password. See Chapter 14 for details of authentication.
`FindByIdAsync(id)`	Finds the user object associated with the specified ID. See the "Implementing the Delete Feature" section.
`FindByNameAsync(name)`	Finds the user object associated with the specified name. I use this method in the "Seeding the Database" section of Chapter 14.
`UpdateAsync(user)`	Pushes changes to a user object back into the database. See the "Implementing the Edit Feature" section.
`Users`	Returns an enumeration of the users. See the "Enumerating User Accounts" section.

■ **Tip** Notice that the names of all of these methods end with `Async`. This is because ASP.NET Identity is implemented almost entirely using C# asynchronous programming features, which means that operations will be performed concurrently and not block other activities. You will see how this works once I start demonstrating how to create and manage user data. There are also synchronous extension methods for each `Async` method. I stick to the asynchronous methods for most examples, but the synchronous equivalents are useful if you need to perform multiple related operations in sequence. I have included an example of this in the "Seeding the Database" section of Chapter 14. The synchronous methods are also useful when you want to call Identity methods from within property getters or setters, which I do in Chapter 15.

I added a class file called `AppUserManager.cs` to the `Infrastructure` folder and used it to define the user manager class, which I have called `AppUserManager`, as shown in Listing 13-7.

Listing 13-7. The Contents of the AppUserManager.cs File

```
using Microsoft.AspNet.Identity;
using Microsoft.AspNet.Identity.EntityFramework;
using Microsoft.AspNet.Identity.Owin;
using Microsoft.Owin;
using Users.Models;

namespace Users.Infrastructure {
    public class AppUserManager : UserManager<AppUser> {
```

```
        public AppUserManager(IUserStore<AppUser> store)
            : base(store) {
        }

        public static AppUserManager Create(
                IdentityFactoryOptions<AppUserManager> options,
                IOwinContext context) {

            AppIdentityDbContext db = context.Get<AppIdentityDbContext>();
            AppUserManager manager = new AppUserManager(new UserStore<AppUser>(db));

            return manager;
        }
    }
}
```

The static `Create` method will be called when Identity needs an instance of the `AppUserManager`, which will happen when I perform operations on user data—something that I will demonstrate once I have finished performing the setup.

To create an instance of the `AppUserManager` class, I need an instance of `UserStore<AppUser>`. The `UserStore<T>` class is the Entity Framework implementation of the `IUserStore<T>` interface, which provides the storage-specific implementation of the methods defined by the `UserManager` class. To create the `UserStore<AppUser>`, I need an instance of the `AppIdentityDbContext` class, which I get through OWIN as follows:

```
...
AppIdentityDbContext db = context.Get<AppIdentityDbContext>();
...
```

The `IOwinContext` implementation passed as an argument to the `Create` method defines a generically typed `Get` method that returns instances of objects that have been registered in the OWIN start class, which I describe in the following section.

Creating the Start Class

The final piece I need to get ASP.NET Identity up and running is a *start class*. In Listing 13-4, I defined an application setting that specified a configuration class for OWIN, like this:

```
...
<add key="owin:AppStartup" value="Users.IdentityConfig" />
...
```

OWIN emerged independently of ASP.NET and has its own conventions. One of them is that there is a class that is instantiated to load and configure middleware and perform any other configuration work that is required. By default, this class is called `Start`, and it is defined in the global namespace. This class contains a method called `Configuration`, which is called by the OWIN infrastructure and passed an implementation of the `Owin.IAppBuilder` interface, which supports setting up the middleware that an application requires. The `Start` class is usually defined as a partial class, with its other class files dedicated to each kind of middleware that is being used.

I freely ignore this convention, given that the only OWIN middleware that I use in MVC framework applications is Identity. I prefer to use the application setting in the `Web.config` file to define a single class in the top-level namespace of the application. To this end, I added a class file called `IdentityConfig.cs` to the `App_Start` folder and used it to define the class shown in Listing 13-8, which is the class that I specified in the `Web.config` folder.

Listing 13-8. The Contents of the IdentityConfig.cs File

```
using Microsoft.AspNet.Identity;
using Microsoft.Owin;
using Microsoft.Owin.Security.Cookies;
using Owin;
using Users.Infrastructure;

namespace Users {
    public class IdentityConfig {
        public void Configuration(IAppBuilder app) {

            app.CreatePerOwinContext<AppIdentityDbContext>(AppIdentityDbContext.Create);
            app.CreatePerOwinContext<AppUserManager>(AppUserManager.Create);

            app.UseCookieAuthentication(new CookieAuthenticationOptions {
                AuthenticationType = DefaultAuthenticationTypes.ApplicationCookie,
                LoginPath = new PathString("/Account/Login"),
            });
        }
    }
}
```

The `IAppBuilder` interface is supplemented by a number of extension methods defined in classes in the `Owin` namespace. The `CreatePerOwinContext` method creates a new instance of the `AppUserManager` and `AppIdentityDbContext` classes for each request. This ensures that each request has clean access to the ASP.NET Identity data and that I don't have to worry about synchronization or poorly cached database data.

The `UseCookieAuthentication` method tells ASP.NET Identity how to use a cookie to identity authenticated users, where the options are specified through the `CookieAuthenticationOptions` class. The important part here is the `LoginPath` property, which specifies a URL that clients should be redirected to when they request content without authentication. I have specified `/Account/Login`, and I will create the controller that handles these redirections in Chapter 14.

Using ASP.NET Identity

Now that the basic setup is out of the way, I can start to use ASP.NET Identity to add support for managing users to the example application. In the sections that follow, I will demonstrate how the Identity API can be used to create administration tools that allow for centralized management of users. Table 13-4 puts ASP.NET Identity into context.

Table 13-4. *Putting Content Caching by Attribute in Context*

Question	Answer
What is it?	ASP.NET Identity is the API used to manage user data and perform authentication and authorization.
Why should I care?	Most applications require users to create accounts and provide credentials to access content and features. ASP.NET Identity provides the facilities for performing these operations.
How is it used by the MVC framework?	ASP.NET Identity isn't used directly by the MVC framework but integrates through the standard MVC authorization features.

Enumerating User Accounts

Centralized user administration tools are useful in just about all applications, even those that allow users to create and manage their own accounts. There will always be some customers who require bulk account creation, for example, and support issues that require inspection and adjustment of user data. From the perspective of this chapter, administration tools are useful because they consolidate a lot of basic user management functions into a small number of classes, making them useful examples to demonstrate the fundamental features of ASP.NET Identity.

I started by adding a controller called Admin to the project, which is shown in Listing 13-9, and which I will use to define my user administration functionality.

Listing 13-9. The Contents of the AdminController.cs File

```
using System.Web;
using System.Web.Mvc;
using Microsoft.AspNet.Identity.Owin;
using Users.Infrastructure;

namespace Users.Controllers {
    public class AdminController : Controller {

        public ActionResult Index() {
            return View(UserManager.Users);
        }

        private AppUserManager UserManager {
            get {
                return HttpContext.GetOwinContext().GetUserManager<AppUserManager>();
            }
        }
    }
}
```

The Index action method enumerates the users managed by the Identity system; of course, there aren't any users at the moment, but there will be soon. The important part of this listing is the way that I obtain an instance of the AppUserManager class, through which I manage user information. I will be using the AppUserManager class repeatedly as I implement the different administration functions, and I defined the UserManager property in the Admin controller to simplify my code.

The Microsoft.Owin.Host.SystemWeb assembly adds extension methods for the HttpContext class, one of which is GetOwinContext. This provides a per-request context object into the OWIN API through an IOwinContext object. The IOwinContext isn't that interesting in an MVC framework application, but there is another extension method called GetUserManager<T> that is used to get instances of the user manager class.

■ **Tip** As you may have gathered, there are lots of extension methods in ASP.NET Identity; overall, the API is something of a muddle as it tries to mix OWIN, abstract Identity functionality, and the concrete Entity Framework storage implementation.

I called the GetUserManager with a generic type parameter to specify the AppUserManager class that I created earlier in the chapter, like this:

```
...
return HttpContext.GetOwinContext().GetUserManager<AppUserManager>();
...
```

Once I have an instance of the AppUserManager class, I can start to query the data store. The AppUserManager.Users property returns an enumeration of user objects—instances of the AppUser class in my application—which can be queried and manipulated using LINQ.

In the Index action method, I pass the value of the Users property to the View method so that I can list details of the users in the view. Listing 13-10 shows the contents of the Views/Admin/Index.cshtml file that I created by right-clicking the Index action method and selecting Add View from the pop-up menu.

Listing 13-10. The Contents of the Index.cshtml File in the /Views/Admin Folder

```
@using Users.Models
@model IEnumerable<AppUser>
@{
    ViewBag.Title = "Index";
}

<div class="panel panel-primary">
    <div class="panel-heading">
        User Accounts
    </div>
    <table class="table table-striped">
        <tr><th>ID</th><th>Name</th><th>Email</th></tr>
        @if (Model.Count() == 0) {
            <tr><td colspan="3" class="text-center">No User Accounts</td></tr>
        } else {
            foreach (AppUser user in Model) {
                <tr>
                    <td>@user.Id</td>
                    <td>@user.UserName</td>
                    <td>@user.Email</td>
                </tr>
            }
        }
    </table>
</div>
@Html.ActionLink("Create", "Create", null, new { @class = "btn btn-primary" })
```

This view contains a table that has rows for each user, with columns for the unique ID, username, and e-mail address. If there are no users in the database, then a message is displayed, as shown in Figure 13-4.

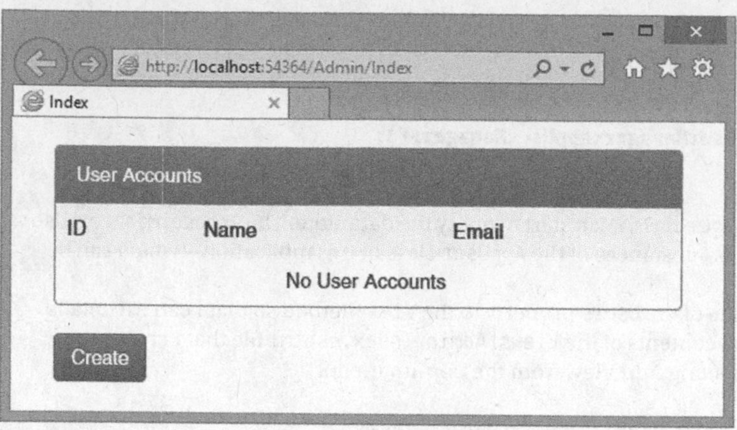

Figure 13-4. *Display the (empty) list of users*

I included a Create link in the view (which I styled as a button using Bootstrap) that targets the `Create` action on the `Admin` controller. I'll implement this action shortly to support adding users.

RESETTING THE DATABASE

When you start the application and navigate to the `/Admin/Index` URL, it will take a few moments before the contents rendered from the view are displayed. This is because the Entity Framework has connected to the database and determined that there is no schema defined. The Code First feature uses the classes I defined earlier in the chapter (and some which are contained in the Identity assemblies) to create the schema so that it is ready to be queried and to store data.

You can see the effect by opening the Visual Studio SQL Server Object Explorer window and expanding entry for the `IdentityDB` database schema, which will include tables with names such as `AspNetUsers` and `AspNetRoles`.

To delete the database, right-click the IdentityDb item and select Delete from the pop-up menu. Check both of the options in the Delete Database dialog and click the OK button to delete the database.

Right-click the Databases item, select Add New Database (as shown in Figure 13-3), and enter **IdentityDb** in the Database Name field. Click OK to create the empty database. The next time you start the application and navigate to the `Admin/Index` URL, the Entity Framework will detect that there is no schema and re-create it.

Creating Users

I am going to use MVC framework model validation for the input my application receives, and the easiest way to do this is to create simple view models for each of the operations that my controller supports. I added a class file called `UserViewModels.cs` to the `Models` folder and used it to define the class shown in Listing 13-11. I'll add further classes to this file as I define models for additional features.

Listing 13-11. The Contents of the UserViewModels.cs File

```
using System.ComponentModel.DataAnnotations;

namespace Users.Models {

    public class CreateModel {
        [Required]
        public string Name { get; set; }
        [Required]
        public string Email { get; set; }
        [Required]
        public string Password { get; set; }
    }
}
```

The initial model I have defined is called `CreateModel`, and it defines the basic properties that I require to create a user account: a username, an e-mail address, and a password. I have used the `Required` attribute from the `System.ComponentModel.DataAnnotations` namespace to denote that values are required for all three properties defined in the model.

I added a pair of `Create` action methods to the `Admin` controller, which are targeted by the link in the `Index` view from the previous section and which uses the standard controller pattern to present a view to the user for a GET request and process form data for a POST request. You can see the new action methods in Listing 13-12.

Listing 13-12. Defining the Create Action Methods in the AdminController.cs File

```
using System.Web;
using System.Web.Mvc;
using Microsoft.AspNet.Identity.Owin;
using Users.Infrastructure;
using Users.Models;
using Microsoft.AspNet.Identity;
using System.Threading.Tasks;

namespace Users.Controllers {
    public class AdminController : Controller {

        public ActionResult Index() {
            return View(UserManager.Users);
        }

        public ActionResult Create() {
            return View();
        }

        [HttpPost]
        public async Task<ActionResult> Create(CreateModel model) {
            if (ModelState.IsValid) {
                AppUser user = new AppUser {UserName = model.Name, Email = model.Email};
                IdentityResult result = await UserManager.CreateAsync(user,
                    model.Password);
```

```
                if (result.Succeeded) {
                    return RedirectToAction("Index");
                } else {
                    AddErrorsFromResult(result);
                }
            }
            return View(model);
        }

        private void AddErrorsFromResult(IdentityResult result) {
            foreach (string error in result.Errors) {
                ModelState.AddModelError("", error);
            }
        }

        private AppUserManager UserManager {
            get {
                return HttpContext.GetOwinContext().GetUserManager<AppUserManager>();
            }
        }
    }
}
```

The important part of this listing is the Create method that takes a CreateModel argument and that will be invoked when the administrator submits their form data. I use the ModelState.IsValid property to check that the data I am receiving contains the values I require, and if it does, I create a new instance of the AppUser class and pass it to the UserManager.CreateAsync method, like this:

```
...
AppUser user = new AppUser {UserName = model.Name, Email = model.Email};
IdentityResult result = await UserManager.CreateAsync(user, model.Password);
...
```

The result from the CreateAsync method is an implementation of the IdentityResult interface, which describes the outcome of the operation through the properties listed in Table 13-5.

***Table 13-5.** The Properties Defined by the IdentityResult Interface*

Name	Description
Errors	Returns a string enumeration that lists the errors encountered while attempting the operation
Succeeded	Returns true if the operation succeeded

USING THE ASP.NET IDENTITY ASYNCHRONOUS METHODS

You will notice that all of the operations for manipulating user data, such as the UserManager.CreateAsync method I used in Listing 13-12, are available as asynchronous methods. Such methods are easily consumed with the async and await keywords. Using asynchronous Identity methods allows your action methods to be executed asynchronously, which can improve the overall throughput of your application.

However, you can also use synchronous extension methods provided by the Identity API. All of the commonly used asynchronous methods have a synchronous wrapper so that the functionality of the UserManager.CreateAsync method can be called through the synchronous UserManager.Create method. I use the asynchronous methods for preference, and I recommend you follow the same approach in your projects. The synchronous methods can be useful for creating simpler code when you need to perform multiple dependent operations, so I used them in the "Seeding the Database" section of Chapter 14 as a demonstration.

I inspect the Succeeded property in the Create action method to determine whether I have been able to create a new user record in the database. If the Succeeded property is true, then I redirect the browser to the Index action so that list of users is displayed:

```
...
if (result.Succeeded) {
    return RedirectToAction("Index");
} else {
    AddErrorsFromResult(result);
}
...
```

If the Succeeded property is false, then I call the AddErrorsFromResult method, which enumerates the messages from the Errors property and adds them to the set of model state errors, taking advantage of the MVC framework model validation feature. I defined the AddErrorsFromResult method because I will have to process errors from other operations as I build the functionality of my administration controller. The last step is to create the view that will allow the administrator to create new accounts. Listing 13-13 shows the contents of the Views/Admin/Create.cshtml file.

Listing 13-13. The Contents of the Create.cshtml File

```
@model Users.Models.CreateModel
@{ ViewBag.Title = "Create User";}
<h2>Create User</h2>
@Html.ValidationSummary(false)
@using (Html.BeginForm()) {
    <div class="form-group">
        <label>Name</label>
        @Html.TextBoxFor(x => x.Name, new { @class = "form-control"})
    </div>
    <div class="form-group">
        <label>Email</label>
        @Html.TextBoxFor(x => x.Email, new { @class = "form-control" })
    </div>
```

```
    <div class="form-group">
        <label>Password</label>
        @Html.PasswordFor(x => x.Password, new { @class = "form-control" })
    </div>
    <button type="submit" class="btn btn-primary">Create</button>
    @Html.ActionLink("Cancel", "Index", null, new { @class = "btn btn-default"})
}
```

There is nothing special about this view—it is a simple form that gathers values that the MVC framework will bind to the properties of the model class that is passed to the Create action method.

Testing the Create Functionality

To test the ability to create a new user account, start the application, navigate to the /Admin/Index URL, and click the Create button. Fill in the form with the values shown in Table 13-6.

Table 13-6. *The Values for Creating an Example User*

Name	Value
Name	Joe
Email	joe@example.com
Password	secret

■ **Tip** Although not widely known by developers, there are domains that are reserved for testing, including example.com. You can see a complete list at https://tools.ietf.org/html/rfc2606.

Once you have entered the values, click the Create button. ASP.NET Identity will create the user account, which will be displayed when your browser is redirected to the Index action method, as shown in Figure 13-5. You will see a different ID value because IDs are randomly generated for each user account.

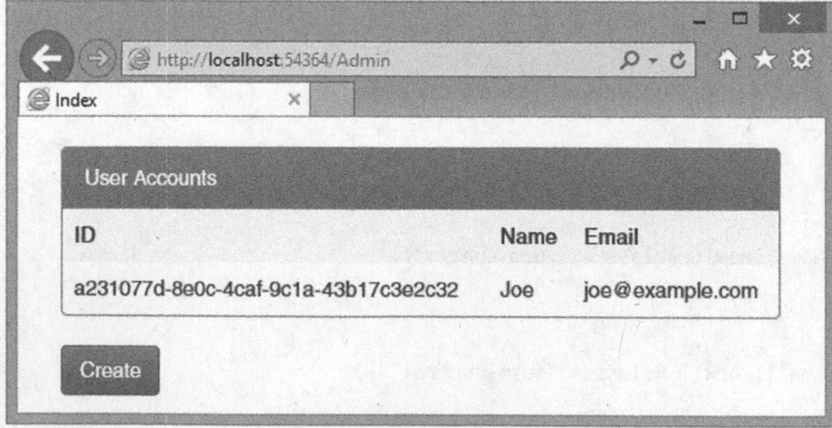

Figure 13-5. *The effect of adding a new user account*

Click the Create button again and enter the same details into the form, using the values in Table 13-6. This time when you submit the form, you will see an error reported through the model validation summary, as shown in Figure 13-6.

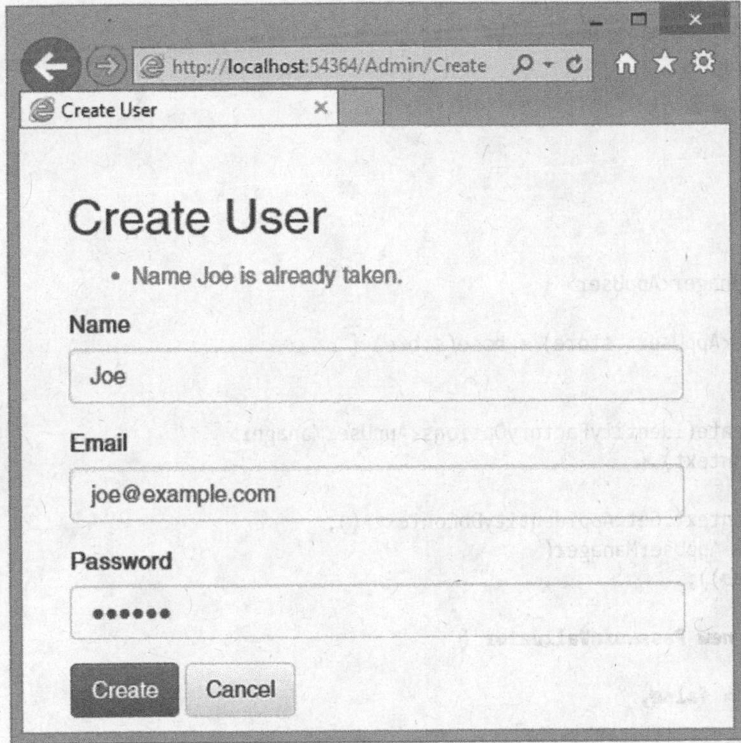

***Figure 13-6.** An error trying to create a new user*

Validating Passwords

One of the most common requirements, especially for corporate applications, is to enforce a password policy. ASP.NET Identity provides the `PasswordValidator` class, which can be used to configure a password policy using the properties described in Table 13-7.

***Table 13-7.** The Properties Defined by the PasswordValidator Class*

Name	Description
`RequiredLength`	Specifies the minimum length of a valid passwords.
`RequireNonLetterOrDigit`	When set to `true`, valid passwords must contain a character that is neither a letter nor a digit.
`RequireDigit`	When set to `true`, valid passwords must contain a digit.
`RequireLowercase`	When set to `true`, valid passwords must contain a lowercase character.
`RequireUppercase`	When set to `true`, valid passwords must contain a uppercase character.

A password policy is defined by creating an instance of the `PasswordValidator` class, setting the property values, and using the object as the value for the `PasswordValidator` property in the `Create` method that OWIN uses to instantiate the `AppUserManager` class, as shown in Listing 13-14.

Listing 13-14. Setting a Password Policy in the AppUserManager.cs File

```
using Microsoft.AspNet.Identity;
using Microsoft.AspNet.Identity.EntityFramework;
using Microsoft.AspNet.Identity.Owin;
using Microsoft.Owin;
using Users.Models;

namespace Users.Infrastructure {
    public class AppUserManager : UserManager<AppUser> {

        public AppUserManager(IUserStore<AppUser> store) : base(store) {
        }

        public static AppUserManager Create(IdentityFactoryOptions<AppUserManager>
                options, IOwinContext context) {

            AppIdentityDbContext db = context.Get<AppIdentityDbContext>();
            AppUserManager manager = new AppUserManager(
                new UserStore<AppUser>(db));

            manager.PasswordValidator = new PasswordValidator {
                RequiredLength = 6,
                RequireNonLetterOrDigit = false,
                RequireDigit = false,
                RequireLowercase = true,
                RequireUppercase = true
            };

            return manager;
        }
    }
}
```

I used the `PasswordValidator` class to specify a policy that requires at least six characters and a mix of uppercase and lowercase characters. You can see how the policy is applied by starting the application, navigating to the `/Admin/Index` URL, clicking the Create button, and trying to create an account that has the password `secret`. The password doesn't meet the new password policy, and an error is added to the model state, as shown in Figure 13-7.

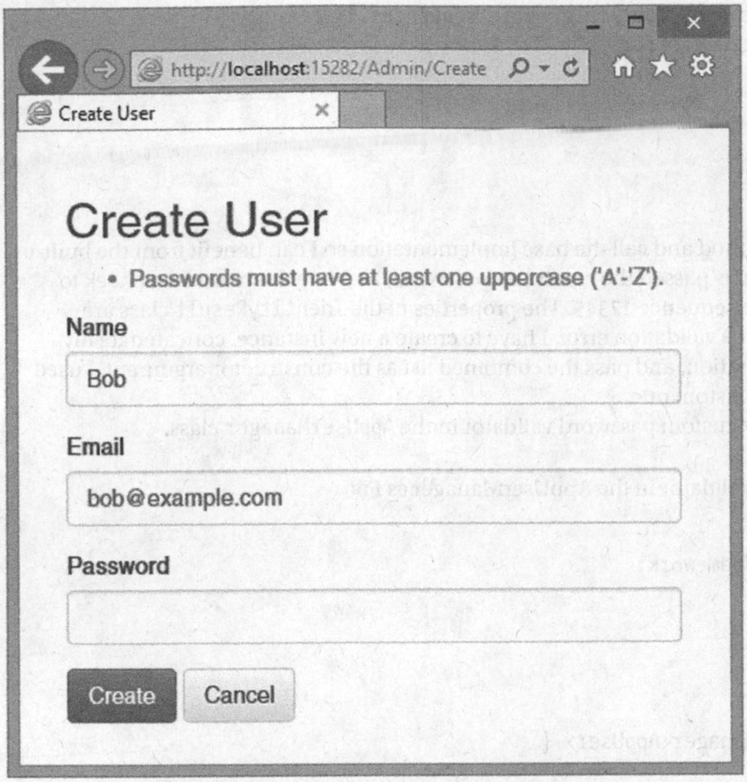

Figure 13-7. Reporting an error when validating a password

Implementing a Custom Password Validator

The built-in password validation is sufficient for most applications, but you may need to implement a custom policy, especially if you are implementing a corporate line-of-business application where complex password policies are common. Extending the built-in functionality is done by deriving a new class from `PasswordValidatator` and overriding the `ValidateAsync` method. As a demonstration, I added a class file called `CustomPasswordValidator.cs` in the `Infrastructure` folder and used it to define the class shown in Listing 13-15.

Listing 13-15. The Contents of the CustomPasswordValidator.cs File

```
using System.Linq;
using System.Threading.Tasks;
using Microsoft.AspNet.Identity;

namespace Users.Infrastructure {

    public class CustomPasswordValidator : PasswordValidator {
        public override async Task<IdentityResult> ValidateAsync(string pass) {
            IdentityResult result = await base.ValidateAsync(pass);
            if (pass.Contains("12345")) {
                var errors = result.Errors.ToList();
```

```
                errors.Add("Passwords cannot contain numeric sequences");
                result = new IdentityResult(errors);
            }
            return result;
        }
    }
}
```

I have overridden the ValidateAsync method and call the base implementation so I can benefit from the built-in validation checks. The ValidateAsync method is passed the candidate password, and I perform my own check to ensure that the password does not contain the sequence 12345. The properties of the IdentityResult class are read-only, which means that if I want to report a validation error, I have to create a new instance, concatenate my error with any errors from the base implementation, and pass the combined list as the constructor argument. I used LINQ to concatenate the base errors with my custom one.

Listing 13-16 shows the application of my custom password validator in the AppUserManager class.

Listing 13-16. Applying a Custom Password Validator in the AppUserManager.cs File

```
using Microsoft.AspNet.Identity;
using Microsoft.AspNet.Identity.EntityFramework;
using Microsoft.AspNet.Identity.Owin;
using Microsoft.Owin;
using Users.Models;

namespace Users.Infrastructure {
    public class AppUserManager : UserManager<AppUser> {

        public AppUserManager(IUserStore<AppUser> store) : base(store) {
        }

        public static AppUserManager Create(IdentityFactoryOptions<AppUserManager>
                options, IOwinContext context) {

            AppIdentityDbContext db = context.Get<AppIdentityDbContext>();
            AppUserManager manager = new AppUserManager(
                new UserStore<AppUser>(db));

            manager.PasswordValidator = new CustomPasswordValidator {
                RequiredLength = 6,
                RequireNonLetterOrDigit = false,
                RequireDigit = false,
                RequireLowercase = true,
                RequireUppercase = true
            };

            return manager;
        }
    }
}
```

To test the custom password validation, try to create a new user account with the password `secret12345`. This will break two of the validation rules—one from the built-in validator and one from my custom implementation. Error messages for both problems are added to the model state and displayed when the Create button is clicked, as shown in Figure 13-8.

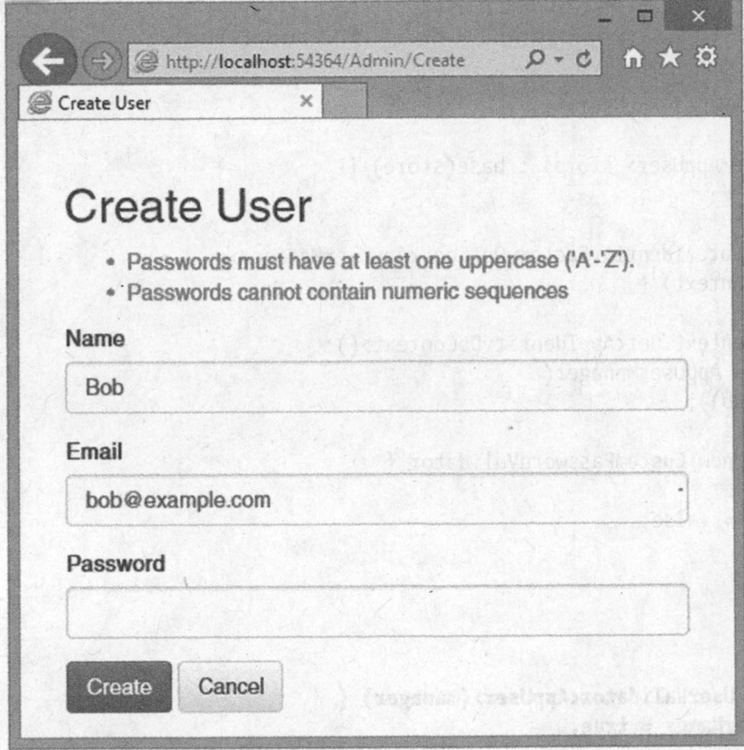

Figure 13-8. *The effect of a custom password validation policy*

Validating User Details

More general validation can be performed by creating an instance of the `UserValidator` class and using the properties it defines to restrict other user property values. Table 13-8 describes the `UserValidator` properties.

Table 13-8. *The Properties Defined by the UserValidator Class*

Name	Description
`AllowOnlyAlphanumericUserNames`	When `true`, usernames can contain only alphanumeric characters.
`RequireUniqueEmail`	When `true`, e-mail addresses must be unique.

Performing validation on user details is done by creating an instance of the `UserValidator` class and assigning it to the `UserValidator` property of the user manager class within the `Create` method that OWIN uses to create instances. Listing 13-17 shows an example of using the built-in validator class.

Listing 13-17. Using the Built-in user Validator Class in the AppUserManager.cs File

```
using Microsoft.AspNet.Identity;
using Microsoft.AspNet.Identity.EntityFramework;
using Microsoft.AspNet.Identity.Owin;
using Microsoft.Owin;
using Users.Models;

namespace Users.Infrastructure {
    public class AppUserManager : UserManager<AppUser> {

        public AppUserManager(IUserStore<AppUser> store) : base(store) {
        }

        public static AppUserManager Create(IdentityFactoryOptions<AppUserManager>
                options, IOwinContext context) {

            AppIdentityDbContext db = context.Get<AppIdentityDbContext>();
            AppUserManager manager = new AppUserManager(
                new UserStore<AppUser>(db));

            manager.PasswordValidator = new CustomPasswordValidator {
                RequiredLength = 6,
                RequireNonLetterOrDigit = false,
                RequireDigit = false,
                RequireLowercase = true,
                RequireUppercase = true
            };

            manager.UserValidator = new UserValidator<AppUser>(manager) {
                AllowOnlyAlphanumericUserNames = true,
                RequireUniqueEmail = true
            };

            return manager;
        }
    }
}
```

The UserValidator class takes a generic type parameter that specifies the type of the user class, which is AppUser in this case. Its constructor argument is the user manager class, which is an instance of the user manager class (which is AppUserManager for my application).

The built-in validation support is rather basic, but you can create a custom validation policy by creating a class that is derived from UserValidator. As a demonstration, I added a class file called CustomUserValidator.cs to the Infrastructure folder and used it to create the class shown in Listing 13-18.

Listing 13-18. The Contents of the CustomUserValidator.cs File

```
using System.Linq;
using System.Threading.Tasks;
using Microsoft.AspNet.Identity;
using Users.Models;
```

```
namespace Users.Infrastructure {

    public class CustomUserValidator : UserValidator<AppUser> {

        public CustomUserValidator(AppUserManager mgr)
            : base(mgr) {
        }

        public override async Task<IdentityResult> ValidateAsync(AppUser user) {
            IdentityResult result = await base.ValidateAsync(user);

            if (!user.Email.ToLower().EndsWith("@example.com")) {
                var errors = result.Errors.ToList();
                errors.Add("Only example.com email addresses are allowed");
                result = new IdentityResult(errors);
            }
            return result;
        }
    }
}
```

The constructor of the derived class must take an instance of the user manager class and call the base implementation so that the built-in validation checks can be performed. Custom validation is implemented by overriding the ValidateAsync method, which takes an instance of the user class and returns an IdentityResult object. My custom policy restricts users to e-mail addresses in the example.com domain and performs the same LINQ manipulation I used for password validation to concatenate my error message with those produced by the base class. Listing 13-19 shows how I applied my custom validation class in the Create method of the AppUserManager class, replacing the default implementation.

Listing 13-19. Using a Custom User Validation Class in the AppUserManager.cs File

```
using Microsoft.AspNet.Identity;
using Microsoft.AspNet.Identity.EntityFramework;
using Microsoft.AspNet.Identity.Owin;
using Microsoft.Owin;
using Users.Models;

namespace Users.Infrastructure {
    public class AppUserManager : UserManager<AppUser> {

        public AppUserManager(IUserStore<AppUser> store) : base(store) {
        }

        public static AppUserManager Create(IdentityFactoryOptions<AppUserManager>
                options, IOwinContext context) {

            AppIdentityDbContext db = context.Get<AppIdentityDbContext>();
            AppUserManager manager = new AppUserManager(
                new UserStore<AppUser>(db));
```

```
            manager.PasswordValidator = new CustomPasswordValidator {
                RequiredLength = 6,
                RequireNonLetterOrDigit = false,
                RequireDigit = false,
                RequireLowercase = true,
                RequireUppercase = true
            };

            manager.UserValidator = new CustomUserValidator(manager) {
                AllowOnlyAlphanumericUserNames = true,
                RequireUniqueEmail = true
            };

            return manager;
        }
    }
}
```

You can see the result if you try to create an account with an e-mail address such as bob@otherdomain.com, as shown in Figure 13-9.

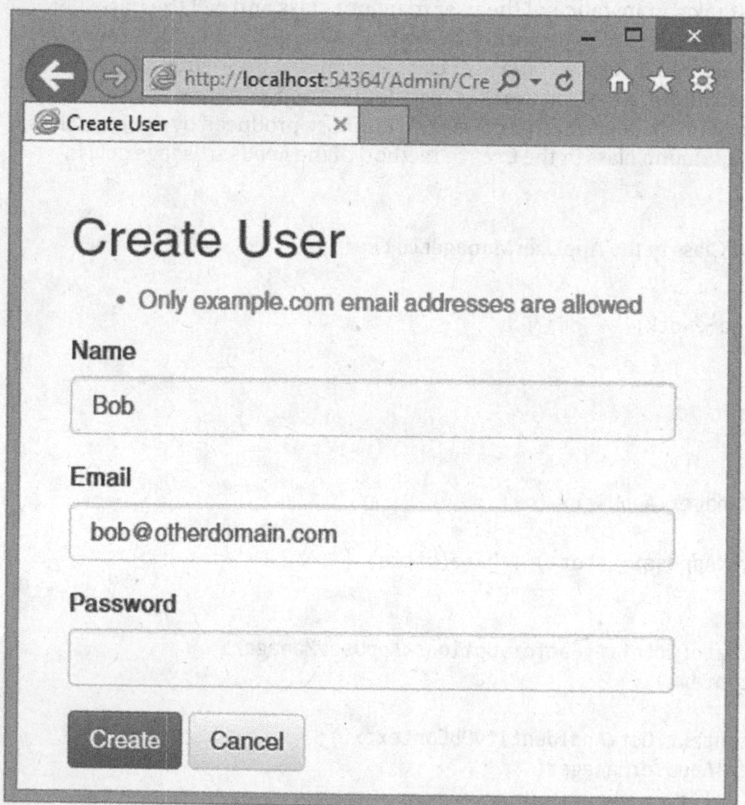

Figure 13-9. *An error message shown by a custom user validation policy*

Completing the Administration Features

I only have to implement the features for editing and deleting users to complete my administration tool. In Listing 13-20, you can see the changes I made to the `Views/Admin/Index.cshtml` file to target `Edit` and `Delete` actions in the `Admin` controller.

Listing 13-20. Adding Edit and Delete Buttons to the Index.cshtml File

```
@using Users.Models
@model IEnumerable<AppUser>
@{ ViewBag.Title = "Index"; }
<div class="panel panel-primary">
    <div class="panel-heading">
        User Accounts
    </div>
    <table class="table table-striped">
        <tr><th>ID</th><th>Name</th><th>Email</th><th></th></tr>
        @if (Model.Count() == 0) {
            <tr><td colspan="4" class="text-center">No User Accounts</td></tr>
        } else {
            foreach (AppUser user in Model) {
                <tr>
                    <td>@user.Id</td>
                    <td>@user.UserName</td>
                    <td>@user.Email</td>
                    <td>
                        @using (Html.BeginForm("Delete", "Admin",
                            new { id = user.Id })) {
                            @Html.ActionLink("Edit", "Edit", new { id = user.Id },
                                    new { @class = "btn btn-primary btn-xs" })
                            <button class="btn btn-danger btn-xs"
                                    type="submit">
                                Delete
                            </button>
                        }
                    </td>
                </tr>
            }
        }
    </table>
</div>
@Html.ActionLink("Create", "Create", null, new { @class = "btn btn-primary" })
```

■ **Tip** You will notice that I have put the `Html.ActionLink` call that targets the `Edit` action method inside the scope of the `Html.Begin` helper. I did this solely so that the Bootstrap styles will style both elements as buttons displayed on a single line.

Implementing the Delete Feature

The user manager class defines a `DeleteAsync` method that takes an instance of the user class and removes it from the database. In Listing 13-21, you can see how I have used the `DeleteAsync` method to implement the delete feature of the `Admin` controller.

Listing 13-21. Deleting Users in the AdminController.cs File

```
using System.Web;
using System.Web.Mvc;
using Microsoft.AspNet.Identity.Owin;
using Users.Infrastructure;
using Users.Models;
using Microsoft.AspNet.Identity;
using System.Threading.Tasks;

namespace Users.Controllers {
    public class AdminController : Controller {

        // ...other action methods omitted for brevity...

        [HttpPost]
        public async Task<ActionResult> Delete(string id) {
            AppUser user = await UserManager.FindByIdAsync(id);
            if (user != null) {
                IdentityResult result = await UserManager.DeleteAsync(user);
                if (result.Succeeded) {
                    return RedirectToAction("Index");
                } else {
                    return View("Error", result.Errors);
                }
            } else {
                return View("Error", new string[] { "User Not Found" });
            }
        }

        private void AddErrorsFromResult(IdentityResult result) {
            foreach (string error in result.Errors) {
                ModelState.AddModelError("", error);
            }
        }

        private AppUserManager UserManager {
            get {
                return HttpContext.GetOwinContext().GetUserManager<AppUserManager>();
            }
        }
    }
}
```

My action method receives the unique ID for the user as an argument, and I use the `FindByIdAsync` method to locate the corresponding user object so that I can pass it to `DeleteAsync` method. The result of the `DeleteAsync` method is an `IdentityResult`, which I process in the same way I did in earlier examples to ensure that any errors are displayed to the user. You can test the delete functionality by creating a new user and then clicking the Delete button that appears alongside it in the `Index` view.

There is no view associated with the `Delete` action, so to display any errors I created a view file called `Error.cshtml` in the `Views/Shared` folder, the contents of which are shown in Listing 13-22.

Listing 13-22. The Contents of the Error.cshtml File

```
@model IEnumerable<string>
@{ ViewBag.Title = "Error";}

<div class="alert alert-danger">
    @switch (Model.Count()) {
        case 0:
            @: Something went wrong. Please try again
            break;
        case 1:
            @Model.First();
            break;
        default:
            @: The following errors were encountered:
            <ul>
                @foreach (string error in Model) {
                    <li>@error</li>
                }
            </ul>
            break;
    }
</div>
@Html.ActionLink("OK", "Index", null, new { @class = "btn btn-default" })
```

■ Tip I put this view in the `Views/Shared` folder so that it can be used by other controllers, including the one I create to manage roles and role membership in Chapter 14.

Implementing the Edit Feature

To complete the administration tool, I need to add support for editing the e-mail address and password for a user account. These are the only properties defined by users at the moment, but I'll show you how to extend the schema with custom properties in Chapter 15. Listing 13-23 shows the `Edit` action methods that I added to the `Admin` controller.

Listing 13-23. Adding the Edit Actions in the AdminController.cs File

```
using System.Web;
using System.Web.Mvc;
using Microsoft.AspNet.Identity.Owin;
using Users.Infrastructure;
using Users.Models;
```

```
using Microsoft.AspNet.Identity;
using System.Threading.Tasks;

namespace Users.Controllers {
    public class AdminController : Controller {

        // ...other action methods omitted for brevity...

        public async Task<ActionResult> Edit(string id) {
            AppUser user = await UserManager.FindByIdAsync(id);
            if (user != null) {
                return View(user);
            } else {
                return RedirectToAction("Index");
            }
        }

        [HttpPost]
        public async Task<ActionResult> Edit(string id, string email, string password) {
            AppUser user = await UserManager.FindByIdAsync(id);
            if (user != null) {
                user.Email = email;
                IdentityResult validEmail
                    = await UserManager.UserValidator.ValidateAsync(user);
                if (!validEmail.Succeeded) {
                    AddErrorsFromResult(validEmail);
                }
                IdentityResult validPass = null;
                if (password != string.Empty) {
                    validPass
                        = await UserManager.PasswordValidator.ValidateAsync(password);
                    if (validPass.Succeeded) {
                        user.PasswordHash =
                            UserManager.PasswordHasher.HashPassword(password);
                    } else {
                        AddErrorsFromResult(validPass);
                    }
                }
                if ((validEmail.Succeeded && validPass == null) || ( validEmail.Succeeded
                        && password != string.Empty && validPass.Succeeded)) {
                    IdentityResult result = await UserManager.UpdateAsync(user);
                    if (result.Succeeded) {
                        return RedirectToAction("Index");
                    } else {
                        AddErrorsFromResult(result);
                    }
                }
```

```
        } else {
            ModelState.AddModelError("", "User Not Found");
        }
        return View(user);
    }

    private void AddErrorsFromResult(IdentityResult result) {
        foreach (string error in result.Errors) {
            ModelState.AddModelError("", error);
        }
    }

    private AppUserManager UserManager {
        get {
            return HttpContext.GetOwinContext().GetUserManager<AppUserManager>();
        }
    }
  }
}
```

The Edit action targeted by GET requests uses the ID string embedded in the Index view to call the FindByIdAsync method in order to get an AppUser object that represents the user.

The more complex implementation receives the POST request, with arguments for the user ID, the new e-mail address, and the password. I have to perform several tasks to complete the editing operation.

The first task is to validate the values I have received. I am working with a simple user object at the moment—although I'll show you how to customize the data stored for users in Chapter 15—but even so, I need to validate the user data to ensure that I don't violate the custom policies defined in the "Validating User Details" and "Validating Passwords" sections. I start by validating the e-mail address, which I do like this:

```
...
user.Email = email;
IdentityResult validEmail = await UserManager.UserValidator.ValidateAsync(user);
if (!validEmail.Succeeded) {
   AddErrorsFromResult(validEmail);
}
...
```

■ **Tip** Notice that I have to change the value of the Email property before I perform the validation because the ValidateAsync method only accepts instances of the user class.

The next step is to change the password, if one has been supplied. ASP.NET Identity stores hashes of passwords, rather than the passwords themselves—this is intended to prevent passwords from being stolen. My next step is to take the validated password and generate the hash code that will be stored in the database so that the user can be authenticated (which I demonstrate in Chapter 14).

Passwords are converted to hashes through an implementation of the IPasswordHasher interface, which is obtained through the AppUserManager.PasswordHasher property. The IPasswordHasher interface defines the HashPassword method, which takes a string argument and returns its hashed value, like this:

```
...
if (password != string.Empty) {
    validPass = await UserManager.PasswordValidator.ValidateAsync(password);
    if (validPass.Succeeded) {
        user.PasswordHash = UserManager.PasswordHasher.HashPassword(password);
    } else {
        AddErrorsFromResult(validPass);
    }
}
...
```

Changes to the user class are not stored in the database until the UpdateAsync method is called, like this:

```
...
if ((validEmail.Succeeded && validPass == null)
    || ( validEmail.Succeeded && password != string.Empty &&
        validPass.Succeeded)) {
    IdentityResult result = await UserManager.UpdateAsync(user);
    if (result.Succeeded) {
        return RedirectToAction("Index");
    } else {
        AddErrorsFromResult(result);
    }
}
...
```

Creating the View

The final component is the view that will render the current values for a user and allow new values to be submitted to the controller. Listing 13-24 shows the contents of the Views/Admin/Edit.cshtml file.

Listing 13-24. The Contents of the Edit.cshtml File

```
@model Users.Models.AppUser
@{ ViewBag.Title = "Edit"; }
@Html.ValidationSummary(false)
<h2>Edit User</h2>

<div class="form-group">
    <label>Name</label>
    <p class="form-control-static">@Model.Id</p>
</div>
@using (Html.BeginForm()) {
    @Html.HiddenFor(x => x.Id)
    <div class="form-group">
        <label>Email</label>
        @Html.TextBoxFor(x => x.Email, new { @class = "form-control" })
    </div>
```

```
    <div class="form-group">
        <label>Password</label>
        <input name="password" type="password" class="form-control" />
    </div>
    <button type="submit" class="btn btn-primary">Save</button>
    @Html.ActionLink("Cancel", "Index", null, new { @class = "btn btn-default" })
}
```

There is nothing special about the view. It displays the user ID, which cannot be changed, as static text and provides a form for editing the e-mail address and password, as shown in Figure 13-10. Validation problems are displayed in the validation summary section of the view, and successfully editing a user account will return to the list of accounts in the system.

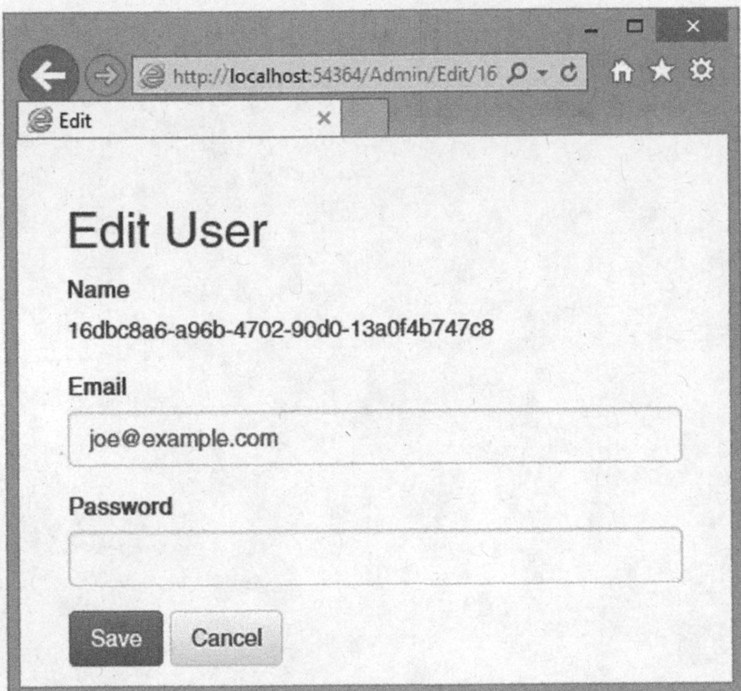

Figure 13-10. *Editing a user account*

Summary

In this chapter, I showed you how to create the configuration and classes required to use ASP.NET Identity and demonstrated how they can be applied to create a user administration tool. In the next chapter, I show you how to perform authentication and authorization with ASP.NET Identity.

CHAPTER 14

Applying ASP.NET Identity

In this chapter, I show you how to apply ASP.NET Identity to authenticate and authorize the user accounts created in the previous chapter. I explain how the ASP.NET platform provides a foundation for authenticating requests and how ASP.NET Identity fits into that foundation to authenticate users and enforce authorization through roles. Table 14-1 summarizes this chapter.

Table 14-1. *Chapter Summary*

Problem	Solution	Listing
Prepare an application for user authentication.	Apply the `Authorize` attribute to restrict access to action methods and define a controller to which users will be redirected to provide credentials.	1–4
Authenticate a user.	Check the name and password using the `FindAsync` method defined by the user manager class and create an implementation of the `IIdentity` interface using the `CreateIdentityMethod`. Set an authentication cookie for subsequent requests by calling the `SignIn` method defined by the authentication manager class.	5
Prepare an application for role-based authorization.	Create a role manager class and register it for instantiation in the OWIN startup class.	6–8
Create and delete roles.	Use the `CreateAsync` and `DeleteAsync` methods defined by the role manager class.	9–12
Manage role membership.	Use the `AddToRoleAsync` and `RemoveFromRoleAsync` methods defined by the user manager class.	13–15
Use roles for authorization.	Set the `Roles` property of the `Authorize` attribute.	16–19
Seed the database with initial content.	Use the database context initialization class.	20, 21

Preparing the Example Project

In this chapter, I am going to continue working on the Users project I created in Chapter 13. No changes to the application components are required.

Authenticating Users

The most fundamental activity for ASP.NET Identity is to authenticate users, and in this section, I explain and demonstrate how this is done. Table 14-2 puts authentication into context.

Table 14-2. *Putting Authentication in Context*

Question	Answer
What is it?	Authentication validates credentials provided by users. Once the user is authenticated, requests that originate from the browser contain a cookie that represents the user identity.
Why should I care?	Authentication is how you check the identity of your users and is the first step toward restricting access to sensitive parts of the application.
How is it used by the MVC framework?	Authentication features are accessed through the `Authorize` attribute, which is applied to controllers and action methods in order to restrict access to authenticated users.

■ **Tip** I use names and passwords stored in the ASP.NET Identity database in this chapter. In Chapter 15, I demonstrate how ASP.NET Identity can be used to authenticate users with a service from Google (Identity also supports authentication for Microsoft, Facebook, and Twitter accounts).

Understanding the Authentication/Authorization Process

The ASP.NET Identity system integrates into the ASP.NET platform, which means you use the standard MVC framework techniques to control access to action methods, such as the `Authorize` attribute. In this section, I am going to apply basic restrictions to the `Index` action method in the `Home` controller and then implement the features that allow users to identify themselves so they can gain access to it. Listing 14-1 shows how I have applied the `Authorize` attribute to the `Home` controller.

Listing 14-1. Securing the Home Controller

```
using System.Web.Mvc;
using System.Collections.Generic;

namespace Users.Controllers {

    public class HomeController : Controller {

        [Authorize]
        public ActionResult Index() {
            Dictionary<string, object> data
                = new Dictionary<string, object>();
            data.Add("Placeholder", "Placeholder");
            return View(data);
        }
    }
}
```

Using the `Authorize` attribute in this way is the most general form of authorization and restricts access to the `Index` action methods to requests that are made by users who have been authenticated by the application.

If you start the application and request a URL that targets the `Index` action on the `Home` controller (`/Home/Index`, `/Home`, or just `/`), you will see the error shown by Figure 14-1.

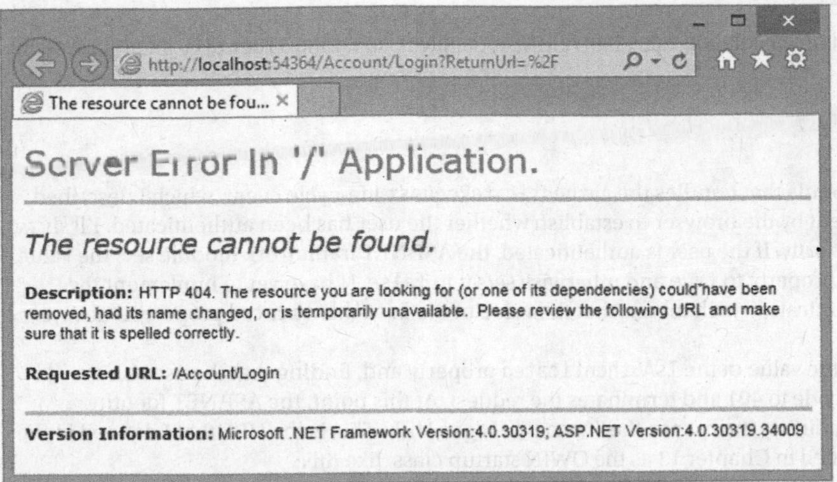

Figure 14-1. Requesting a protected URL

The ASP.NET platform provides some useful information about the user through the `HttpContext` object, which is used by the `Authorize` attribute to check the status of the current request and see whether the user has been authenticated. The `HttpContext.User` property returns an implementation of the `IPrincipal` interface, which is defined in the `System.Security.Principal` namespace. The `IPrincipal` interface defines the property and method shown in Table 14-3.

Table 14-3. The Members Defined by the IPrincipal Interface

Name	Description
`Identity`	Returns an implementation of the `IIdentity` interface that describes the user associated with the request.
`IsInRole(role)`	Returns `true` if the user is a member of the specified role. See the "Authorizing Users with Roles" section for details of managing authorizations with roles.

The implementation of `IIdentity` interface returned by the `IPrincipal.Identity` property provides some basic, but useful, information about the current user through the properties I have described in Table 14-4.

Table 14-4. The Properties Defined by the IIdentity Interface

Name	Description
`AuthenticationType`	Returns a string that describes the mechanism used to authenticate the user
`IsAuthenticated`	Returns `true` if the user has been authenticated
`Name`	Returns the name of the current user

■ **Tip** In Chapter 15 I describe the implementation class that ASP.NET Identity uses for the `IIdentity` interface, which is called `ClaimsIdentity`.

ASP.NET Identity contains a module that handles the `AuthenticateRequest` life-cycle event, which I described in Chapter 3, and uses the cookies sent by the browser to establish whether the user has been authenticated. I'll show you how these cookies are created shortly. If the user is authenticated, the ASP.NET framework module sets the value of the `IIdentity.IsAuthenticated` property to `true` and otherwise sets it to `false`. (I have yet to implement the feature that will allow users to authenticate, which means that the value of the `IsAuthenticated` property is always `false` in the example application.)

The `Authorize` module checks the value of the `IsAuthenticated` property and, finding that the user isn't authenticated, sets the result status code to 401 and terminates the request. At this point, the ASP.NET Identity module intercepts the request and redirects the user to the `/Account/Login` URL. This is the URL that I defined in the `IdentityConfig` class, which I specified in Chapter 13 as the OWIN startup class, like this:

```
using Microsoft.AspNet.Identity;
using Microsoft.Owin;
using Microsoft.Owin.Security.Cookies;
using Owin;
using Users.Infrastructure;

namespace Users {
    public class IdentityConfig {
        public void Configuration(IAppBuilder app) {

            app.CreatePerOwinContext<AppUserManager>(AppUserManager.Create);

            app.UseCookieAuthentication(new CookieAuthenticationOptions {
                AuthenticationType = DefaultAuthenticationTypes.ApplicationCookie,
                LoginPath = new PathString("/Account/Login"),
            });
        }
    }
}
```

The browser requests the `/Account/Login` URL, but since it doesn't correspond to any controller or action in the example project, the server returns a 404 – Not Found response, leading to the error message shown in Figure 14-1.

Preparing to Implement Authentication

Even though the request ends in an error message, the request in the previous section illustrates how the ASP.NET Identity system fits into the standard ASP.NET request life cycle. The next step is to implement a controller that will receive requests for the `/Account/Login` URL and authenticate the user. I started by adding a new model class to the `UserViewModels.cs` file, as shown in Listing 14-2.

Listing 14-2. Adding a New Model Class to the UserViewModels.cs File

```
using System.ComponentModel.DataAnnotations;

namespace Users.Models {

    public class CreateModel {
        [Required]
        public string Name { get; set; }
        [Required]
        public string Email { get; set; }
        [Required]
        public string Password { get; set; }
    }

    public class LoginModel {
        [Required]
        public string Name { get; set; }
        [Required]
        public string Password { get; set; }
    }
}
```

The new model has `Name` and `Password` properties, both of which are decorated with the `Required` attribute so that I can use model validation to check that the user has provided values.

■ **Tip** In a real project, I would use client-side validation to check that the user has provided name and password values before submitting the form to the server, but I am going to keep things focused on Identity and the server-side functionality in this chapter. See *Pro ASP.NET MVC 5* for details of client-side form validation.

I added an `Account` controller to the project, as shown in Listing 14-3, with `Login` action methods to collect and process the user's credentials. I have not implemented the authentication logic in the listing because I am going to define the view and then walk through the process of validating user credentials and signing users into the application.

Listing 14-3. The Contents of the AccountController.cs File

```
using System.Threading.Tasks;
using System.Web.Mvc;
using Users.Models;

namespace Users.Controllers {

    [Authorize]
    public class AccountController : Controller {

        [AllowAnonymous]
        public ActionResult Login(string returnUrl) {
            if (ModelState.IsValid) {
            }
```

```
            ViewBag.returnUrl = returnUrl;
            return View();
        }

        [HttpPost]
        [AllowAnonymous]
        [ValidateAntiForgeryToken]
        public async Task<ActionResult> Login(LoginModel details, string returnUrl) {
            return View(details);
        }
    }
}
```

Even though it doesn't authenticate users yet, the Account controller contains some useful infrastructure that I want to explain separately from the ASP.NET Identity code that I'll add to the Login action method shortly.

First, notice that both versions of the Login action method take an argument called returnUrl. When a user requests a restricted URL, they are redirected to the /Account/Login URL with a query string that specifies the URL that the user should be sent back to once they have been authenticated. You can see this if you start the application and request the /Home/Index URL. Your browser will be redirected, like this:

```
/Account/Login?ReturnUrl=%2FHome%2FIndex
```

The value of the ReturnUrl query string parameter allows me to redirect the user so that navigating between open and secured parts of the application is a smooth and seamless process.

Next, notice the attributes that I have applied to the Account controller. Controllers that manage user accounts contain functionality that should be available only to authenticated users, such as password reset, for example. To that end, I have applied the Authorize attribute to the controller class and then used the AllowAnonymous attribute on the individual action methods. This restricts action methods to authenticated users by default but allows unauthenticated users to log in to the application.

Finally, I have applied the ValidateAntiForgeryToken attribute, which works in conjunction with the Html.AntiForgeryToken helper method in the view and guards against cross-site request forgery. Cross-site forgery exploits the trust that your user has for your application and it is especially important to use the helper and attribute for authentication requests.

■ **Tip** You can learn more about cross-site request forgery at http://en.wikipedia.org/wiki/Cross-site_request_forgery.

My last preparatory step is to create the view that will be rendered to gather credentials from the user. Listing 14-4 shows the contents of the Views/Account/Login.cshtml file, which I created by right-clicking the Index action method and selecting Add View from the pop-up menu.

Listing 14-4. The Contents of the Login.cshtml File

```
@model Users.Models.LoginModel
@{ ViewBag.Title = "Login";}
<h2>Log In</h2>

@Html.ValidationSummary()
```

```
@using (Html.BeginForm()) {
    @Html.AntiForgeryToken();
    <input type="hidden" name="returnUrl" value="@ViewBag.returnUrl" />
    <div class="form-group">
        <label>Name</label>
        @Html.TextBoxFor(x => x.Name, new { @class = "form-control" })
    </div>
    <div class="form-group">
        <label>Password</label>
        @Html.PasswordFor(x => x.Password, new { @class = "form-control" })
    </div>
    <button class="btn btn-primary" type="submit">Log In</button>
}
```

The only notable aspects of this view are using the `Html.AntiForgeryToken` helper and creating a hidden input element to preserve the `returnUrl` argument. In all other respects, this is a standard Razor view, but it completes the preparations for authentication and demonstrates the way that unauthenticated requests are intercepted and redirected. To test the new controller, start the application and request the `/Home/Index` URL. You will be redirected to the `/Account/Login` URL, as shown in Figure 14-2.

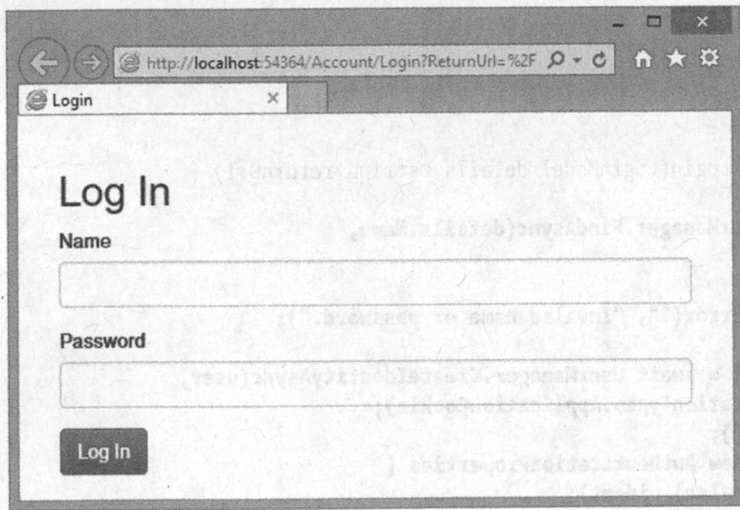

***Figure 14-2.** Prompting the user for authentication credentials*

Adding User Authentication

Requests for protected URLs are being correctly redirected to the `Account` controller, but the credentials provided by the user are not yet used for authentication. In Listing 14-5, you can see how I have completed the implementation of the `Login` action.

Listing 14-5. Adding Authentication to the AccountController.cs File

```
using System.Threading.Tasks;
using System.Web.Mvc;
using Users.Models;
using Microsoft.Owin.Security;
using System.Security.Claims;
using Microsoft.AspNet.Identity;
using Microsoft.AspNet.Identity.Owin;
using Users.Infrastructure;
using System.Web;

namespace Users.Controllers {

    [Authorize]
    public class AccountController : Controller {

        [AllowAnonymous]
        public ActionResult Login(string returnUrl) {
            ViewBag.returnUrl = returnUrl;
            return View();
        }

        [HttpPost]
        [AllowAnonymous]
        [ValidateAntiForgeryToken]
        public async Task<ActionResult> Login(LoginModel details, string returnUrl) {
            if (ModelState.IsValid) {
                AppUser user = await UserManager.FindAsync(details.Name,
                    details.Password);
                if (user == null) {
                    ModelState.AddModelError("", "Invalid name or password.");
                } else {
                    ClaimsIdentity ident = await UserManager.CreateIdentityAsync(user,
                        DefaultAuthenticationTypes.ApplicationCookie);
                    AuthManager.SignOut();
                    AuthManager.SignIn(new AuthenticationProperties {
                        IsPersistent = false}, ident);
                    return Redirect(returnUrl);
                }
            }
            ViewBag.returnUrl = returnUrl;
            return View(details);
        }

        private IAuthenticationManager AuthManager {
            get {
                return HttpContext.GetOwinContext().Authentication;
            }
        }
```

```
        private AppUserManager UserManager {
            get {
                return HttpContext.GetOwinContext().GetUserManager<AppUserManager>();
            }
        }
    }
}
```

The simplest part is checking the credentials, which I do through the FindAsync method of the AppUserManager class, which you will remember as the user manager class from Chapter 13:

```
...
AppUser user = await UserManager.FindAsync(details.Name, details.Password);
...
```

I will be using the AppUserManager class repeatedly in the Account controller, so I defined a property called UserManager that returns the instance of the class using the GetOwinContext extension method for the HttpContext class, just as I did for the Admin controller in Chapter 13.

The FindAsync method takes the account name and password supplied by the user and returns an instance of the user class (AppUser in the example application) if the user account exists *and* if the password is correct. If there is no such account or the password doesn't match the one stored in the database, then the FindAsync method returns null, in which case I add an error to the model state that tells the user that something went wrong.

If the FindAsync method does return an AppUser object, then I need to create the cookie that the browser will send in subsequent requests to show they are authenticated. Here are the relevant statements:

```
...
ClaimsIdentity ident = await UserManager.CreateIdentityAsync(user,
    DefaultAuthenticationTypes.ApplicationCookie);
AuthManager.SignOut();
AuthManager.SignIn(new AuthenticationProperties {IsPersistent = false}, ident);
return Redirect(returnUrl);
...
```

The first step is to create a ClaimsIdentity object that identifies the user. The ClaimsIdentity class is the ASP.NET Identity implementation of the IIdentity interface that I described in Table 14-4 and that you can see used in the "Using Roles for Authorization" section later in this chapter.

■ **Tip** Don't worry about why the class is called ClaimsIdentity at the moment. I explain what claims are and how they can be used in Chapter 15.

Instances of ClaimsIdentity are created by calling the user manager CreateIdentityAsync method, passing in a user object and a value from the DefaultAuthenticationTypes enumeration. The ApplicationCookie value is used when working with individual user accounts.

The next step is to invalidate any existing authentication cookies and create the new one. I defined the AuthManager property in the controller because I'll need access to the object it provides repeatedly as I build the functionality in this chapter. The property returns an implementation of the IAuthenticationManager interface that is responsible for performing common authentication options. I have described the most useful methods provided by the IAuthenticationManager interface in Table 14-5.

Table 14-5. The Most Useful Methods Defined by the IAuthenticationManager Interface

Name	Description
`SignIn(options, identity)`	Signs the user in, which generally means creating the cookie that identifies authenticated requests
`SignOut()`	Signs the user out, which generally means invalidating the cookie that identifies authenticated requests

The arguments to the `SignIn` method are an `AuthenticationProperties` object that configures the authentication process and the `ClaimsIdentity` object. I set the `IsPersistent` property defined by the `AuthenticationProperties` object to `true` to make the authentication cookie persistent at the browser, meaning that the user doesn't have to authenticate again when starting a new session. (There are other properties defined by the `AuthenticationProperties` class, but the `IsPersistent` property is the only one that is widely used at the moment.)

The final step is to redirect the user to the URL they requested before the authentication process started, which I do by calling the `Redirect` method.

CONSIDERING TWO-FACTOR AUTHENTICATION

I have performed single-factor authentication in this chapter, which is where the user is able to authenticate using a single piece of information known to them in advance: the password.

ASP.NET Identity also supports two-factor authentication, where the user needs something extra, usually something that is given to the user at the moment they want to authenticate. The most common examples are a value from a SecureID token or an authentication code that is sent as an e-mail or text message (strictly speaking, the two factors can be anything, including fingerprints, iris scans, and voice recognition, although these are options that are rarely required for most web applications).

Security is increased because an attacker needs to know the user's password *and* have access to whatever provides the second factor, such an e-mail account or cell phone.

I don't show two-factor authentication in the book for two reasons. The first is that it requires a lot of preparatory work, such as setting up the infrastructure that distributes the second-factor e-mails and texts and implementing the validation logic, all of which is beyond the scope of this book.

The second reason is that two-factor authentication forces the user to remember to jump through an additional hoop to authenticate, such as remembering their phone or keeping a security token nearby, something that isn't always appropriate for web applications. I carried a SecureID token of one sort or another for more than a decade in various jobs, and I lost count of the number of times that I couldn't log in to an employer's system because I left the token at home.

If you are interested in two-factor security, then I recommend relying on a third-party provider such as Google for authentication, which allows the user to choose whether they want the additional security (and inconvenience) that two-factor authentication provides. I demonstrate third-party authentication in Chapter 15.

Testing Authentication

To test user authentication, start the application and request the /Home/Index URL. When redirected to the /Account/Login URL, enter the details of one of the users I listed at the start of the chapter (for instance, the name joe and the password MySecret). Click the Log In button, and your browser will be redirected back to the /Home/Index URL, but this time it will submit the authentication cookie that grants it access to the action method, as shown in Figure 14-3.

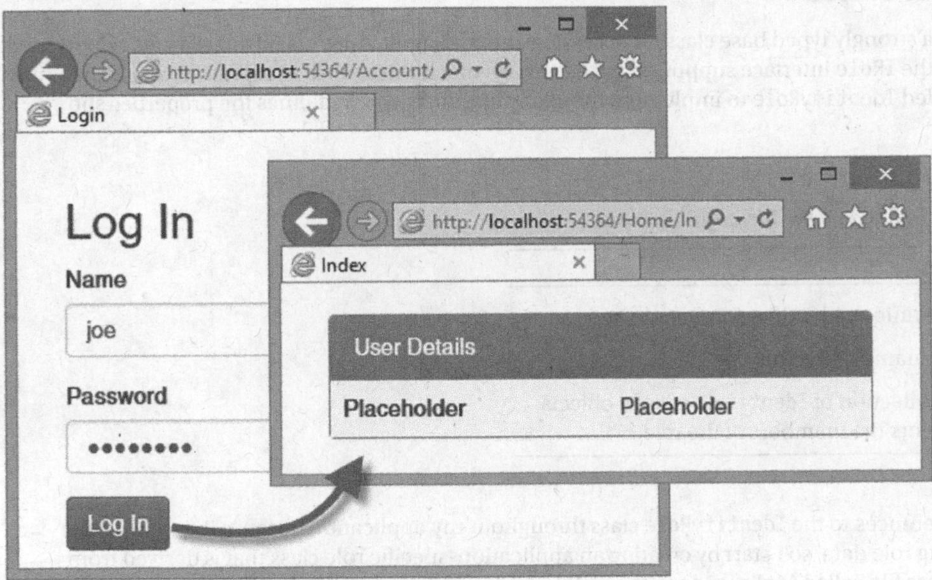

Figure 14-3. Authenticating a user

■ **Tip** You can use the browser F12 tools to see the cookies that are used to identify authenticated requests.

Authorizing Users with Roles

In the previous section, I applied the Authorize attribute in its most basic form, which allows any authenticated user to execute the action method. In this section, I will show you how to refine authorization to give finer-grained control over which users can perform which actions. Table 14-6 puts authorization in context.

Table 14-6. Putting Authorization in Context

Question	Answer
What is it?	Authorization is the process of granting access to controllers and action methods to certain users, generally based on role membership.
Why should I care?	Without roles, you can differentiate only between users who are authenticated and those who are not. Most applications will have different types of users, such as customers and administrators.
How is it used by the MVC framework?	Roles are used to enforce authorization through the Authorize attribute, which is applied to controllers and action methods.

■ **Tip** In Chapter 15, I show you a different approach to authorization using *claims*, which are an advanced ASP.NET Identity feature.

Adding Support for Roles

ASP.NET Identity provides a strongly typed base class for accessing and managing roles called `RoleManager<T>`, where `T` is the implementation of the `IRole` interface supported by the storage mechanism used to represent roles. The Entity Framework uses a class called `IdentityRole` to implement the `IRole` interface, which defines the properties shown in Table 14-7.

Table 14-7. *The Properties Defined by the IdentityRole Class*

Name	Description
`Id`	Defines the unique identifier for the role
`Name`	Defines the name of the role
`Users`	Returns a collection of `IdentityUserRole` objects that represents the members of the role

I don't want to leak references to the `IdentityRole` class throughout my application because it ties me to the Entity Framework for storing role data, so I start by creating an application-specific role class that is derived from `IdentityRole`. I added a class file called `AppRole.cs` to the `Models` folder and used it to define the class shown in Listing 14-6.

Listing 14-6 The Contents of the AppRole.cs File

```
using Microsoft.AspNet.Identity.EntityFramework;

namespace Users.Models {
    public class AppRole : IdentityRole {

        public AppRole() : base() {}

        public AppRole(string name) : base(name) { }
    }
}
```

The `RoleManager<T>` class operates on instances of the `IRole` implementation class through the methods and properties shown in Table 14-8.

Table 14-8. *The Members Defined by the RoleManager<T> Class*

Name	Description
CreateAsync(role)	Creates a new role
DeleteAsync(role)	Deletes the specified role
FindByIdAsync(id)	Finds a role by its ID
FindByNameAsync(name)	Finds a role by its name
RoleExistsAsync(name)	Returns true if a role with the specified name exists
UpdateAsync(role)	Stores changes to the specified role
Roles	Returns an enumeration of the roles that have been defined

These methods follow the same basic pattern of the UserManager<T> class that I described in Chapter 13. Following the pattern I used for managing users, I added a class file called AppRoleManager.cs to the Infrastructure folder and used it to define the class shown in Listing 14-7.

Listing 14-7 The Contents of the AppRoleManager.cs File

```
using System;
using Microsoft.AspNet.Identity;
using Microsoft.AspNet.Identity.EntityFramework;
using Microsoft.AspNet.Identity.Owin;
using Microsoft.Owin;
using Users.Models;

namespace Users.Infrastructure {

    public class AppRoleManager : RoleManager<AppRole>, IDisposable {

        public AppRoleManager(RoleStore<AppRole> store)
            : base(store) {
        }

        public static AppRoleManager Create(
                IdentityFactoryOptions<AppRoleManager> options,
                IOwinContext context) {
            return new AppRoleManager(new
                RoleStore<AppRole>(context.Get<AppIdentityDbContext>()));
        }
    }
}
```

This class defines a Create method that will allow the OWIN start class to create instances for each request where Identity data is accessed, which means I don't have to disseminate details of how role data is stored throughout the application. I can just obtain and operate on instances of the AppRoleManager class. You can see how I have registered the role manager class with the OWIN start class, IdentityConfig, in Listing 14-8. This ensures that instances of the AppRoleManager class are created using the same Entity Framework database context that is used for the AppUserManager class.

Listing 14-8. Creating Instances of the AppRoleManager Class in the IdentityConfig.cs File

```
using Microsoft.AspNet.Identity;
using Microsoft.Owin;
using Microsoft.Owin.Security.Cookies;
using Owin;
using Users.Infrastructure;

namespace Users {
    public class IdentityConfig {
        public void Configuration(IAppBuilder app) {

            app.CreatePerOwinContext<AppIdentityDbContext>(AppIdentityDbContext.Create);
            app.CreatePerOwinContext<AppUserManager>(AppUserManager.Create);
            app.CreatePerOwinContext<AppRoleManager>(AppRoleManager.Create);

            app.UseCookieAuthentication(new CookieAuthenticationOptions {
                AuthenticationType = DefaultAuthenticationTypes.ApplicationCookie,
                LoginPath = new PathString("/Account/Login"),
            });
        }
    }
}
```

Creating and Deleting Roles

Having prepared the application for working with roles, I am going to create an administration tool for managing them. I will start the basics and define action methods and views that allow roles to be created and deleted. I added a controller called RoleAdmin to the project, which you can see in Listing 14-9.

Listing 14-9. The Contents of the RoleAdminController.cs File

```
using System.ComponentModel.DataAnnotations;
using System.Linq;
using System.Threading.Tasks;
using System.Web;
using System.Web.Mvc;
using Microsoft.AspNet.Identity;
using Microsoft.AspNet.Identity.Owin;
using Users.Infrastructure;
using Users.Models;

namespace Users.Controllers {
    public class RoleAdminController : Controller {

        public ActionResult Index() {
            return View(RoleManager.Roles);
        }

        public ActionResult Create() {
            return View();
        }
```

```
        [HttpPost]
        public async Task<ActionResult> Create([Required]string name) {
            if (ModelState.IsValid) {
                IdentityResult result
                    = await RoleManager.CreateAsync(new AppRole(name));
                if (result.Succeeded) {
                    return RedirectToAction("Index");
                } else {
                    AddErrorsFromResult(result);
                }
            }
            return View(name);
        }

        [HttpPost]
        public async Task<ActionResult> Delete(string id) {
            AppRole role = await RoleManager.FindByIdAsync(id);
            if (role != null) {
                IdentityResult result = await RoleManager.DeleteAsync(role);
                if (result.Succeeded) {
                    return RedirectToAction("Index");
                } else {
                    return View("Error", result.Errors);
                }
            } else {
                return View("Error", new string[] { "Role Not Found" });
            }
        }

        private void AddErrorsFromResult(IdentityResult result) {
            foreach (string error in result.Errors) {
                ModelState.AddModelError("", error);
            }
        }

        private AppUserManager UserManager {
            get {
                return HttpContext.GetOwinContext().GetUserManager<AppUserManager>();
            }
        }

        private AppRoleManager RoleManager {
            get {
                return HttpContext.GetOwinContext().GetUserManager<AppRoleManager>();
            }
        }
    }
}
```

I have applied many of the same techniques that I used in the Admin controller in Chapter 13, including a UserManager property that obtains an instance of the AppUserManager class and an AddErrorsFromResult method that processes the errors reported in an IdentityResult object and adds them to the model state.

I have also defined a RoleManager property that obtains an instance of the AppRoleManager class, which I used in the action methods to obtain and manipulate the roles in the application. I am not going to describe the action methods in detail because they follow the same pattern I used in Chapter 13, using the AppRoleManager class in place of AppUserManager and calling the methods I described in Table 14-8.

Creating the Views

The views for the RoleAdmin controller are standard HTML and Razor markup, but I have included them in this chapter so that you can re-create the example. I want to display the names of the users who are members of each role. The Entity Framework IdentityRole class defines a Users property that returns a collection of IdentityUserRole user objects representing the members of the role. Each IdentityUserRole object has a UserId property that returns the unique ID of a user, and I want to get the username for each ID. I added a class file called IdentityHelpers.cs to the Infrastructure folder and used it to define the class shown in Listing 14-10.

Listing 14-10. The Contents of the IdentityHelpers.cs File

```
using System.Web;
using System.Web.Mvc;
using Microsoft.AspNet.Identity.Owin;

namespace Users.Infrastructure {
    public static class IdentityHelpers {
        public static MvcHtmlString GetUserName(this HtmlHelper html, string id) {
            AppUserManager mgr
                = HttpContext.Current.GetOwinContext().GetUserManager<AppUserManager>();
            return new MvcHtmlString(mgr.FindByIdAsync(id).Result.UserName);
        }
    }
}
```

Custom HTML helper methods are defined as extensions on the HtmlHelper class. My helper, which is called GetUsername, takes a string argument containing a user ID, obtains an instance of the AppUserManager through the GetOwinContext.GetUserManager method (where GetOwinContext is an extension method on the HttpContext class), and uses the FindByIdAsync method to locate the AppUser instance associated with the ID and to return the value of the UserName property.

Listing 14-11 shows the contents of the Index.cshtml file from the Views/RoleAdmin folder, which I created by right-clicking the Index action method in the code editor and selecting Add View from the pop-up menu.

Listing 14-11. The Contents of the Index.cshtml File in the Views/RoleAdmin Folder

```
@using Users.Models
@using Users.Infrastructure
@model IEnumerable<AppRole>
@{ ViewBag.Title = "Roles"; }
<div class="panel panel-primary">
    <div class="panel-heading">Roles</div>
    <table class="table table-striped">
        <tr><th>ID</th><th>Name</th><th>Users</th><th></th></tr>
        @if (Model.Count() == 0) {
```

```
            <tr><td colspan="4" class="text-center">No Roles</td></tr>
        } else {
            foreach (AppRole role in Model) {
                <tr>
                    <td>@role.Id</td>
                    <td>@role.Name</td>
                    <td>
                        @if (role.Users == null || role.Users.Count == 0) {
                            @: No Users in Role
                        } else {
                            <p>@string.Join(", ", role.Users.Select(x =>
                                Html.GetUserName(x.UserId)))</p>
                        }
                    </td>
                    <td>
                        @using (Html.BeginForm("Delete", "RoleAdmin",
                            new { id = role.Id })) {
                            @Html.ActionLink("Edit", "Edit", new { id = role.Id },
                                    new { @class = "btn btn-primary btn-xs" })
                            <button class="btn btn-danger btn-xs"
                                    type="submit">
                                Delete
                            </button>
                        }
                    </td>
                </tr>
            }
        }
    </table>
</div>
@Html.ActionLink("Create", "Create", null, new { @class = "btn btn-primary" })
```

This view displays a list of the roles defined by the application, along with the users who are members, and I use the GetUserName helper method to get the name for each user.

Listing 14-12 shows the Views/RoleAdmin/Create.cshtml file, which I created to allow new roles to be created.

Listing 14-12. The Contents of the Create.cshtml File in the Views/RoleAdmin Folder

```
@model string
@{ ViewBag.Title = "Create Role";}
<h2>Create Role</h2>
@Html.ValidationSummary(false)
@using (Html.BeginForm()) {
    <div class="form-group">
        <label>Name</label>
        <input name="name" value="@Model" class="form-control" />
    </div>
    <button type="submit" class="btn btn-primary">Create</button>
    @Html.ActionLink("Cancel", "Index", null, new { @class = "btn btn-default" })
}
```

The only information required to create a new view is a name, which I gather using a standard input element and submit the value to the Create action method.

Testing Creating and Deleting Roles

To test the new controller, start the application and navigate to the /RoleAdmin/Index URL. To create a new role, click the Create button, enter a name in the input element, and click the second Create button. The new view will be saved to the database and displayed when the browser is redirected to the Index action, as shown in Figure 14-4. You can remove the role from the application by clicking the Delete button.

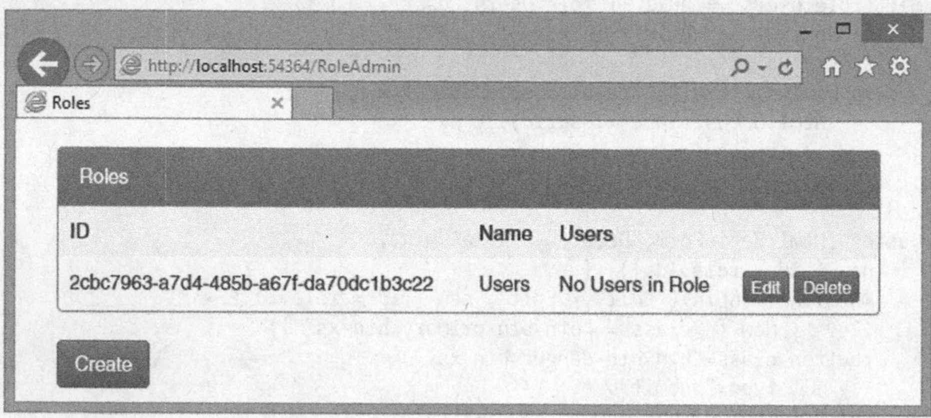

Figure 14-4. *Creating a new role*

Managing Role Memberships

To authorize users, it isn't enough to just create and delete roles; I also have to be able to manage role memberships, assigning and removing users from the roles that the application defines. This isn't a complicated process, but it invokes taking the role data from the AppRoleManager class and then calling the methods defined by the AppUserMangager class that associate users with roles.

I started by defining view models that will let me represent the membership of a role and receive a new set of membership instructions from the user. Listing 14-13 shows the additions I made to the UserViewModels.cs file.

Listing 14-13. Adding View Models to the UserViewModels.cs File

```
using System.ComponentModel.DataAnnotations;
using System.Collections.Generic;

namespace Users.Models {

    public class CreateModel {
        [Required]
        public string Name { get; set; }
        [Required]
        public string Email { get; set; }
        [Required]
        public string Password { get; set; }
    }
```

```
    public class LoginModel {
        [Required]
        public string Name { get; set; }
        [Required]
        public string Password { get; set; }
    }

    public class RoleEditModel {
        public AppRole Role { get; set; }
        public IEnumerable<AppUser> Members { get; set; }
        public IEnumerable<AppUser> NonMembers { get; set; }
    }

    public class RoleModificationModel {
        [Required]
        public string RoleName { get; set; }
        public string[] IdsToAdd { get; set; }
        public string[] IdsToDelete { get; set; }
    }
}
```

The RoleEditModel class will let me pass details of a role and details of the users in the system, categorized by membership. I use AppUser objects in the view model so that I can extract the name and ID for each user in the view that will allow memberships to be edited. The RoleModificationModel class is the one that I will receive from the model binding system when the user submits their changes. It contains arrays of user IDs rather than AppUser objects, which is what I need to change role memberships.

Having defined the view models, I can add the action methods to the controller that will allow role memberships to be defined. Listing 14-14 shows the changes I made to the RoleAdmin controller.

Listing 14-14. Adding Action Methods in the RoleAdminController.cs File

```
using System.ComponentModel.DataAnnotations;
using System.Linq;
using System.Threading.Tasks;
using System.Web;
using System.Web.Mvc;
using Microsoft.AspNet.Identity;
using Microsoft.AspNet.Identity.Owin;
using Users.Infrastructure;
using Users.Models;
using System.Collections.Generic;

namespace Users.Controllers {
    public class RoleAdminController : Controller {

        // ...other action methods omitted for brevity...

        public async Task<ActionResult> Edit(string id) {
            AppRole role = await RoleManager.FindByIdAsync(id);
            string[] memberIDs = role.Users.Select(x => x.UserId).ToArray();
            IEnumerable<AppUser> members
                = UserManager.Users.Where(x => memberIDs.Any(y => y == x.Id));
```

```
            IEnumerable<AppUser> nonMembers = UserManager.Users.Except(members);
            return View(new RoleEditModel {
                Role = role,
                Members = members,
                NonMembers = nonMembers
            });
        }

        [HttpPost]
        public async Task<ActionResult> Edit(RoleModificationModel model) {
            IdentityResult result;
            if (ModelState.IsValid) {
                foreach (string userId in model.IdsToAdd ?? new string[] { }) {
                    result = await UserManager.AddToRoleAsync(userId, model.RoleName);
                    if (!result.Succeeded) {
                        return View("Error", result.Errors);
                    }
                }
                foreach (string userId in model.IdsToDelete ?? new string[] { }) {
                    result = await UserManager.RemoveFromRoleAsync(userId,
                        model.RoleName);
                    if (!result.Succeeded) {
                        return View("Error", result.Errors);
                    }
                }
                return RedirectToAction("Index");
            }
            return View("Error", new string[] { "Role Not Found" });
        }

        private void AddErrorsFromResult(IdentityResult result) {
            foreach (string error in result.Errors) {
                ModelState.AddModelError("", error);
            }
        }

        private AppUserManager UserManager {
            get {
                return HttpContext.GetOwinContext().GetUserManager<AppUserManager>();
            }
        }

        private AppRoleManager RoleManager {
            get {
                return HttpContext.GetOwinContext().GetUserManager<AppRoleManager>();
            }
        }
    }
}
```

The majority of the code in the GET version of the Edit action method is responsible for generating the sets of members and nonmembers of the selected role, which is done using LINQ. Once I have grouped the users, I call the View method, passing a new instance of the RoleEditModel class I defined in Listing 14-13.

The POST version of the Edit method is responsible for adding and removing users to and from roles. The AppUserManager class inherits a number of role-related methods from its base class, which I have described in Table 14-9.

Table 14-9. *The Role-Related Methods Defined by the UserManager<T> Class*

Name	Description
AddToRoleAsync(id, name)	Adds the user with the specified ID to the role with the specified name
GetRolesAsync(id)	Returns a list of the names of the roles of which the user with the specified ID is a member
IsInRoleAsync(id, name)	Returns true if the user with the specified ID is a member of the role with the specified name
RemoveFromRoleAsync(id, name)	Removes the user with the specified ID as a member from the role with the specified name

An oddity of these methods is that the role-related methods operate on user IDs and role *names*, even though roles also have unique identifiers. It is for this reason that my RoleModificationModel view model class has a RoleName property.

Listing 14-15 shows the view for the Edit.cshtml file, which I added to the Views/RoleAdmin folder and used to define the markup that allows the user to edit role memberships.

Listing 14-15. The Contents of the Edit.cshtml File in the Views/RoleAdmin Folder

```
@using Users.Models
@model RoleEditModel
@{ ViewBag.Title = "Edit Role";}
@Html.ValidationSummary()
@using (Html.BeginForm()) {
    <input type="hidden" name="roleName" value="@Model.Role.Name" />
    <div class="panel panel-primary">
        <div class="panel-heading">Add To @Model.Role.Name</div>
        <table class="table table-striped">
            @if (Model.NonMembers.Count() == 0) {
                <tr><td colspan="2">All Users Are Members</td></tr>
            } else {
                <tr><td>User ID</td><td>Add To Role</td></tr>
                foreach (AppUser user in Model.NonMembers) {
                    <tr>
                        <td>@user.UserName</td>
                        <td>
                            <input type="checkbox" name="IdsToAdd" value="@user.Id">
                        </td>
                    </tr>
                }
            }
        </table>
    </div>
```

```
    <div class="panel panel-primary">
        <div class="panel-heading">Remove from @Model.Role.Name</div>
        <table class="table table-striped">
            @if (Model.Members.Count() == 0) {
                <tr><td colspan="2">No Users Are Members</td></tr>
            } else {
                <tr><td>User ID</td><td>Remove From Role</td></tr>
                foreach (AppUser user in Model.Members) {
                    <tr>
                        <td>@user.UserName</td>
                        <td>
                            <input type="checkbox" name="IdsToDelete" value="@user.Id">
                        </td>
                    </tr>
                }
            }
        </table>
    </div>
    <button type="submit" class="btn btn-primary">Save</button>
    @Html.ActionLink("Cancel", "Index", null, new { @class = "btn btn-default" })
}
```

The view contains two tables: one for users who are not members of the selected role and one for those who are members. Each user's name is displayed along with a check box that allows the membership to be changed.

Testing Editing Role Membership

Adding the `AppRoleManager` class to the application causes the Entity Framework to delete the contents of the database and rebuild the schema, which means that any users you created in the previous chapter have been removed. So that there are users to assign to roles, start the application and navigate to the `/Admin/Index` URL and create users with the details in Table 14-10.

***Table 14-10.** The Values for Creating Example User*

Name	Email	Password
Alice	alice@example.com	MySecret
Bob	bob@example.com	MySecret
Joe	joe@example.com	MySecret

■ **Tip** Deleting the user database is fine for an example application but tends to be a problem in real applications. I show you how to gracefully manage changes to the database schema in Chapter 15.

To test managing role memberships, navigate to the `/RoleAdmin/Index` URL and create a role called `Users`, following the instructions from the "Testing, Creating, and Deleting Roles" section. Click the Edit button and check the boxes so that Alice and Joe are members of the role but Bob is not, as shown in Figure 14-5.

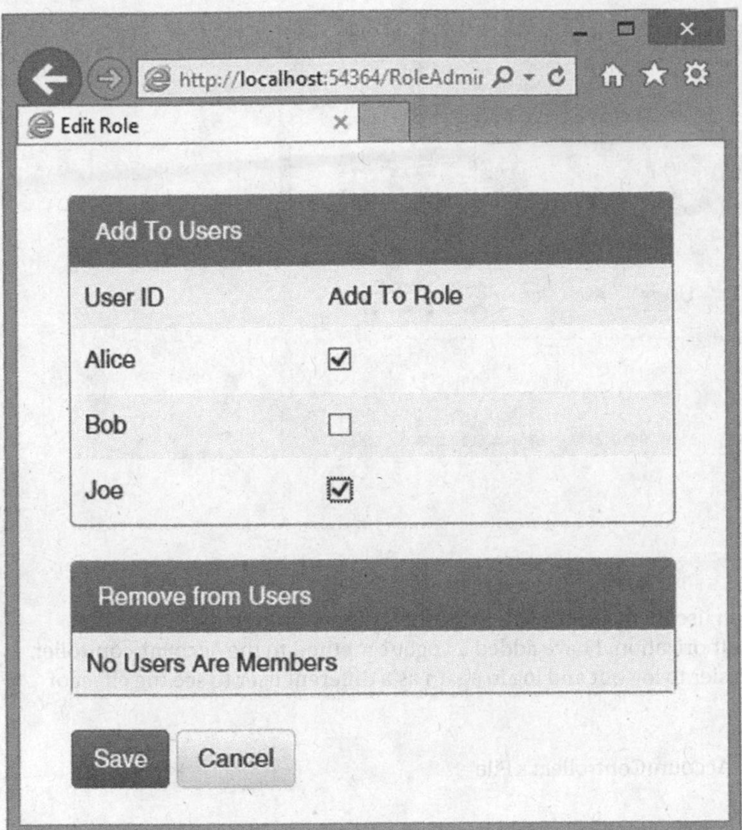

***Figure 14-5.** Editing role membership*

■ **Tip** If you get an error that tells you there is already an open a data reader, then you didn't set the `MultipleActiveResultSets` setting to `true` in the connection string in Chapter 13.

Click the Save button, and the controller will update the role memberships and redirect the browser to the `Index` action. The summary of the `Users` role will show that Alice and Joe are now members, as illustrated by Figure 14-6.

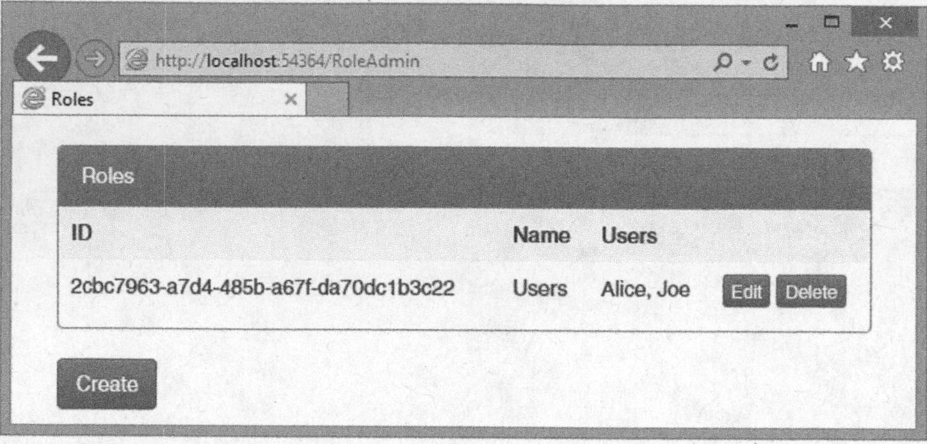

Figure 14-6. *The effect of adding users to a role*

Using Roles for Authorization

Now that I have the ability to manage roles, I can use them as the basis for authorization through the `Authorize` attribute. To make it easier to test role-based authorization, I have added a `Logout` method to the `Account` controller, as shown in Listing 14-16, which will make it easier to log out and log in again as a different user to see the effect of role membership.

Listing 14-16. Adding a Logout Method to the AccountController.cs File

```
using System.Threading.Tasks;
using System.Web.Mvc;
using Users.Models;
using Microsoft.Owin.Security;
using System.Security.Claims;
using Microsoft.AspNet.Identity;
using Microsoft.AspNet.Identity.Owin;
using Users.Infrastructure;
using System.Web;

namespace Users.Controllers {

    [Authorize]
    public class AccountController : Controller {

        [AllowAnonymous]
        public ActionResult Login(string returnUrl) {
            ViewBag.returnUrl = returnUrl;
            return View();
        }

        [HttpPost]
        [AllowAnonymous]
        [ValidateAntiForgeryToken]
```

```
        public async Task<ActionResult> Login(LoginModel details, string returnUrl) {
            // ...statements omitted for brevity...
        }

        [Authorize]
        public ActionResult Logout() {
            AuthManager.SignOut();
            return RedirectToAction("Index", "Home");
        }

        private IAuthenticationManager AuthManager {
            get {
                return HttpContext.GetOwinContext().Authentication;
            }
        }

        private AppUserManager UserManager {
            get {
                return HttpContext.GetOwinContext().GetUserManager<AppUserManager>();
            }
        }
    }
}
```

I have updated the Home controller to add a new action method and pass some information about the authenticated user to the view, as shown in Listing 14-17.

Listing 14-17. Adding an Action Method and Account Information to the HomeController.cs File

```
using System.Web.Mvc;
using System.Collections.Generic;
using System.Web;
using System.Security.Principal;

namespace Users.Controllers {

    public class HomeController : Controller {

        [Authorize]
        public ActionResult Index() {
            return View(GetData("Index"));
        }

        [Authorize(Roles="Users")]
        public ActionResult OtherAction() {
            return View("Index", GetData("OtherAction"));
        }

        private Dictionary<string, object> GetData(string actionName) {
            Dictionary<string, object> dict
                = new Dictionary<string, object>();
```

```
            dict.Add("Action", actionName);
            dict.Add("User", HttpContext.User.Identity.Name);
            dict.Add("Authenticated", HttpContext.User.Identity.IsAuthenticated);
            dict.Add("Auth Type", HttpContext.User.Identity.AuthenticationType);
            dict.Add("In Users Role", HttpContext.User.IsInRole("Users"));
            return dict;
        }
    }
}
```

I have left the Authorize attribute unchanged for the Index action method, but I have set the Roles property when applying the attribute to the OtherAction method, specifying that only members of the Users role should be able to access it. I also defined a GetData method, which adds some basic information about the user identity, using the properties available through the HttpContext object. The final change I made was to the Index.cshtml file in the Views/Home folder, which is used by both actions in the Home controller, to add a link that targets the Logout method in the Account controller, as shown in Listing 14-18.

Listing 14-18. Adding a Sign-Out Link to the Index.cshtml File in the Views/Home Folder

```
@{ ViewBag.Title = "Index"; }

<div class="panel panel-primary">
    <div class="panel-heading">User Details</div>
    <table class="table table-striped">
        @foreach (string key in Model.Keys) {
            <tr>
                <th>@key</th>
                <td>@Model[key]</td>
            </tr>
        }
    </table>
</div>

@Html.ActionLink("Sign Out", "Logout", "Account", null, new {@class = "btn btn-primary"})
```

■ **Tip** The Authorize attribute can also be used to authorize access based on a list of individual usernames. This is an appealing feature for small projects, but it means you have to change the code in your controllers each time the set of users you are authorizing changes, and that usually means having to go through the test-and-deploy cycle again. Using roles for authorization isolates the application from changes in individual user accounts and allows you to control access to the application through the memberships stored by ASP.NET Identity.

To test the authentication, start the application and navigate to the /Home/Index URL. Your browser will be redirected so that you can enter user credentials. It doesn't matter which of the user details from Table 14-10 you choose to authenticate with because the Authorize attribute applied to the Index action allows access to any authenticated user.

However, if you now request the /Home/OtherAction URL, the user details you chose from Table 14-10 will make a difference because only Alice and Joe are members of the Users role, which is required to access the OtherAction method. If you log in as Bob, then your browser will be redirected so that you can be prompted for credentials once again.

Redirecting an already authenticated user for more credentials is rarely a useful thing to do, so I have modified the Login action method in the Account controller to check to see whether the user is authenticated and, if so, redirect them to the shared Error view. Listing 14-19 shows the changes.

Listing 14-19. Detecting Already Authenticated Users in the AccountController.cs File

```
using System.Threading.Tasks;
using System.Web.Mvc;
using Users.Models;
using Microsoft.Owin.Security;
using System.Security.Claims;
using Microsoft.AspNet.Identity;
using Microsoft.AspNet.Identity.Owin;
using Users.Infrastructure;
using System.Web;

namespace Users.Controllers {

    [Authorize]
    public class AccountController : Controller {

        [AllowAnonymous]
        public ActionResult Login(string returnUrl) {
            if (HttpContext.User.Identity.IsAuthenticated) {
                return View("Error", new string[] { "Access Denied" });
            }
            ViewBag.returnUrl = returnUrl;
            return View();
        }

        [HttpPost]
        [AllowAnonymous]
        [ValidateAntiForgeryToken]
        public async Task<ActionResult> Login(LoginModel details, string returnUrl) {
            // ...code omitted for brevity...
        }

        [Authorize]
        public ActionResult Logout() {
            AuthManager.SignOut();
            return RedirectToAction("Index", "Home");
        }

        private IAuthenticationManager AuthManager {
            get {
                return HttpContext.GetOwinContext().Authentication;
            }
        }
```

```
        private AppUserManager UserManager {
            get {
                return HttpContext.GetOwinContext().GetUserManager<AppUserManager>();
            }
        }
    }
}
```

Figure 14-7 shows the responses generated for the user Bob when requesting the /Home/Index and /Home/OtherAction URLs.

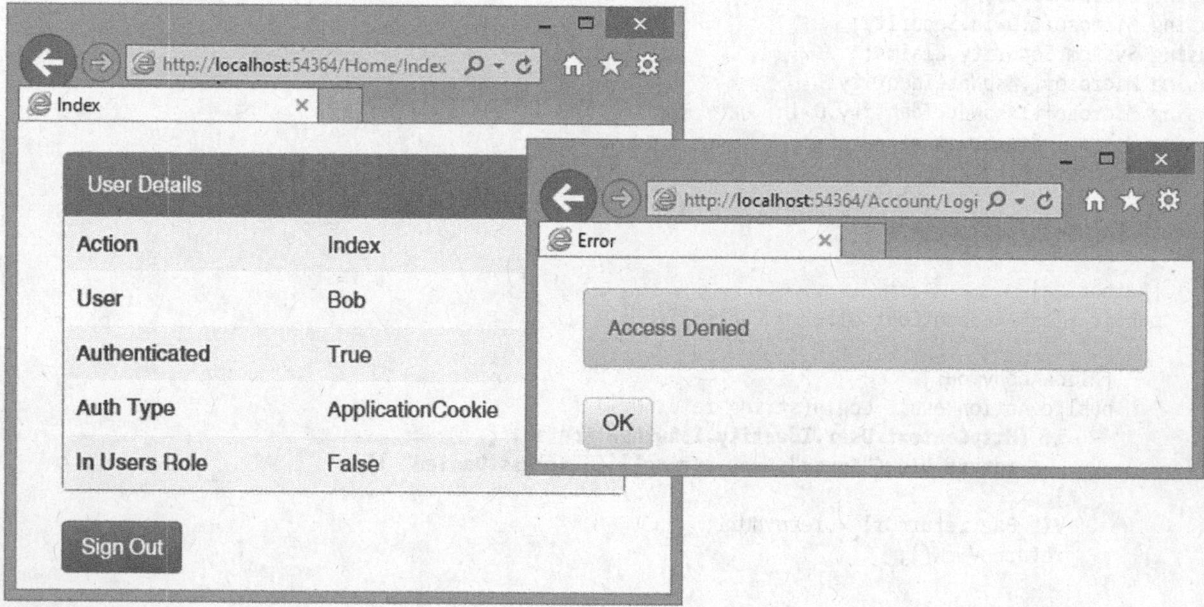

Figure 14-7. Using roles to control access to action methods

■ **Tip** Roles are loaded when the user logs in, which means if you change the roles for the user you are currently authenticated as, the changes won't take effect until you log out and authenticate.

Seeding the Database

One lingering problem in my example project is that access to my Admin and RoleAdmin controllers is not restricted. This is a classic chicken-and-egg problem because in order to restrict access, I need to create users and roles, but the Admin and RoleAdmin controllers are the user management tools, and if I protect them with the Authorize attribute, there won't be any credentials that will grant me access to them, especially when I first deploy the application.

The solution to this problem is to seed the database with some initial data when the Entity Framework Code First feature creates the schema. This allows me to automatically create users and assign them to roles so that there is a base level of content available in the database.

The database is seeded by adding statements to the PerformInitialSetup method of the IdentityDbInit class, which is the application-specific Entity Framework database setup class. Listing 14-20 shows the changes I made to create an administration user.

Listing 14-20. Seeding the Database in the AppIdentityDbContext.cs File

```
using System.Data.Entity;
using Microsoft.AspNet.Identity.EntityFramework;
using Users.Models;
using Microsoft.AspNet.Identity;

namespace Users.Infrastructure {
    public class AppIdentityDbContext : IdentityDbContext<AppUser> {

        public AppIdentityDbContext() : base("IdentityDb") { }

        static AppIdentityDbContext() {
            Database.SetInitializer<AppIdentityDbContext>(new IdentityDbInit());
        }

        public static AppIdentityDbContext Create() {
            return new AppIdentityDbContext();
        }
    }

    public class IdentityDbInit
            : DropCreateDatabaseIfModelChanges<AppIdentityDbContext> {
        protected override void Seed(AppIdentityDbContext context) {
            PerformInitialSetup(context);
            base.Seed(context);
        }

        public void PerformInitialSetup(AppIdentityDbContext context) {
            AppUserManager userMgr = new AppUserManager(new UserStore<AppUser>(context));
            AppRoleManager roleMgr = new AppRoleManager(new RoleStore<AppRole>(context));

            string roleName = "Administrators";
            string userName = "Admin";
            string password = "MySecret";
            string email = "admin@example.com";

            if (!roleMgr.RoleExists(roleName)) {
                roleMgr.Create(new AppRole(roleName));
            }

            AppUser user = userMgr.FindByName(userName);
            if (user == null) {
                userMgr.Create(new AppUser { UserName = userName, Email = email },
                    password);
                user = userMgr.FindByName(userName);
            }
```

```
            if (!userMgr.IsInRole(user.Id, roleName)) {
                userMgr.AddToRole(user.Id, roleName);
            }
        }
    }
}
```

■ **Tip** For this example, I used the synchronous extension methods to locate and manage the role and user. As I explained in Chapter 13, I prefer the asynchronous methods by default, but the synchronous methods can be useful when you need to perform a sequence of related operations.

I have to create instances of `AppUserManager` and `AppRoleManager` directly because the `PerformInitialSetup` method is called before the OWIN configuration is complete. I use the `RoleManager` and `AppManager` objects to create a role called `Administrators` and a user called `Admin` and add the user to the role.

■ **Tip** Read Chapter 15 before you add database seeding to your project. I describe database migrations, which allow you to take control of schema changes in the database and which put the seeding logic in a different place.

With this change, I can use the `Authorize` attribute to protect the `Admin` and `RoleAdmin` controllers. Listing 14-21 shows the change I made to the `Admin` controller.

Listing 14-21. Restricting Access in the AdminController.cs File

```
using System.Web;
using System.Web.Mvc;
using Microsoft.AspNet.Identity.Owin;
using Users.Infrastructure;
using Users.Models;
using Microsoft.AspNet.Identity;
using System.Threading.Tasks;

namespace Users.Controllers {

    [Authorize(Roles = "Administrators")]
    public class AdminController : Controller {
        // ...statements omitted for brevity...
    }
}
```

Listing 14-22 shows the corresponding change I made to the `RoleAdmin` controller.

Listing 14-22. Restricting Access in the RoleAdminController.cs File

```
using System.ComponentModel.DataAnnotations;
using System.Linq;
using System.Threading.Tasks;
using System.Web;
```

```
using System.Web.Mvc;
using Microsoft.AspNet.Identity;
using Microsoft.AspNet.Identity.Owin;
using Users.Infrastructure;
using Users.Models;
using System.Collections.Generic;

namespace Users.Controllers {

    [Authorize(Roles = "Administrators")]
    public class RoleAdminController : Controller {
        // ...statements omitted for brevity...
    }
}
```

The database is seeded only when the schema is created, which means I need to reset the database to complete the process. This isn't something you would do in a real application, of course, but I wanted to wait until I demonstrated how authentication and authorization worked before creating the administrator account.

To delete the database, open the Visual Studio SQL Server Object Explorer window and locate and right-click the `IdentityDb` item. Select Delete from the pop-up menu and check both of the options in the Delete Database dialog window. Click the OK button to delete the database.

Now create an empty database to which the schema will be added by right-clicking the Databases item, selecting Add New Database, and entering **IdentityDb** in the Database Name field. Click OK to create the empty database.

■ **Tip** There are step-by-step instructions with screenshots in Chapter 13 for creating the database.

Now start the application and request the `/Admin/Index` or `/RoleAdmin/Index` URL. There will be a delay while the schema is created and the database is seeded, and then you will be prompted to enter your credentials. Use `Admin` as the name and `MySecret` as the password, and you will be granted access to the controllers.

■ **Caution** Deleting the database removes the user accounts you created using the details in Table 14-10, which is why you would not perform this task on a live database containing user details.

Summary

In this chapter, I showed you how to use ASP.NET Identity to authenticate and authorize users. I explained how the ASP.NET life-cycle events provide a foundation for authenticating requests, how to collect and validate credentials users, and how to restrict access to action methods based on the roles that a user is a member of. In the next chapter, I demonstrate some of the advanced features that ASP.NET Identity provides.

CHAPTER 15

Advanced ASP.NET Identity

In this chapter, I finish my description of ASP.NET Identity by showing you some of the advanced features it offers. I demonstrate how you can extend the database schema by defining custom properties on the user class and how to use database migrations to apply those properties without deleting the data in the ASP.NET Identity database. I also explain how ASP.NET Identity supports the concept of claims and demonstrate how they can be used to flexibly authorize access to action methods. I finish the chapter—and the book—by showing you how ASP.NET Identity makes it easy to authenticate users through third parties. I demonstrate authentication with Google accounts, but ASP.NET Identity has built-in support for Microsoft, Facebook, and Twitter accounts as well. Table 15-1 summarizes this chapter.

Table 15-1. *Chapter Summary*

Problem	Solution	Listing
Store additional information about users.	Define custom user properties.	1–3, 8–11
Update the database schema without deleting user data.	Perform a database migration.	4–7
Perform fine-grained authorization.	Use claims.	12–14
Add claims about a user.	Use the `ClaimsIdentity.AddClaims` method.	15–19
Authorize access based on claim values.	Create a custom authorization filter attribute.	20–21
Authenticate through a third party.	Install the NuGet package for the authentication provider, redirect requests to that provider, and specify a callback URL that creates the user account.	22–25

Preparing the Example Project

In this chapter, I am going to continue working on the Users project I created in Chapter 13 and enhanced in Chapter 14. No changes to the application are required, but start the application and make sure that there are users in the database. Figure 15-1 shows the state of my database, which contains the users Admin, Alice, Bob, and Joe from the previous chapter. To check the users, start the application and request the `/Admin/Index` URL and authenticate as the Admin user.

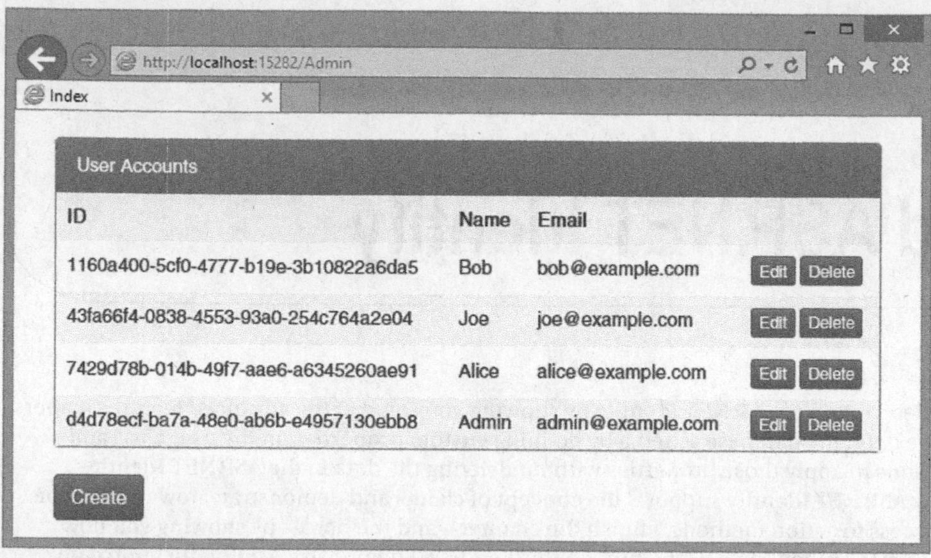

***Figure 15-1.** The initial users in the Identity database*

I also need some roles for this chapter. I used the `RoleAdmin` controller to create roles called `Users` and `Employees` and assigned the users to those roles, as described in Table 15-2.

***Table 15-2.** The Types of Web Forms Code Nuggets*

Role	Members
`Users`	`Alice, Joe`
`Employees`	`Alice, Bob`

Figure 15-2 shows the required role configuration displayed by the `RoleAdmin` controller.

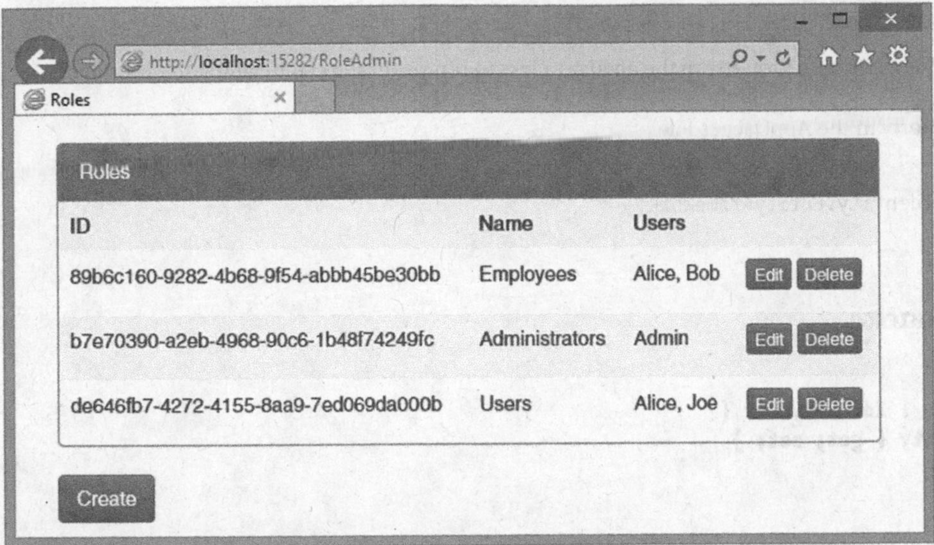

***Figure 15-2.** Configuring the roles required for this chapter*

Adding Custom User Properties

When I created the AppUser class to represent users in Chapter 13, I noted that the base class defined a basic set of properties to describe the user, such as e-mail address and telephone number. Most applications need to store more information about users, including persistent application preferences and details such as addresses—in short, any data that is useful to running the application and that should last between sessions. In ASP.NET Membership, this was handled through the user profile system, but ASP.NET Identity takes a different approach.

Because the ASP.NET Identity system uses Entity Framework to store its data by default, defining additional user information is just a matter of adding properties to the user class and letting the Code First feature create the database schema required to store them. Table 15-3 puts custom user properties in context.

***Table 15-3.** Putting Cusotm User Properties in Context*

Question	Answer
What is it?	Custom user properties allow you to store additional information about your users, including their preferences and settings.
Why should I care?	A persistent store of settings means that the user doesn't have to provide the same information each time they log in to the application.
How is it used by the MVC framework?	This feature isn't used directly by the MVC framework, but it is available for use in action methods.

Defining Custom Properties

Listing 15-1 shows how I added a simple property to the AppUser class to represent the city in which the user lives.

Listing 15-1. Adding a Property in the AppUser.cs File

```
using System;
using Microsoft.AspNet.Identity.EntityFramework;

namespace Users.Models {
    public enum Cities {
        LONDON, PARIS, CHICAGO
    }

    public class AppUser : IdentityUser {
        public Cities City { get; set; }
    }
}
```

I have defined an enumeration called Cities that defines values for some large cities and added a property called City to the AppUser class. To allow the user to view and edit their City property, I added actions to the Home controller, as shown in Listing 15-2.

Listing 15-2. Adding Support for Custom User Properties in the HomeController.cs File

```
using System.Web.Mvc;
using System.Collections.Generic;
using System.Web;
using System.Security.Principal;
using System.Threading.Tasks;
using Users.Infrastructure;
using Microsoft.AspNet.Identity;
using Microsoft.AspNet.Identity.Owin;
using Users.Models;

namespace Users.Controllers {

    public class HomeController : Controller {

        [Authorize]
        public ActionResult Index() {
            return View(GetData("Index"));
        }

        [Authorize(Roles = "Users")]
        public ActionResult OtherAction() {
            return View("Index", GetData("OtherAction"));
        }
```

```
    private Dictionary<string, object> GetData(string actionName) {
        Dictionary<string, object> dict
            = new Dictionary<string, object>();
        dict.Add("Action", actionName);
        dict.Add("User", HttpContext.User.Identity.Name);
        dict.Add("Authenticated", HttpContext.User.Identity.IsAuthenticated);
        dict.Add("Auth Type", HttpContext.User.Identity.AuthenticationType);
        dict.Add("In Users Role", HttpContext.User.IsInRole("Users"));
        return dict;
    }

    [Authorize]
    public ActionResult UserProps() {
        return View(CurrentUser);
    }

    [Authorize]
    [HttpPost]
    public async Task<ActionResult> UserProps(Cities city) {
        AppUser user = CurrentUser;
        user.City = city;
        await UserManager.UpdateAsync(user);
        return View(user);
    }

    private AppUser CurrentUser {
        get {
            return UserManager.FindByName(HttpContext.User.Identity.Name);
        }
    }

    private AppUserManager UserManager {
        get {
            return HttpContext.GetOwinContext().GetUserManager<AppUserManager>();
        }
    }
  }
}
```

I added a CurrentUser property that uses the AppUserManager class to retrieve an AppUser instance to represent the current user. I pass the AppUser object as the view model object in the GET version of the UserProps action method, and the POST method uses it to update the value of the new City property. Listing 15-3 shows the UserProps.cshtml view, which displays the City property value and contains a form to change it.

Listing 15-3. The Contents of the UserProps.cshtml File in the Views/Home Folder

```
@using Users.Models
@model AppUser
@{ ViewBag.Title = "UserProps";}
```

```
<div class="panel panel-primary">
    <div class="panel-heading">
        Custom User Properties
    </div>
    <table class="table table-striped">
        <tr><th>City</th><td>@Model.City</td></tr>
    </table>
</div>

@using (Html.BeginForm()) {
    <div class="form-group">
        <label>City</label>
        @Html.DropDownListFor(x => x.City, new SelectList(Enum.GetNames(typeof(Cities))))
    </div>
    <button class="btn btn-primary" type="submit">Save</button>
}
```

■ **Caution** Don't start the application when you have created the view. In the sections that follow, I demonstrate how to preserve the contents of the database, and if you start the application now, the ASP.NET Identity users will be deleted.

Preparing for Database Migration

The default behavior for the Entity Framework Code First feature is to drop the tables in the database and re-create them whenever classes that drive the schema have changed. You saw this in Chapter 14 when I added support for roles: When the application was started, the database was reset, and the user accounts were lost.

Don't start the application yet, but if you were to do so, you would see a similar effect. Deleting data during development is usually not a problem, but doing so in a production setting is usually disastrous because it deletes all of the real user accounts and causes a panic while the backups are restored. In this section, I am going to demonstrate how to use the database migration feature, which updates a Code First schema in a less brutal manner and preserves the existing data it contains.

The first step is to issue the following command in the Visual Studio Package Manager Console:

```
Enable-Migrations -EnableAutomaticMigrations
```

This enables the database migration support and creates a `Migrations` folder in the Solution Explorer that contains a `Configuration.cs` class file, the contents of which are shown in Listing 15-4.

Listing 15-4. The Contents of the Configuration.cs File

```
namespace Users.Migrations {
    using System;
    using System.Data.Entity;
    using System.Data.Entity.Migrations;
    using System.Linq;
```

```
    internal sealed class Configuration
            : DbMigrationsConfiguration<Users.Infrastructure.AppIdentityDbContext> {
        public Configuration() {
            AutomaticMigrationsEnabled = true;
            ContextKey = "Users.Infrastructure.AppIdentityDbContext";
        }

        protected override void Seed(Users.Infrastructure.AppIdentityDbContext context) {
            // This method will be called after migrating to the latest version.

            // You can use the DbSet<T>.AddOrUpdate() helper extension method
            // to avoid creating duplicate seed data. E.g.
            //
            //   context.People.AddOrUpdate(
            //     p => p.FullName,
            //     new Person { FullName = "Andrew Peters" },
            //     new Person { FullName = "Brice Lambson" },
            //     new Person { FullName = "Rowan Miller" }
            //   );
            //
        }
    }
}
```

■ **Tip** You might be wondering why you are entering a database migration command into the console used to manage NuGet packages. The answer is that the Package Manager Console is really *PowerShell*, which is a general-purpose tool that is mislabeled by Visual Studio. You can use the console to issue a wide range of helpful commands. See `http://go.microsoft.com/fwlink/?LinkID=108518` for details.

The class will be used to migrate existing content in the database to the new schema, and the Seed method will be called to provide an opportunity to update the existing database records. In Listing 15-5, you can see how I have used the Seed method to set a default value for the new City property I added to the AppUser class. (I have also updated the class file to reflect my usual coding style.)

Listing 15-5. Managing Existing Content in the Configuration.cs File

```
using System.Data.Entity.Migrations;
using Microsoft.AspNet.Identity;
using Microsoft.AspNet.Identity.EntityFramework;
using Users.Infrastructure;
using Users.Models;

namespace Users.Migrations {

    internal sealed class Configuration
            : DbMigrationsConfiguration<AppIdentityDbContext> {
```

```
        public Configuration() {
            AutomaticMigrationsEnabled = true;
            ContextKey = "Users.Infrastructure.AppIdentityDbContext";
        }

        protected override void Seed(AppIdentityDbContext context) {

            AppUserManager userMgr = new AppUserManager(new UserStore<AppUser>(context));
            AppRoleManager roleMgr = new AppRoleManager(new RoleStore<AppRole>(context));

            string roleName = "Administrators";
            string userName = "Admin";
            string password = "MySecret";
            string email = "admin@example.com";

            if (!roleMgr.RoleExists(roleName)) {
                roleMgr.Create(new AppRole(roleName));
            }

            AppUser user = userMgr.FindByName(userName);
            if (user == null) {
                userMgr.Create(new AppUser { UserName = userName, Email = email },
                    password);
                user = userMgr.FindByName(userName);
            }

            if (!userMgr.IsInRole(user.Id, roleName)) {
                userMgr.AddToRole(user.Id, roleName);
            }

            foreach (AppUser dbUser in userMgr.Users) {
                dbUser.City = Cities.PARIS;
            }
            context.SaveChanges();
        }
    }
}
```

You will notice that much of the code that I added to the Seed method is taken from the IdentityDbInit class, which I used to seed the database with an administration user in Chapter 14. This is because the new Configuration class added to support database migrations will replace the seeding function of the IdentityDbInit class, which I'll update shortly. Aside from ensuring that there is an admin user, the statements in the Seed method that are important are the ones that set the initial value for the City property I added to the AppUser class, as follows:

```
...
foreach (AppUser dbUser in userMgr.Users) {
    dbUser.City = Cities.PARIS;
}
context.SaveChanges();
...
```

You don't have to set a default value for new properties—I just wanted to demonstrate that the Seed method in the Configuration class can be used to update the existing user records in the database.

■ **Caution** Be careful when setting values for properties in the Seed method for real projects because the values will be applied every time you change the schema, overriding any values that the user has set since the last schema update was performed. I set the value of the City property just to demonstrate that it can be done.

Changing the Database Context Class

The reason that I added the seeding code to the Configuration class is that I need to change the IdentityDbInit class. At present, the IdentityDbInit class is derived from the descriptively named DropCreateDatabaseIfModelChanges<AppIdentityDbContext> class, which, as you might imagine, drops the entire database when the Code First classes change. Listing 15-6 shows the changes I made to the IdentityDbInit class to prevent it from affecting the database.

Listing 15-6. Preventing Database Schema Changes in the AppIdentityDbContext.cs File

```
using System.Data.Entity;
using Microsoft.AspNet.Identity.EntityFramework;
using Users.Models;
using Microsoft.AspNet.Identity;

namespace Users.Infrastructure {
    public class AppIdentityDbContext : IdentityDbContext<AppUser> {

        public AppIdentityDbContext() : base("IdentityDb") { }

        static AppIdentityDbContext() {
            Database.SetInitializer<AppIdentityDbContext>(new IdentityDbInit());
        }

        public static AppIdentityDbContext Create() {
            return new AppIdentityDbContext();
        }
    }

    public class IdentityDbInit : NullDatabaseInitializer<AppIdentityDbContext> {
    }
}
```

I have removed the methods defined by the class and changed its base to NullDatabaseInitializer<AppIdentityDbContext>, which prevents the schema from being altered.

Performing the Migration

All that remains is to generate and apply the migration. First, run the following command in the Package Manager Console:

```
Add-Migration CityProperty
```

This creates a new migration called CityProperty (I like my migration names to reflect the changes I made). A class new file will be added to the Migrations folder, and its name reflects the time at which the command was run and the name of the migration. My file is called 201402262244036_CityProperty.cs, for example. The contents of this file contain the details of how Entity Framework will change the database during the migration, as shown in Listing 15-7.

Listing 15-7. The Contents of the 201402262244036_ CityProperty.cs File

```
namespace Users.Migrations {
    using System;
    using System.Data.Entity.Migrations;

    public partial class Init : DbMigration {
        public override void Up() {
            AddColumn("dbo.AspNetUsers", "City", c => c.Int(nullable: false));
        }

        public override void Down() {
            DropColumn("dbo.AspNetUsers", "City");
        }
    }
}
```

The Up method describes the changes that have to be made to the schema when the database is upgraded, which in this case means adding a City column to the AspNetUsers table, which is the one that is used to store user records in the ASP.NET Identity database.

The final step is to perform the migration. Without starting the application, run the following command in the Package Manager Console:

```
Update-Database -TargetMigration CityProperty
```

The database schema will be modified, and the code in the Configuration.Seed method will be executed. The existing user accounts will have been preserved and enhanced with a City property (which I set to Paris in the Seed method).

Testing the Migration

To test the effect of the migration, start the application, navigate to the /Home/UserProps URL, and authenticate as one of the Identity users (for example, as Alice with the password MySecret). Once authenticated, you will see the current value of the City property for the user and have the opportunity to change it, as shown in Figure 15-3.

Figure 15-3. *Displaying and changing a custom user property*

Defining an Additional Property

Now that database migrations are set up, I am going to define a further property just to demonstrate how subsequent changes are handled and to show a more useful (and less dangerous) example of using the `Configuration.Seed` method. Listing 15-8 shows how I added a `Country` property to the `AppUser` class.

Listing 15-8. Adding Another Property in the AppUserModels.cs File

```
using System;
using Microsoft.AspNet.Identity.EntityFramework;

namespace Users.Models {

    public enum Cities {
        LONDON, PARIS, CHICAGO
    }

    public enum Countries {
        NONE, UK, FRANCE, USA
    }

    public class AppUser : IdentityUser {
        public Cities City { get; set; }
        public Countries Country { get; set; }

        public void SetCountryFromCity(Cities city) {
            switch (city) {
                case Cities.LONDON:
                    Country = Countries.UK;
                    break;
```

```
                case Cities.PARIS:
                    Country = Countries.FRANCE;
                    break;
                case Cities.CHICAGO:
                    Country = Countries.USA;
                    break;
                default:
                    Country = Countries.NONE;
                    break;
            }
        }
    }
}
```

I have added an enumeration to define the country names and a helper method that selects a country value based on the City property. Listing 15-9 shows the change I made to the Configuration class so that the Seed method sets the Country property based on the City, but only if the value of Country is NONE (which it will be for all users when the database is migrated because the Entity Framework sets enumeration columns to the first value).

Listing 15-9. Modifying the Database Seed in the Configuration.cs File

```
using System.Data.Entity.Migrations;
using Microsoft.AspNet.Identity;
using Microsoft.AspNet.Identity.EntityFramework;
using Users.Infrastructure;
using Users.Models;

namespace Users.Migrations {

    internal sealed class Configuration
            : DbMigrationsConfiguration<AppIdentityDbContext> {

        public Configuration() {
            AutomaticMigrationsEnabled = true;
            ContextKey = "Users.Infrastructure.AppIdentityDbContext";
        }

        protected override void Seed(AppIdentityDbContext context) {

            AppUserManager userMgr = new AppUserManager(new UserStore<AppUser>(context));
            AppRoleManager roleMgr = new AppRoleManager(new RoleStore<AppRole>(context));

            string roleName = "Administrators";
            string userName = "Admin";
            string password = "MySecret";
            string email = "admin@example.com";

            if (!roleMgr.RoleExists(roleName)) {
                roleMgr.Create(new AppRole(roleName));
            }
```

```
            AppUser user = userMgr.FindByName(userName);
            if (user == null) {
                userMgr.Create(new AppUser { UserName = userName, Email = email },
                    password);
                user = userMgr.FindByName(userName);
            }

            if (!userMgr.IsInRole(user.Id, roleName)) {
                userMgr.AddToRole(user.Id, roleName);
            }

            foreach (AppUser dbUser in userMgr.Users) {
                if (dbUser.Country == Countries.NONE) {
                    dbUser.SetCountryFromCity(dbUser.City);
                }
            }

            context.SaveChanges();
        }
    }
}
```

This kind of seeding is more useful in a real project because it will set a value for the Country property only if one has not already been set—subsequent migrations won't be affected, and user selections won't be lost.

Adding Application Support

There is no point defining additional user properties if they are not available in the application, so Listing 15-10 shows the change I made to the Views/Home/UserProps.cshtml file to display the value of the Country property.

Listing 15-10. Displaying an Additional Property in the UserProps.cshtml File

```
@using Users.Models
@model AppUser
@{ ViewBag.Title = "UserProps";}

<div class="panel panel-primary">
    <div class="panel-heading">
        Custom User Properties
    </div>
    <table class="table table-striped">
        <tr><th>City</th><td>@Model.City</td></tr>
        <tr><th>Country</th><td>@Model.Country</td></tr>
    </table>
</div>

@using (Html.BeginForm()) {
    <div class="form-group">
        <label>City</label>
        @Html.DropDownListFor(x => x.City, new SelectList(Enum.GetNames(typeof(Cities))))
    </div>
    <button class="btn btn-primary" type="submit">Save</button>
}
```

Listing 15-11 shows the corresponding change I made to the Home controller to update the Country property when the City value changes.

Listing 15-11. Setting Custom Properties in the HomeController.cs File

```
using System.Web.Mvc;
using System.Collections.Generic;
using System.Web;
using System.Security.Principal;
using System.Threading.Tasks;
using Users.Infrastructure;
using Microsoft.AspNet.Identity;
using Microsoft.AspNet.Identity.Owin;

using Users.Models;

namespace Users.Controllers {

    public class HomeController : Controller {

        // ...other action methods omitted for brevity...

        [Authorize]
        public ActionResult UserProps() {
            return View(CurrentUser);
        }

        [Authorize]
        [HttpPost]
        public async Task<ActionResult> UserProps(Cities city) {
            AppUser user = CurrentUser;
            user.City = city;
            user.SetCountryFromCity(city);
            await UserManager.UpdateAsync(user);
            return View(user);
        }

        // ...properties omitted for brevity...
    }
}
```

Performing the Migration

All that remains is to create and apply a new migration. Enter the following command into the Package Manager Console:

```
Add-Migration CountryProperty
```

This will generate another file in the Migrations folder that contains the instruction to add the Country column. To apply the migration, execute the following command:

```
Update-Database -TargetMigration CountryProperty
```

The migration will be performed, and the value of the Country property will be set based on the value of the existing City property for each user. You can check the new user property by starting the application and authenticating and navigating to the /Home/UserProps URL, as shown in Figure 15-4.

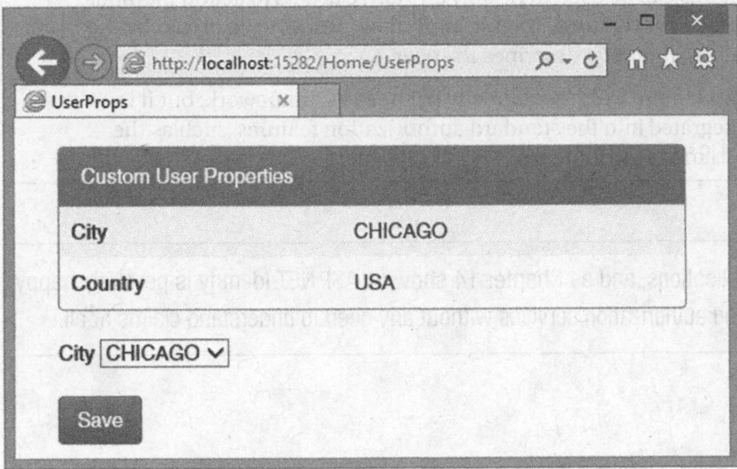

Figure 15-4. Creating an additional user property

■ **Tip** Although I am focused on the process of upgrading the database, you can also migrate back to a previous version by specifying an earlier migration. Use the -Force argument make changes that cause data loss, such as removing a column.

Working with Claims

In older user-management systems, such as ASP.NET Membership, the application was assumed to be the authoritative source of all information about the user, essentially treating the application as a closed world and trusting the data that is contained within it.

This is such an ingrained approach to software development that it can be hard to recognize that's what is happening, but you saw an example of the closed-world technique in Chapter 14 when I authenticated users against the credentials stored in the database and granted access based on the roles associated with those credentials. I did the same thing again in this chapter when I added properties to the user class. Every piece of information that I needed to manage user authentication and authorization came from within my application—and that is a perfectly satisfactory approach for many web applications, which is why I demonstrated these techniques in such depth.

ASP.NET Identity also supports an alternative approach for dealing with users, which works well when the MVC framework application isn't the sole source of information about users and which can be used to authorize users in more flexible and fluid ways than traditional roles allow.

This alternative approach uses *claims*, and in this section I'll describe how ASP.NET Identity supports *claims-based authorization.* Table 15-4 puts claims in context.

***Table 15-4.** Putting Claims in Context*

Question	Answer
What is it?	Claims are pieces of information about users that you can use to make authorization decisions. Claims can be obtained from external systems as well as from the local Identity database.
Why should I care?	Claims can be used to flexibly authorize access to action methods. Unlike conventional roles, claims allow access to be driven by the information that describes the user.
How is it used by the MVC framework?	This feature isn't used directly by the MVC framework, but it is integrated into the standard authorization features, such as the `Authorize` attribute.

■ **Tip** You don't have to use claims in your applications, and as Chapter 14 showed, ASP.NET Identity is perfectly happy providing an application with the authentication and authorization services without any need to understand claims at all.

Understanding Claims

A *claim* is a piece of information about the user, along with some information about where the information came from. The easiest way to unpack claims is through some practical demonstrations, without which any discussion becomes too abstract to be truly useful. To get started, I added a `Claims` controller to the example project, the definition of which you can see in Listing 15-12.

Listing 15-12. The Contents of the ClaimsController.cs File

```
using System.Security.Claims;
using System.Web;
using System.Web.Mvc;

namespace Users.Controllers {
    public class ClaimsController : Controller {

        [Authorize]
        public ActionResult Index() {
            ClaimsIdentity ident = HttpContext.User.Identity as ClaimsIdentity;
            if (ident == null) {
                return View("Error", new string[] { "No claims available" });
            } else {
                return View(ident.Claims);
            }
        }
    }
}
```

■ **Tip** You may feel a little lost as I define the code for this example. Don't worry about the details for the moment—just stick with it until you see the output from the action method and view that I define. More than anything else, that will help put claims into perspective.

You can get the claims associated with a user in different ways. One approach is to use the `Claims` property defined by the user class, but in this example, I have used the `HttpContext.User.Identity` property to demonstrate the way that ASP.NET Identity is integrated with the rest of the ASP.NET platform. As I explained in Chapter 13, the `HttpContext.User.Identity` property returns an implementation of the `IIdentity` interface, which is a `ClaimsIdentity` object when working using ASP.NET Identity. The `ClaimsIdentity` class is defined in the `System.Security.Claims` namespace, and Table 15-5 shows the members it defines that are relevant to this chapter.

***Table 15-5.** The Members Defined by the ClaimsIdentity Class*

Name	Description
`Claims`	Returns an enumeration of `Claim` objects representing the claims for the user.
`AddClaim(claim)`	Adds a claim to the user identity.
`AddClaims(claims)`	Adds an enumeration of `Claim` objects to the user identity.
`HasClaim(predicate)`	Returns true if the user identity contains a claim that matches the specified predicate. See the "Applying Claims" section for an example predicate.
`RemoveClaim(claim)`	Removes a claim from the user identity.

Other members are available, but the ones in the table are those that are used most often in web applications, for reason that will become obvious as I demonstrate how claims fit into the wider ASP.NET platform.

In Listing 15-12, I cast the `IIdentity` implementation to the `ClaimsIdentity` type and pass the enumeration of `Claim` objects returned by the `ClaimsIdentity.Claims` property to the `View` method. A `Claim` object represents a single piece of data about the user, and the `Claim` class defines the properties shown in Table 15-6.

***Table 15-6.** The Properties Defined by the Claim Class*

Name	Description
`Issuer`	Returns the name of the system that provided the claim
`Subject`	Returns the `ClaimsIdentity` object for the user who the claim refers to
`Type`	Returns the type of information that the claim represents
`Value`	Returns the piece of information that the claim represents

Listing 15-13 shows the contents of the `Index.cshtml` file that I created in the `Views/Claims` folder and that is rendered by the `Index` action of the `Claims` controller. The view adds a row to a table for each claim about the user.

Listing 15-13. The Contents of the Index.cshtml File in the Views/Claims Folder

```
@using System.Security.Claims
@using Users.Infrastructure
@model IEnumerable<Claim>
@{ ViewBag.Title = "Claims"; }

<div class="panel panel-primary">
    <div class="panel-heading">
        Claims
    </div>
    <table class="table table-striped">
        <tr>
            <th>Subject</th><th>Issuer</th>
            <th>Type</th><th>Value</th>
        </tr>
        @foreach (Claim claim in Model.OrderBy(x => x.Type)) {
            <tr>
                <td>@claim.Subject.Name</td>
                <td>@claim.Issuer</td>
                <td>@Html.ClaimType(claim.Type)</td>
                <td>@claim.Value</td>
            </tr>
        }
    </table>
</div>
```

The value of the Claim.Type property is a URI for a Microsoft schema, which isn't especially useful. The popular schemas are used as the values for fields in the System.Security.Claims.ClaimTypes class, so to make the output from the Index.cshtml view easier to read, I added an HTML helper to the IdentityHelpers.cs file, as shown in Listing 15-14. It is this helper that I use in the Index.cshtml file to format the value of the Claim.Type property.

Listing 15-14. Adding a Helper to the IdentityHelpers.cs File

```
using System.Web;
using System.Web.Mvc;
using Microsoft.AspNet.Identity.Owin;
using System;
using System.Linq;
using System.Reflection;
using System.Security.Claims;

namespace Users.Infrastructure {
    public static class IdentityHelpers {

        public static MvcHtmlString GetUserName(this HtmlHelper html, string id) {
            AppUserManager mgr
                = HttpContext.Current.GetOwinContext().GetUserManager<AppUserManager>();
            return new MvcHtmlString(mgr.FindByIdAsync(id).Result.UserName);
        }
```

```
        public static MvcHtmlString ClaimType(this HtmlHelper html, string claimType) {
            FieldInfo[] fields = typeof(ClaimTypes).GetFields();
            foreach (FieldInfo field in fields) {
                if (field.GetValue(null).ToString() == claimType) {
                    return new MvcHtmlString(field.Name);
                }
            }
            return new MvcHtmlString(string.Format("{0}",
                claimType.Split('/', '.').Last()));
        }
    }
}
```

■ **Note** The helper method isn't at all efficient because it reflects on the fields of the `ClaimType` class for each claim that is displayed, but it is sufficient for my purposes in this chapter. You won't often need to display the claim type in real applications.

To see why I have created a controller that uses claims without really explaining what they are, start the application, authenticate as the user Alice (with the password `MySecret`), and request the `/Claims/Index` URL. Figure 15-5 shows the content that is generated.

http://localhost:15282/Claims/Index

Claims

Claims

Subject	Issuer	Type	Value
Alice	LOCAL AUTHORITY	SecurityStamp	bf5adfe6-a6c7-4169-80be-127526d5216f
Alice	LOCAL AUTHORITY	identityprovider	ASP.NET Identity
Alice	LOCAL AUTHORITY	Role	Employees
Alice	LOCAL AUTHORITY	Role	Users
Alice	LOCAL AUTHORITY	Name	Alice
Alice	LOCAL AUTHORITY	NameIdentifier	7ef3b837-0e55-4b94-af02-bad1fd4c4c41

Figure 15-5. *The output from the Index action of the Claims controller*

It can be hard to make out the detail in the figure, so I have reproduced the content in Table 15-7.

Table 15-7. The Data Shown in Figure 15-5

Subject	Issuer	Type	Value
Alice	LOCAL AUTHORITY	SecurityStamp	Unique ID
Alice	LOCAL AUTHORITY	IdentityProvider	ASP.NET Identity
Alice	LOCAL AUTHORITY	Role	Employees
Alice	LOCAL AUTHORITY	Role	Users
Alice	LOCAL AUTHORITY	Name	Alice
Alice	LOCAL AUTHORITY	NameIdentifier	Alice's user ID

The table shows the most important aspect of claims, which is that I have already been using them when I implemented the traditional authentication and authorization features in Chapter 14. You can see that some of the claims relate to user identity (the Name claim is Alice, and the NameIdentifier claim is Alice's unique user ID in my ASP.NET Identity database).

Other claims show membership of roles—there are two Role claims in the table, reflecting the fact that Alice is assigned to both the Users and Employees roles. There is also a claim about how Alice has been authenticated: The IdentityProvider is set to ASP.NET Identity.

The difference when this information is expressed as a set of claims is that you can determine where the data came from. The Issuer property for all the claims shown in the table is set to LOCAL AUTHORITY, which indicates that the user's identity has been established by the application.

So, now that you have seen some example claims, I can more easily describe what a claim is. A claim is any piece of information about a user that is available to the application, including the user's identity and role memberships. And, as you have seen, the information I have been defining about my users in earlier chapters is automatically made available as claims by ASP.NET Identity.

Creating and Using Claims

Claims are interesting for two reasons. The first reason is that an application can obtain claims from multiple sources, rather than just relying on a local database for information about the user. You will see a real example of this when I show you how to authenticate users through a third-party system in the "Using Third-Party Authentication" section, but for the moment I am going to add a class to the example project that simulates a system that provides claims information. Listing 15-15 shows the contents of the LocationClaimsProvider.cs file that I added to the Infrastructure folder.

Listing 15-15. The Contents of the LocationClaimsProvider.cs File

```
using System.Collections.Generic;
using System.Security.Claims;

namespace Users.Infrastructure {

    public static class LocationClaimsProvider {

        public static IEnumerable<Claim> GetClaims(ClaimsIdentity user) {
            List<Claim> claims = new List<Claim>();
            if (user.Name.ToLower() == "alice") {
                    claims.Add(CreateClaim(ClaimTypes.PostalCode, "DC 20500"));
                    claims.Add(CreateClaim(ClaimTypes.StateOrProvince, "DC"));
```

```
        } else {
                claims.Add(CreateClaim(ClaimTypes.PostalCode, "NY 10036"));
                claims.Add(CreateClaim(ClaimTypes.StateOrProvince, "NY"));
        }
        return claims;
    }

    private static Claim CreateClaim(string type, string value) {
        return new Claim(type, value, ClaimValueTypes.String, "RemoteClaims");
    }
  }
}
```

The GetClaims method takes a ClaimsIdentity argument and uses the Name property to create claims about the user's ZIP code and state. This class allows me to simulate a system such as a central HR database, which would be the authoritative source of location information about staff, for example.

Claims are associated with the user's identity during the authentication process, and Listing 15-16 shows the changes I made to the Login action method of the Account controller to call the LocationClaimsProvider class.

Listing 15-16. Associating Claims with a User in the AccountController.cs File

```
...
[HttpPost]
[AllowAnonymous]
[ValidateAntiForgeryToken]
public async Task<ActionResult> Login(LoginModel details, string returnUrl) {
    if (ModelState.IsValid) {
        AppUser user = await UserManager.FindAsync(details.Name,
            details.Password);
        if (user == null) {
            ModelState.AddModelError("", "Invalid name or password.");
        } else {
            ClaimsIdentity ident = await UserManager.CreateIdentityAsync(user,
                DefaultAuthenticationTypes.ApplicationCookie);
            ident.AddClaims(LocationClaimsProvider.GetClaims(ident));
            AuthManager.SignOut();
            AuthManager.SignIn(new AuthenticationProperties {
                IsPersistent = false
            }, ident);
            return Redirect(returnUrl);
        }
    }
    ViewBag.returnUrl = returnUrl;
    return View(details);
}
...
```

You can see the effect of the location claims by starting the application, authenticating as a user, and requesting the /Claim/Index URL. Figure 15-6 shows the claims for Alice. You may have to sign out and sign back in again to see the change.

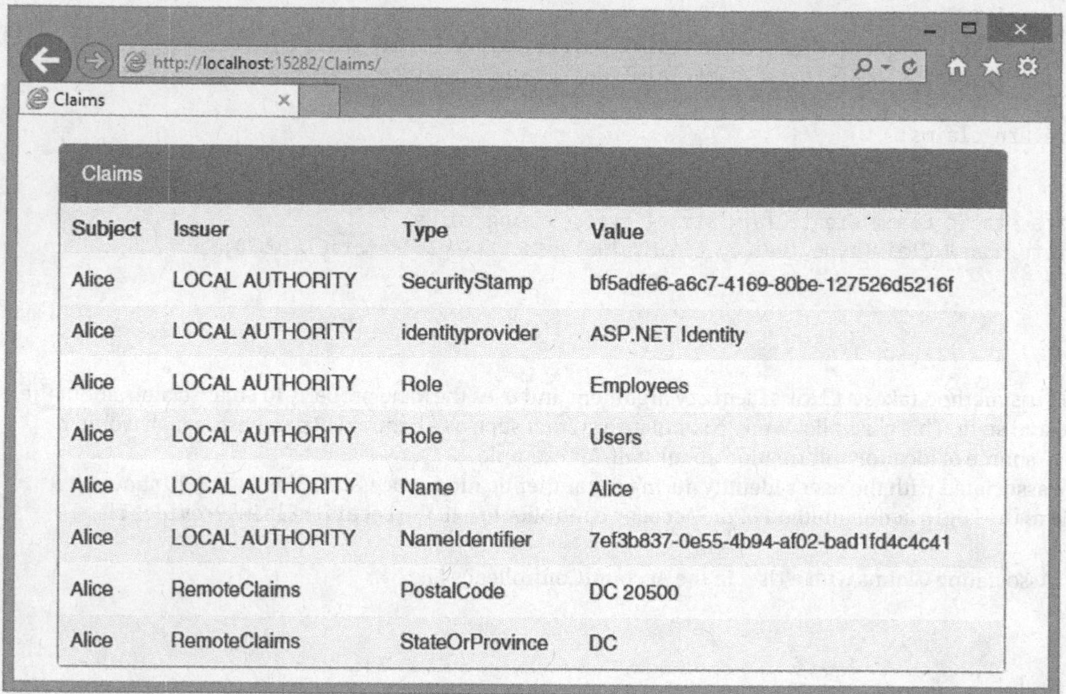

Subject	Issuer	Type	Value
Alice	LOCAL AUTHORITY	SecurityStamp	bf5adfe6-a6c7-4169-80be-127526d5216f
Alice	LOCAL AUTHORITY	identityprovider	ASP.NET Identity
Alice	LOCAL AUTHORITY	Role	Employees
Alice	LOCAL AUTHORITY	Role	Users
Alice	LOCAL AUTHORITY	Name	Alice
Alice	LOCAL AUTHORITY	NameIdentifier	7ef3b837-0e55-4b94-af02-bad1fd4c4c41
Alice	RemoteClaims	PostalCode	DC 20500
Alice	RemoteClaims	StateOrProvince	DC

***Figure 15-6.** Defining additional claims for users*

Obtaining claims from multiple locations means that the application doesn't have to duplicate data that is held elsewhere and allows integration of data from external parties. The `Claim.Issuer` property tells you where a claim originated from, which helps you judge how accurate the data is likely to be and how much weight you should give the data in your application. Location data obtained from a central HR database is likely to be more accurate and trustworthy than data obtained from an external mailing list provider, for example.

Applying Claims

The second reason that claims are interesting is that you can use them to manage user access to your application more flexibly than with standard roles. The problem with roles is that they are static, and once a user has been assigned to a role, the user remains a member until explicitly removed. This is, for example, how long-term employees of big corporations end up with incredible access to internal systems: They are assigned the roles they require for each new job they get, but the old roles are rarely removed. (The unexpectedly broad systems access sometimes becomes apparent during the investigation into how someone was able to ship the contents of the warehouse to their home address—true story.)

Claims can be used to authorize users based directly on the information that is known about them, which ensures that the authorization changes when the data changes. The simplest way to do this is to generate `Role` claims based on user data that are then used by controllers to restrict access to action methods. Listing 15-17 shows the contents of the `ClaimsRoles.cs` file that I added to the `Infrastructure`.

Listing 15-17. The Contents of the ClaimsRoles.cs File

```
using System.Collections.Generic;
using System.Security.Claims;

namespace Users.Infrastructure {
    public class ClaimsRoles {

        public static IEnumerable<Claim> CreateRolesFromClaims(ClaimsIdentity user) {
            List<Claim> claims = new List<Claim>();
            if (user.HasClaim(x => x.Type == ClaimTypes.StateOrProvince
                    && x.Issuer == "RemoteClaims" && x.Value == "DC")
                && user.HasClaim(x => x.Type == ClaimTypes.Role
                    && x.Value == "Employees")) {
                claims.Add(new Claim(ClaimTypes.Role, "DCStaff"));
            }
            return claims;
        }
    }
}
```

The gnarly looking `CreateRolesFromClaims` method uses lambda expressions to determine whether the user has a `StateOrProvince` claim from the `RemoteClaims` issuer with a value of `DC` and a `Role` claim with a value of `Employees`. If the user has both claims, then a `Role` claim is returned for the `DCStaff` role. Listing 15-18 shows how I call the `CreateRolesFromClaims` method from the `Login` action in the `Account` controller.

Listing 15-18. Generating Roles Based on Claims in the AccountController.cs File

```
...
[HttpPost]
[AllowAnonymous]
[ValidateAntiForgeryToken]
public async Task<ActionResult> Login(LoginModel details, string returnUrl) {
    if (ModelState.IsValid) {
        AppUser user = await UserManager.FindAsync(details.Name,
            details.Password);
        if (user == null) {
            ModelState.AddModelError("", "Invalid name or password.");
        } else {
            ClaimsIdentity ident = await UserManager.CreateIdentityAsync(user,
                DefaultAuthenticationTypes.ApplicationCookie);
            ident.AddClaims(LocationClaimsProvider.GetClaims(ident));
            ident.AddClaims(ClaimsRoles.CreateRolesFromClaims(ident));
            AuthManager.SignOut();
            AuthManager.SignIn(new AuthenticationProperties {
                IsPersistent = false
            }, ident);
            return Redirect(returnUrl);
        }
    }
    ViewBag.returnUrl = returnUrl;
    return View(details);
}
...
```

I can then restrict access to an action method based on membership of the DCStaff role. Listing 15-19 shows a new action method I added to the Claims controller to which I have applied the Authorize attribute.

Listing 15-19. Adding a New Action Method to the ClaimsController.cs File

```
using System.Security.Claims;
using System.Web;
using System.Web.Mvc;

namespace Users.Controllers {
    public class ClaimsController : Controller {

        [Authorize]
        public ActionResult Index() {
            ClaimsIdentity ident = HttpContext.User.Identity as ClaimsIdentity;
            if (ident == null) {
                return View("Error", new string[] { "No claims available" });
            } else {
                return View(ident.Claims);
            }
        }

        [Authorize(Roles="DCStaff")]
        public string OtherAction() {
            return "This is the protected action";
        }
    }
}
```

Users will be able to access OtherAction only if their claims grant them membership to the DCStaff role. Membership of this role is generated dynamically, so a change to the user's employment status or location information will change their authorization level.

Authorizing Access Using Claims

The previous example is an effective demonstration of how claims can be used to keep authorizations fresh and accurate, but it is a little indirect because I generate roles based on claims data and then enforce my authorization policy based on the membership of that role. A more direct and flexible approach is to enforce authorization directly by creating a custom authorization filter attribute. Listing 15-20 shows the contents of the ClaimsAccessAttribute.cs file, which I added to the Infrastructure folder and used to create such a filter.

Listing 15-20. The Contents of the ClaimsAccessAttribute.cs File

```
using System.Security.Claims;
using System.Web;
using System.Web.Mvc;

namespace Users.Infrastructure {
    public class ClaimsAccessAttribute : AuthorizeAttribute {
```

```
        public string Issuer { get; set; }
        public string ClaimType { get; set; }
        public string Value { get; set; }

        protected override bool AuthorizeCore(HttpContextBase context) {
            return context.User.Identity.IsAuthenticated
                && context.User.Identity is ClaimsIdentity
                && ((ClaimsIdentity)context.User.Identity).HasClaim(x =>
                    x.Issuer == Issuer && x.Type == ClaimType && x.Value == Value
                );
        }
    }
}
```

The attribute I have defined is derived from the AuthorizeAttribute class, which makes it easy to create custom authorization policies in MVC framework applications by overriding the AuthorizeCore method. My implementation grants access if the user is authenticated, the IIdentity implementation is an instance of ClaimsIdentity, and the user has a claim with the issuer, type, and value matching the class properties. Listing 15-21 shows how I applied the attribute to the Claims controller to authorize access to the OtherAction method based on one of the location claims created by the LocationClaimsProvider class.

Listing 15-21. Performing Authorization on Claims in the ClaimsController.cs File

```
using System.Security.Claims;
using System.Web;
using System.Web.Mvc;
using Users.Infrastructure;

namespace Users.Controllers {
    public class ClaimsController : Controller {

        [Authorize]
        public ActionResult Index() {
            ClaimsIdentity ident = HttpContext.User.Identity as ClaimsIdentity;
            if (ident == null) {
                return View("Error", new string[] { "No claims available" });
            } else {
                return View(ident.Claims);
            }
        }

        [ClaimsAccess(Issuer="RemoteClaims", ClaimType=ClaimTypes.PostalCode,
            Value="DC 20500")]
        public string OtherAction() {
            return "This is the protected action";
        }
    }
}
```

My authorization filter ensures that only users whose location claims specify a ZIP code of DC 20500 can invoke the OtherAction method.

Using Third-Party Authentication

One of the benefits of a claims-based system such as ASP.NET Identity is that any of the claims can come from an external system, even those that identify the user to the application. This means that other systems can authenticate users on behalf of the application, and ASP.NET Identity builds on this idea to make it simple and easy to add support for authenticating users through third parties such as Microsoft, Google, Facebook, and Twitter.

There are some substantial benefits of using third-party authentication: Many users will already have an account, users can elect to use two-factor authentication, and you don't have to manage user credentials in the application. In the sections that follow, I'll show you how to set up and use third-party authentication for Google users, which Table 15-8 puts into context.

***Table 15-8.** Putting Third-Party Authentication in Context*

Question	Answer
What is it?	Authenticating with third parties lets you take advantage of the popularity of companies such as Google and Facebook.
Why should I care?	Users don't like having to remember passwords for many different sites. Using a provider with large-scale adoption can make your application more appealing to users of the provider's services.
How is it used by the MVC framework?	This feature isn't used directly by the MVC framework.

■ **Note** The reason I have chosen to demonstrate Google authentication is that it is the only option that doesn't require me to register my application with the authentication service. You can get details of the registration processes required at `http://bit.ly/1cqLTrE`.

Enabling Google Authentication

ASP.NET Identity comes with built-in support for authenticating users through their Microsoft, Google, Facebook, and Twitter accounts as well more general support for any authentication service that supports `OAuth`. The first step is to add the NuGet package that includes the Google-specific additions for ASP.NET Identity. Enter the following command into the Package Manager Console:

```
Install-Package Microsoft.Owin.Security.Google -version 2.0.2
```

There are NuGet packages for each of the services that ASP.NET Identity supports, as described in Table 15-9.

Table 15-9. *The NuGet Authenticaton Packages*

Name	Description
`Microsoft.Owin.Security.Google`	Authenticates users with Google accounts
`Microsoft.Owin.Security.Facebook`	Authenticates users with Facebook accounts
`Microsoft.Owin.Security.Twitter`	Authenticates users with Twitter accounts
`Microsoft.Owin.Security.MicrosoftAccount`	Authenticates users with Microsoft accounts
`Microsoft.Owin.Security.OAuth`	Authenticates users against any OAuth 2.0 service

Once the package is installed, I enable support for the authentication service in the OWIN startup class, which is defined in the `App_Start/IdentityConfig.cs` file in the example project. Listing 15-22 shows the change that I have made.

Listing 15-22. Enabling Google Authentication in the IdentityConfig.cs File

```
using Microsoft.AspNet.Identity;
using Microsoft.Owin;
using Microsoft.Owin.Security.Cookies;
using Owin;
using Users.Infrastructure;
using Microsoft.Owin.Security.Google;

namespace Users {
    public class IdentityConfig {
        public void Configuration(IAppBuilder app) {

            app.CreatePerOwinContext<AppIdentityDbContext>(AppIdentityDbContext.Create);
            app.CreatePerOwinContext<AppUserManager>(AppUserManager.Create);
            app.CreatePerOwinContext<AppRoleManager>(AppRoleManager.Create);

            app.UseCookieAuthentication(new CookieAuthenticationOptions {
                AuthenticationType = DefaultAuthenticationTypes.ApplicationCookie,
                LoginPath = new PathString("/Account/Login"),
            });

            app.UseExternalSignInCookie(DefaultAuthenticationTypes.ExternalCookie);
            app.UseGoogleAuthentication();
        }
    }
}
```

Each of the packages that I listed in Table 15-9 contains an extension method that enables the corresponding service. The extension method for the Google service is called `UseGoogleAuthentication`, and it is called on the `IAppBuilder` implementation that is passed to the `Configuration` method.

Next I added a button to the `Views/Account/Login.cshtml` file, which allows users to log in via Google. You can see the change in Listing 15-23.

Listing 15-23. Adding a Google Login Button to the Login.cshtml File

```
@model Users.Models.LoginModel
@{ ViewBag.Title = "Login";}
<h2>Log In</h2>

@Html.ValidationSummary()

@using (Html.BeginForm()) {
    @Html.AntiForgeryToken();
    <input type="hidden" name="returnUrl" value="@ViewBag.returnUrl" />
    <div class="form-group">
        <label>Name</label>
        @Html.TextBoxFor(x => x.Name, new { @class = "form-control" })
    </div>
    <div class="form-group">
        <label>Password</label>
        @Html.PasswordFor(x => x.Password, new { @class = "form-control" })
    </div>
    <button class="btn btn-primary" type="submit">Log In</button>
}

@using (Html.BeginForm("GoogleLogin", "Account")) {
    <input type="hidden" name="returnUrl" value="@ViewBag.returnUrl" />
    <button class="btn btn-primary" type="submit">Log In via Google</button>
}
```

The new button submits a form that targets the GoogleLogin action on the Account controller. You can see this method—and the other changes I made the controller—in Listing 15-24.

Listing 15-24. Adding Support for Google Authentication to the AccountController.cs File

```
using System.Threading.Tasks;
using System.Web.Mvc;
using Users.Models;
using Microsoft.Owin.Security;
using System.Security.Claims;
using Microsoft.AspNet.Identity;
using Microsoft.AspNet.Identity.Owin;
using Users.Infrastructure;
using System.Web;

namespace Users.Controllers {

    [Authorize]
    public class AccountController : Controller {

        [AllowAnonymous]
        public ActionResult Login(string returnUrl) {
            if (HttpContext.User.Identity.IsAuthenticated) {
                return View("Error", new string[] { "Access Denied" });
            }
```

```
    ViewBag.returnUrl = returnUrl;
    return View();
}

[HttpPost]
[AllowAnonymous]
[ValidateAntiForgeryToken]
public async Task<ActionResult> Login(LoginModel details, string returnUrl) {
    if (ModelState.IsValid) {
        AppUser user = await UserManager.FindAsync(details.Name,
            details.Password);
        if (user == null) {
            ModelState.AddModelError("", "Invalid name or password.");
        } else {
            ClaimsIdentity ident = await UserManager.CreateIdentityAsync(user,
                DefaultAuthenticationTypes.ApplicationCookie);

            ident.AddClaims(LocationClaimsProvider.GetClaims(ident));
            ident.AddClaims(ClaimsRoles.CreateRolesFromClaims(ident));

            AuthManager.SignOut();
            AuthManager.SignIn(new AuthenticationProperties {
                    IsPersistent = false
                }, ident);
            return Redirect(returnUrl);
        }
    }
    ViewBag.returnUrl = returnUrl;
    return View(details);
}

[HttpPost]
[AllowAnonymous]
public ActionResult GoogleLogin(string returnUrl) {
    var properties = new AuthenticationProperties {
        RedirectUri = Url.Action("GoogleLoginCallback",
            new { returnUrl = returnUrl})
    };
    HttpContext.GetOwinContext().Authentication.Challenge(properties, "Google");
    return new HttpUnauthorizedResult();
}

[AllowAnonymous]
public async Task<ActionResult> GoogleLoginCallback(string returnUrl) {
    ExternalLoginInfo loginInfo = await AuthManager.GetExternalLoginInfoAsync();
    AppUser user = await UserManager.FindAsync(loginInfo.Login);
    if (user == null) {
        user = new AppUser {
            Email = loginInfo.Email,
            UserName = loginInfo.DefaultUserName,
            City = Cities.LONDON, Country = Countries.UK
        };
```

```
                IdentityResult result = await UserManager.CreateAsync(user);
                if (!result.Succeeded) {
                    return View("Error", result.Errors);
                } else {
                    result = await UserManager.AddLoginAsync(user.Id, loginInfo.Login);
                    if (!result.Succeeded) {
                        return View("Error", result.Errors);
                    }
                }
            }

            ClaimsIdentity ident = await UserManager.CreateIdentityAsync(user,
                DefaultAuthenticationTypes.ApplicationCookie);
            ident.AddClaims(loginInfo.ExternalIdentity.Claims);
            AuthManager.SignIn(new AuthenticationProperties {
                IsPersistent = false }, ident);
            return Redirect(returnUrl ?? "/");
        }

        [Authorize]
        public ActionResult Logout() {
            AuthManager.SignOut();
            return RedirectToAction("Index", "Home");
        }

        private IAuthenticationManager AuthManager {
            get {
                return HttpContext.GetOwinContext().Authentication;
            }
        }

        private AppUserManager UserManager {
            get {
                return HttpContext.GetOwinContext().GetUserManager<AppUserManager>();
            }
        }
    }
}
```

The GoogleLogin method creates an instance of the AuthenticationProperties class and sets the RedirectUri property to a URL that targets the GoogleLoginCallback action in the same controller. The next part is a magic phrase that causes ASP.NET Identity to respond to an unauthorized error by redirecting the user to the Google authentication page, rather than the one defined by the application:

```
...
HttpContext.GetOwinContext().Authentication.Challenge(properties, "Google");
return new HttpUnauthorizedResult();
...
```

This means that when the user clicks the Log In via Google button, their browser is redirected to the Google authentication service and then redirected back to the GoogleLoginCallback action method once they are authenticated.

I get details of the external login by calling the GetExternalLoginInfoAsync of the IAuthenticationManager implementation, like this:

```
...
ExternalLoginInfo loginInfo = await AuthManager.GetExternalLoginInfoAsync();
...
```

The ExternalLoginInfo class defines the properties shown in Table 15-10.

***Table 15-10.** The Properties Defined by the ExternalLoginInfo Class*

Name	Description
DefaultUserName	Returns the username
Email	Returns the e-mail address
ExternalIdentity	Returns a ClaimsIdentity that identities the user
Login	Returns a UserLoginInfo that describes the external login

I use the FindAsync method defined by the user manager class to locate the user based on the value of the ExternalLoginInfo.Login property, which returns an AppUser object if the user has been authenticated with the application before:

```
...
AppUser user = await UserManager.FindAsync(loginInfo.Login);
...
```

If the FindAsync method doesn't return an AppUser object, then I know that this is the first time that this user has logged into the application, so I create a new AppUser object, populate it with values, and save it to the database. I also save details of how the user logged in so that I can find them next time:

```
...
result = await UserManager.AddLoginAsync(user.Id, loginInfo.Login);
...
```

All that remains is to generate an identity the user, copy the claims provided by Google, and create an authentication cookie so that the application knows the user has been authenticated:

```
...
ClaimsIdentity ident = await UserManager.CreateIdentityAsync(user,
    DefaultAuthenticationTypes.ApplicationCookie);
ident.AddClaims(loginInfo.ExternalIdentity.Claims);
AuthManager.SignIn(new AuthenticationProperties { IsPersistent = false }, ident);
...
```

Testing Google Authentication

There is one further change that I need to make before I can test Google authentication: I need to change the account verification I set up in Chapter 13 because it prevents accounts from being created with e-mail addresses that are not within the `example.com` domain. Listing 15-25 shows how I removed the verification from the `AppUserManager` class.

Listing 15-25. Disabling Account Validation in the AppUserManager.cs File

```
using Microsoft.AspNet.Identity;
using Microsoft.AspNet.Identity.EntityFramework;
using Microsoft.AspNet.Identity.Owin;
using Microsoft.Owin;
using Users.Models;

namespace Users.Infrastructure {
    public class AppUserManager : UserManager<AppUser> {

        public AppUserManager(IUserStore<AppUser> store)
            : base(store) {
        }

        public static AppUserManager Create(
                IdentityFactoryOptions<AppUserManager> options,
                IOwinContext context) {

            AppIdentityDbContext db = context.Get<AppIdentityDbContext>();
            AppUserManager manager = new AppUserManager(new UserStore<AppUser>(db));

            manager.PasswordValidator = new CustomPasswordValidator {
                RequiredLength = 6,
                RequireNonLetterOrDigit = false,
                RequireDigit = false,
                RequireLowercase = true,
                RequireUppercase = true
            };

            //manager.UserValidator = new CustomUserValidator(manager) {
            //    AllowOnlyAlphanumericUserNames = true,
            //    RequireUniqueEmail = true
            //};

            return manager;
        }
    }
}
```

■ **Tip** You can use validation for externally authenticated accounts, but I am just going to disable the feature for simplicity.

To test authentication, start the application, click the Log In via Google button, and provide the credentials for a valid Google account. When you have completed the authentication process, your browser will be redirected back to the application. If you navigate to the `/Claims/Index` URL, you will be able to see how claims from the Google system have been added to the user's identity, as shown in Figure 15-7.

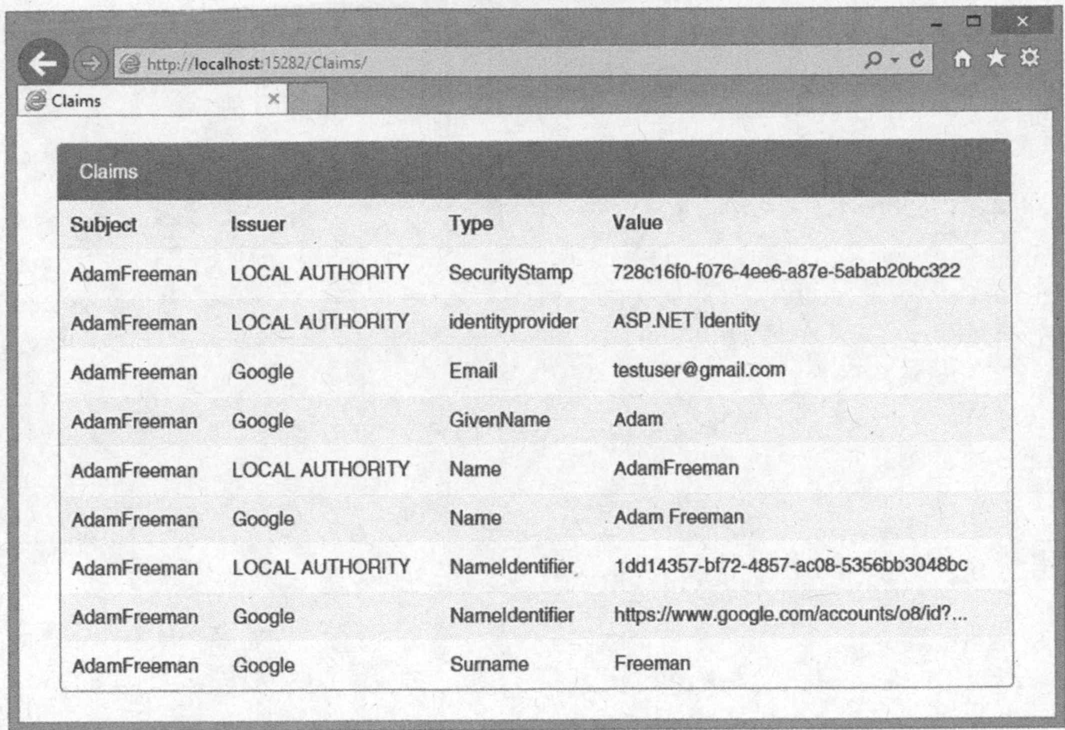

Subject	Issuer	Type	Value
AdamFreeman	LOCAL AUTHORITY	SecurityStamp	728c16f0-f076-4ee6-a87e-5abab20bc322
AdamFreeman	LOCAL AUTHORITY	identityprovider	ASP.NET Identity
AdamFreeman	Google	Email	testuser@gmail.com
AdamFreeman	Google	GivenName	Adam
AdamFreeman	LOCAL AUTHORITY	Name	AdamFreeman
AdamFreeman	Google	Name	Adam Freeman
AdamFreeman	LOCAL AUTHORITY	NameIdentifier	1dd14357-bf72-4857-ac08-5356bb3048bc
AdamFreeman	Google	NameIdentifier	https://www.google.com/accounts/o8/id?...
AdamFreeman	Google	Surname	Freeman

Figure 15-7. *Claims from Google*

Summary

In this chapter, I showed you some of the advanced features that ASP.NET Identity supports. I demonstrated the use of custom user properties and how to use database migrations to preserve data when you upgrade the schema to support them. I explained how claims work and how they can be used to create more flexible ways of authorizing users. I finished the chapter by showing you how to authenticate users via Google, which builds on the ideas behind the use of claims.

And that is all I have to teach you about the ASP.NET platform and how it supports MVC framework applications. I started by exploring the request handling life cycle and how it can be extended, managed, and disrupted. I then took you on a tour of the services that ASP.NET provides, showing you how they can be used to enhance and optimize your applications and improve the experience you deliver to your users. When writing MVC framework applications, it is easy to take the ASP.NET platform for granted, but this book has shown you just how much low-level functionality is available and how valuable it can be. I wish you every success in your web application projects, and I can only hope you have enjoyed reading this book as much as I enjoyed writing it.

Index

B

C

■ D, E

■ I

■ J, K

■ L

■ M

■ N

■ O

P, Q

R

S

T

U

V

W, X, Y, Z

Apress®
THE EXPERT'S VOICE™